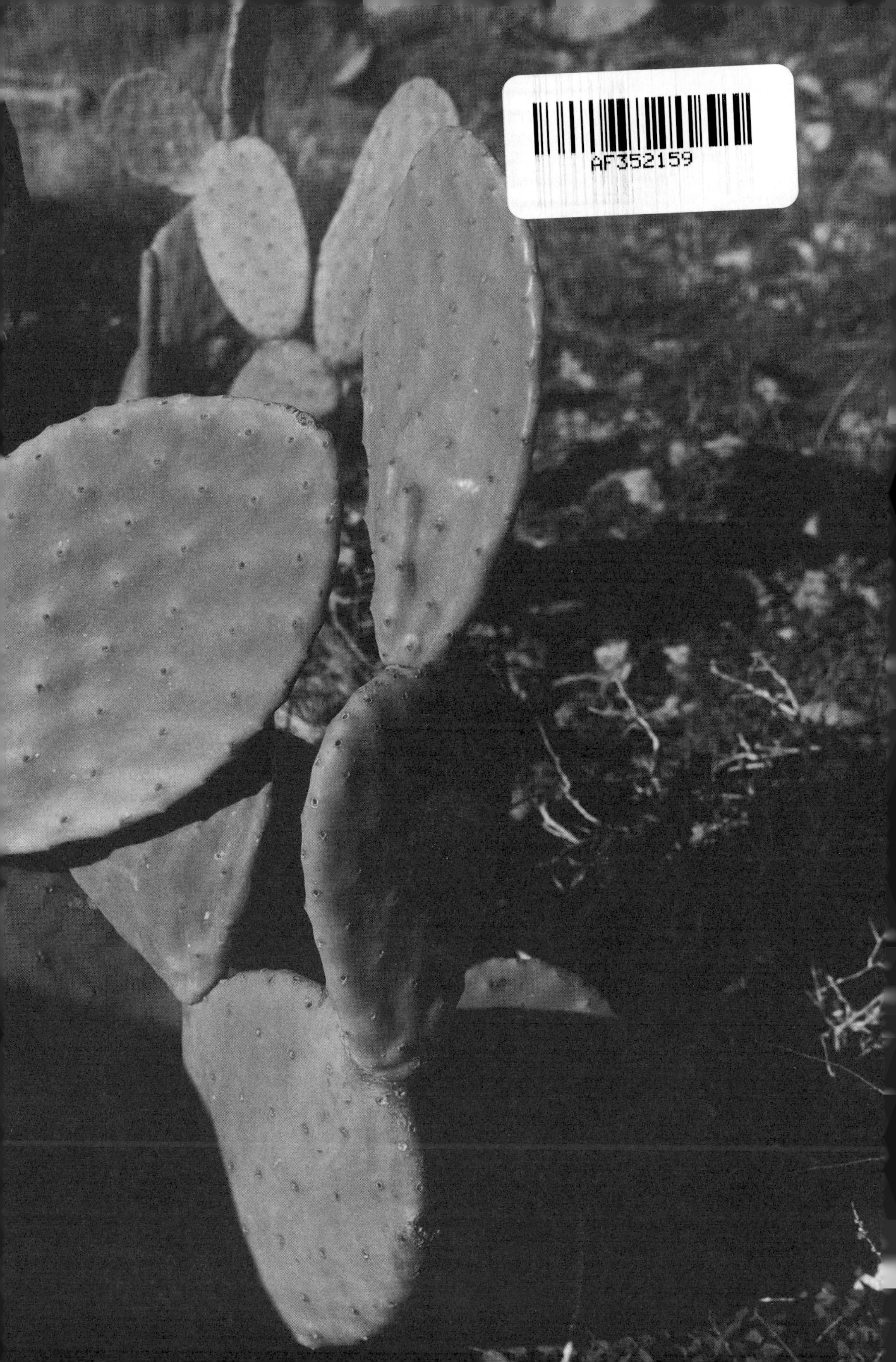
AF352159

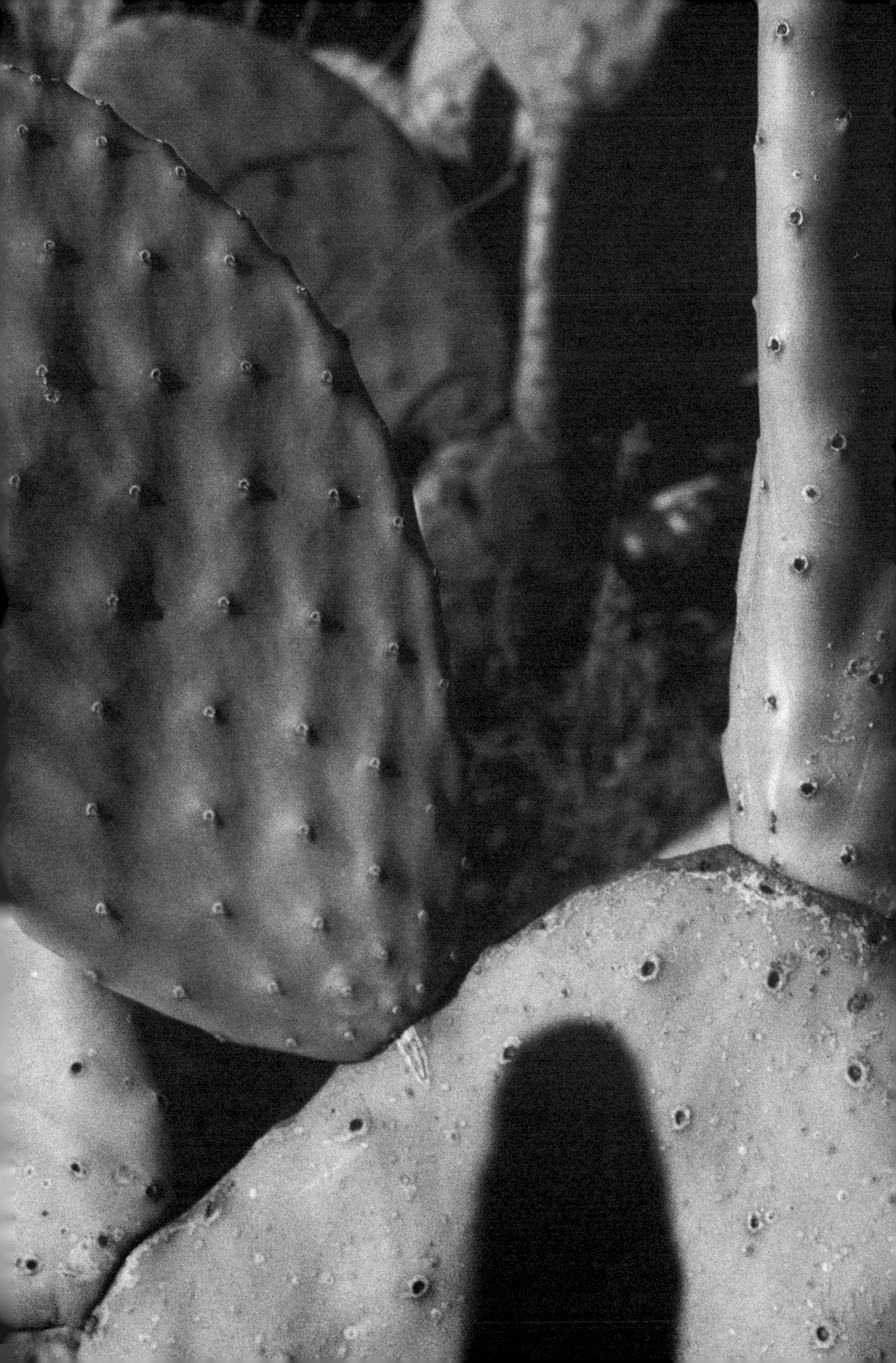

FINDING,
TRANSMITTING,
RECEIVING

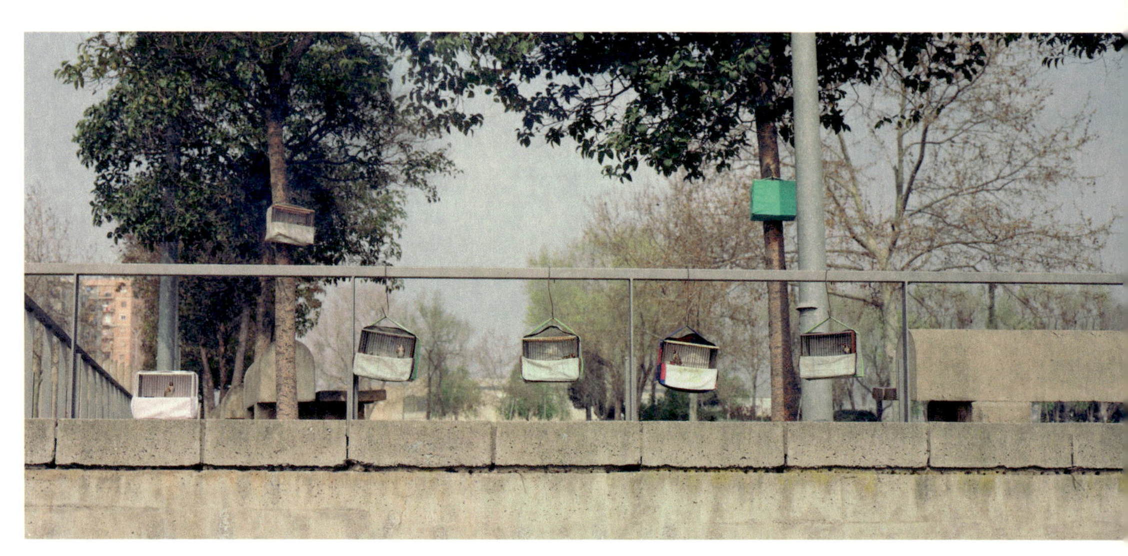

FINDING, TRANSMITTING, RECEIVING

Hannah Collins

black dog
publishing

Designed by Avni Patel

Black Dog Publishing Limited
Unit 4.4 Tea Building
56 Shoreditch High Street
London, E1 6JJ
Tel: +44 (0)20 7613 1922
Fax: +44 (0)20 7613 1944
Email: info@blackdogonline.com

British Library Cataloguing-in-Publication Data.
A CIP record for this book is available from the British Library.
ISBN10 1 904772 79 x
ISBN13 978 1 904772 79 8

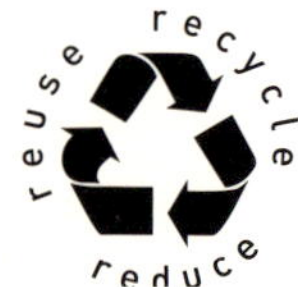

architecture art design
fashion history photography
theory and things

www.blackdogonline.com

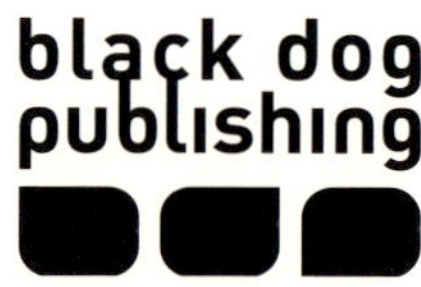

Printed on GardaPat 13 Klassica, acid-free and FSC certified by the international
certification body Woodmark Soil Association on 20 April 2006.

Printed in Turkey, by Ofset Yapımevi

Foreword

If art once presented a window onto the world, modern art resolutely created a world in its own right. Whether through an emphasis on materiality and form or through the evocation of a broader social context, this tendency can be understood as an engagement with the real. The viewer has been invited to enter and become immersed in works of art that combine a symbolic reading with a phenomenal one.

While photography lays claim to the real through its documentary and indexical nature, few artists have been able to defy the pictorial limits of the image by dissolving the picture frame, blurring the boundary between the image and the space in which it is viewed.

An important exception has been the artist Hannah Collins. Her photographs can be experienced as an image and as a kind of architecture; as two-dimensional surface and as sculpture.

One of her earliest works pictures a room and is itself room sized. The scale is one-on-one. *Thin Protective Coverings*, 1986, is a giant, canvas-mounted black and white photograph of a constructed environment made up of flattened cardboard boxes. The image appears to continue the floor and wall of any space in which it is hung. Yet the solidity of the room's structure is disintegrated into an overlapping mosaic of cardboard sheets. This remarkable image has a powerful sculptural quality. At the same time it evokes the makeshift architecture of the homeless; and the unofficial structures of the *favela*. Imposing in its architectonic scale and imagery, the work combines fragility with tenacity; ubiquitous, transitory and disposable, cardboard is a mainstay of surviving life on the streets. The reference to 'coverings' also suggests skin, our own thin, protective covering.

Collins' evocation of the tactile, sensual qualities of the material world combines with her use of scale to give her photographs a spatial, even phenomenological quality that, to paraphrase Rosalind Krauss, locates her work in an expanded field.

There are some other important features of the photographs and film works gathered together in this book. Collins is interested in revealing the archeology of urban space, showing how the built environment bares the traces of the past and intimations of a future. She also pictures the architecture of survival, documenting places created by those who have been displaced.

Juxtaposed with her photographs of buildings and cityscapes, there is an ongoing engagement with the still life and the beauty and interconnectedness of organic things.

Finally there are portraits; animated and speaking for themselves, through film; or, most recently, brought back from the dead through found negatives or prints.

"Photography alludes to the past and the future only in so far as they exist in the present, the past through its surviving relics, the future through prophecy visible in the present."[1]

Collins has lived and worked in London, Barcelona and California. She has also made work in India, North Africa, Poland, Russia and Turkey. In each location she documents the omnipresence of a universal modernism and the global features of modernity. At the same time her lens reveals the cracks and fissures through which the ancient and the culturally specific become visible. Her images move between panoramic cityscapes bristling with television aerials or festooned with billboard posters; and the marbled texture of a single slab of stone cladding.

The surface of the world becomes itself a kind of photograph, exposed to time, to the light of millennia, recording the deep shift of tectonic plates, or the surface patinas of changing civilisations. The epic sweep of a roof-scape or modernist urban facade is juxtaposed with a fragment; it might be the corner of a street, a gate, a brick wall. Collins combines the 'fast time' of technological and cultural change, the dynamo of the modern, with the slow time of geology, forgotten settlements and activities. A building or conurbation may even bare the signs of trauma, such as her pictures of the streets around Auschwitz, or overgrown cemeteries. Her archeology of urban space is also an attempt to confront the present with the past, to show how social history is part of the everyday present.

Collins is also drawn to people who by choice, by virtue of their identity or as victims of circumstance, pursue an existence at the edge of urban space and of legality. Just as her architectural typologies speak of shelter, communal life and labour — she also pictures the structures and topologies that invoke their opposite — homelessness, exile, alienation, unemployment. Yet in the same way as her photographs show how the surfaces of modernity are ruptured by signs of the past, so her portraits of exiled or nomadic communities and individuals show how they inject their specific geographic and cultural histories into the ruthless homogeneity of the global present.

Through stills and the moving image, Collins has tracked how groups and individuals can maintain communal rituals and a sense of dignity when they are relegated to the edge of the dominant social order, prohibited from truly occupying the public arena. This existence of contingency finds its expression in temporary habitats and the colonisation of those public spaces deemed to occupy the margins. Or they might be found spaces that are co-opted for living — a motorway underpass where a gypsy keeps his horses, the no-go concrete zones between public housing tower blocks, a bench in the park. These spaces become co-opted to provide meeting places, areas for negotiation and zones of departure.

Collins has photographed and interviewed gypsy communities who live at the edge of the *polis*; and individual refugees who live among us yet are invisible. This documentation has been extrapolated into narrative through a series of films where she has given a voice to three exiles. Their parallel lives, lack symbolic representation; they are like ghosts among the citizenry, illegal, invisible, impotent. Collins has sought them out to give them visibility through the lens.

She has also pictured those who have disappeared entirely, their passing marked by gravestones, memorials and, of course, photographs themselves. Juxtaposed in the pages of this book with an image of an earthy hole in the ground, a waterfall and a giant staircase, are a series of sepia photographs Collins deploys as found objects. These works are reprints of nineteenth century photographs of family groups or individuals. They are anonymous, yet recognisable as part of the genre of portraiture. Collins draws attention to the details — the leaves hand painted on the wallpaper behind a figure that look like fingerprints; a large male hand grasping a tiny female one; two women's heads at the back of a family group; the label on the back of a print with the name of the photographer's studio embellished with a graphic flourish. We will never know anything of the subjectivity, history or significance of the subjects of these photographs, which can be understood as 'found objects'.

In an important paper on the readymade and the found object in modern and contemporary art, art historian Margaret Iversen comments:

The found object shares with the readymade a lack of obvious aesthetic quality and little intervention on the part of the artist beyond putting the object into circulation, but in almost every other respect it is dissimilar. The difference is attributable to Breton's positioning the found object in a different space — the space of the unconscious.[2]

By dissecting elements of these generic formal portraits, isolating features such as heads, patterns, gestures, Collins triggers an empathetic sense of recognition. She gives them an emotional and psychic charge by highlighting what Iversen has described as "the texture of the real".

Alongside her meditative studies of modern and historic topographies, Collins has always maintained an engagement with the interiority of the still life. Although her exquisitely sensual studies of organic forms and man-made objects can be understood within the genre of the still life, they are not so much prearranged compositions on a table as sensual moments, oases of physicality, grasped from the flux of the everyday. The folds of a cotton sheet caress the eye; the crystals of a chandelier dazzle the gaze; a box of dried sardines triggers an olfactory response. They relate to basic human functions such as eating, sleeping; at the same time they offer moments of intense beauty.

This book has been structured by the artist to follow certain themes. The first section, titled *Events and Conditions* offers a sequence of urban and suburban images. The second section, titled *Finding, Transmitting, Receiving* demonstrates how space is transformed into situation. *Ghosts* is a chapter where the 'dead' images of historic portrait photography come to life. *Scripts* documents Collins' recent film projects. The final section, *Pavilions*, moves between the great iconic Barcelona Pavilion of Mies van der Rohe, an Israeli/ Bedouin tent and the surprisingly baroque interior of a Russian high-rise apartment. These exteriors and interiors leave us with the two polarities in Collins' work — the utopian and the dystopian, folded within one another through Collins' sculptural and architectural photographic practice.

Iwona Blazwick

1.   Szarkowski, John, from *The Photographer's Eye*, catalogue essay, New York: Museum of Modern Art, 1969
2.   Iversen, Margeret, 'Readymade to Found Object', lecture, *Big Ideas*, Whitechapel Gallery, London, 2004

Events and Conditions

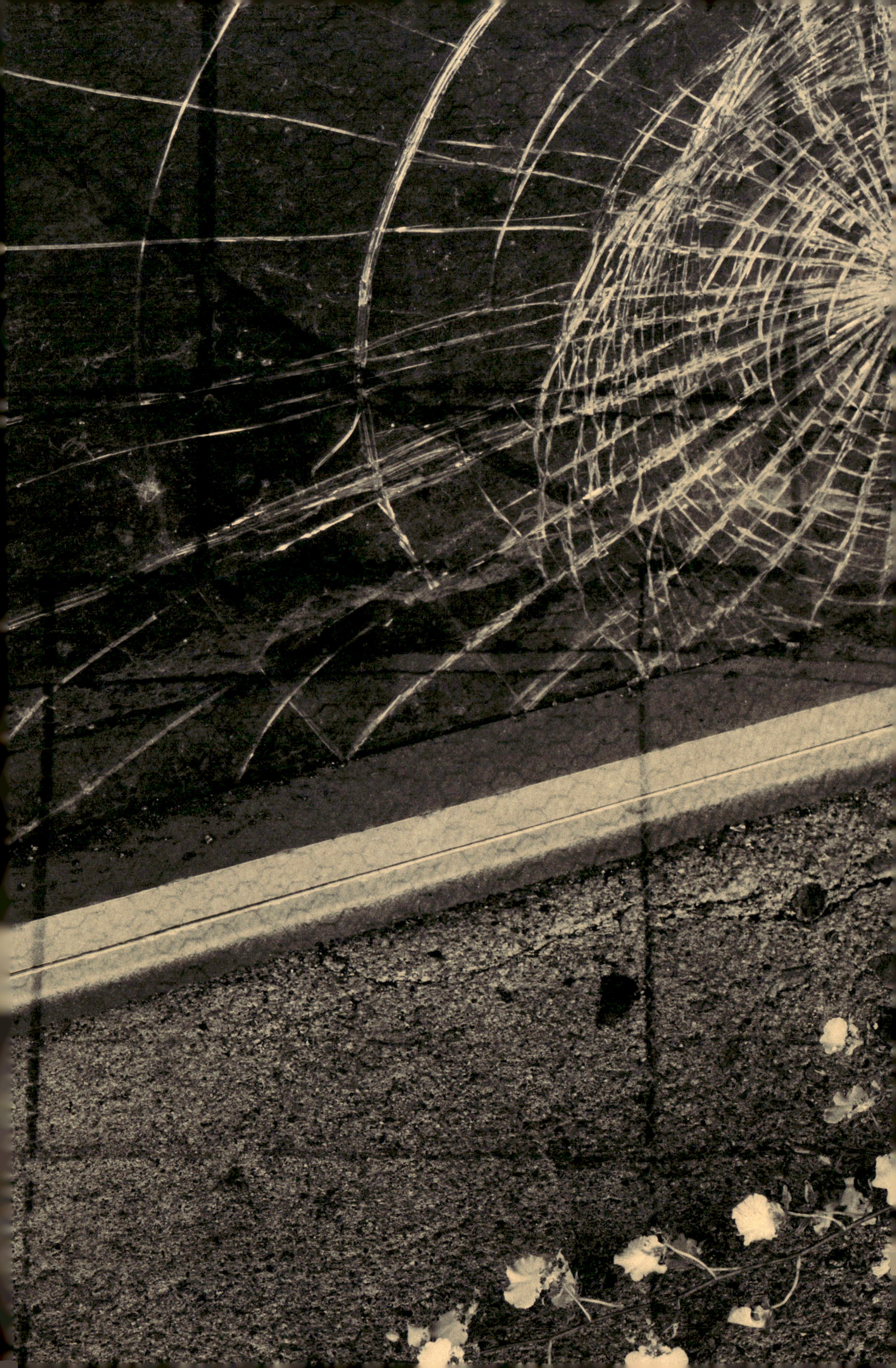

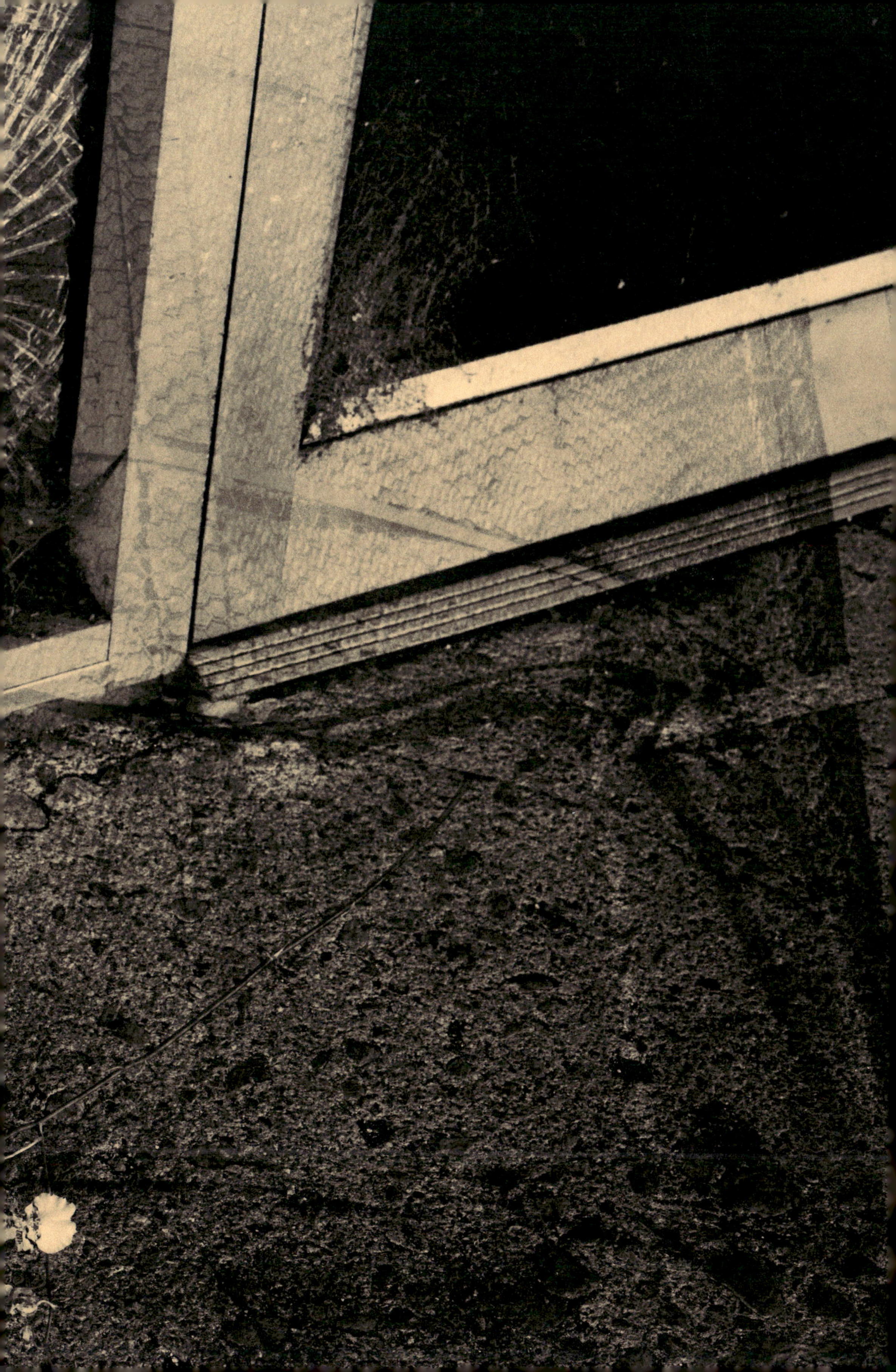

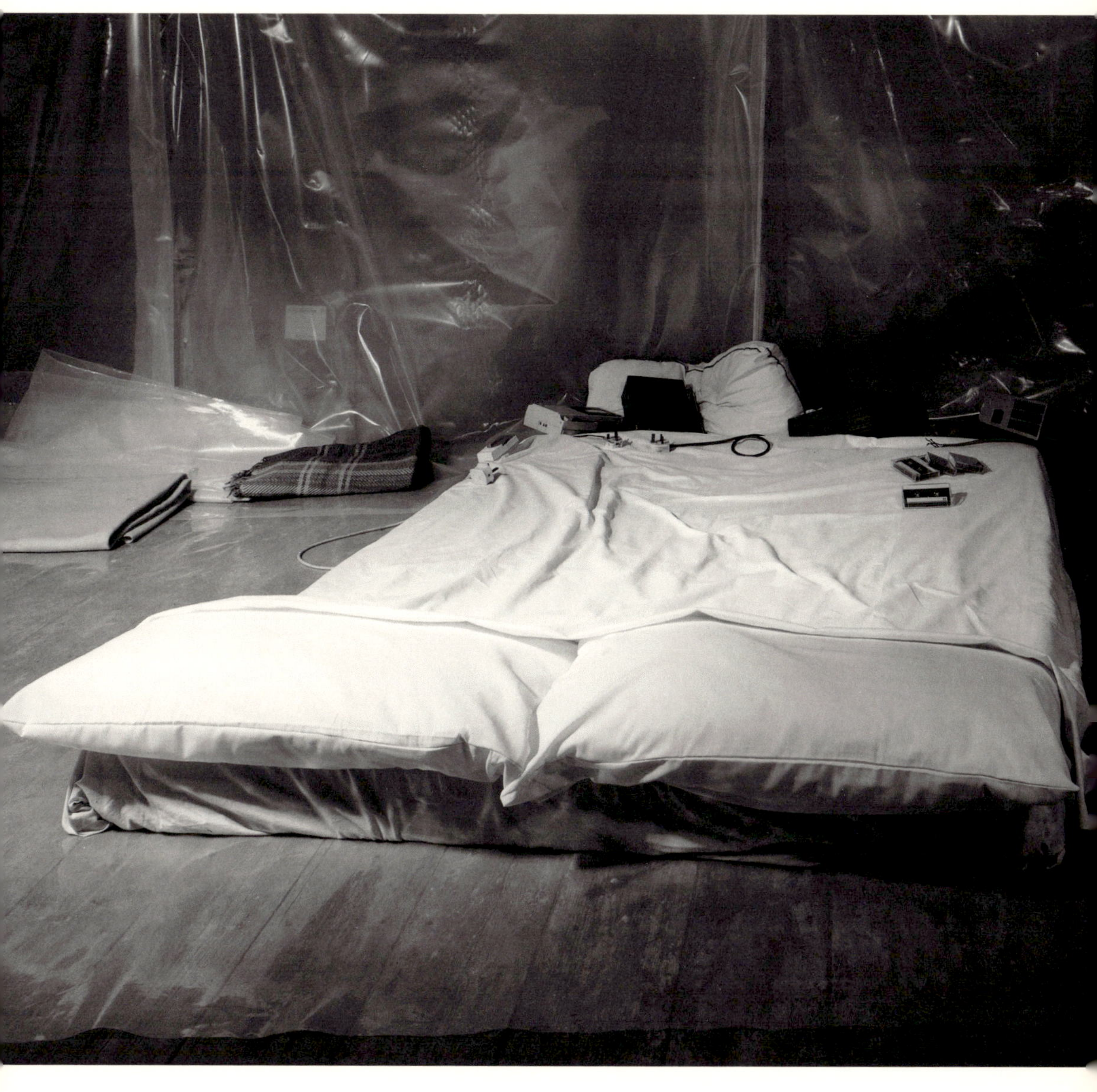

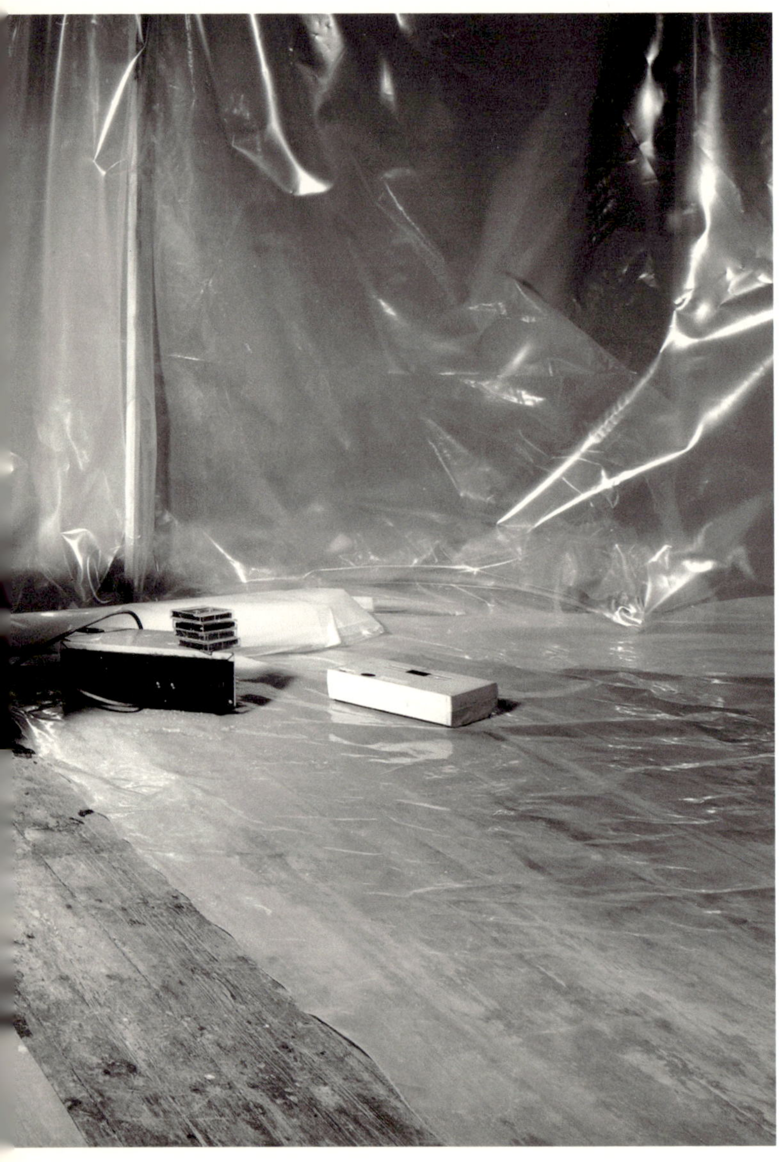

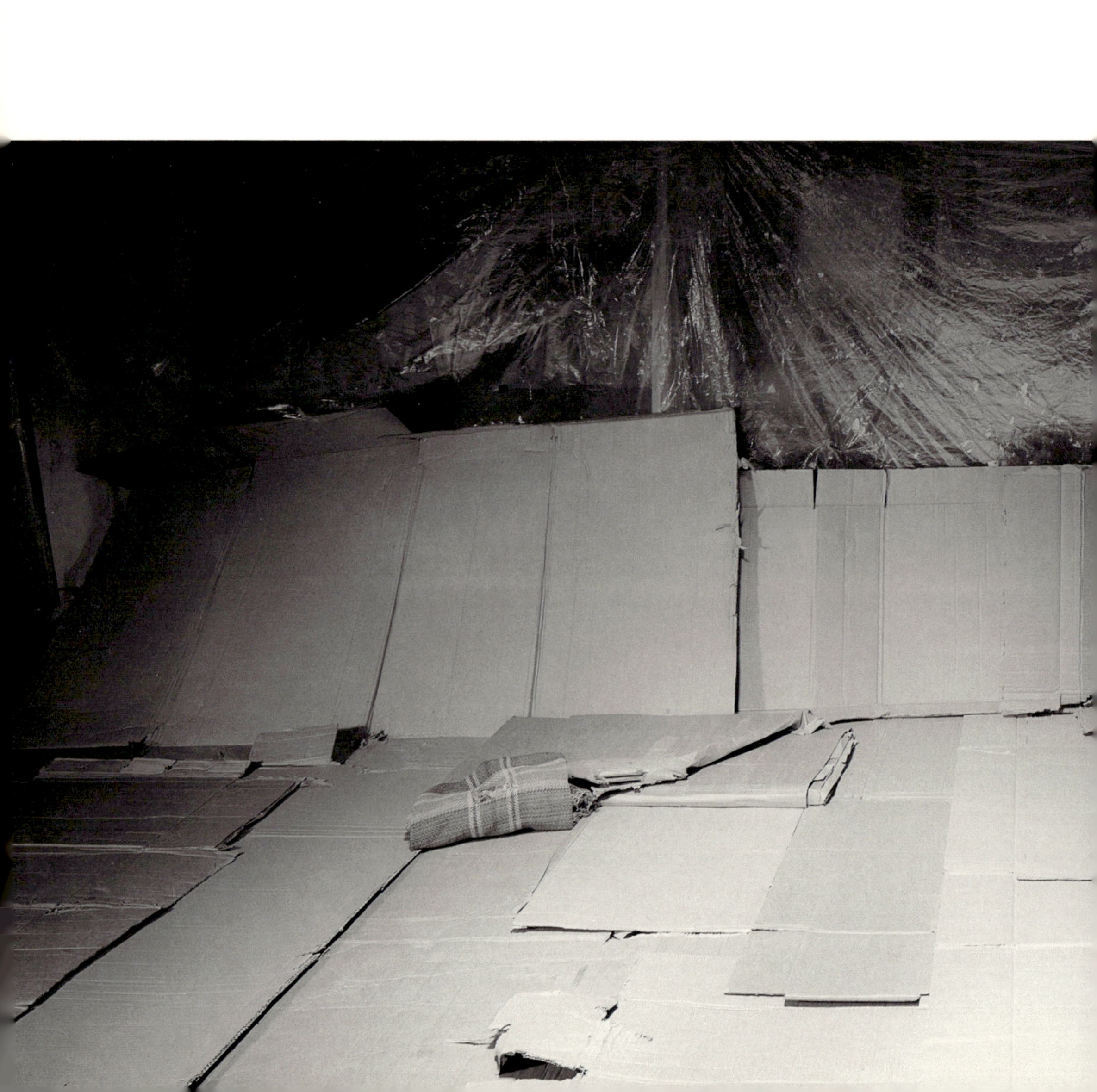

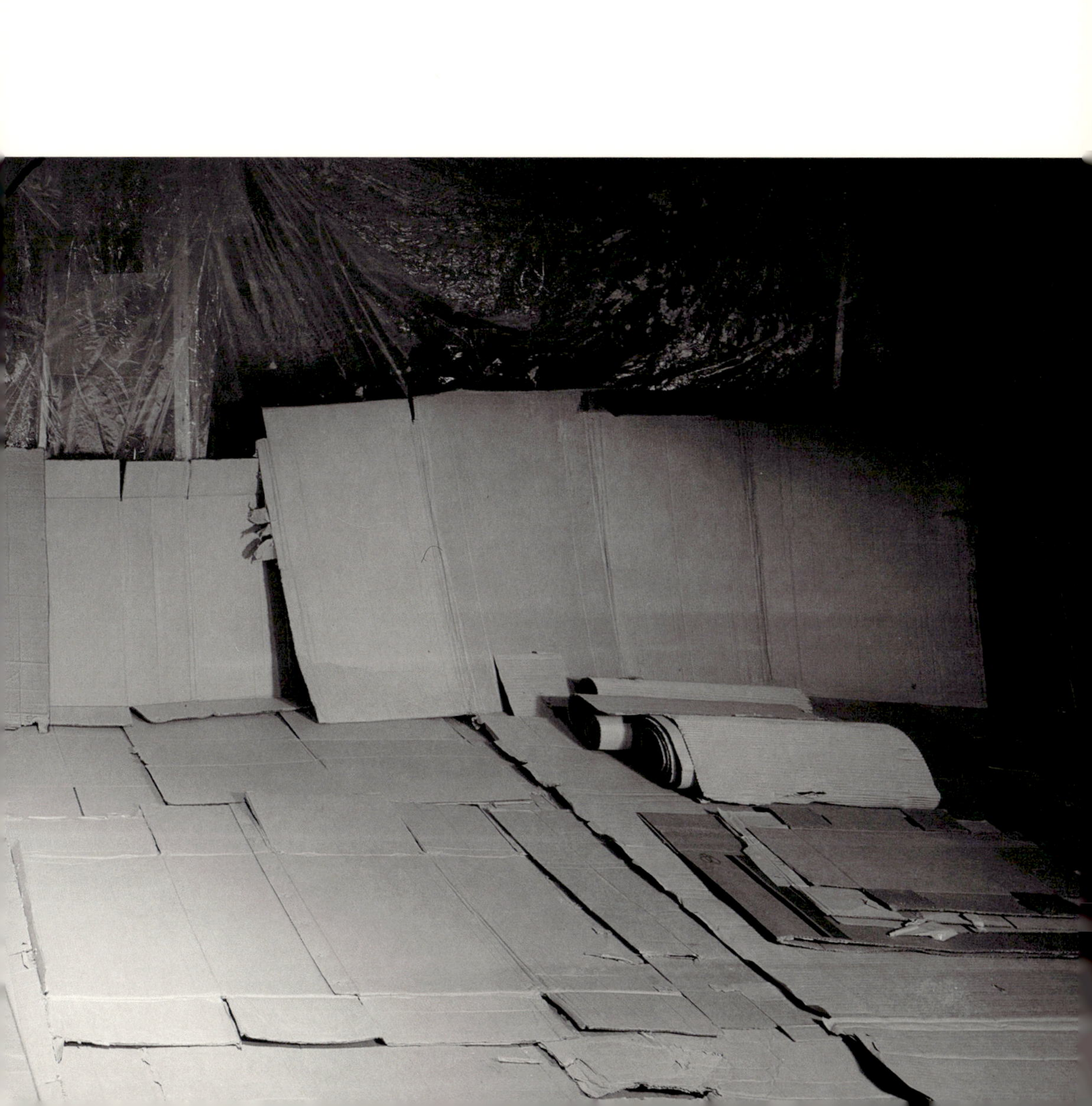

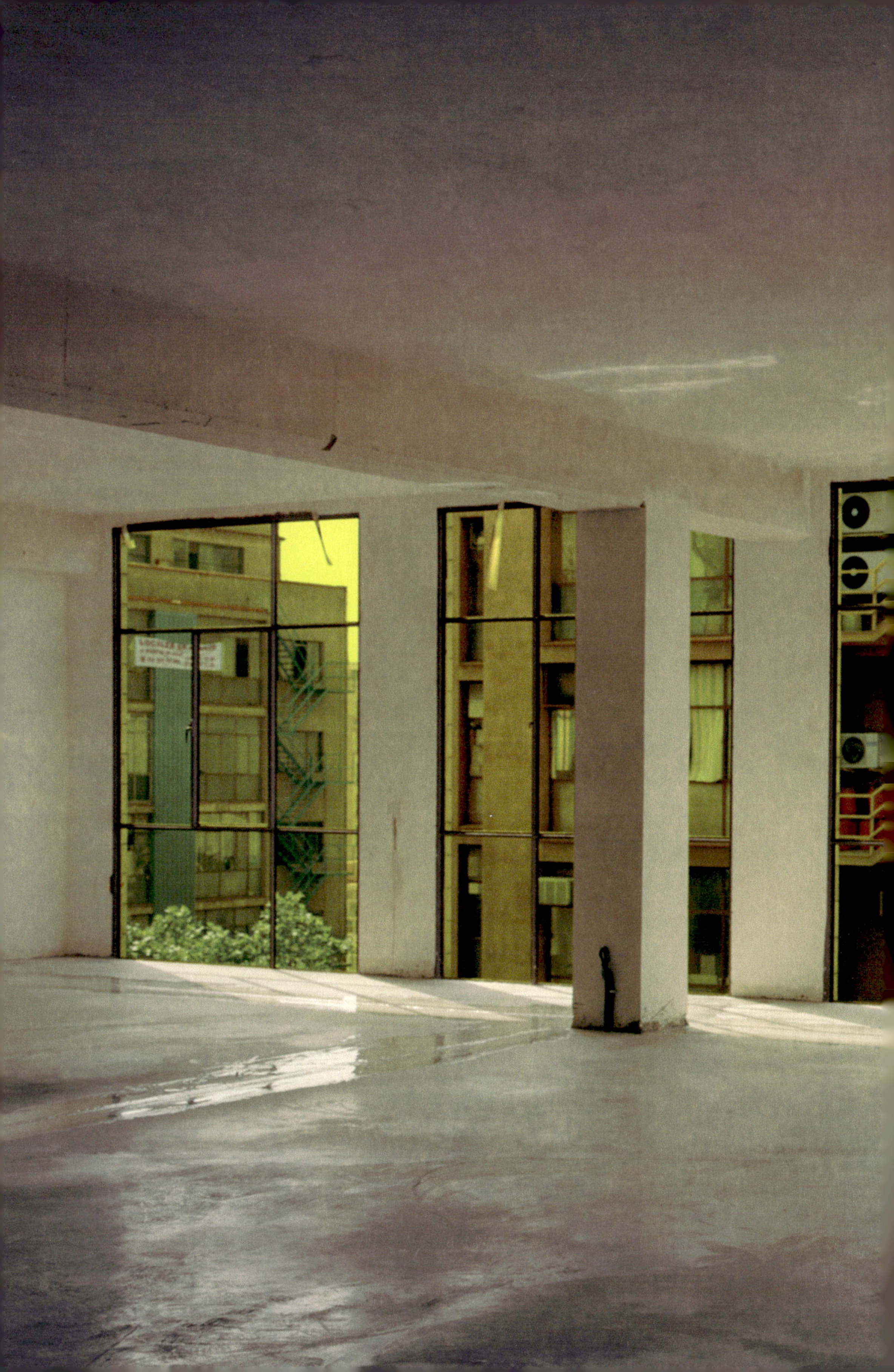

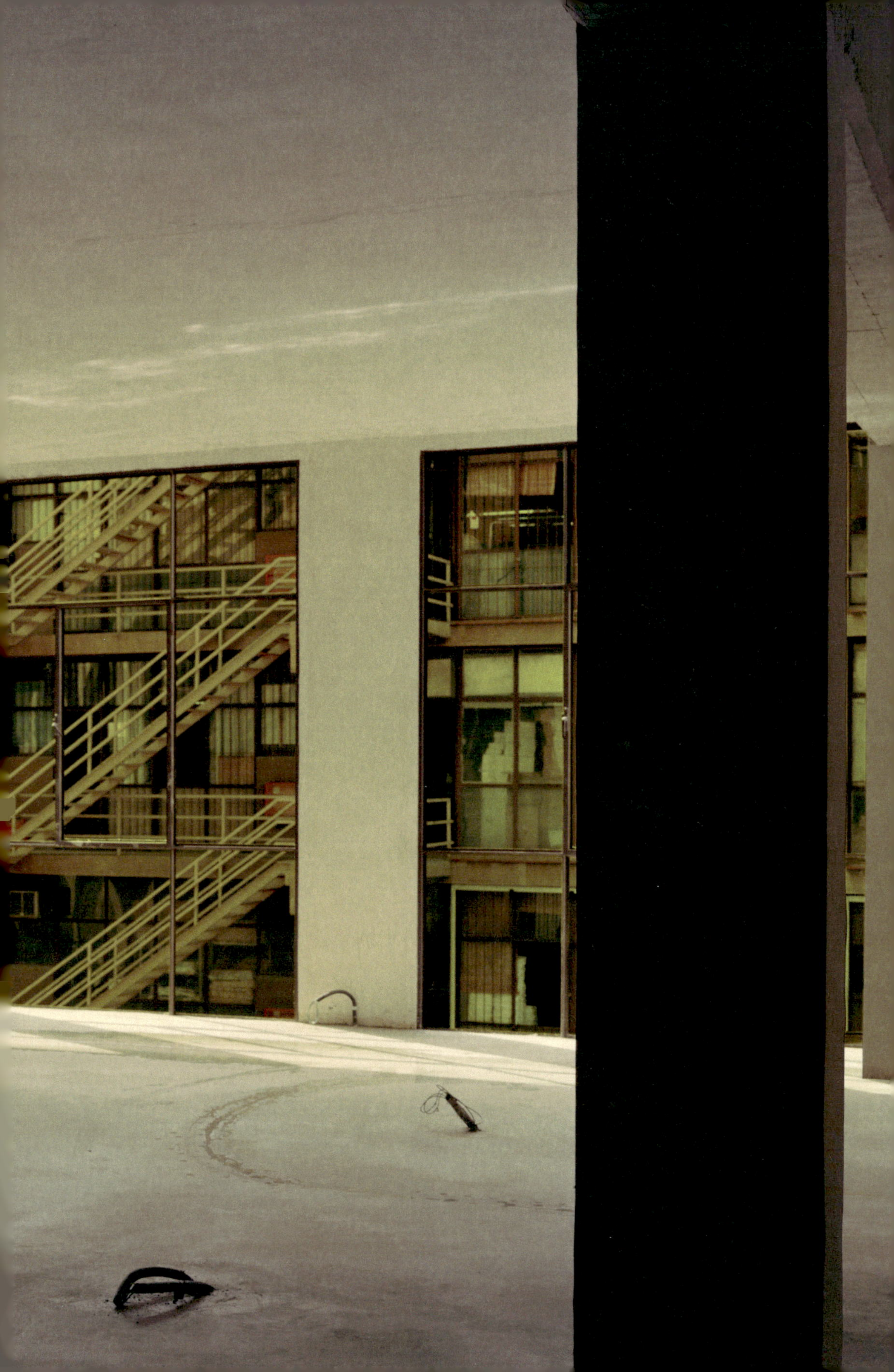

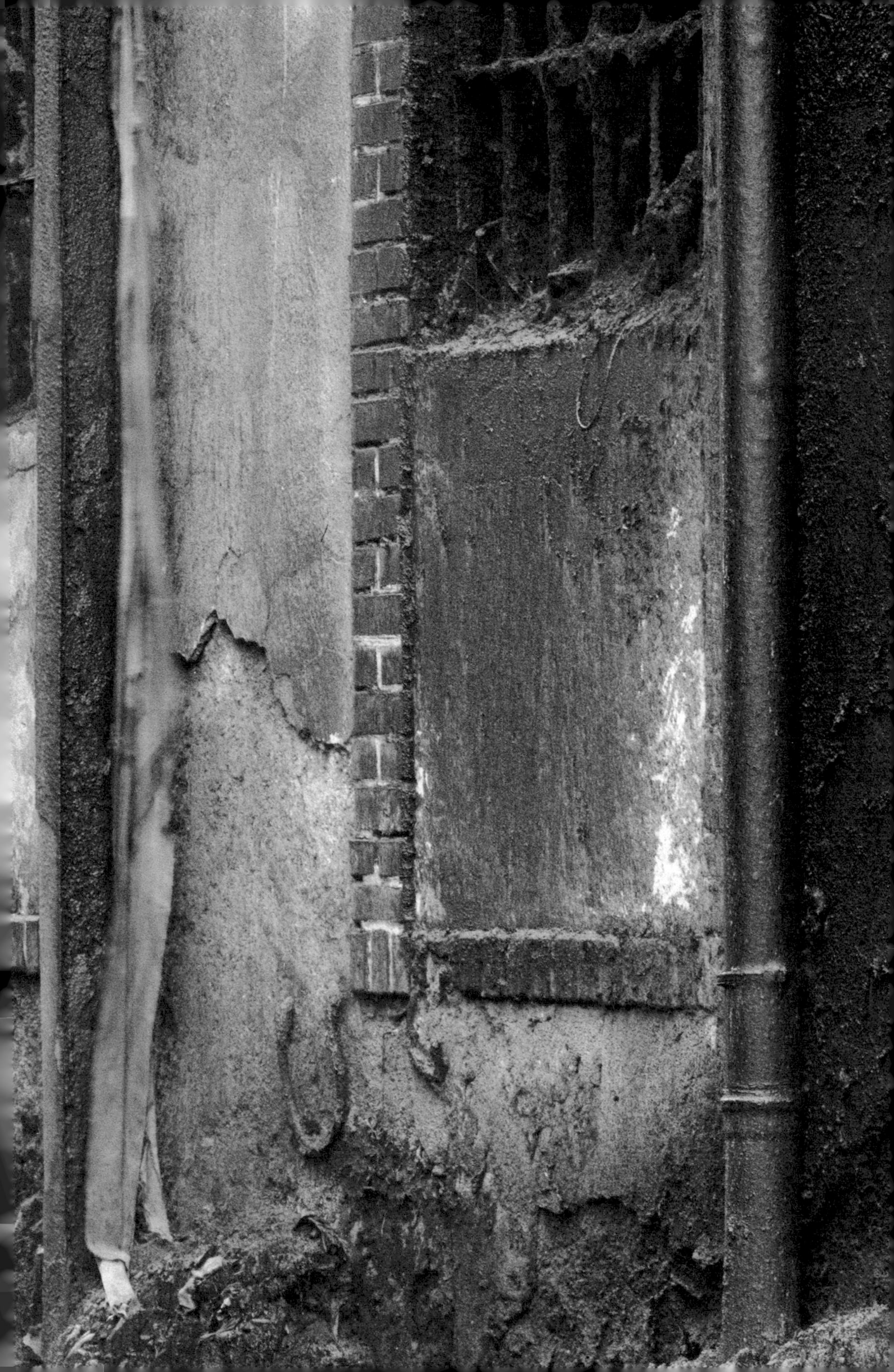

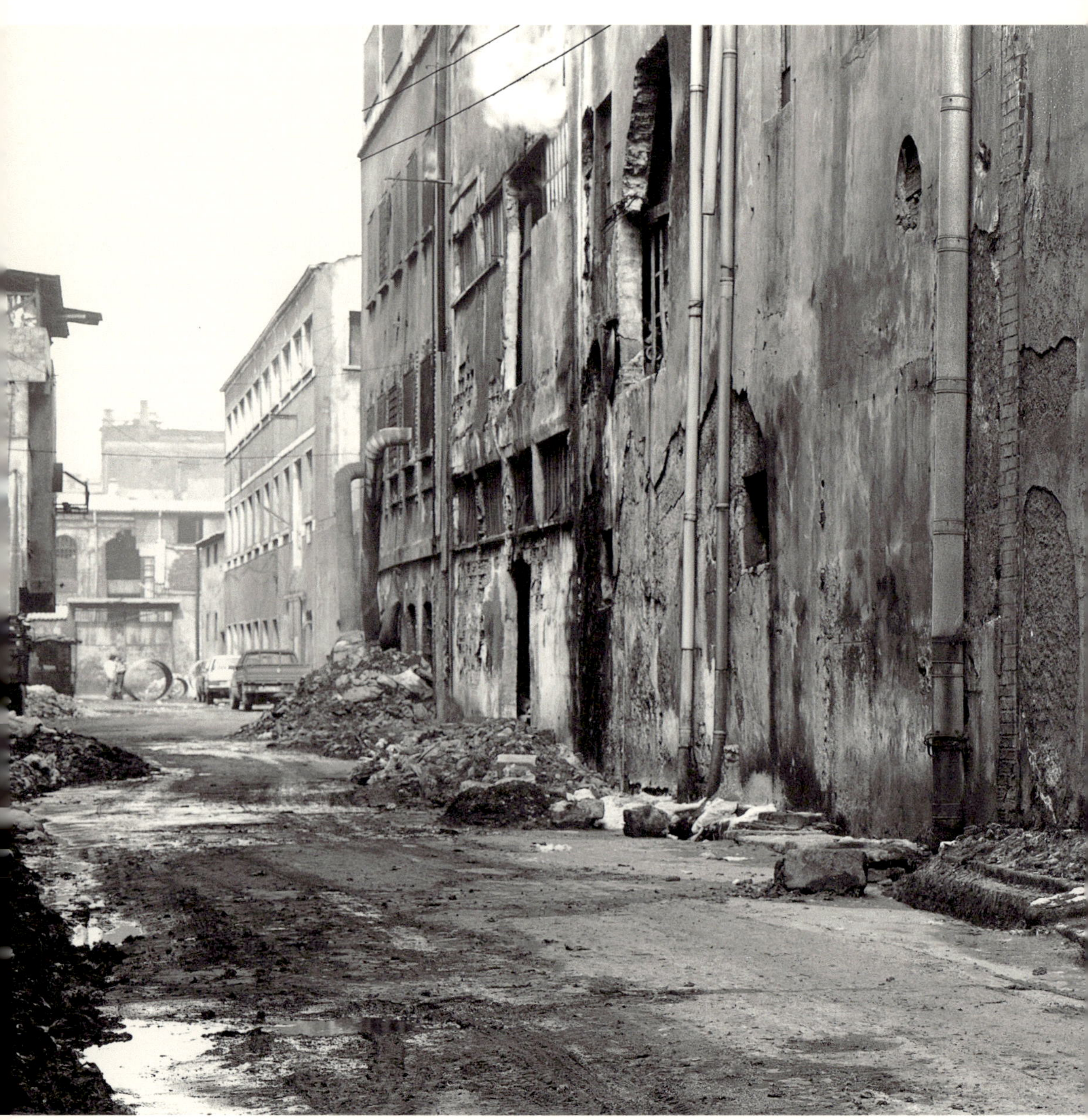

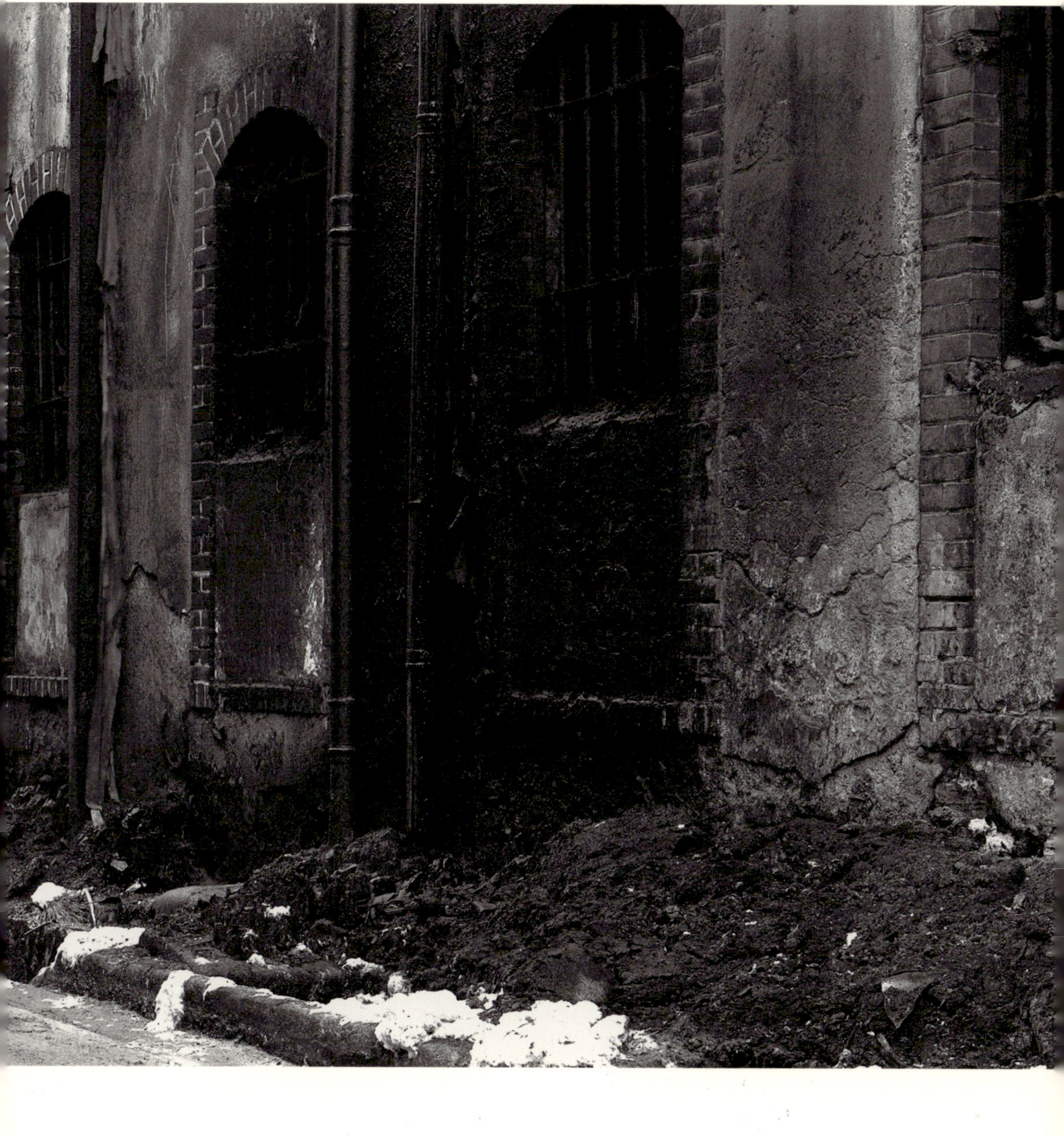

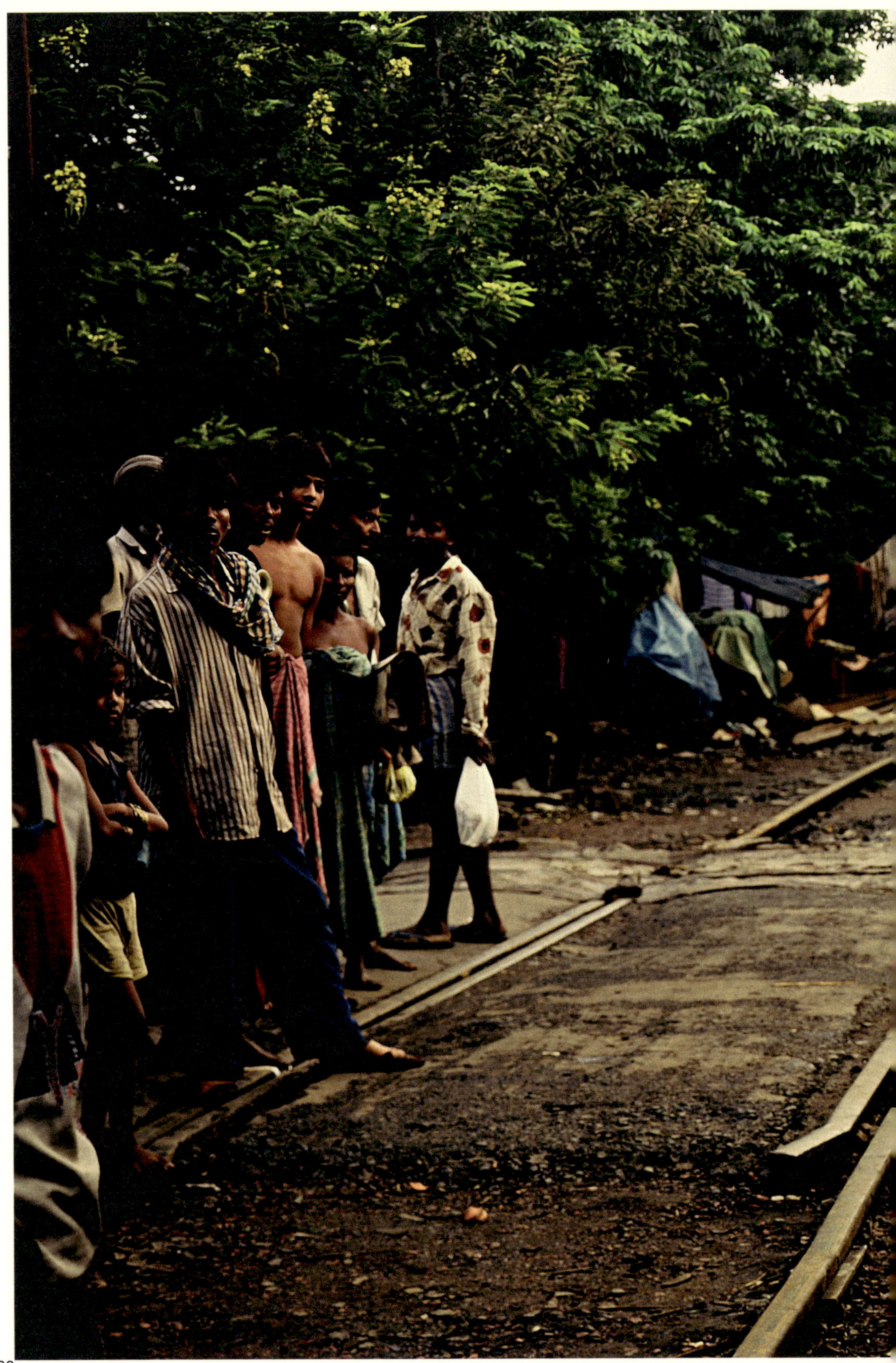

1.22

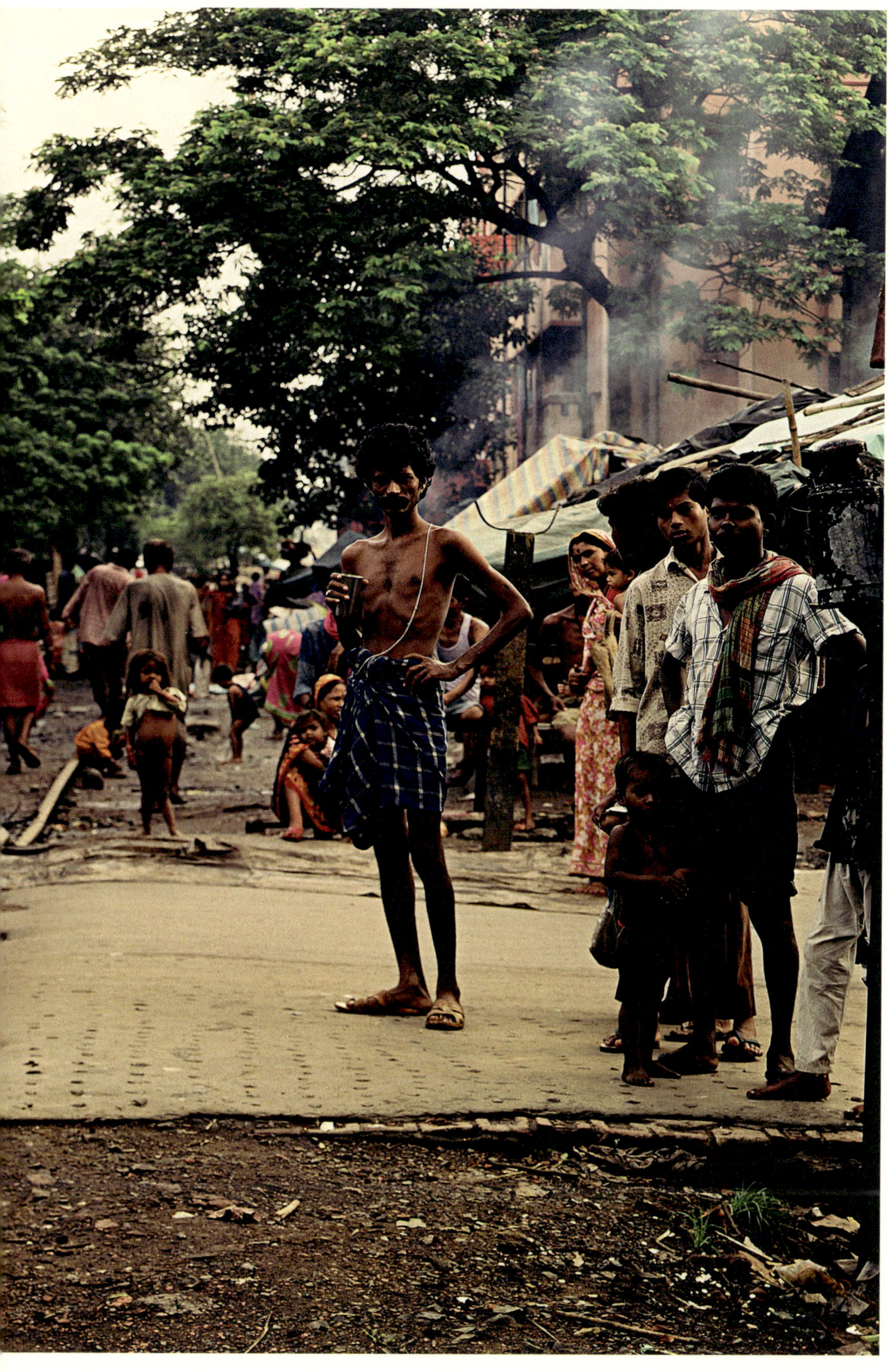

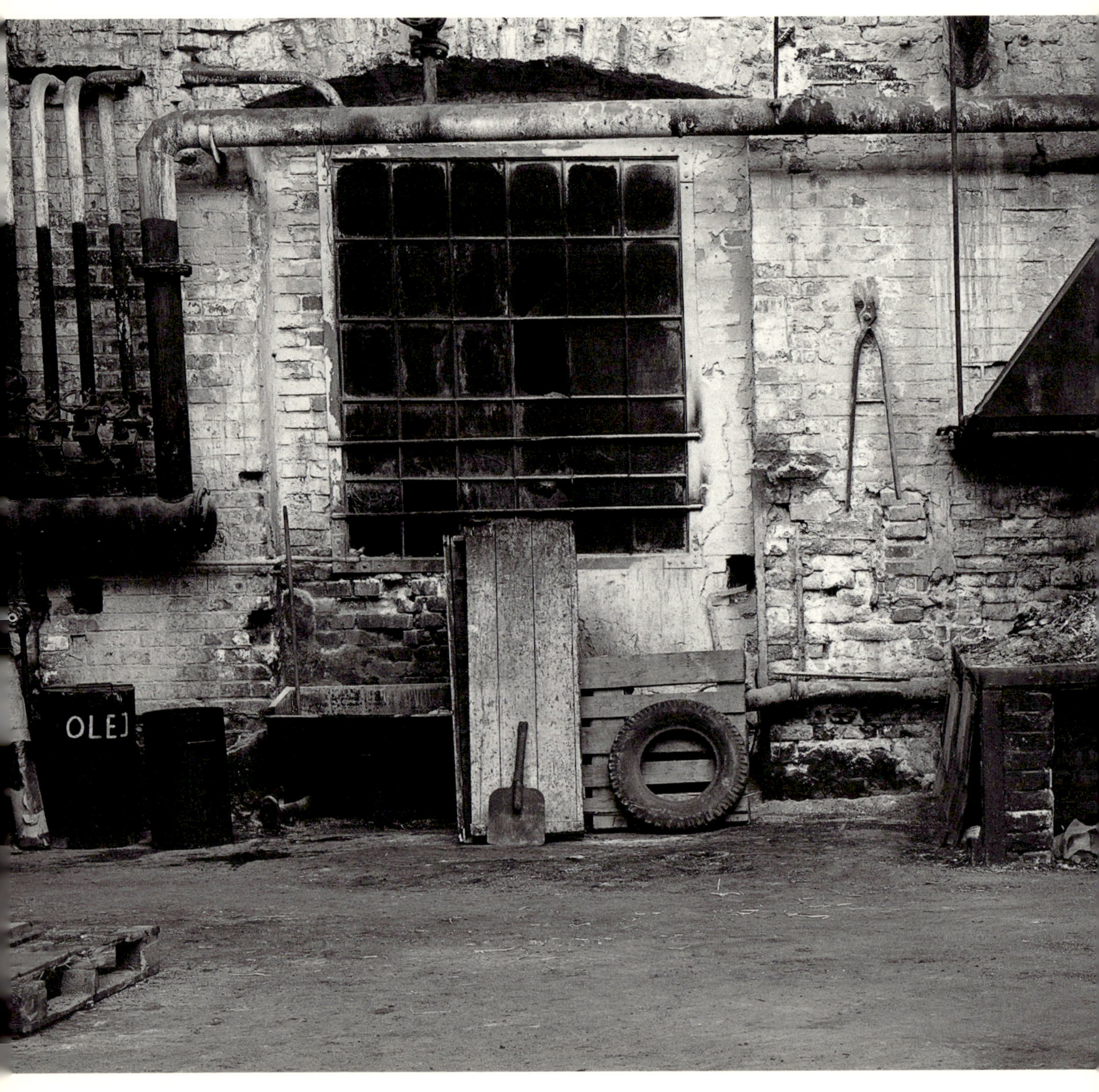

1.24

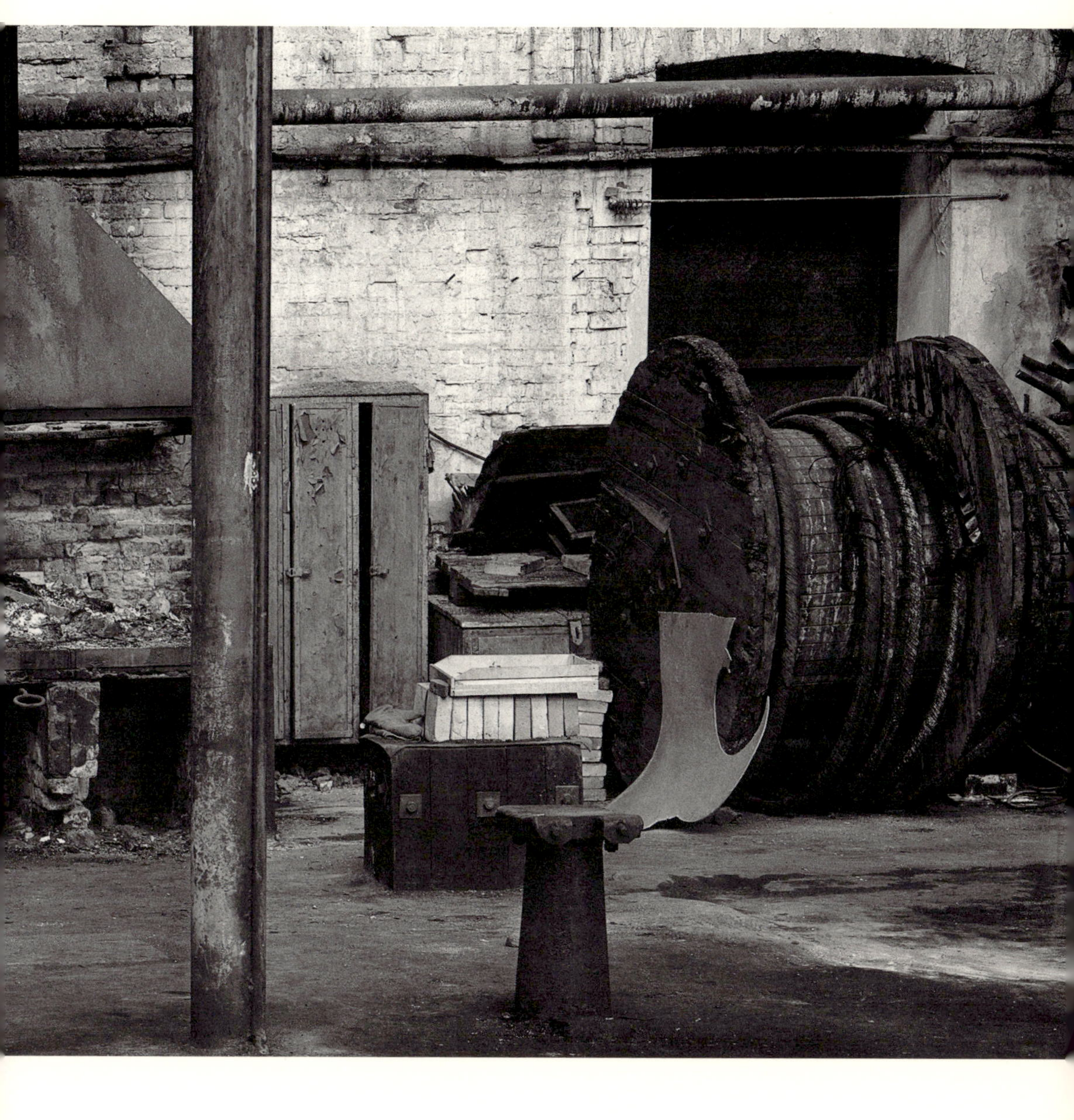

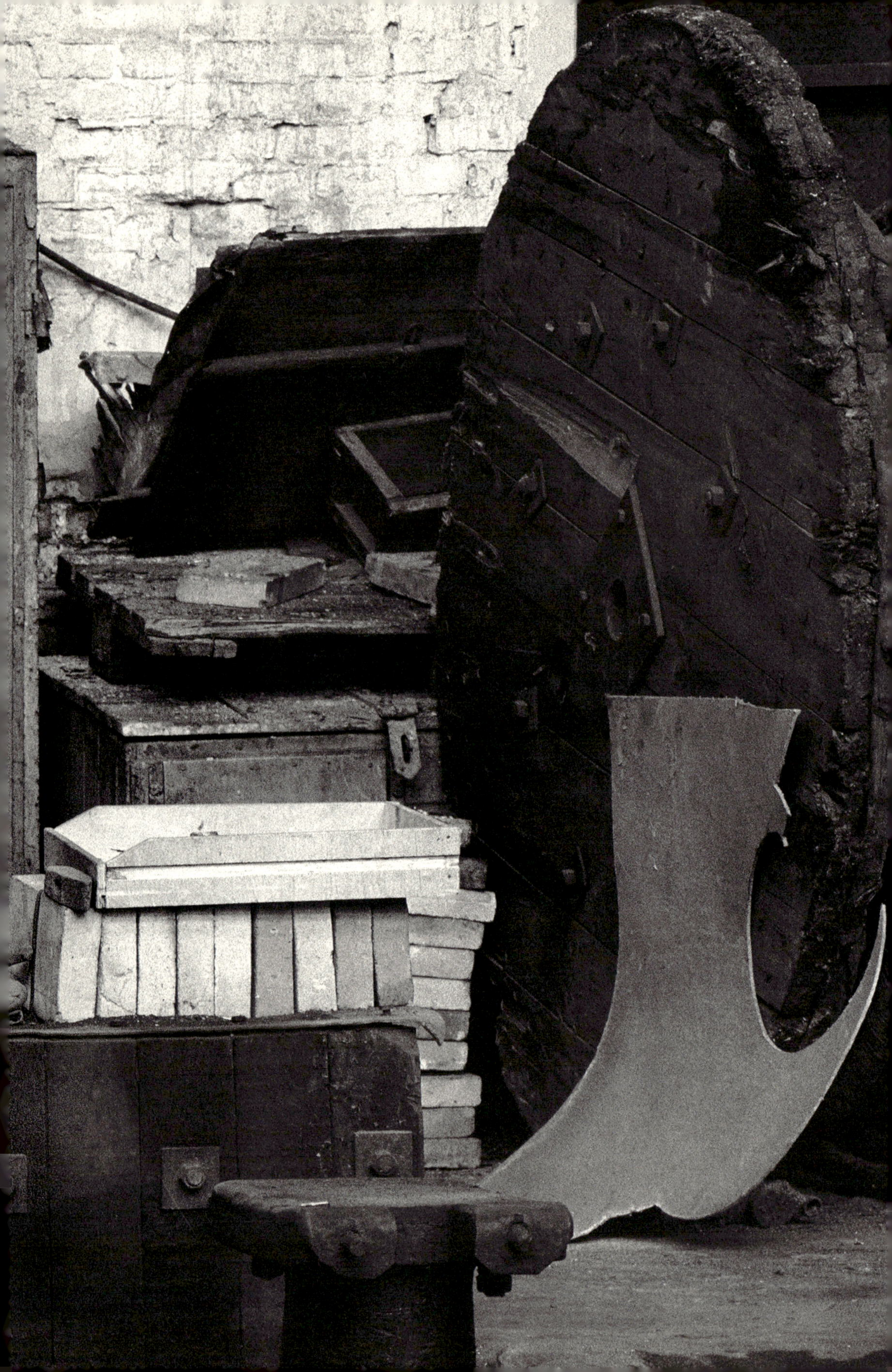

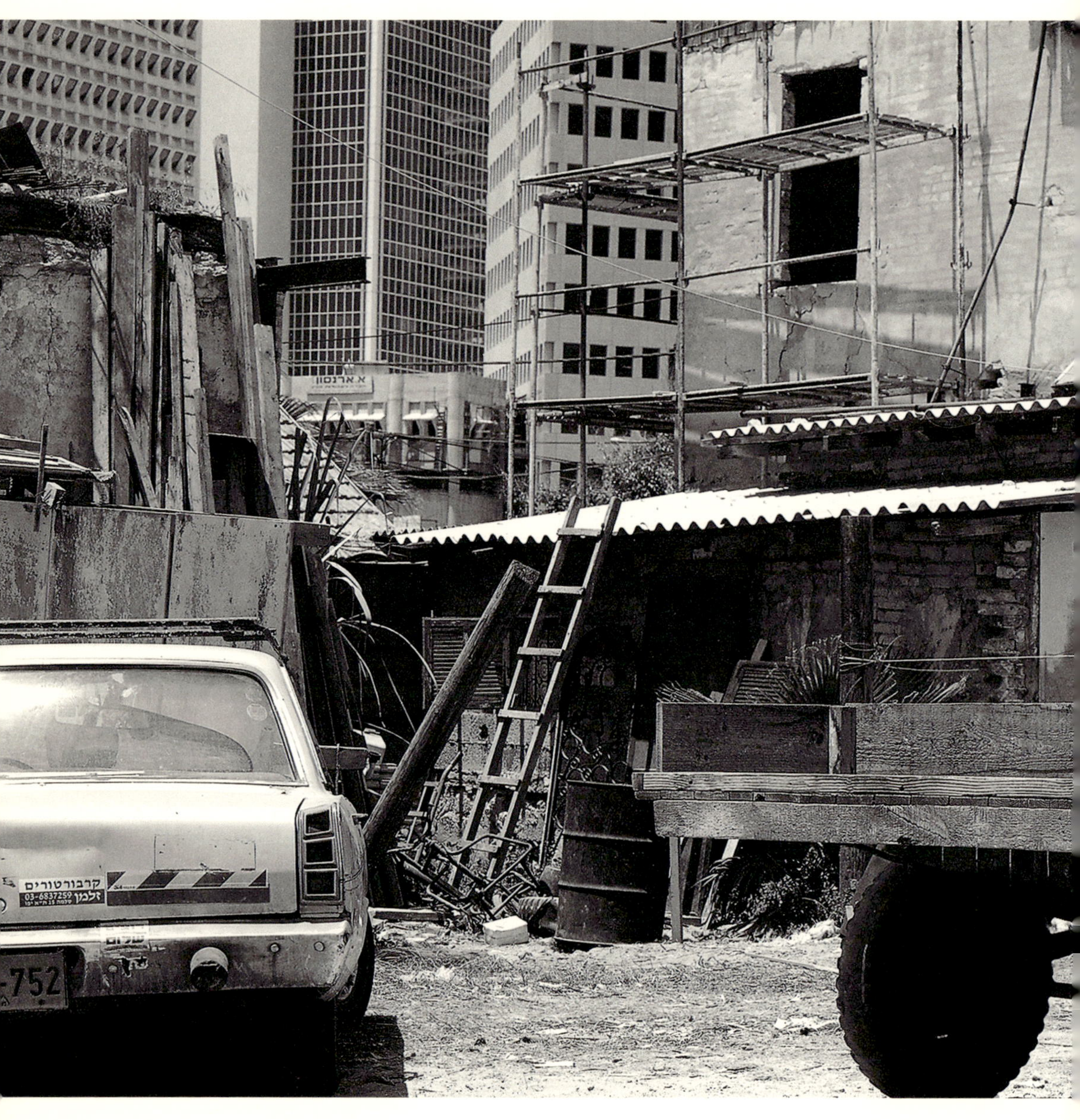

1.28

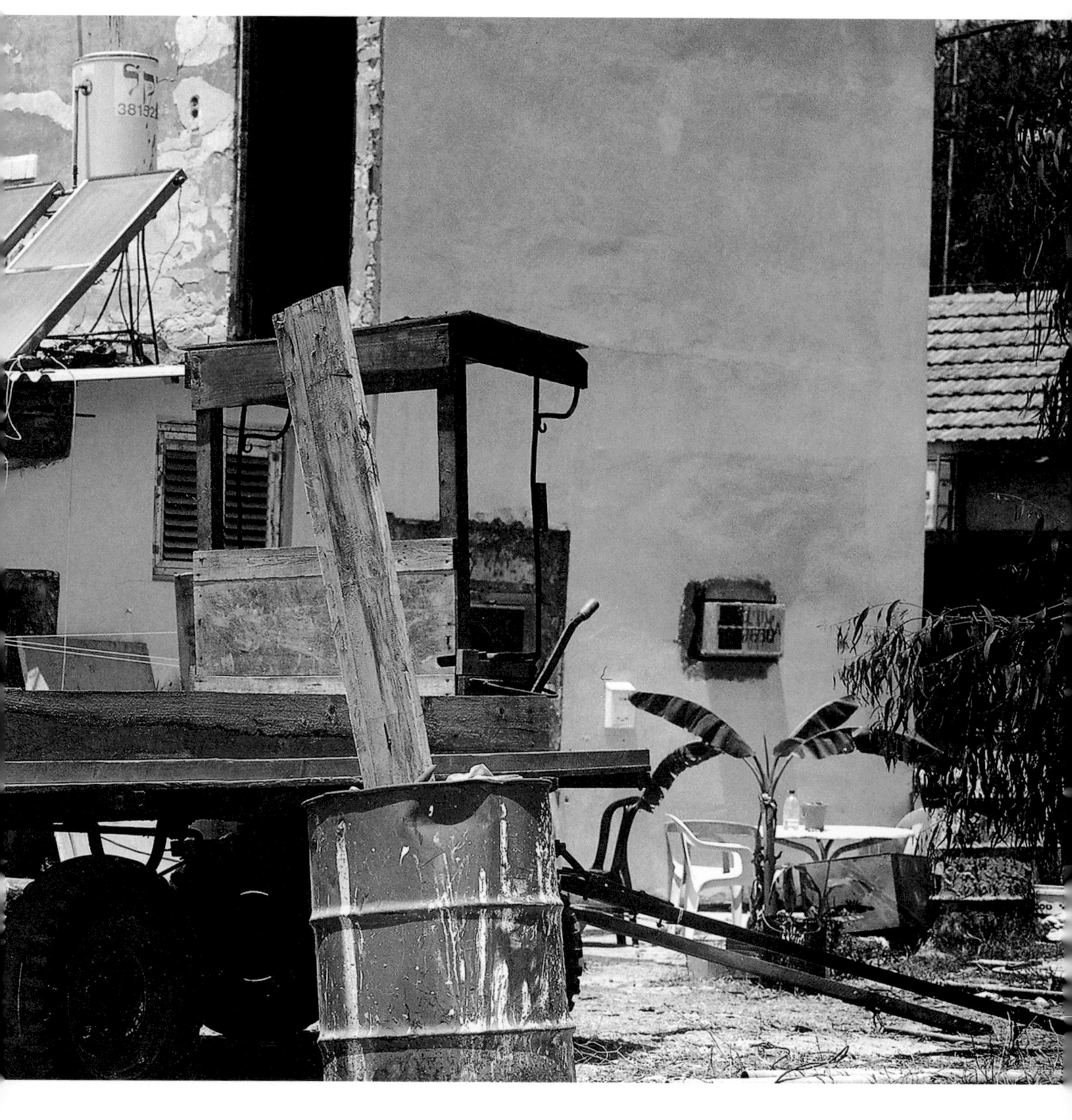

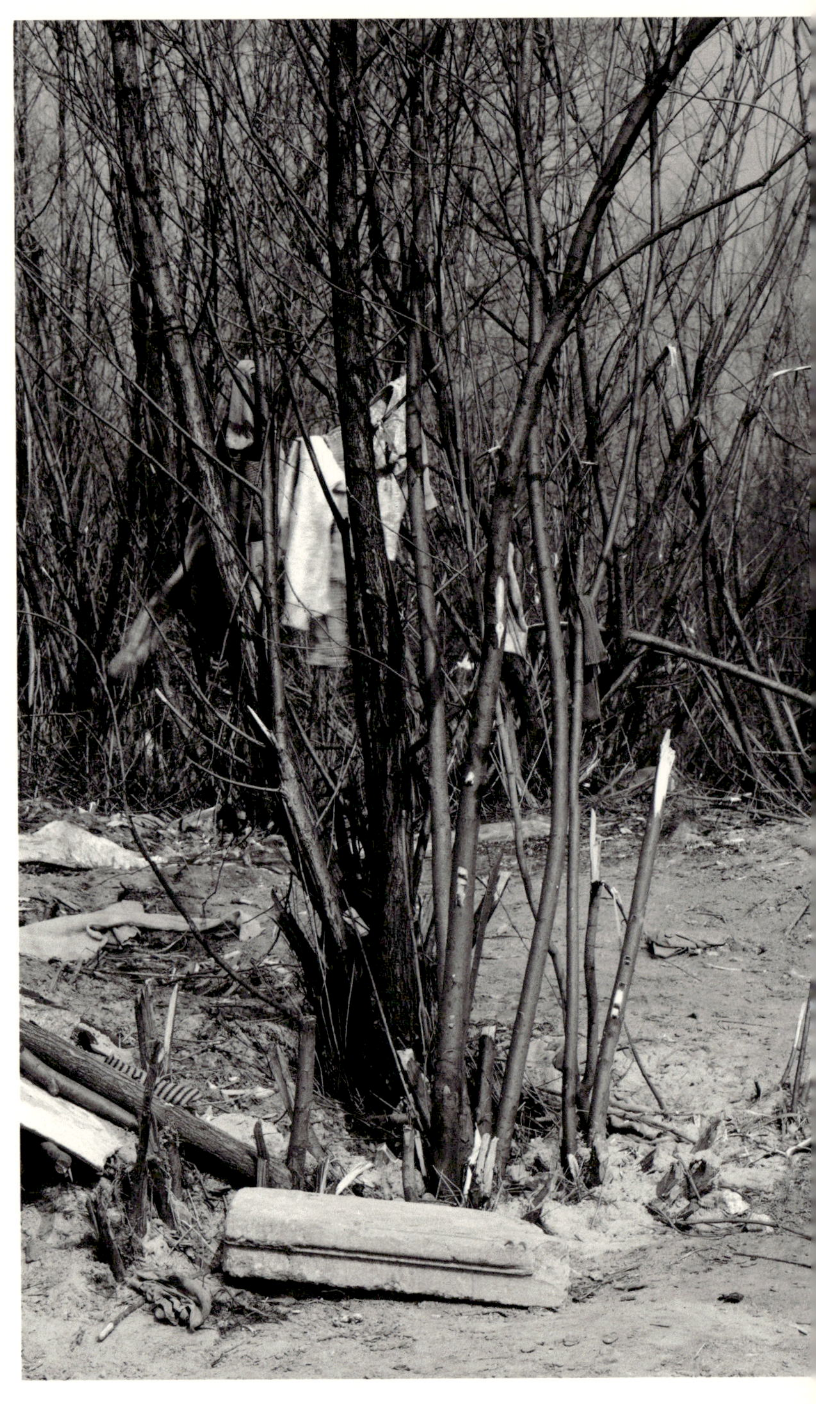

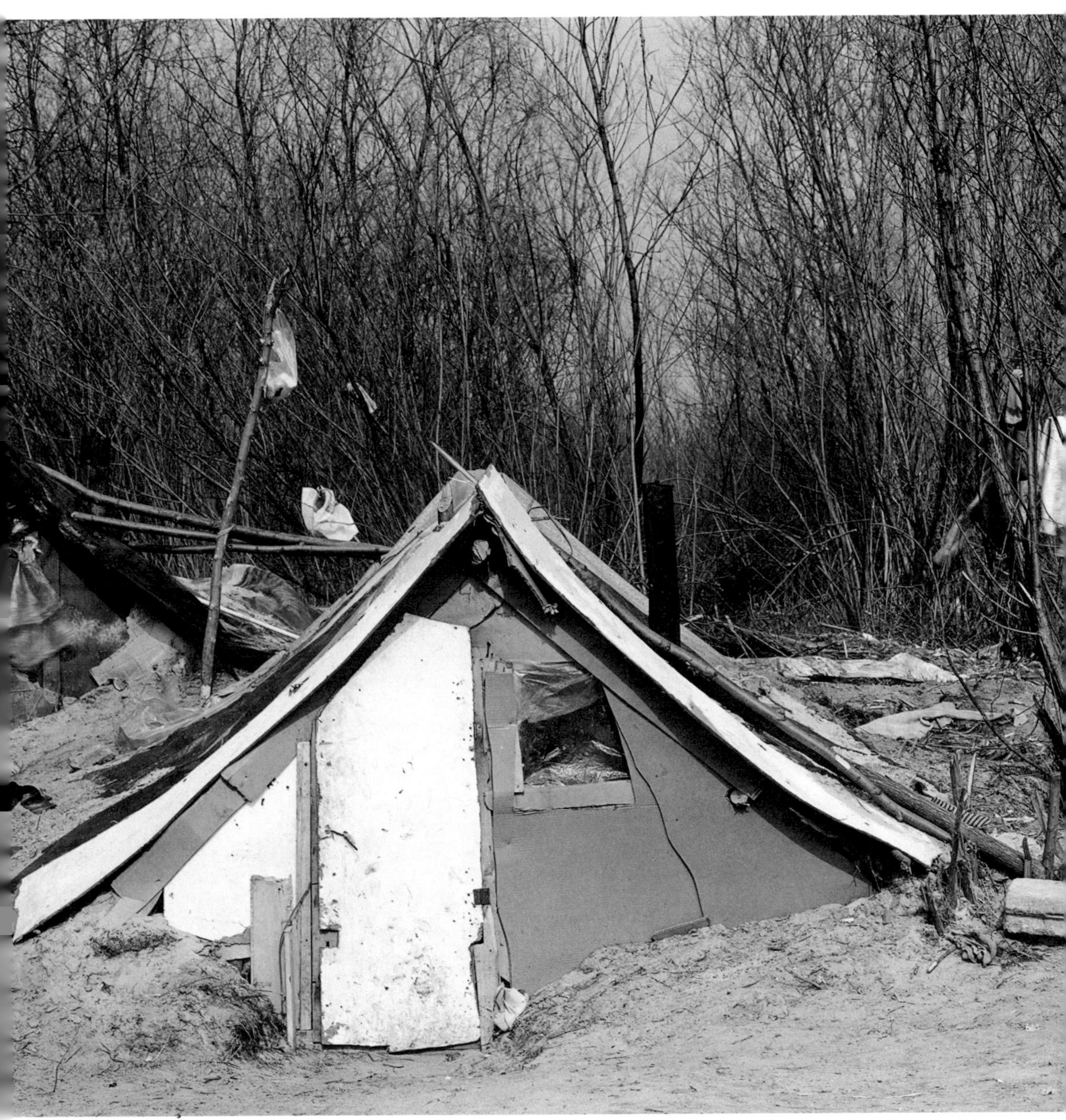

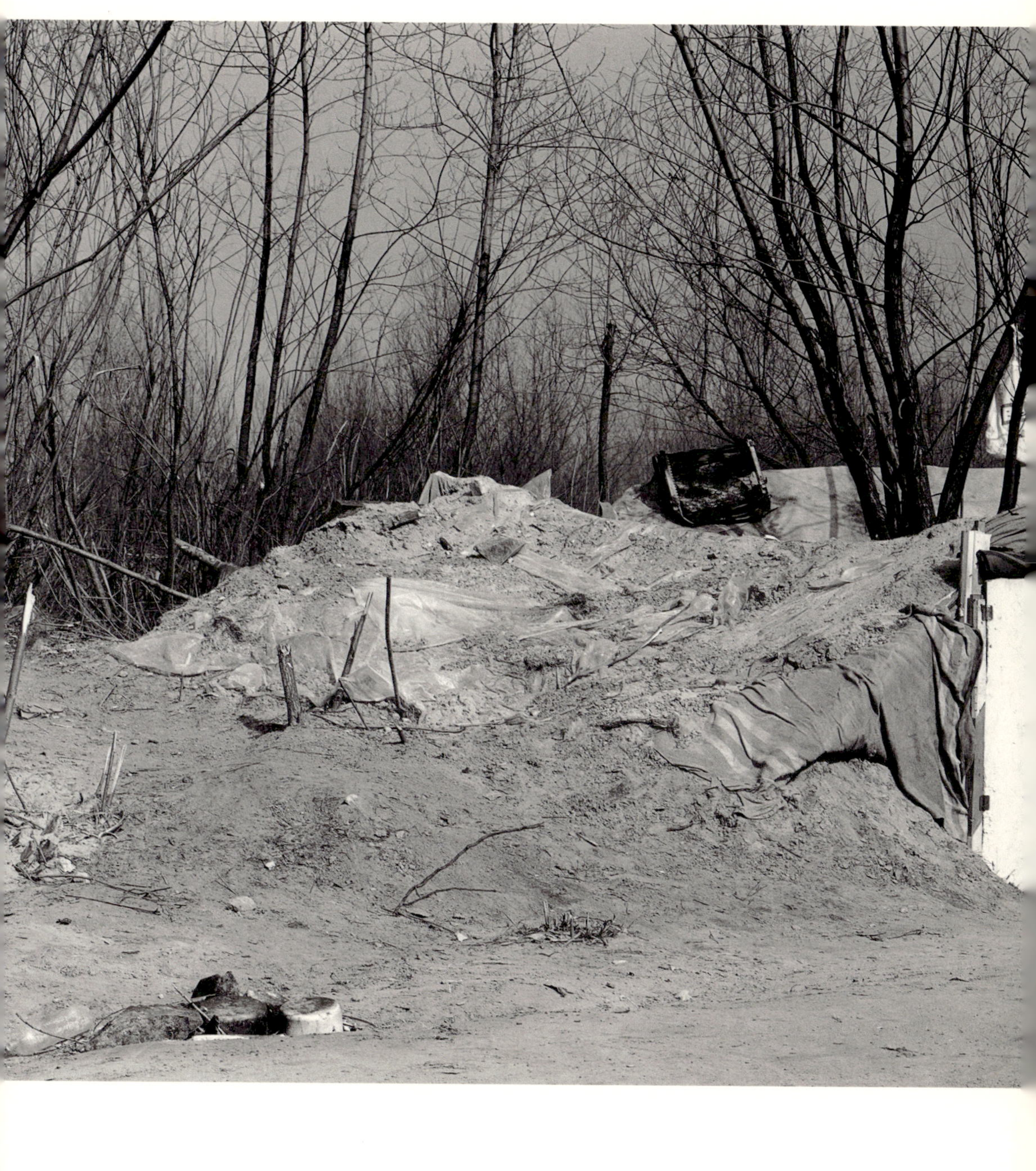

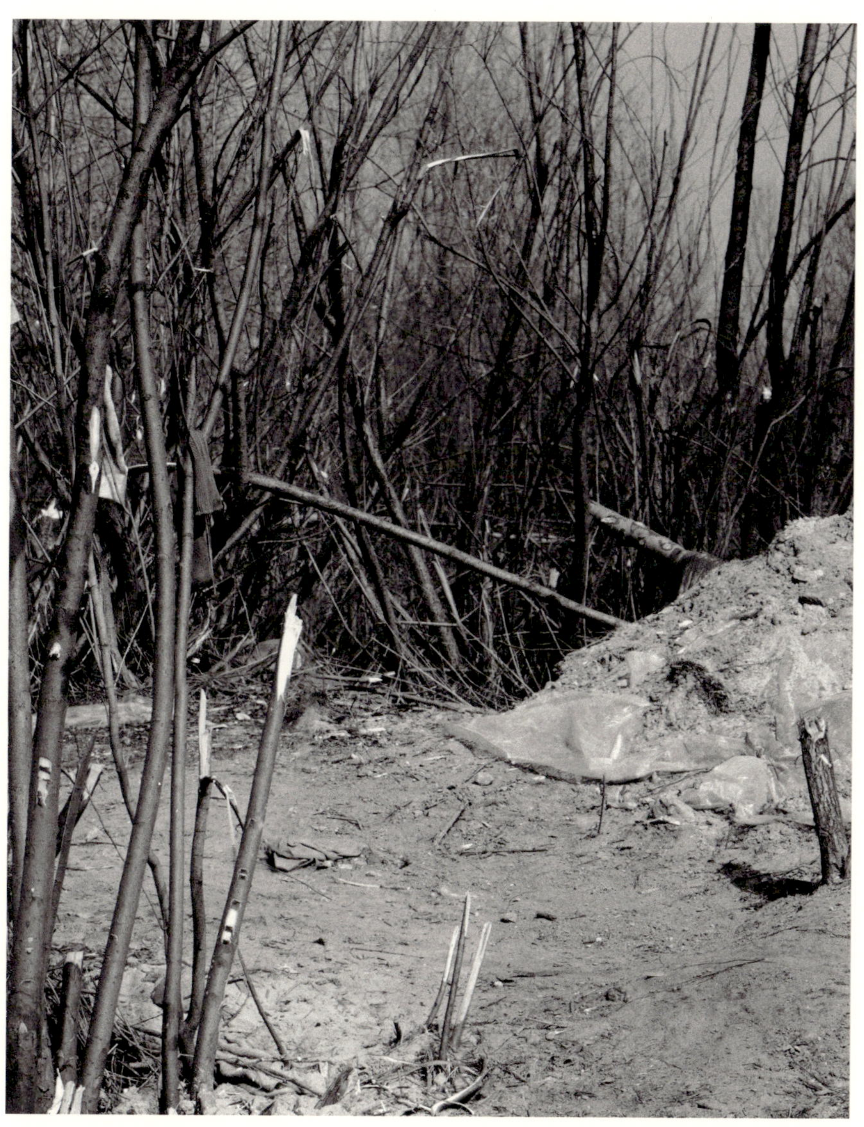

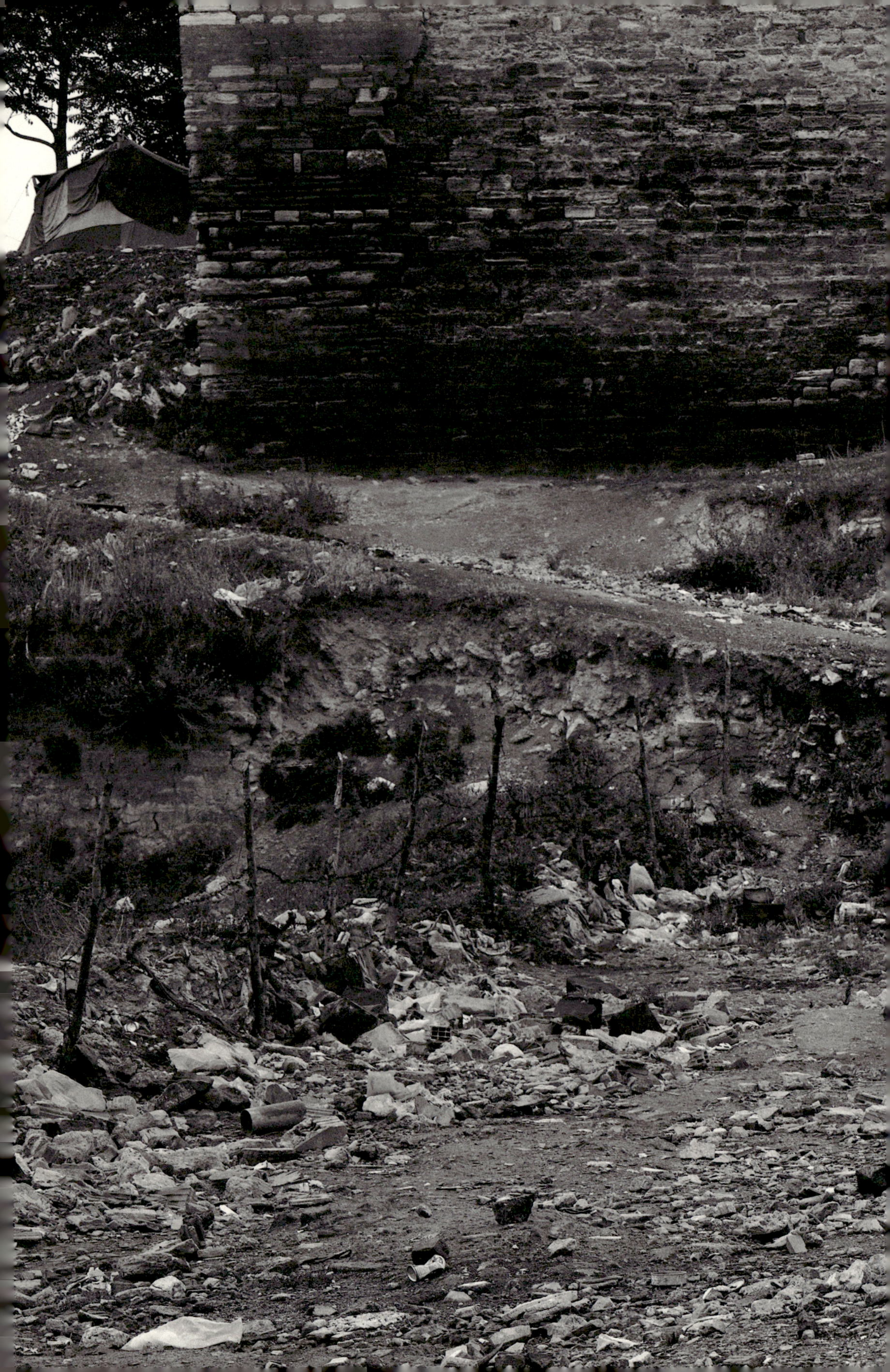

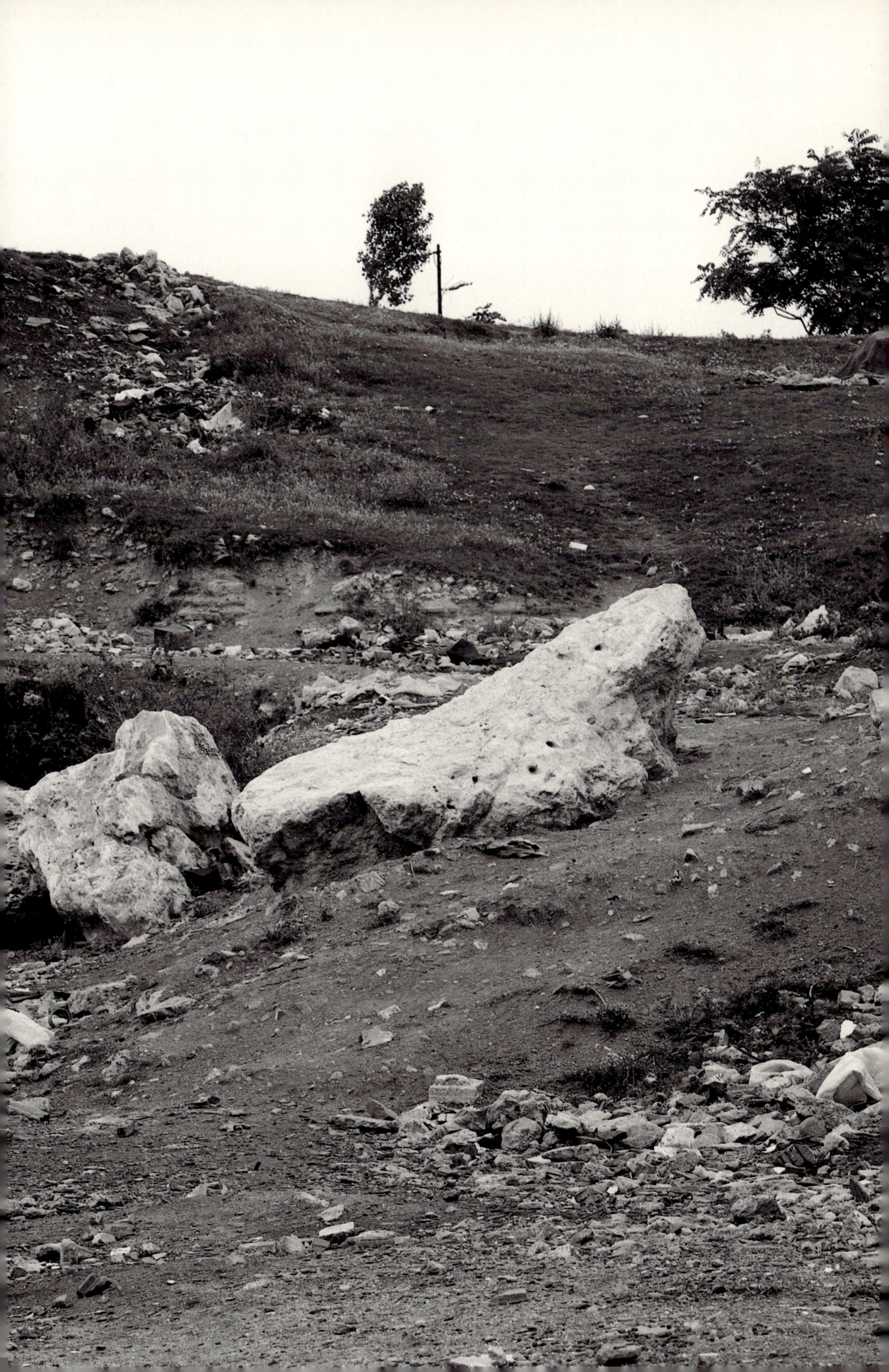

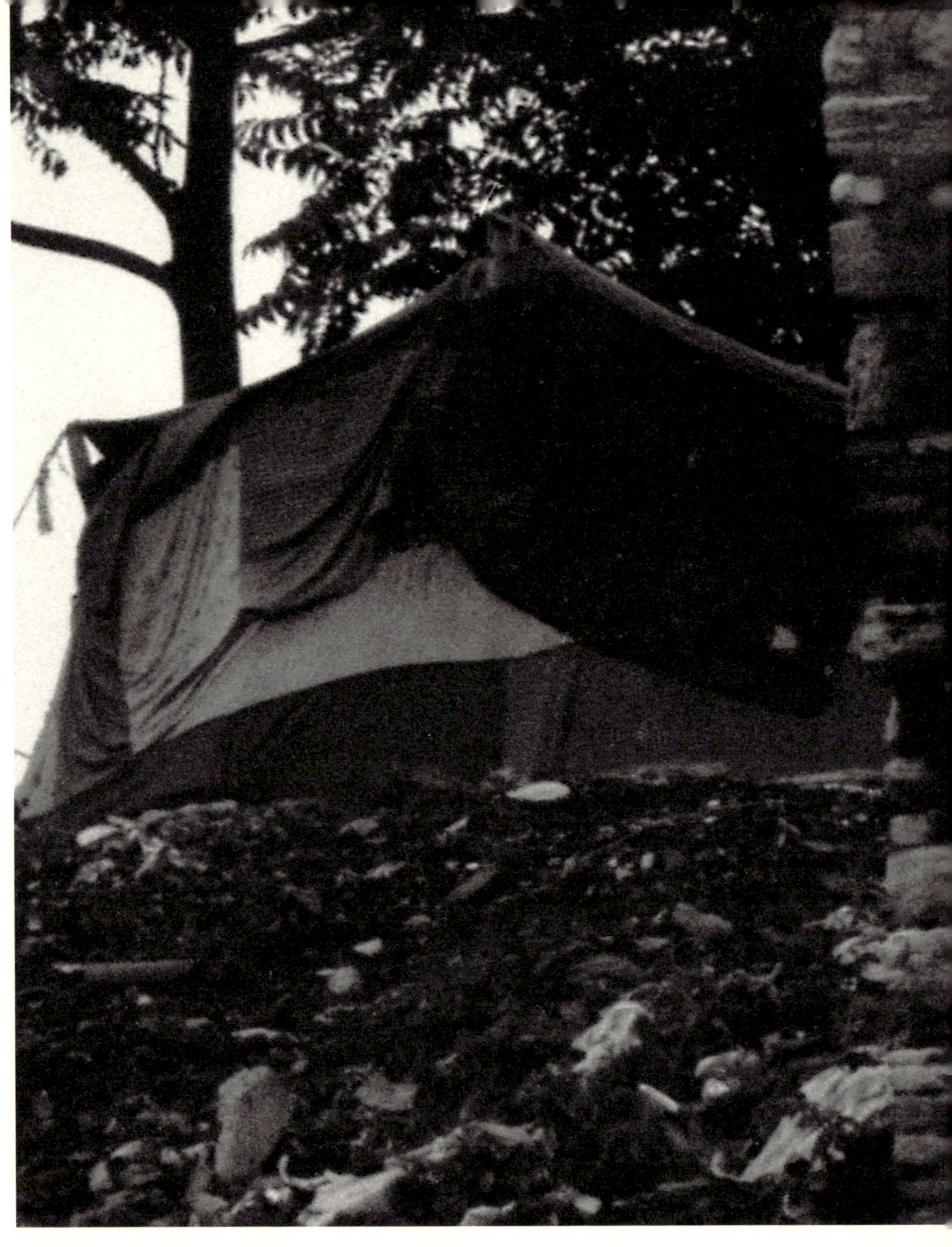

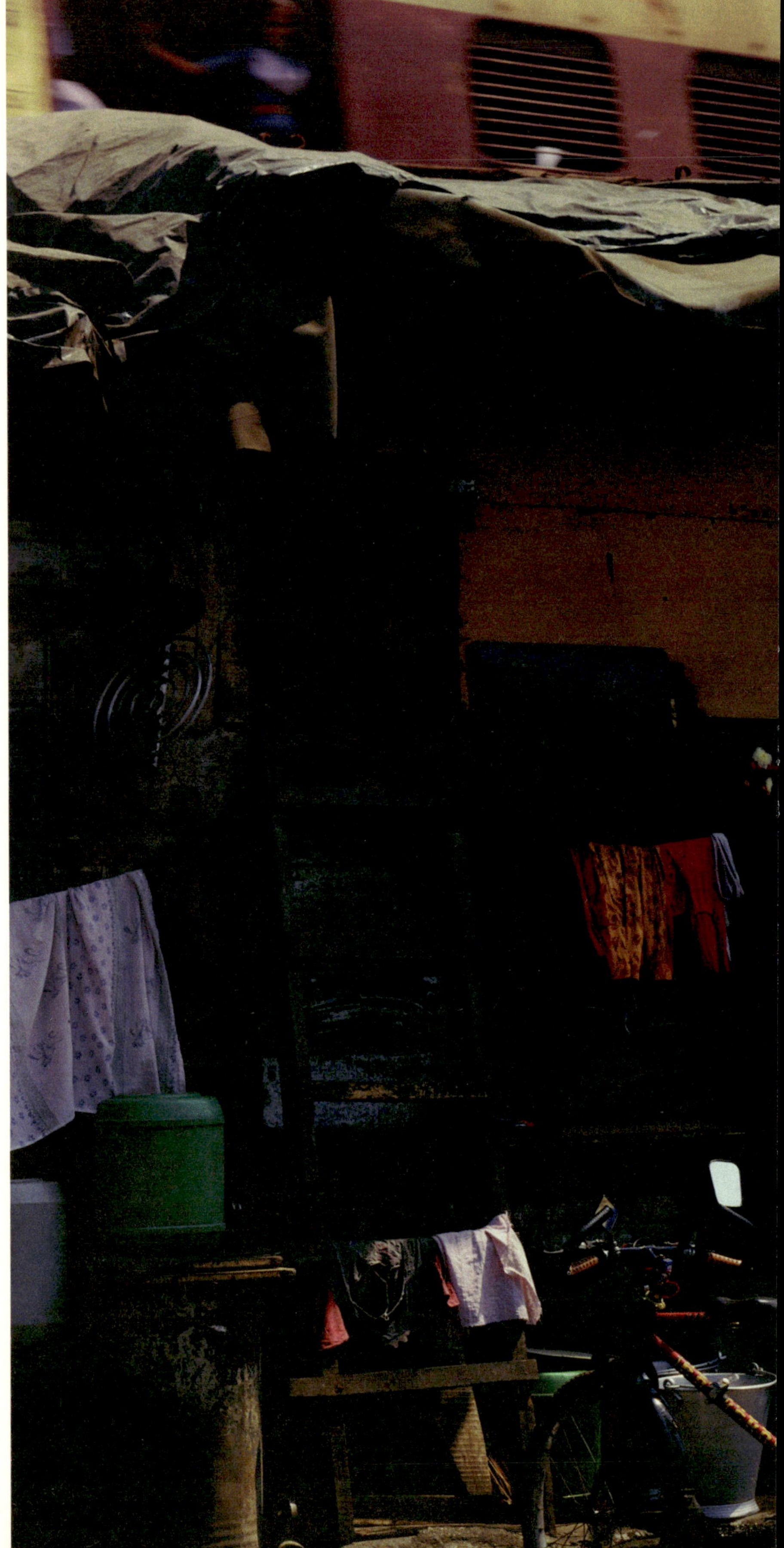

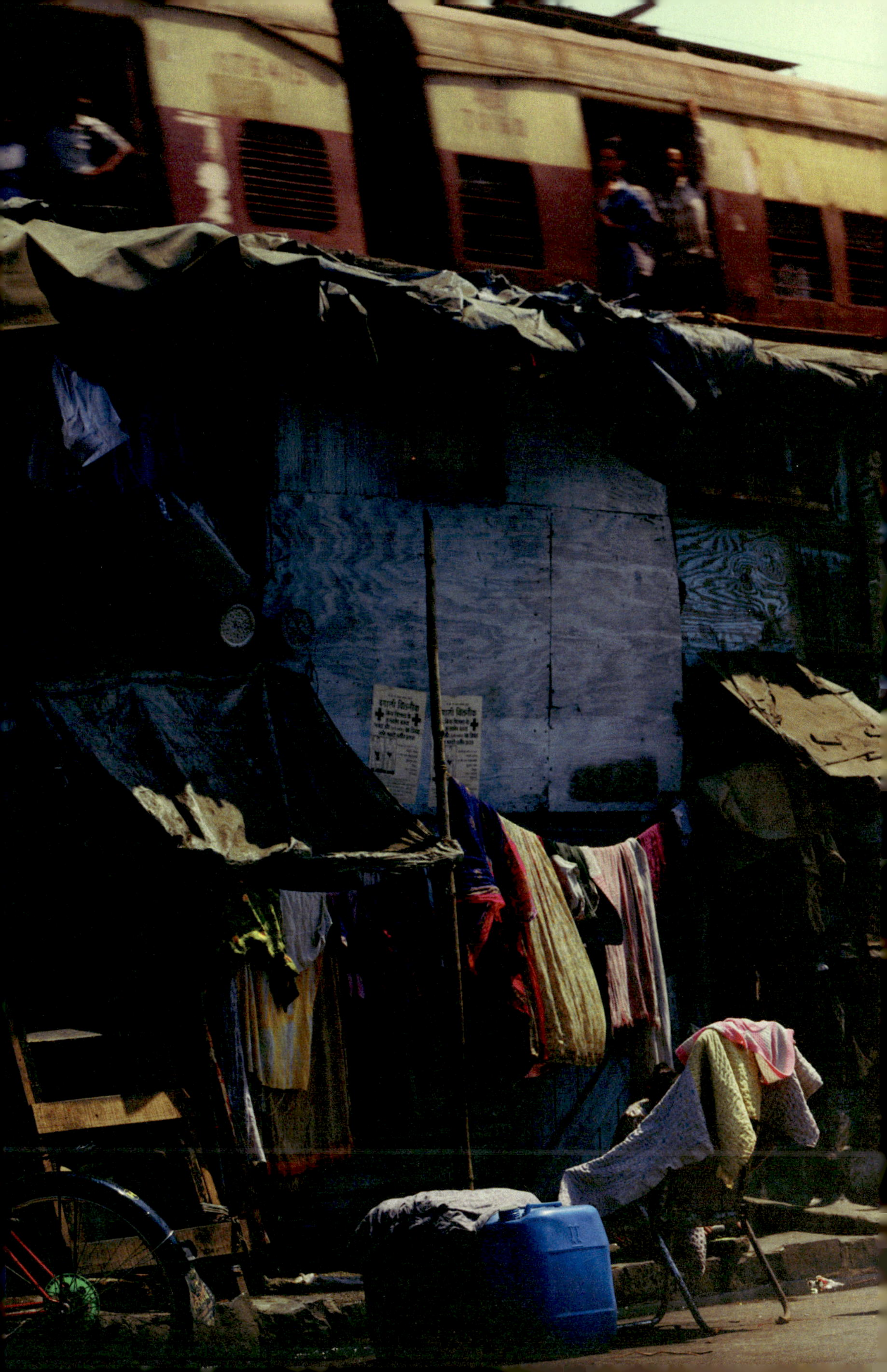

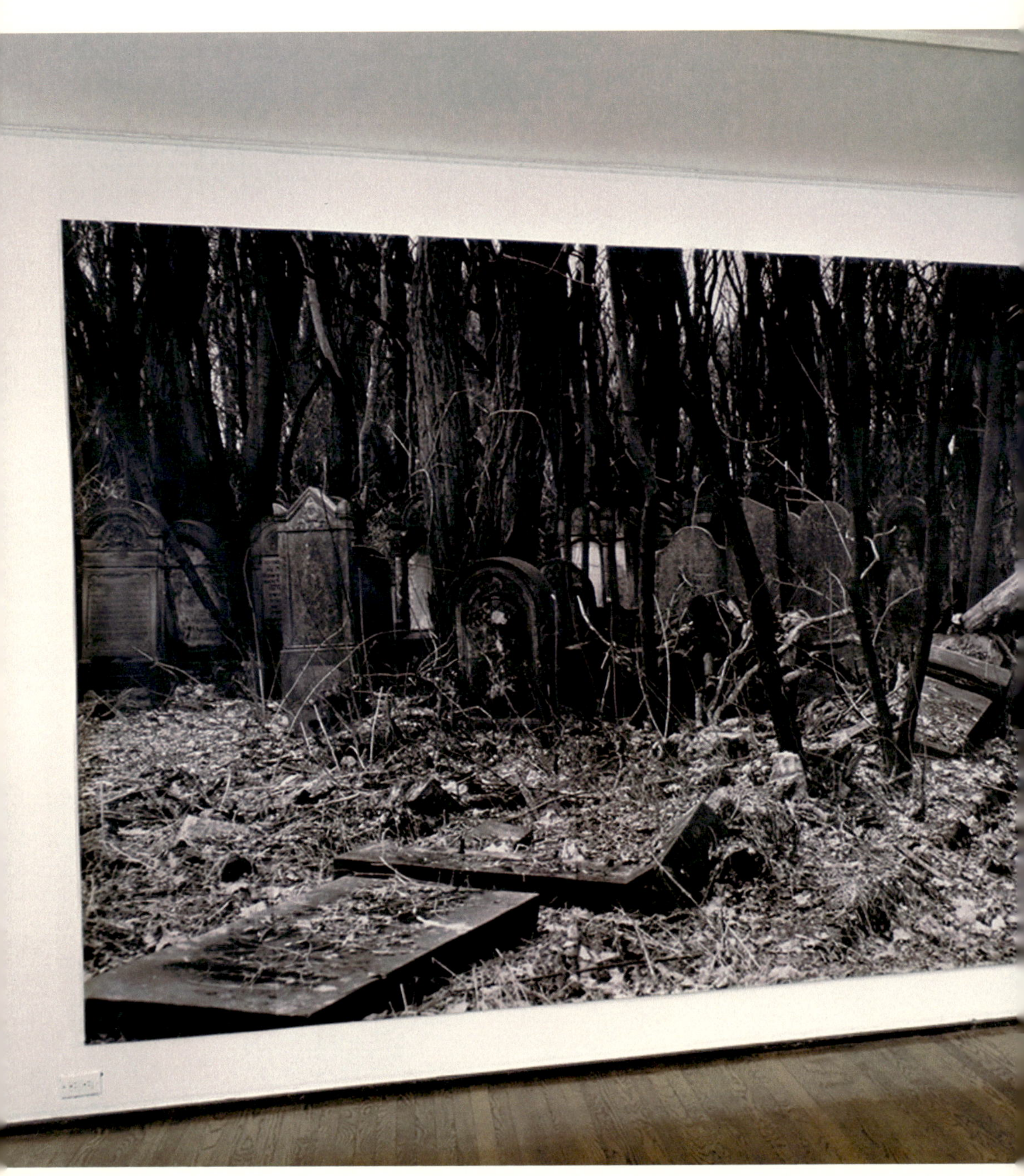

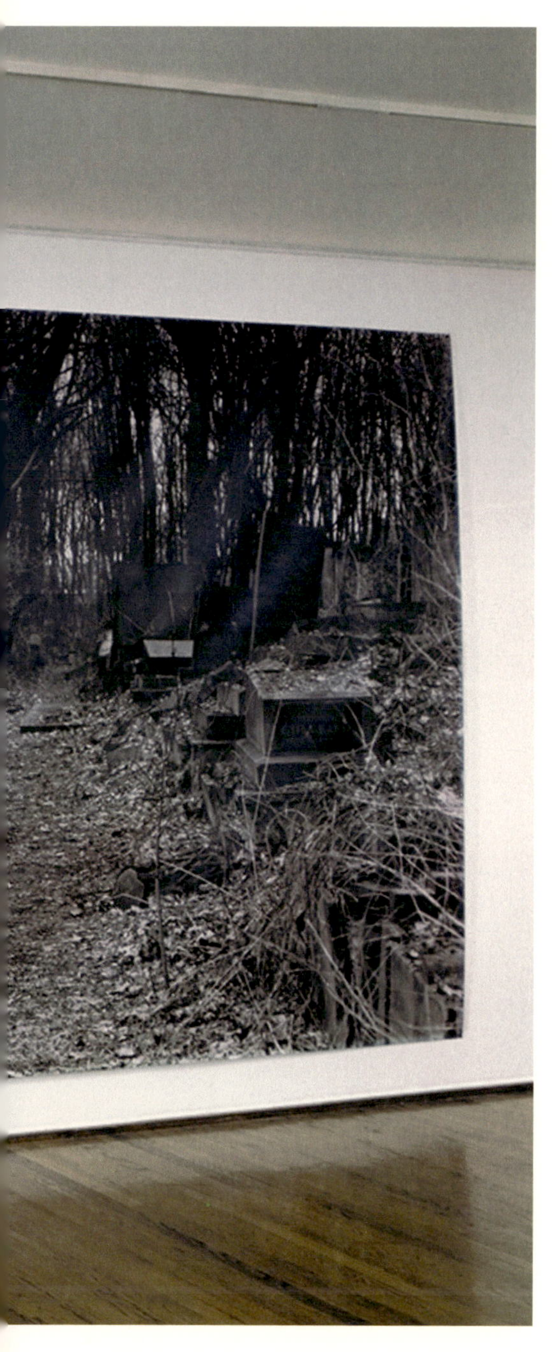

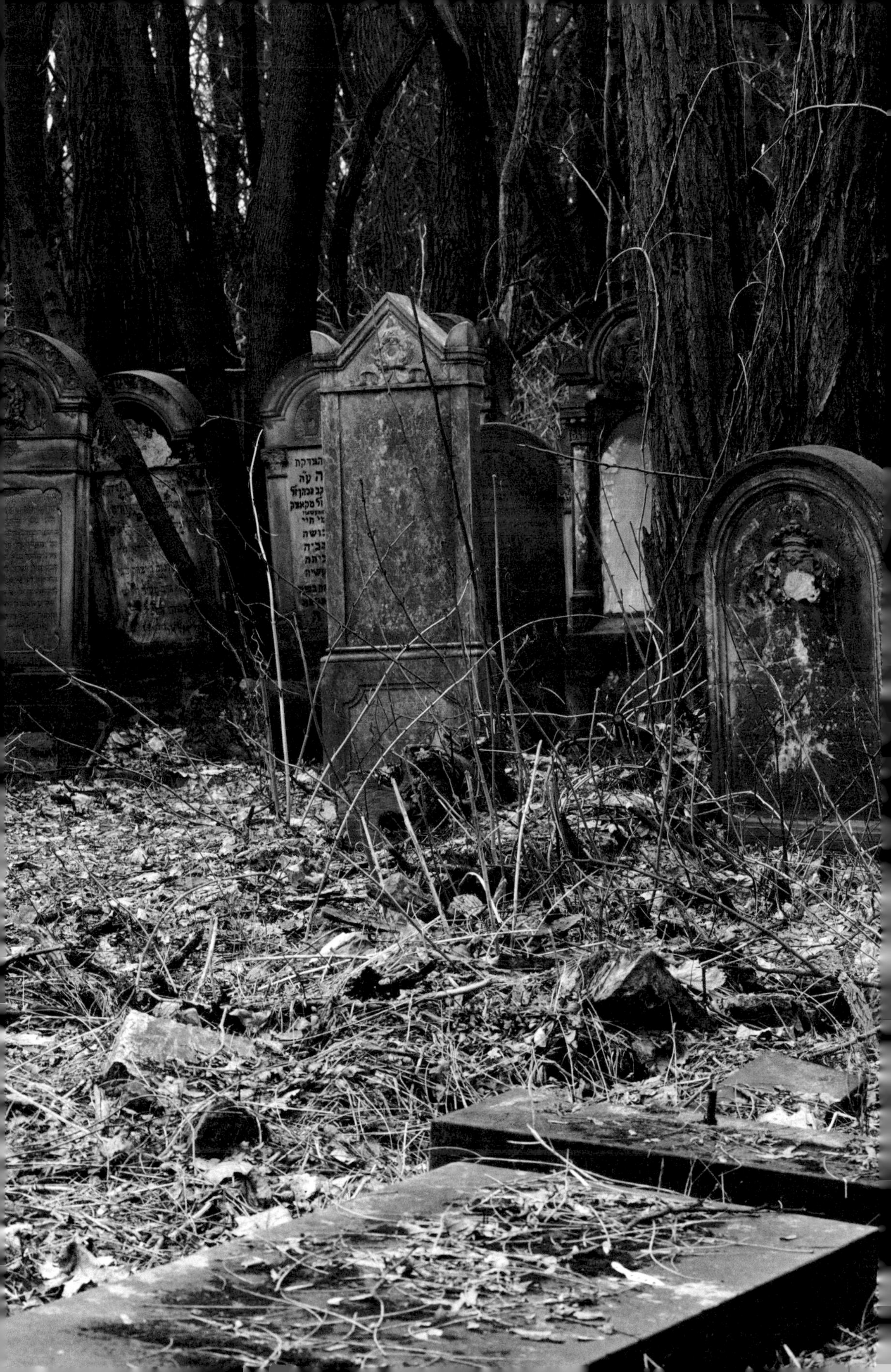

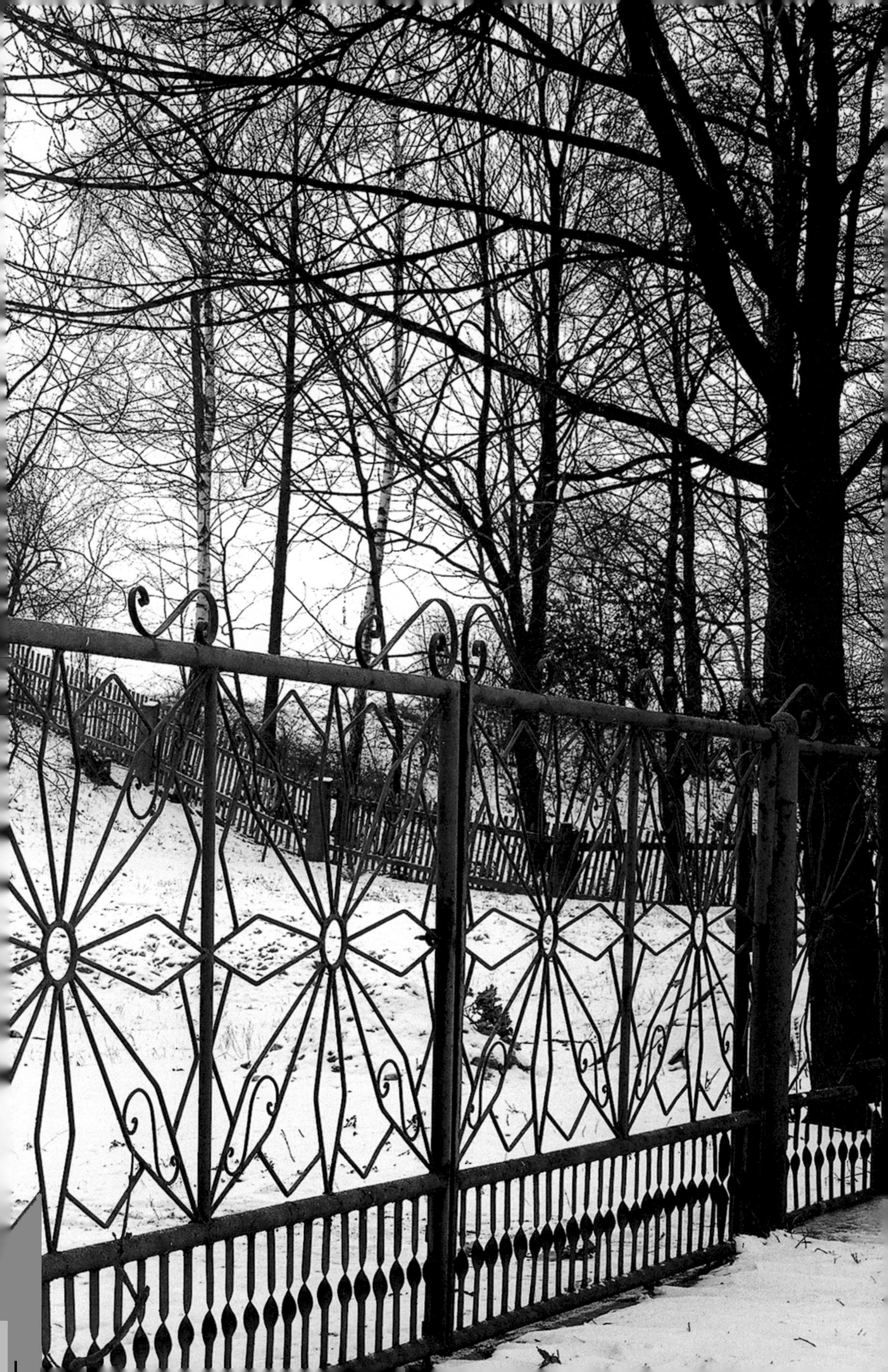

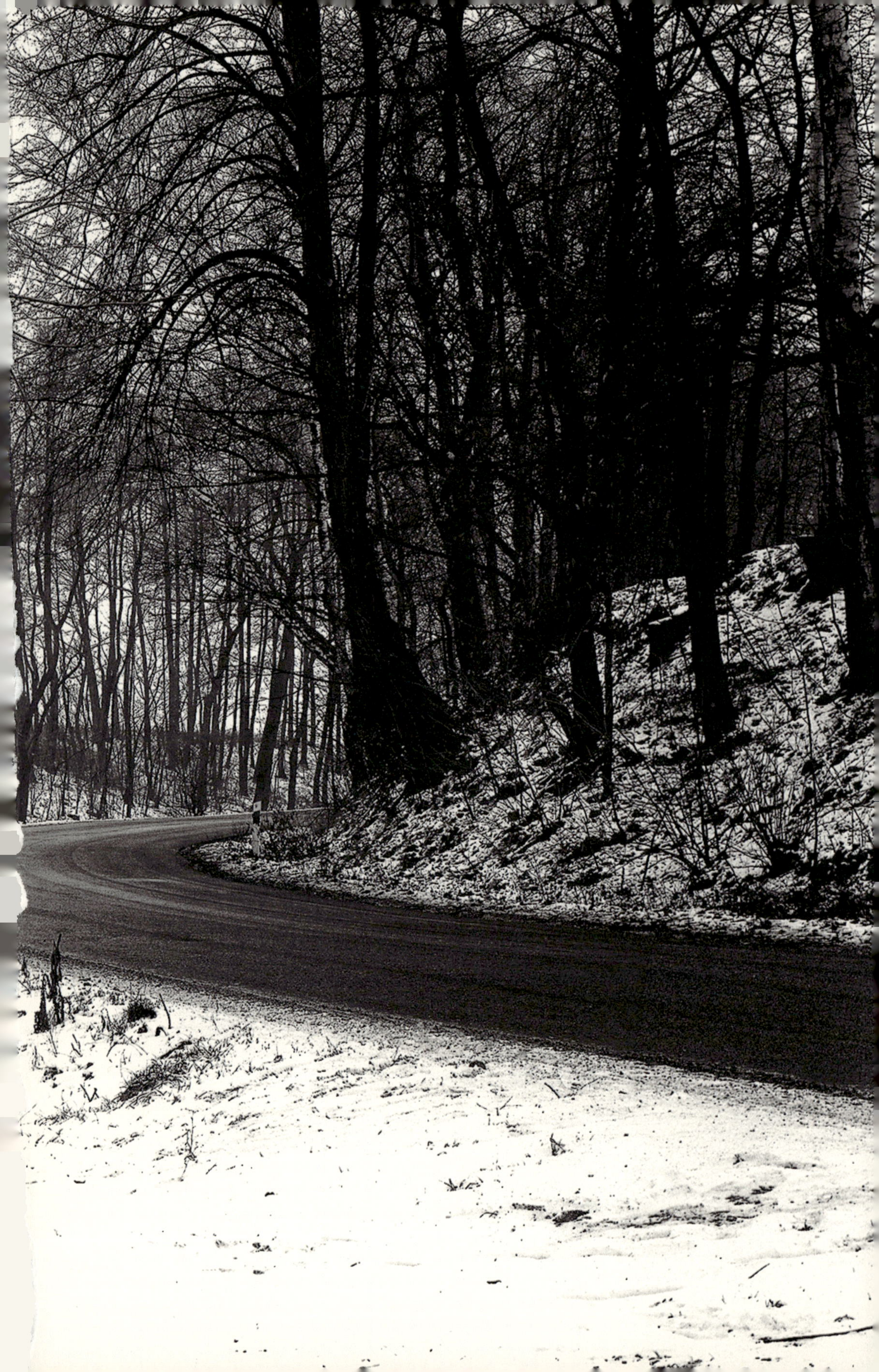

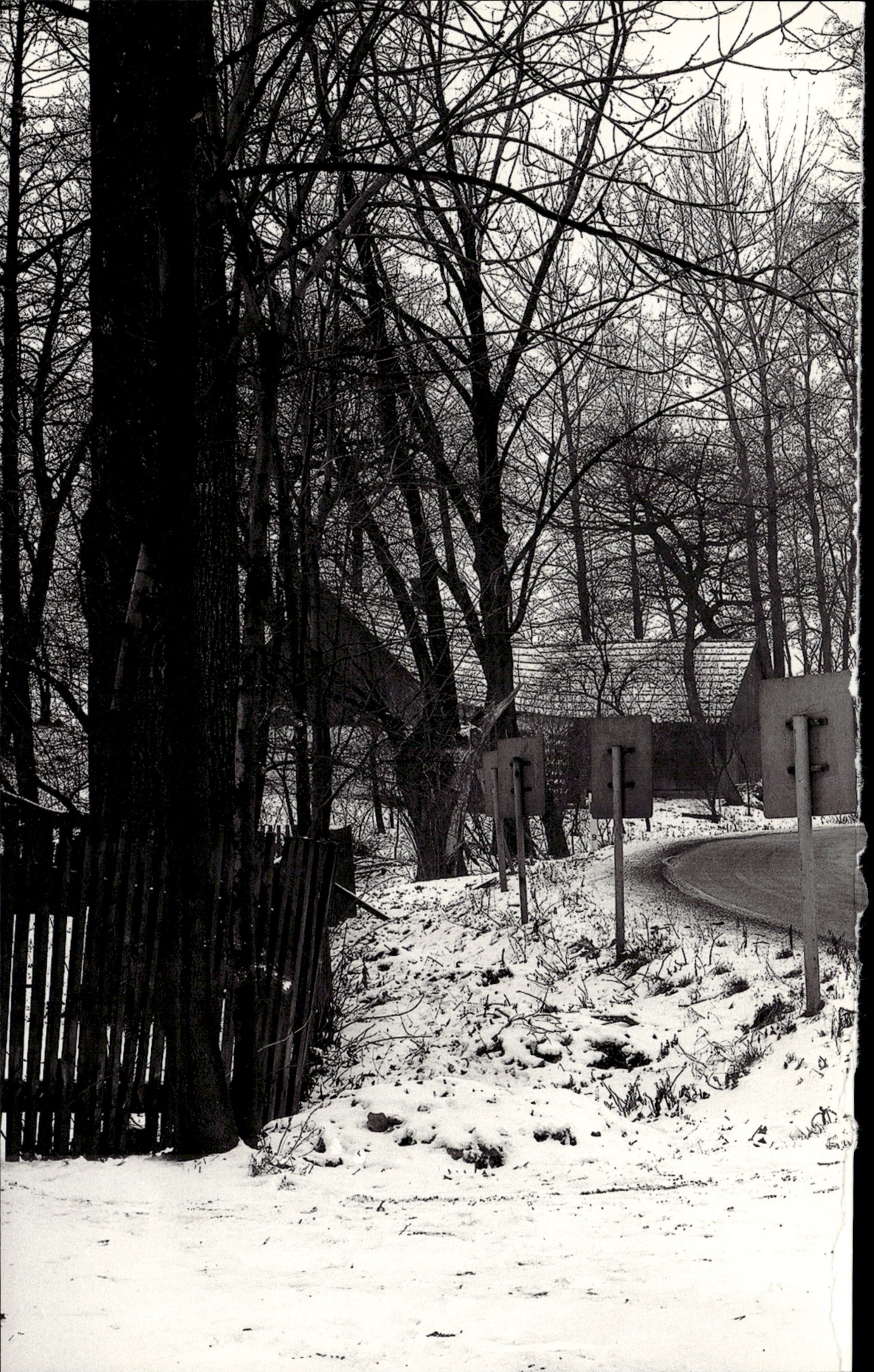

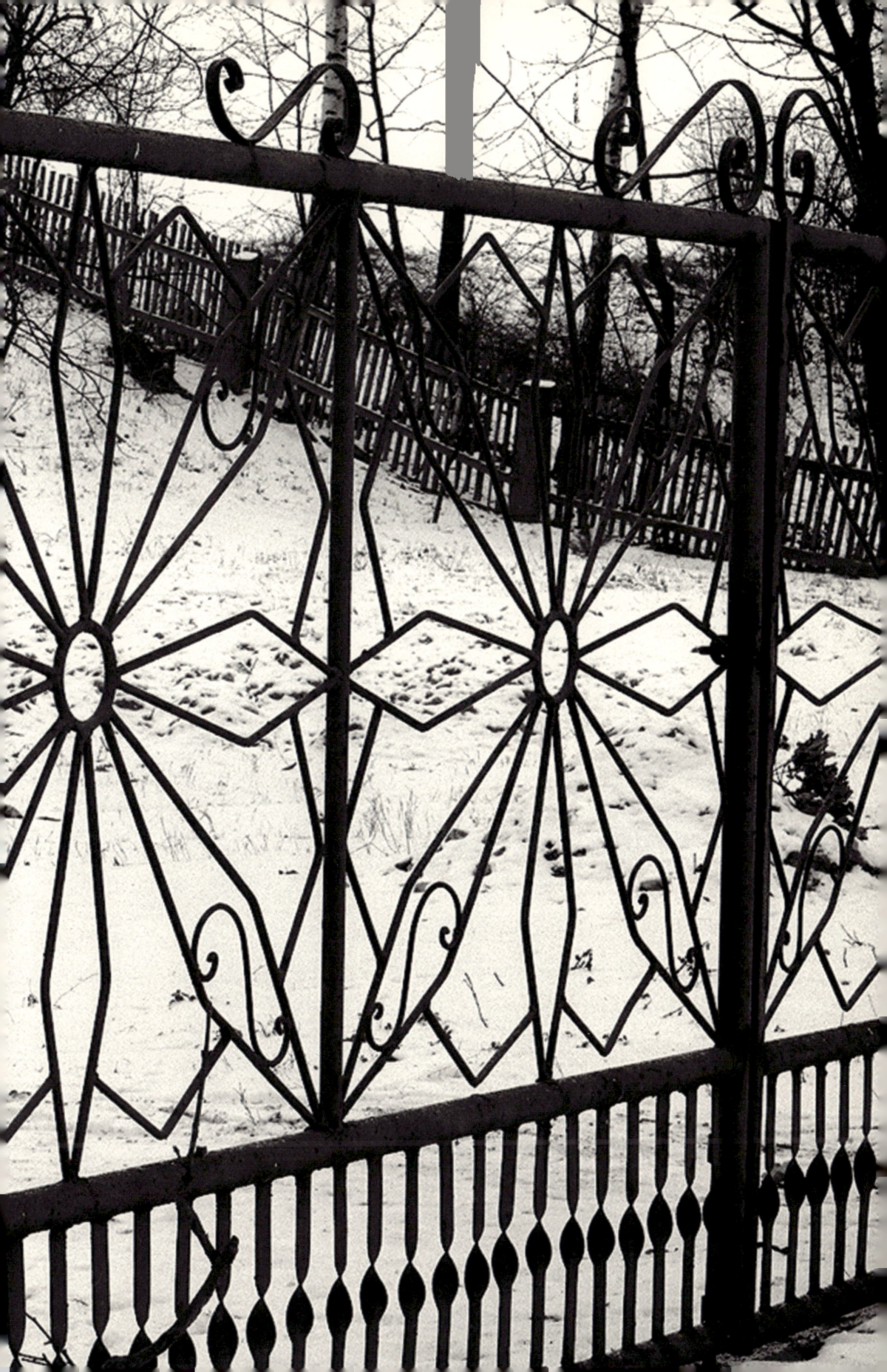

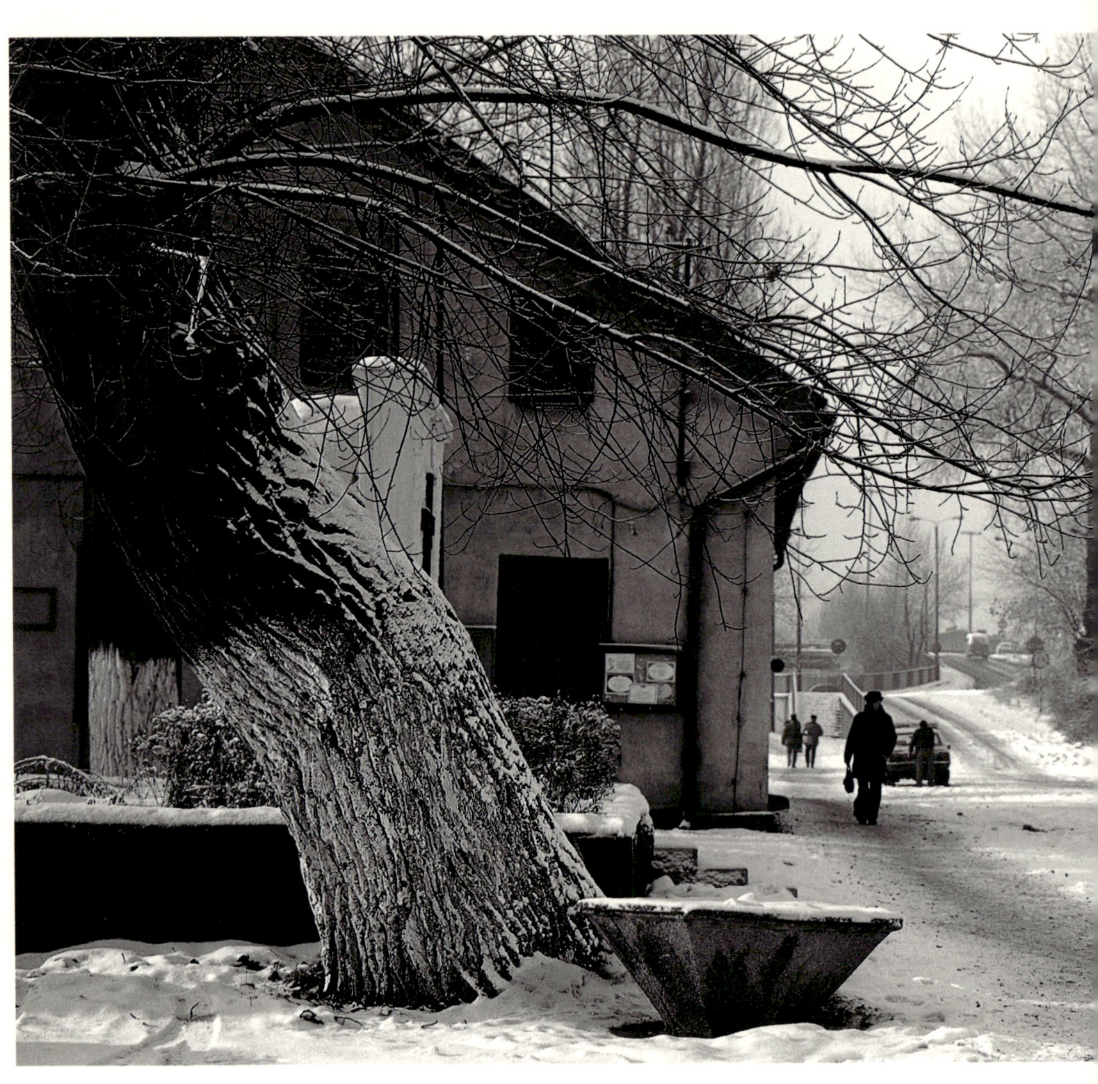

1.50

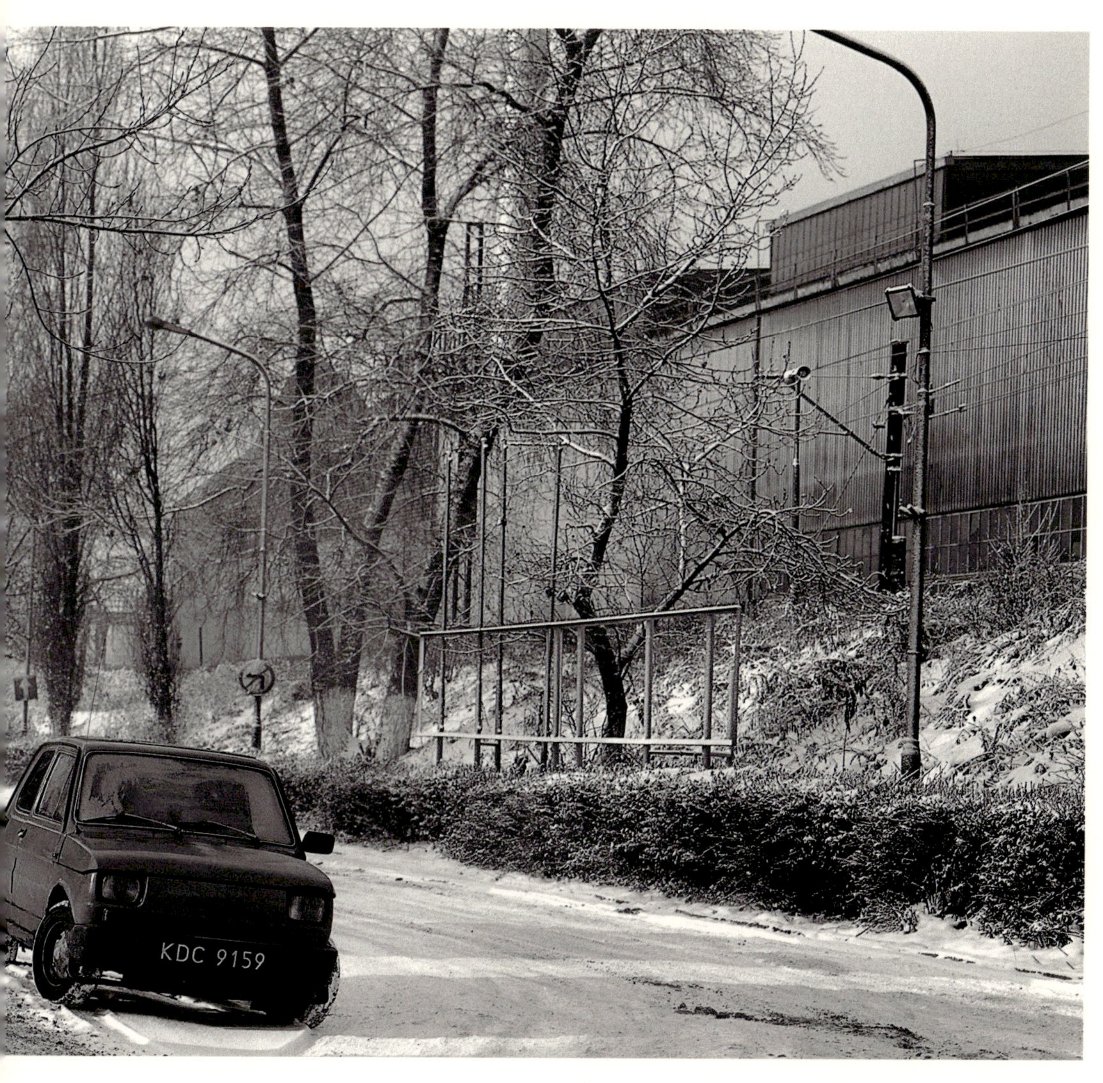

KDC 9159

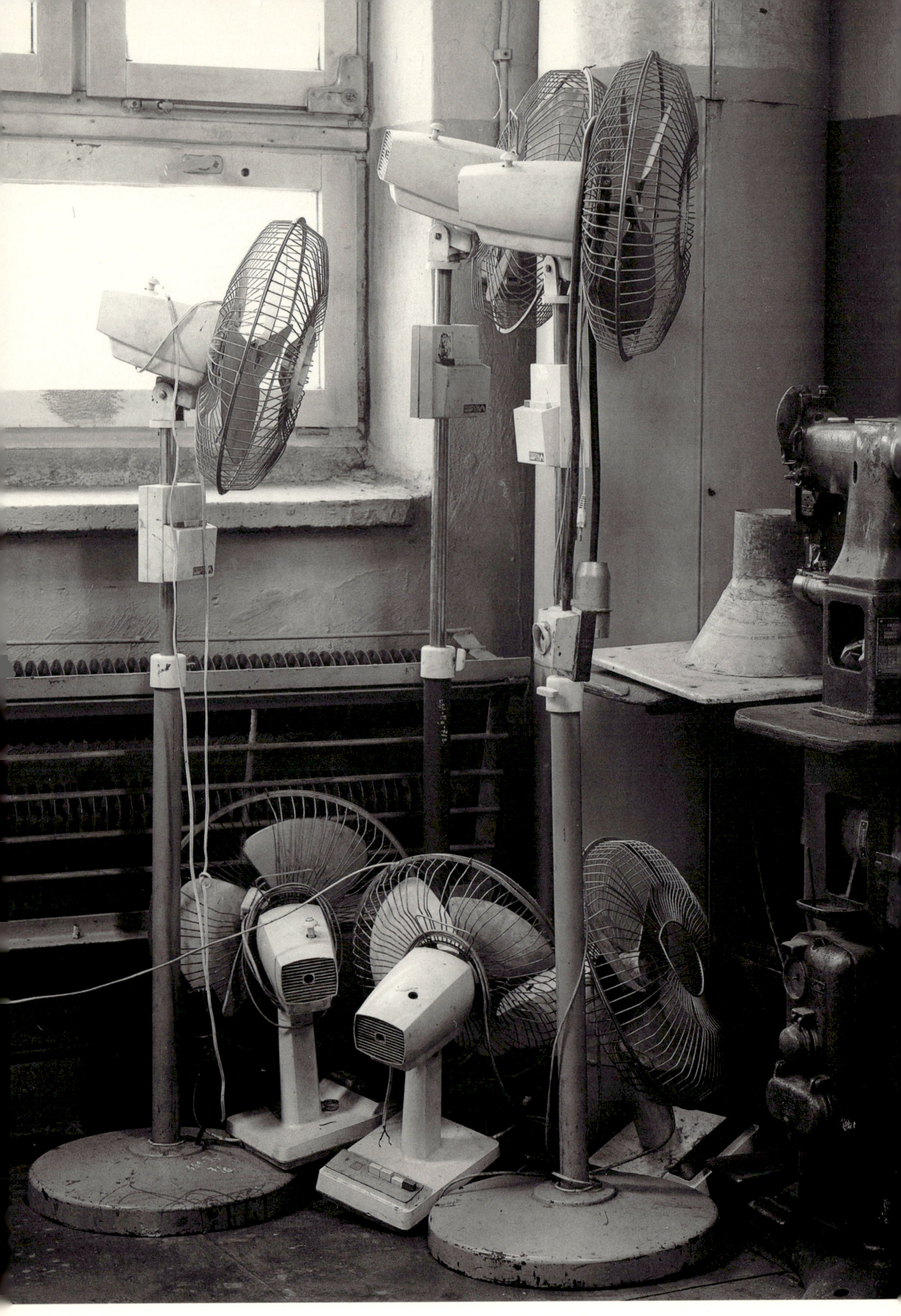

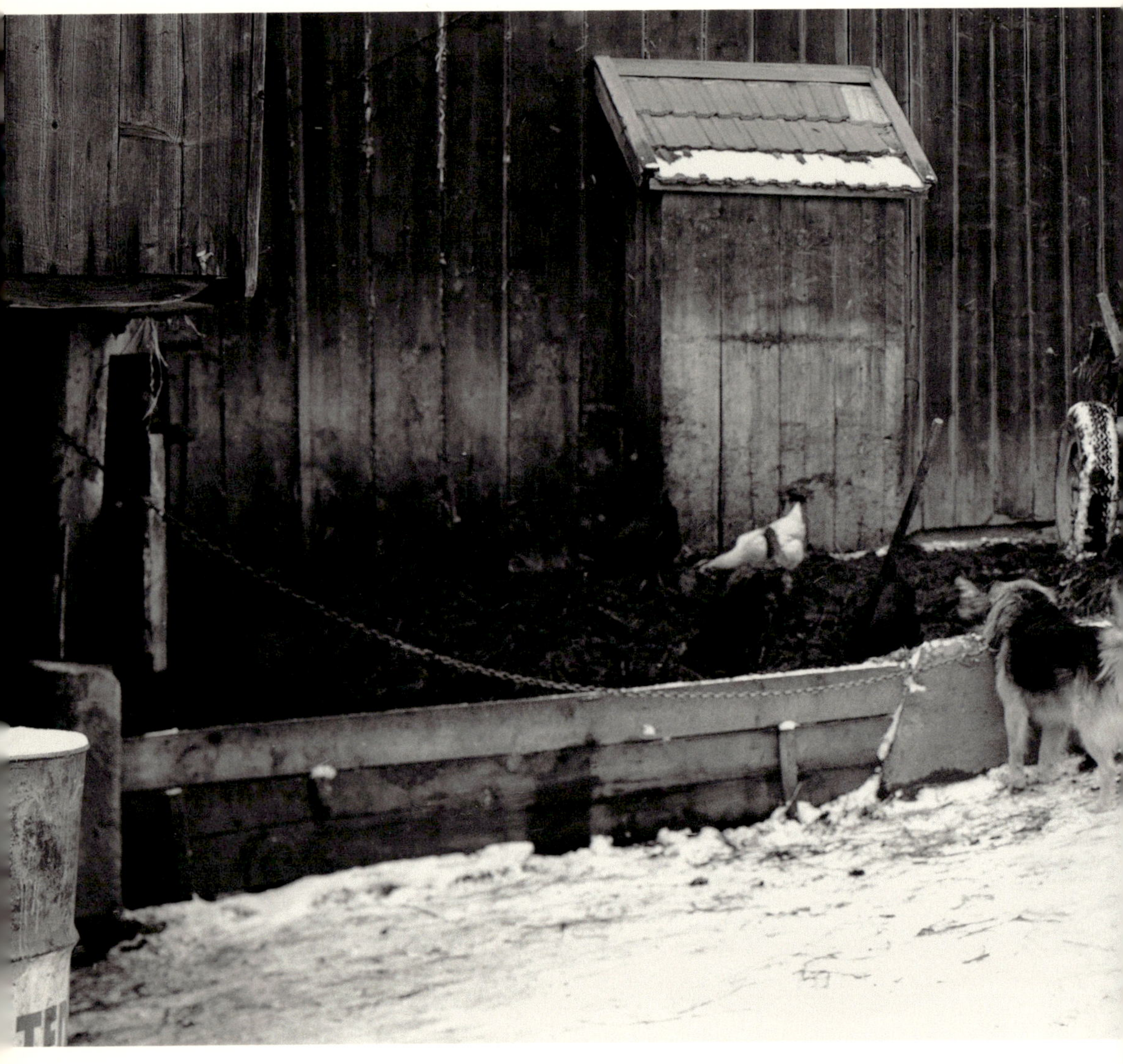

1.54

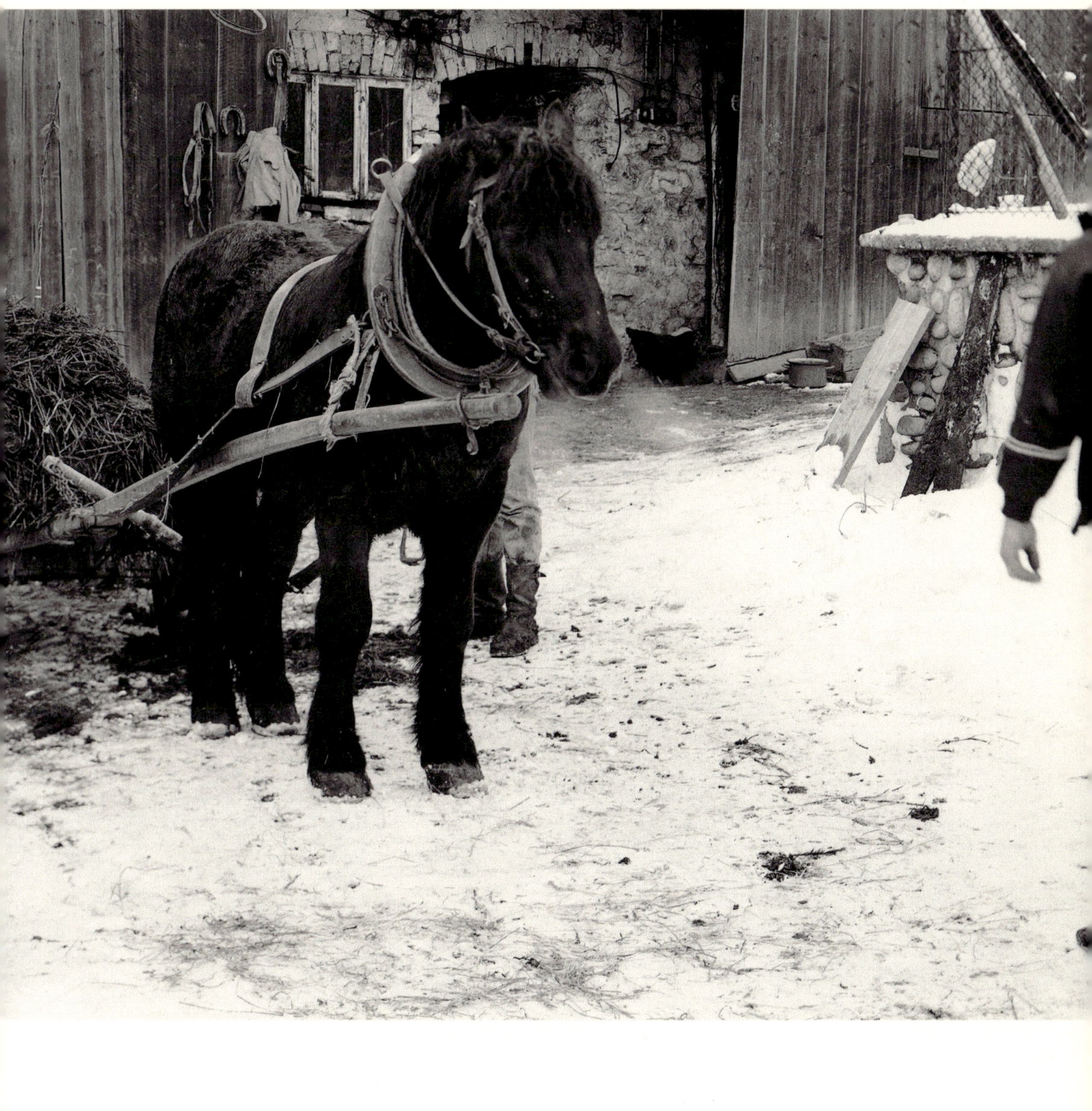

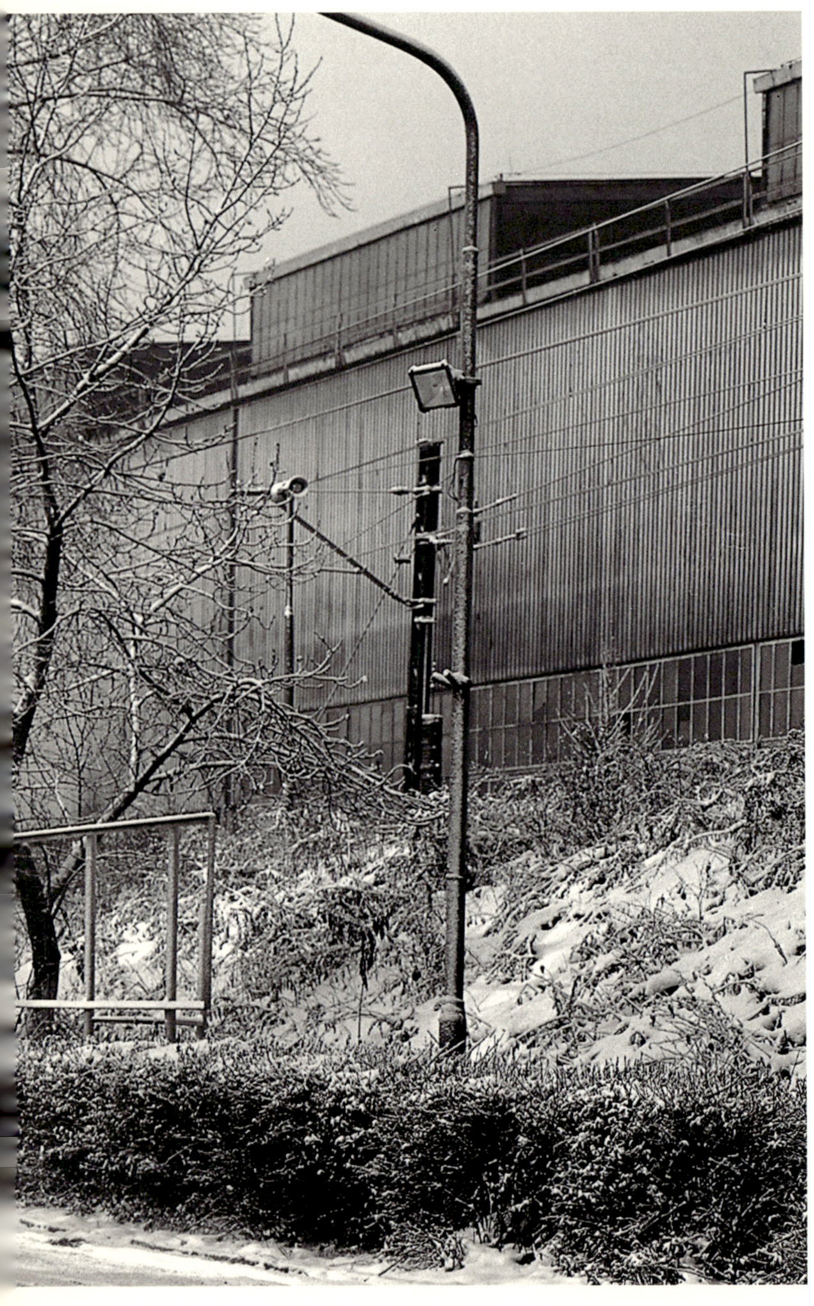

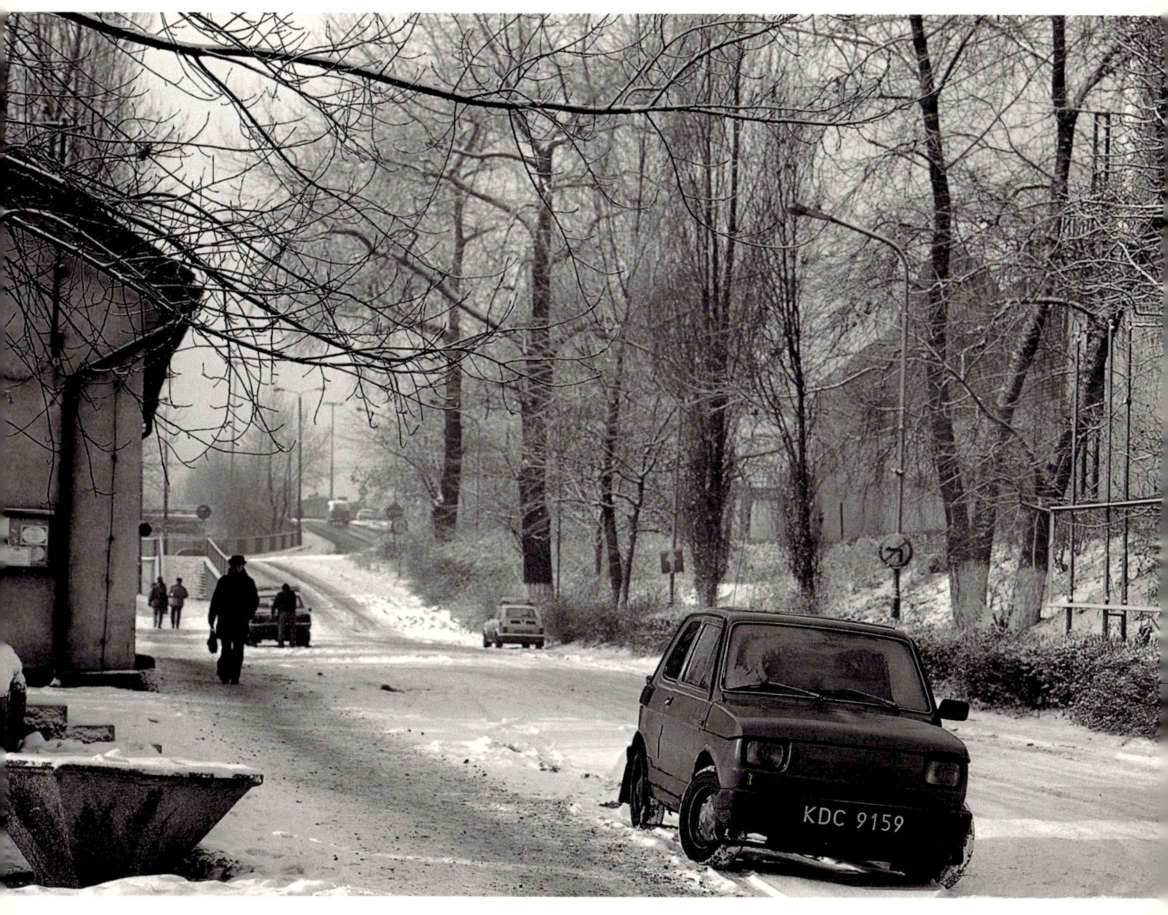

KDC 9159

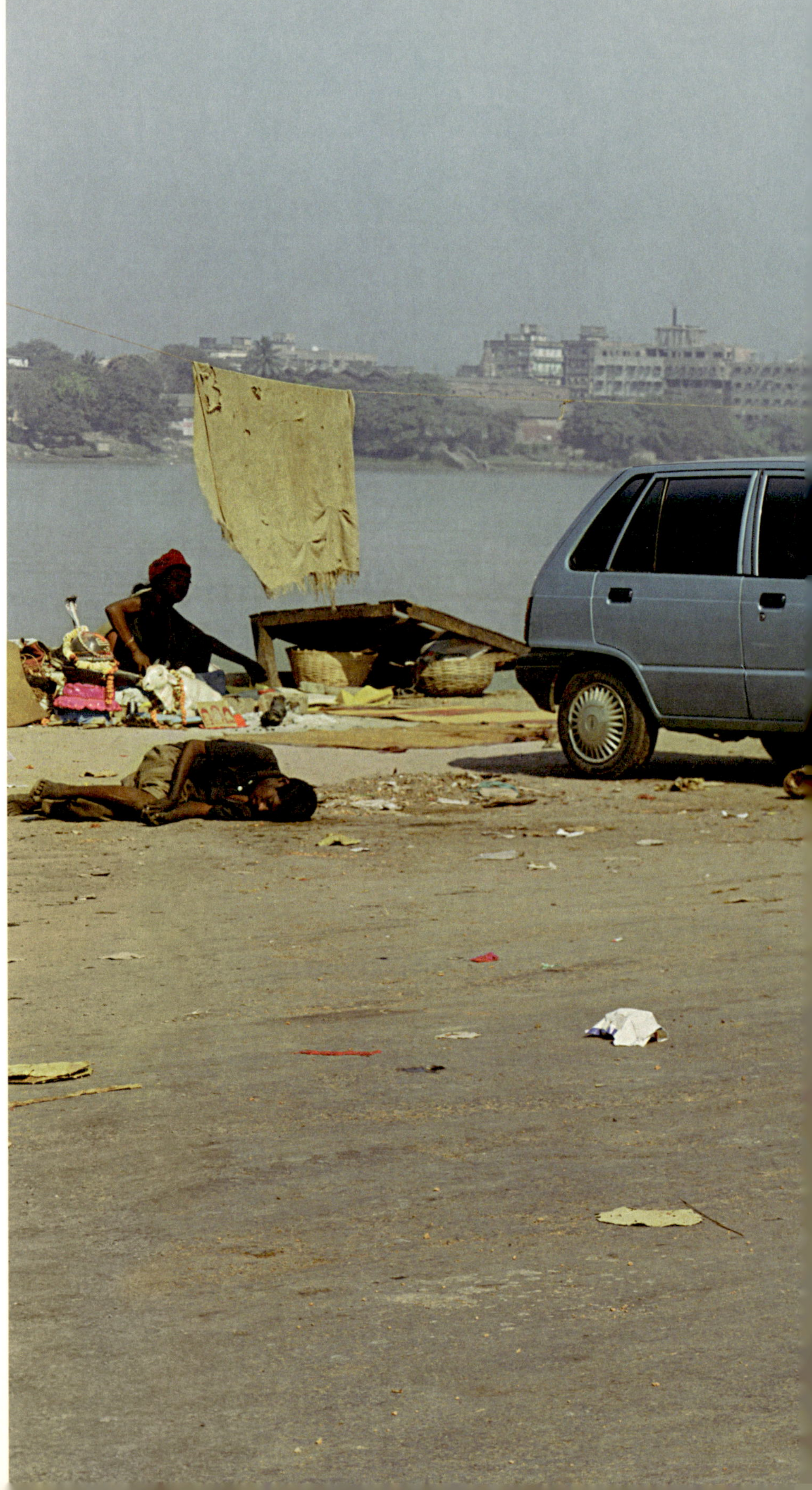

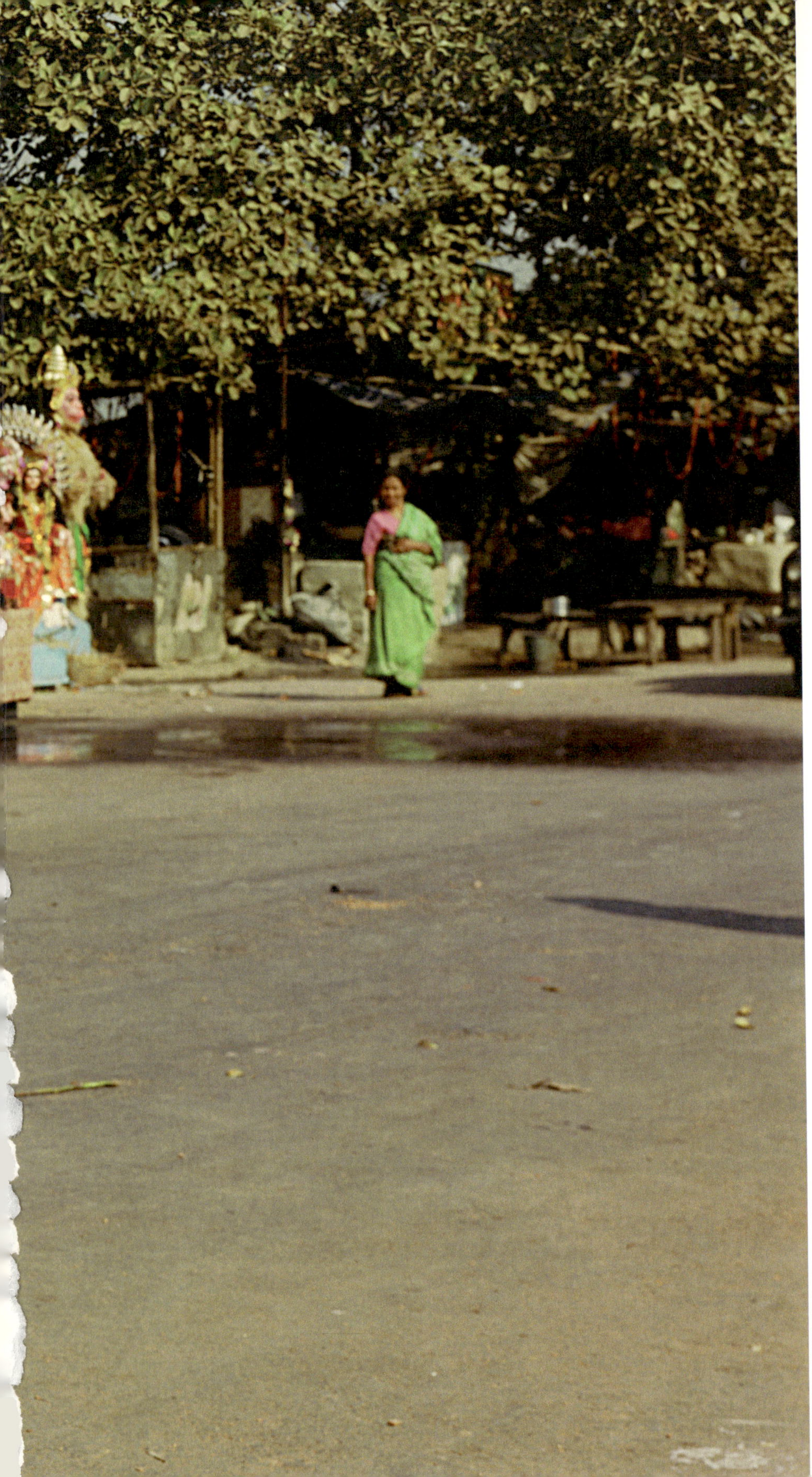

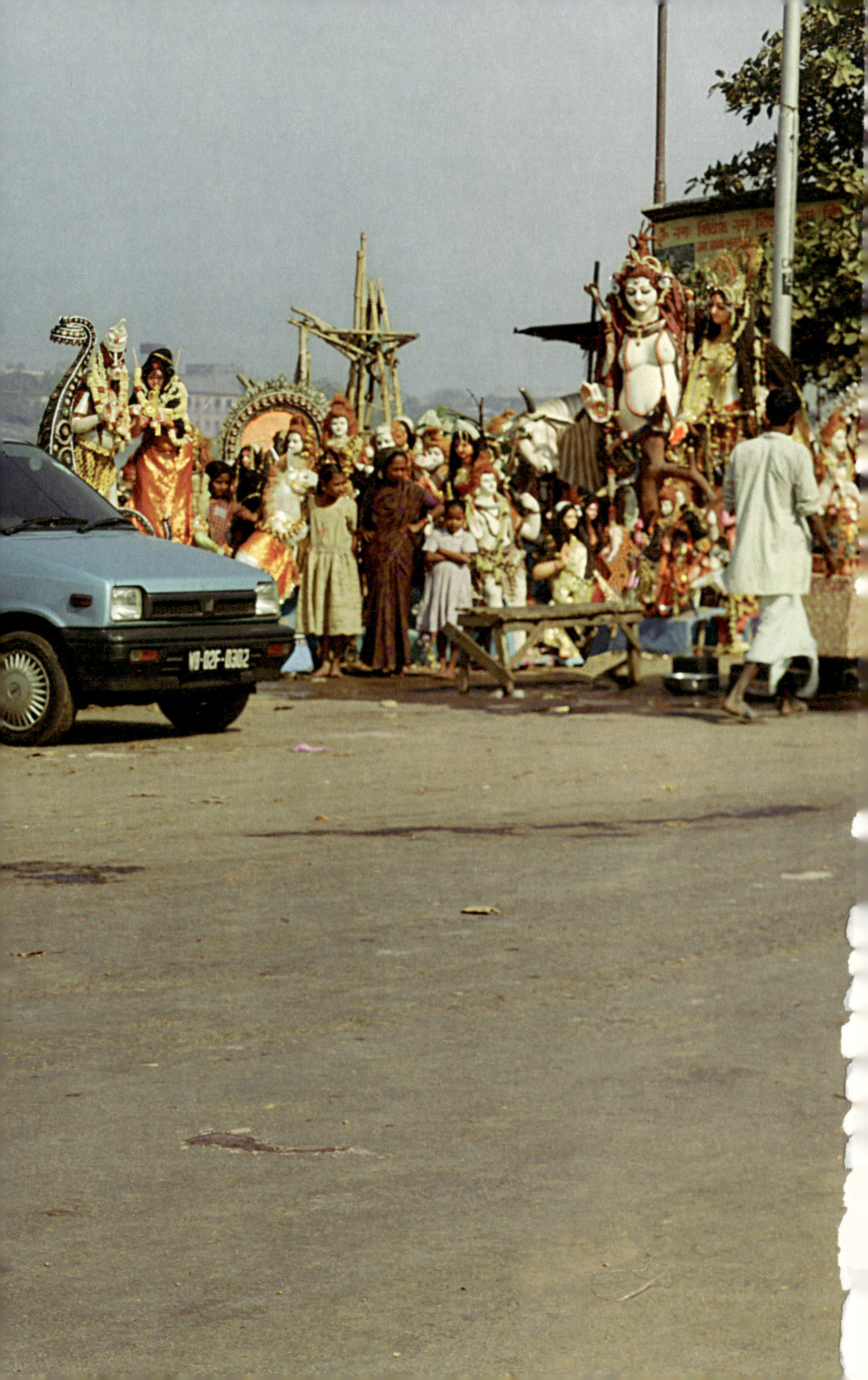

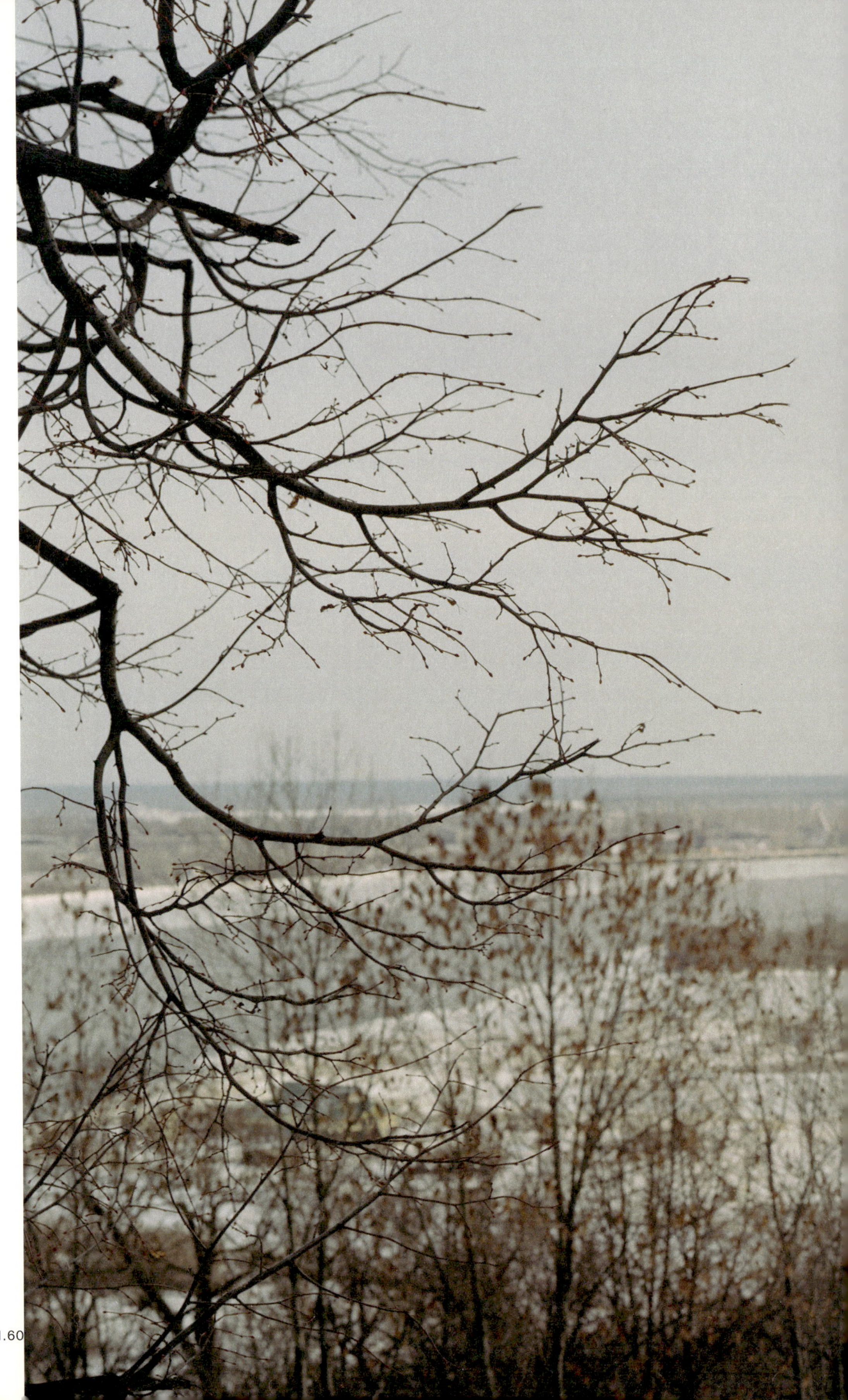

1.60

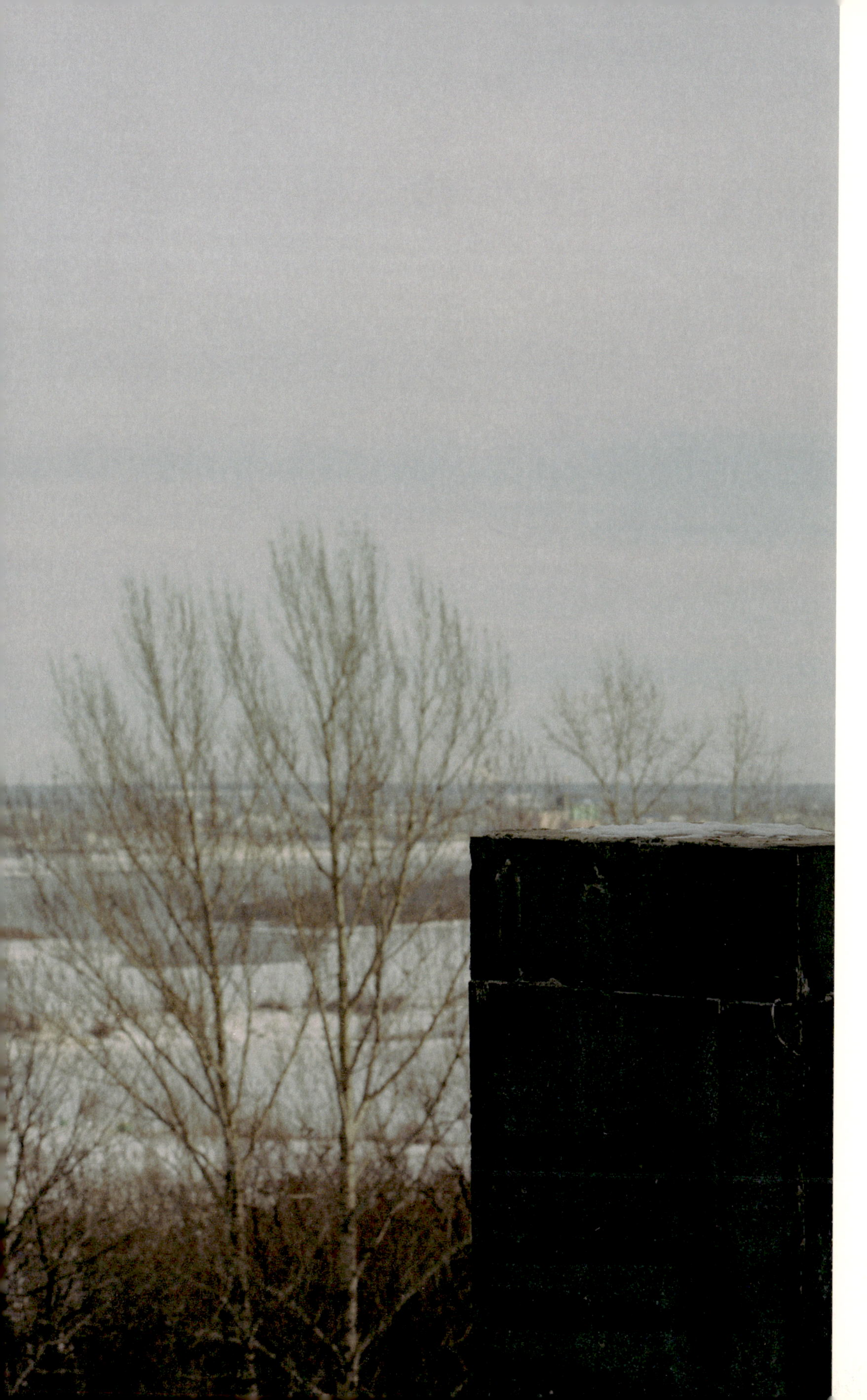

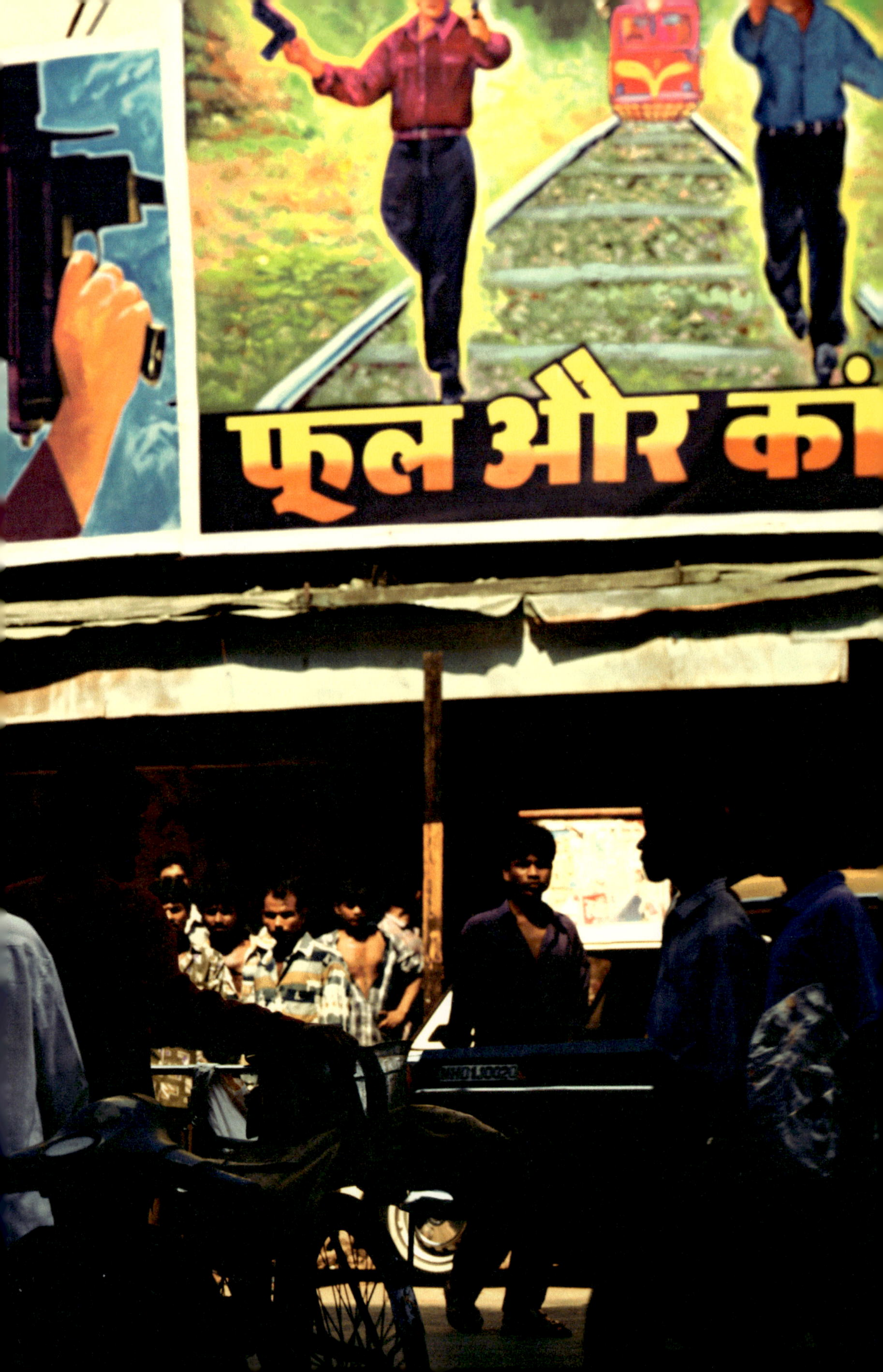
फूल और कां

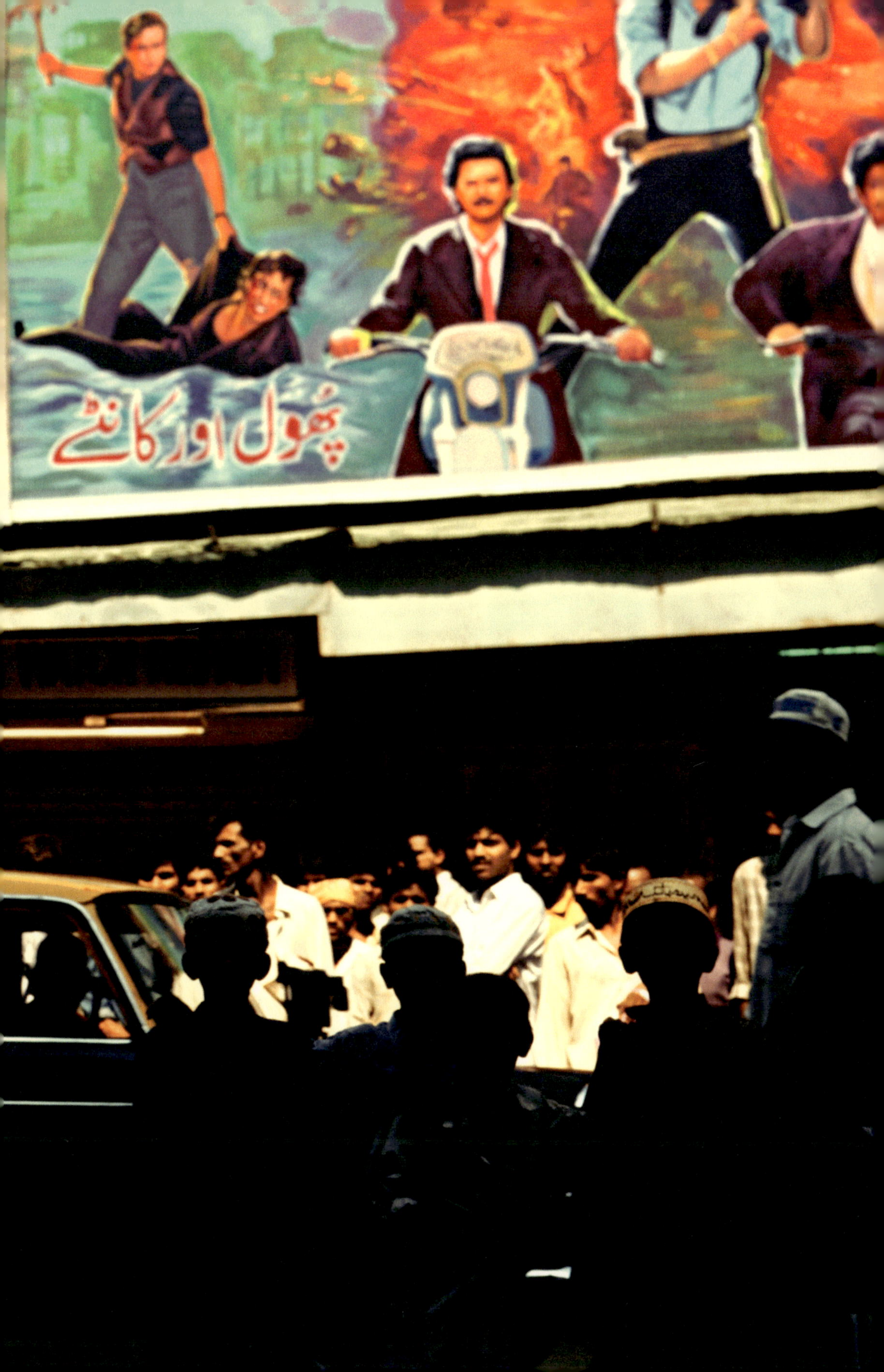

پھول اور کانٹے

Finding, Transmitting, Receiving

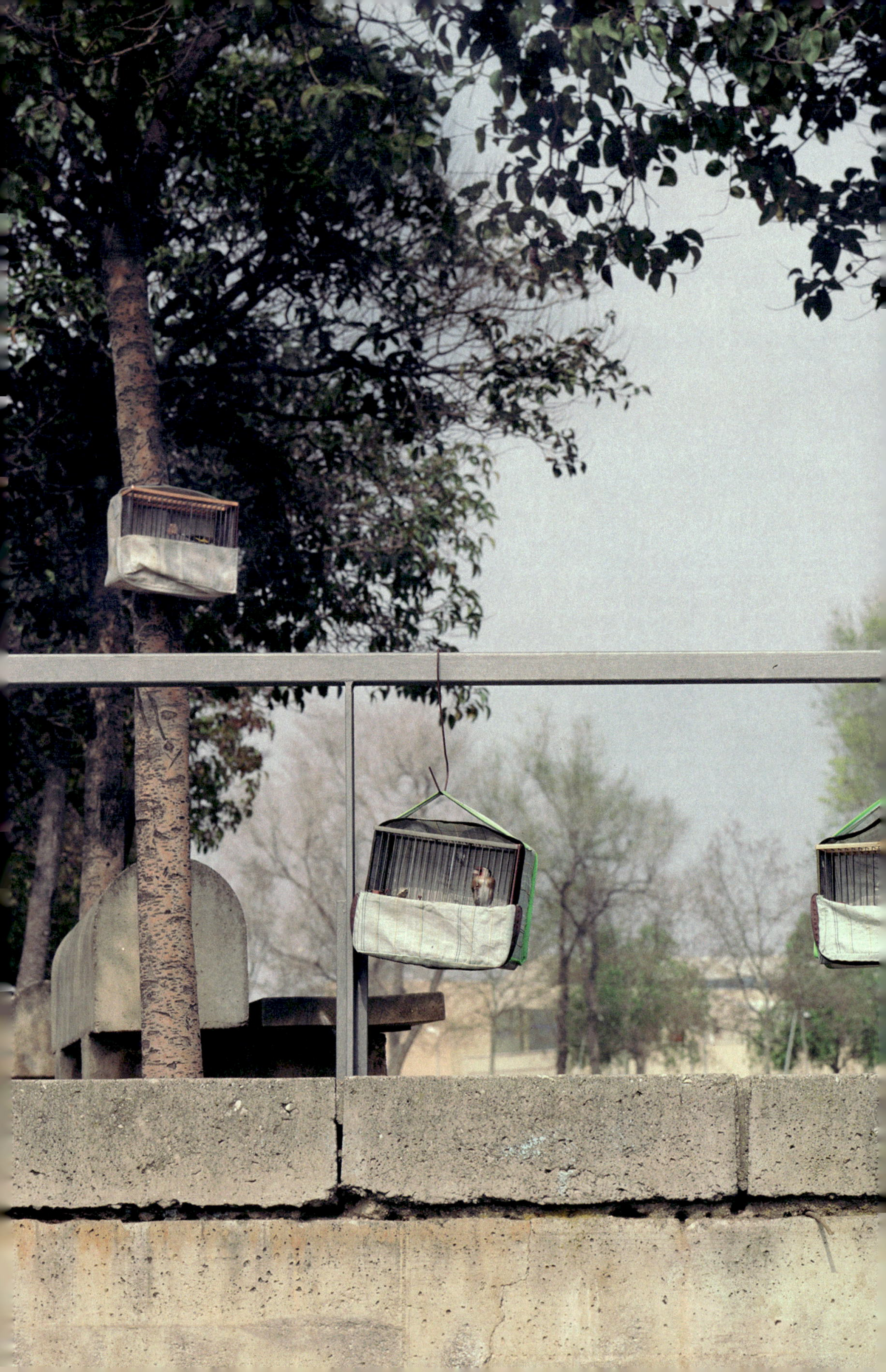

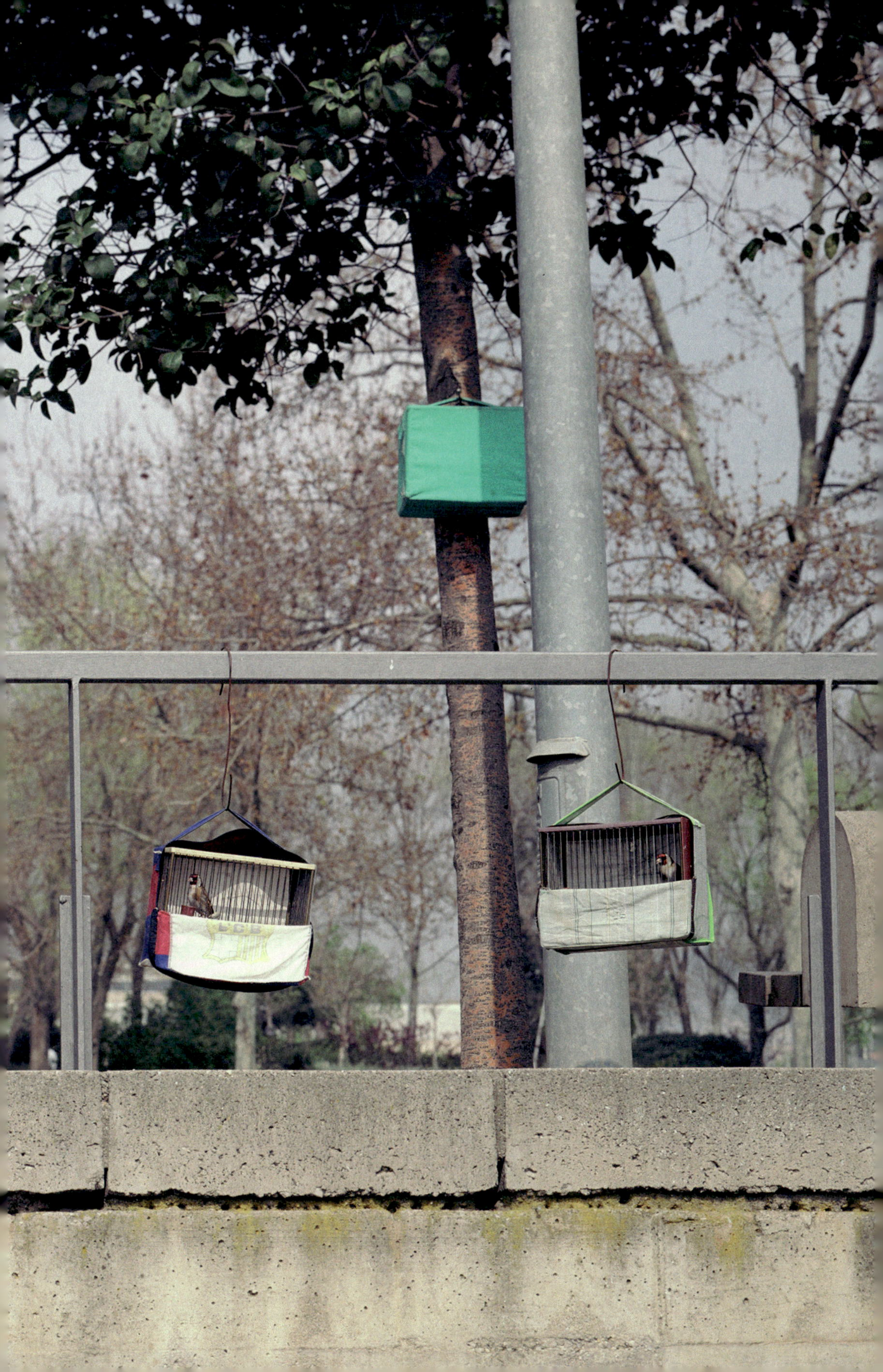

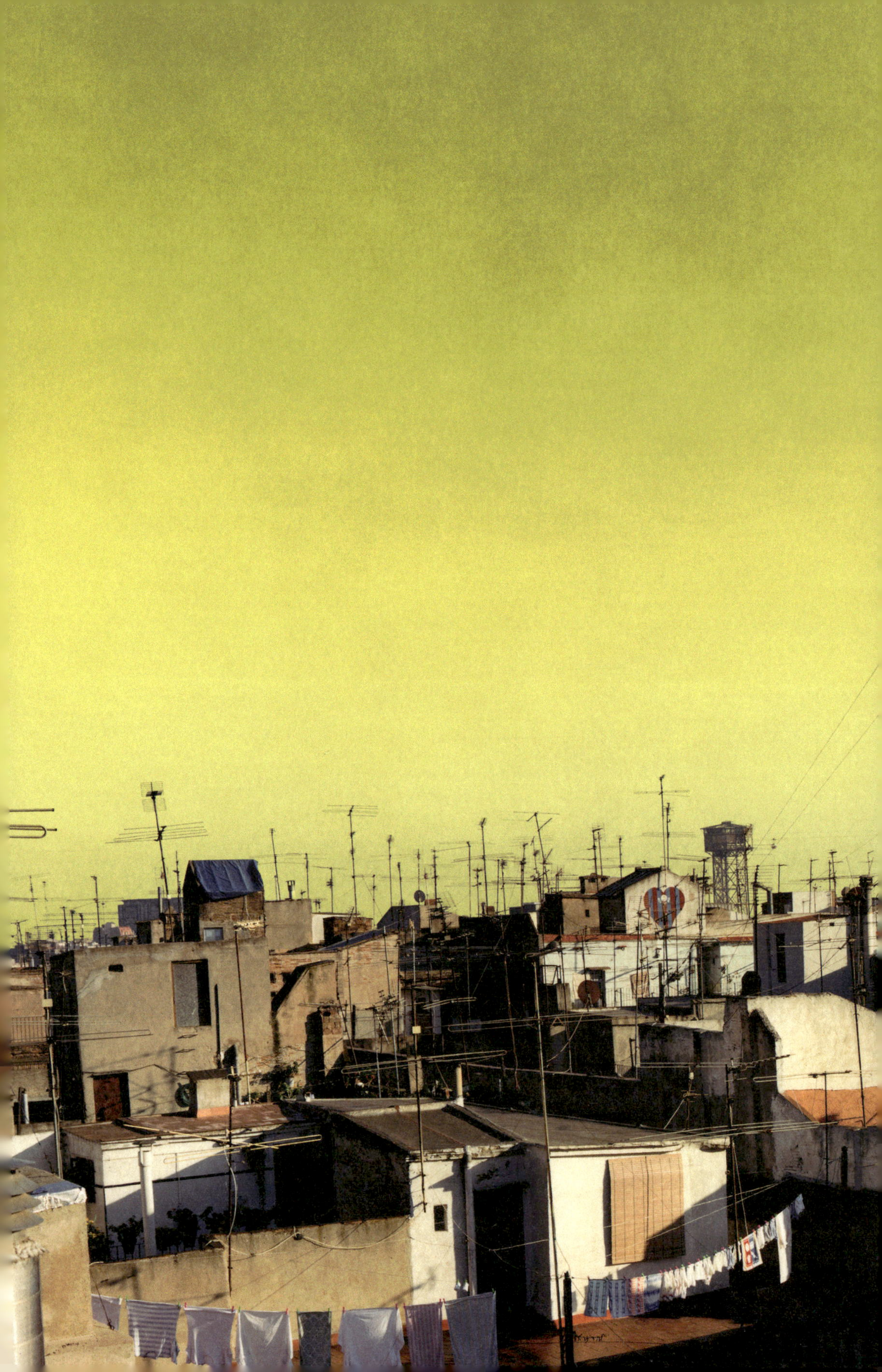

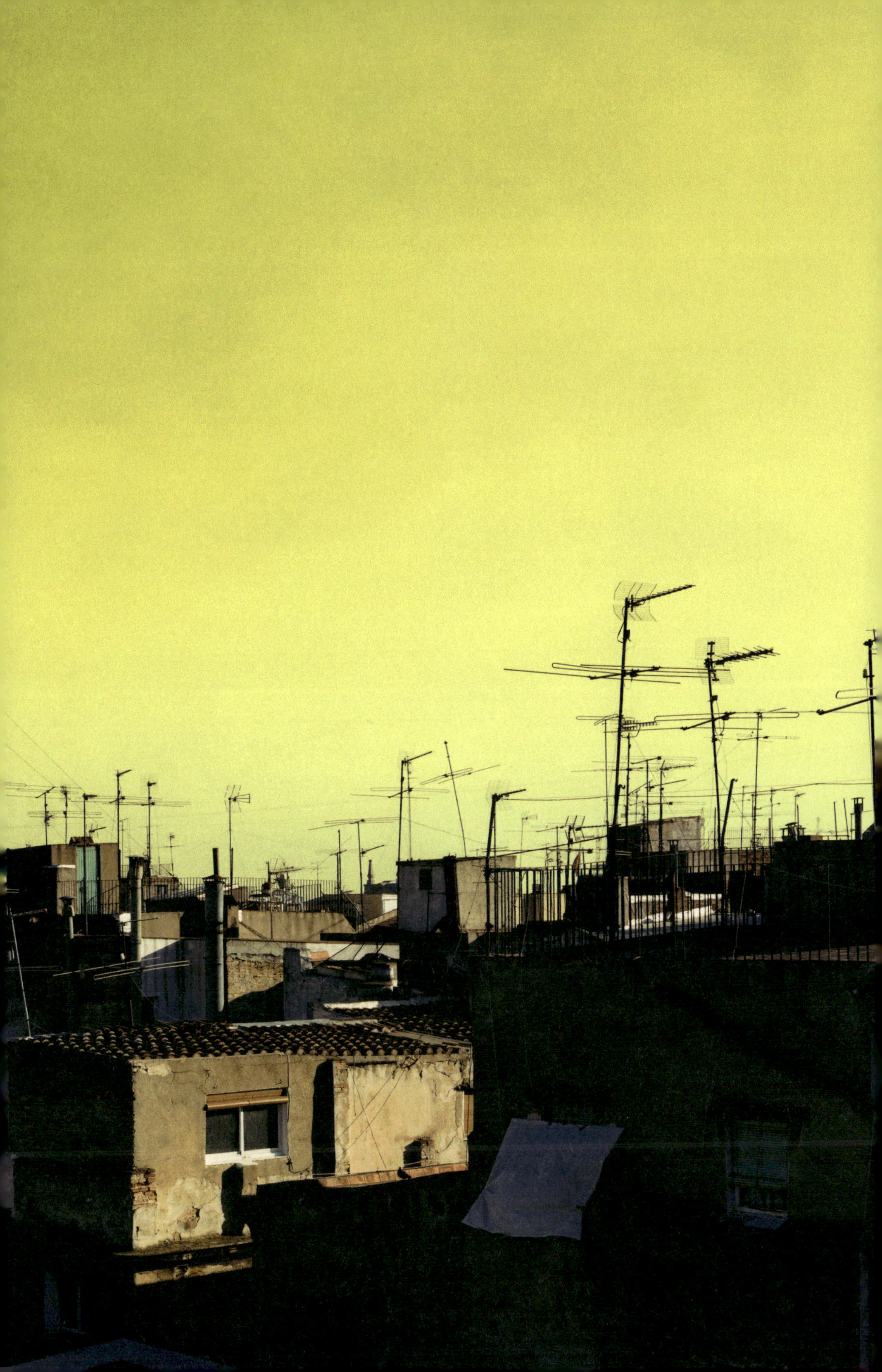

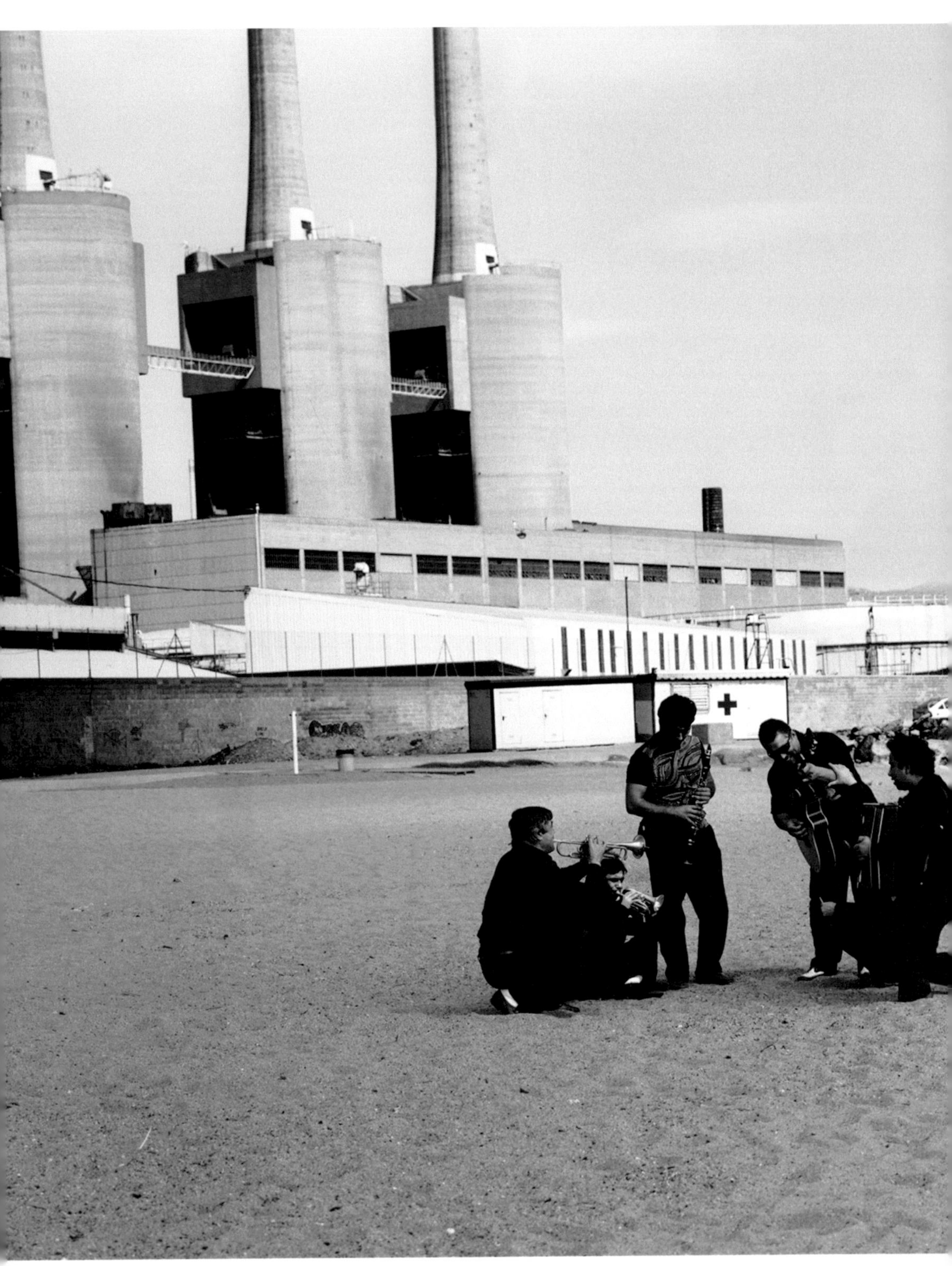

2.10

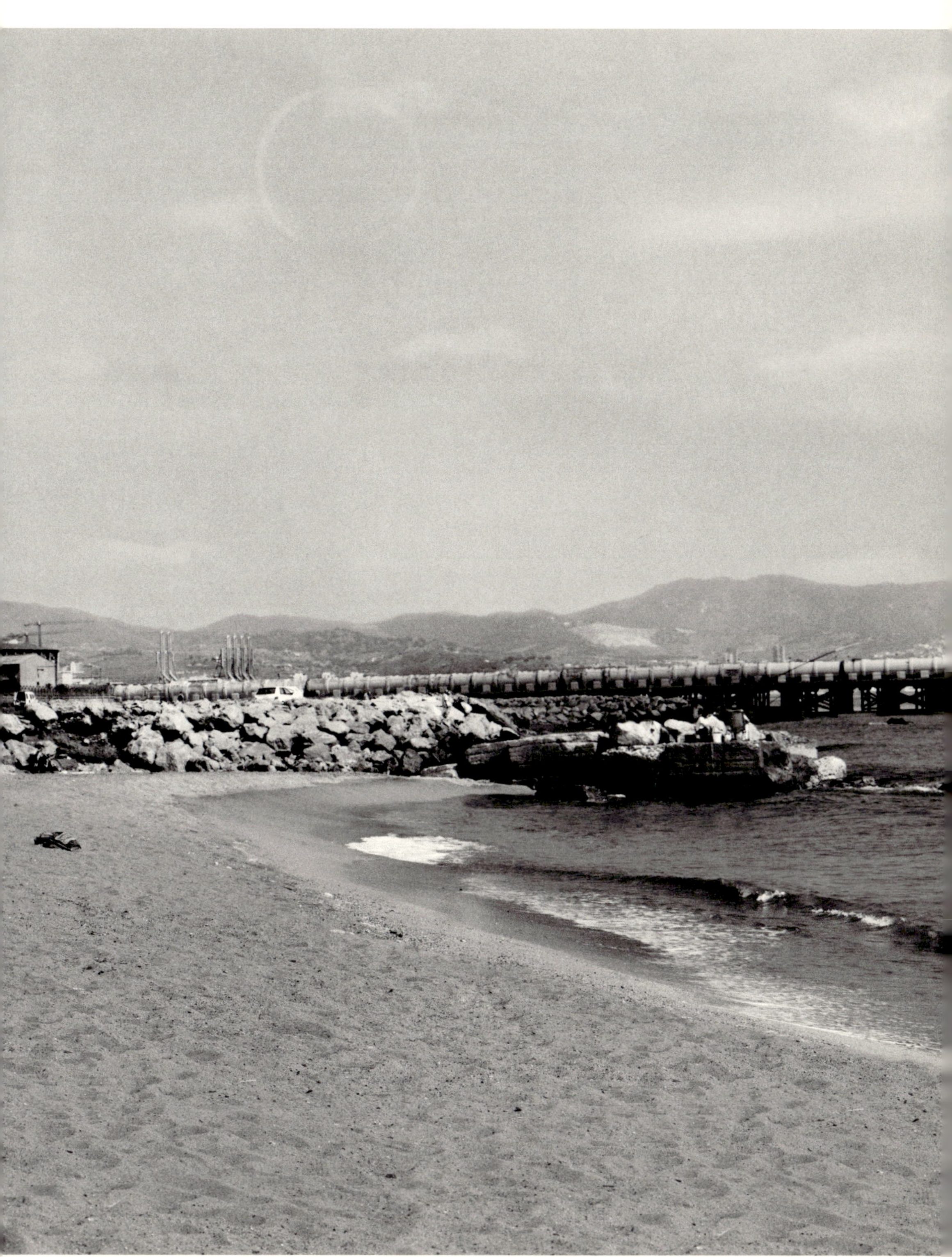

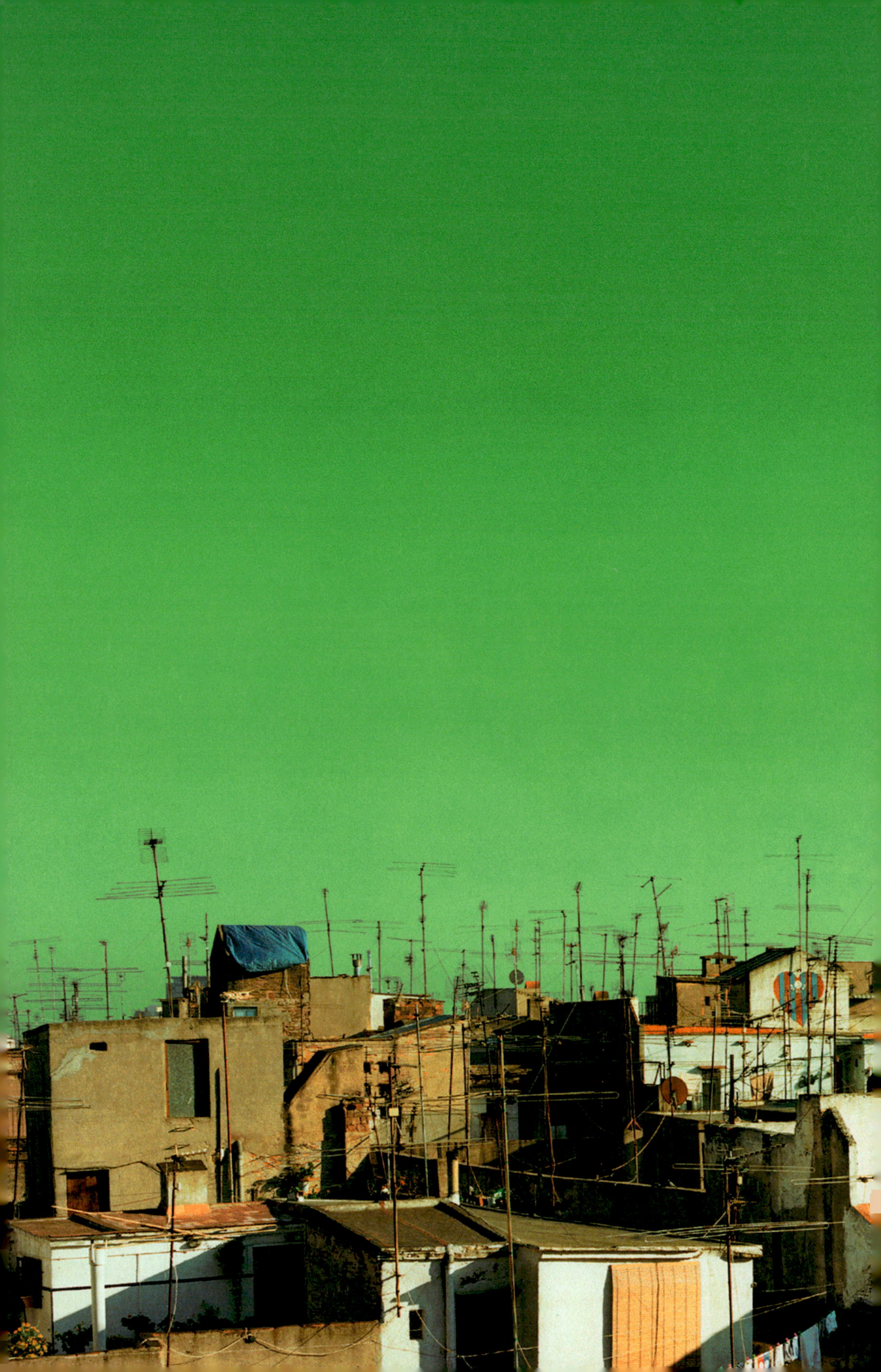

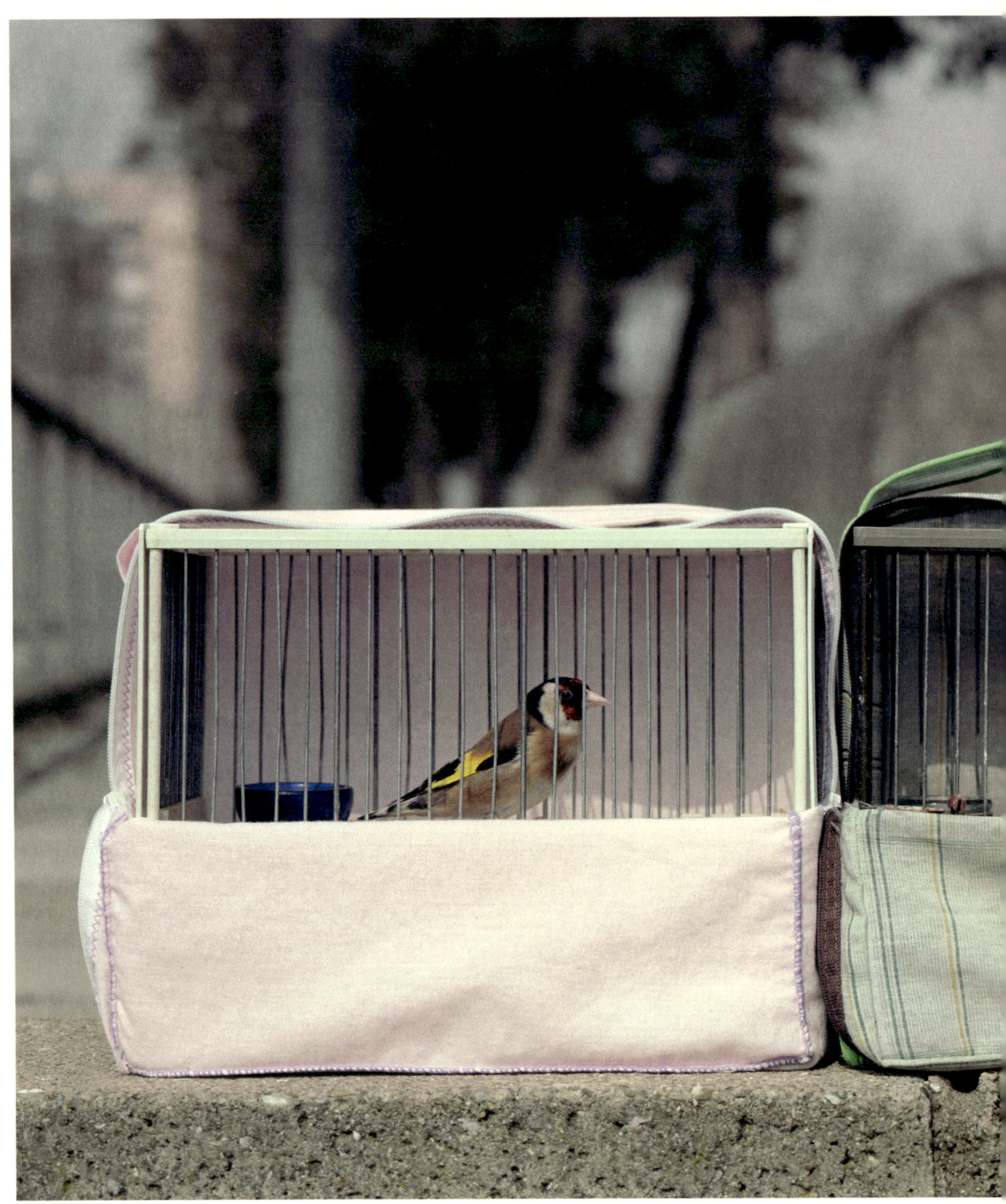

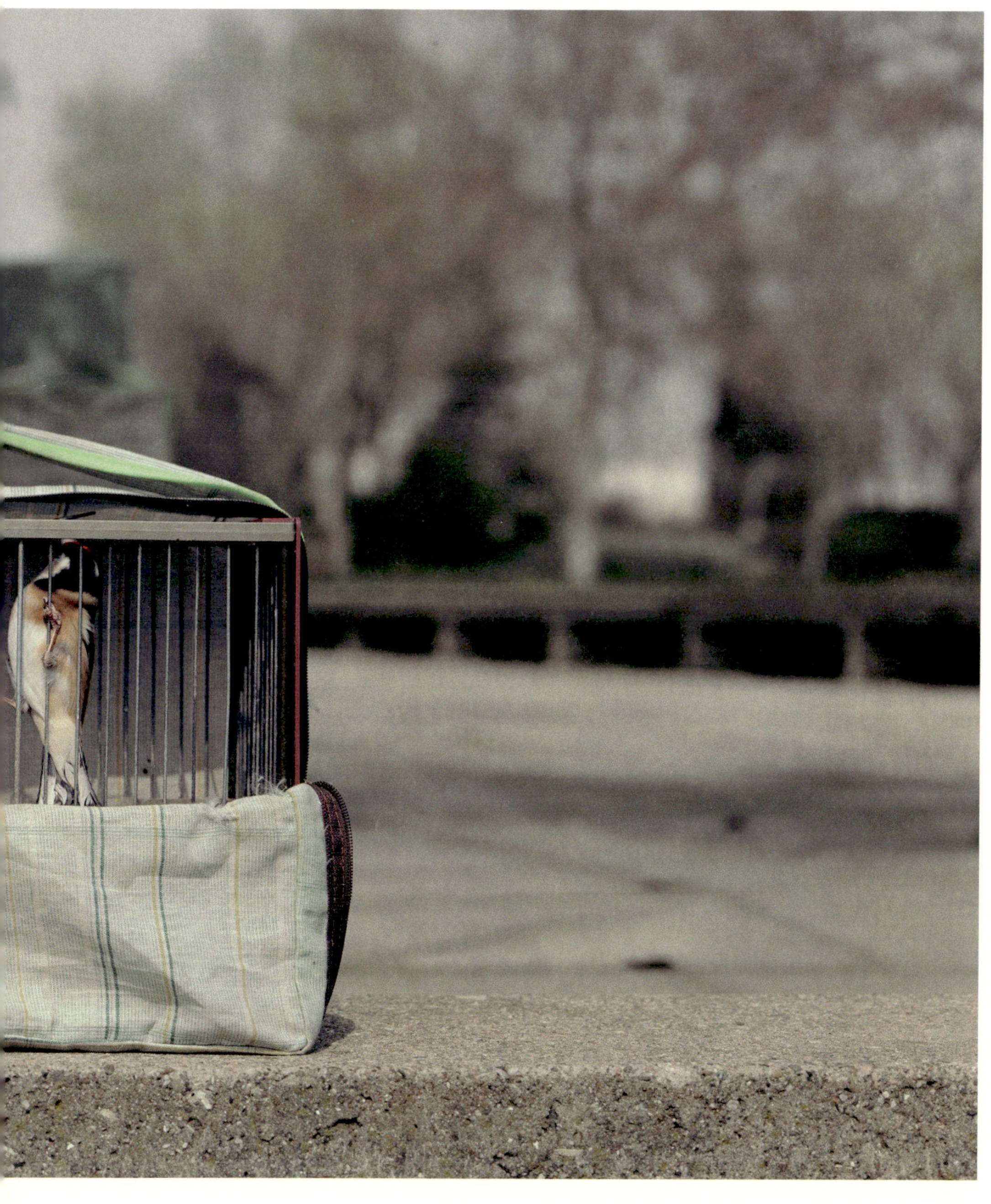

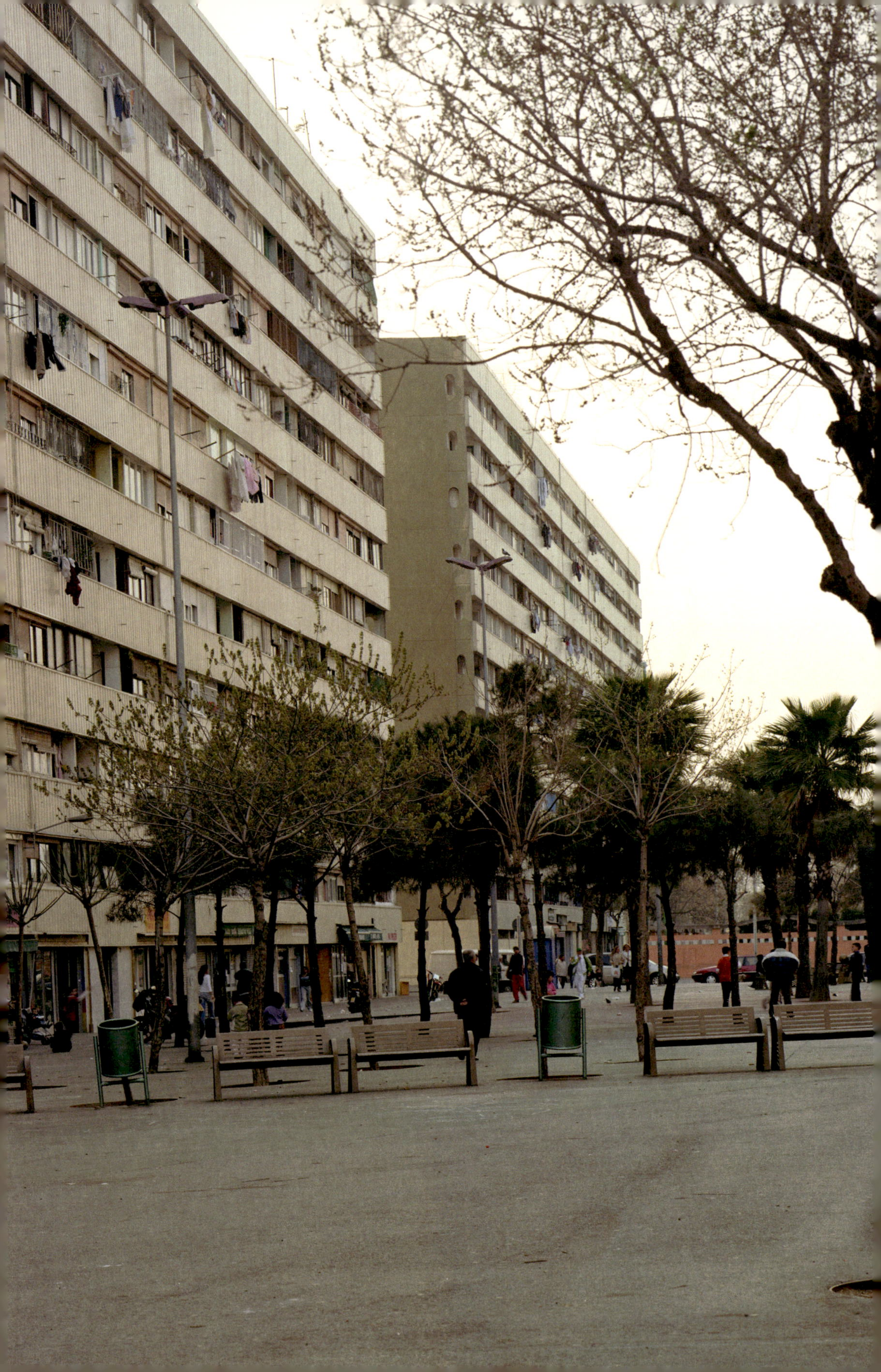

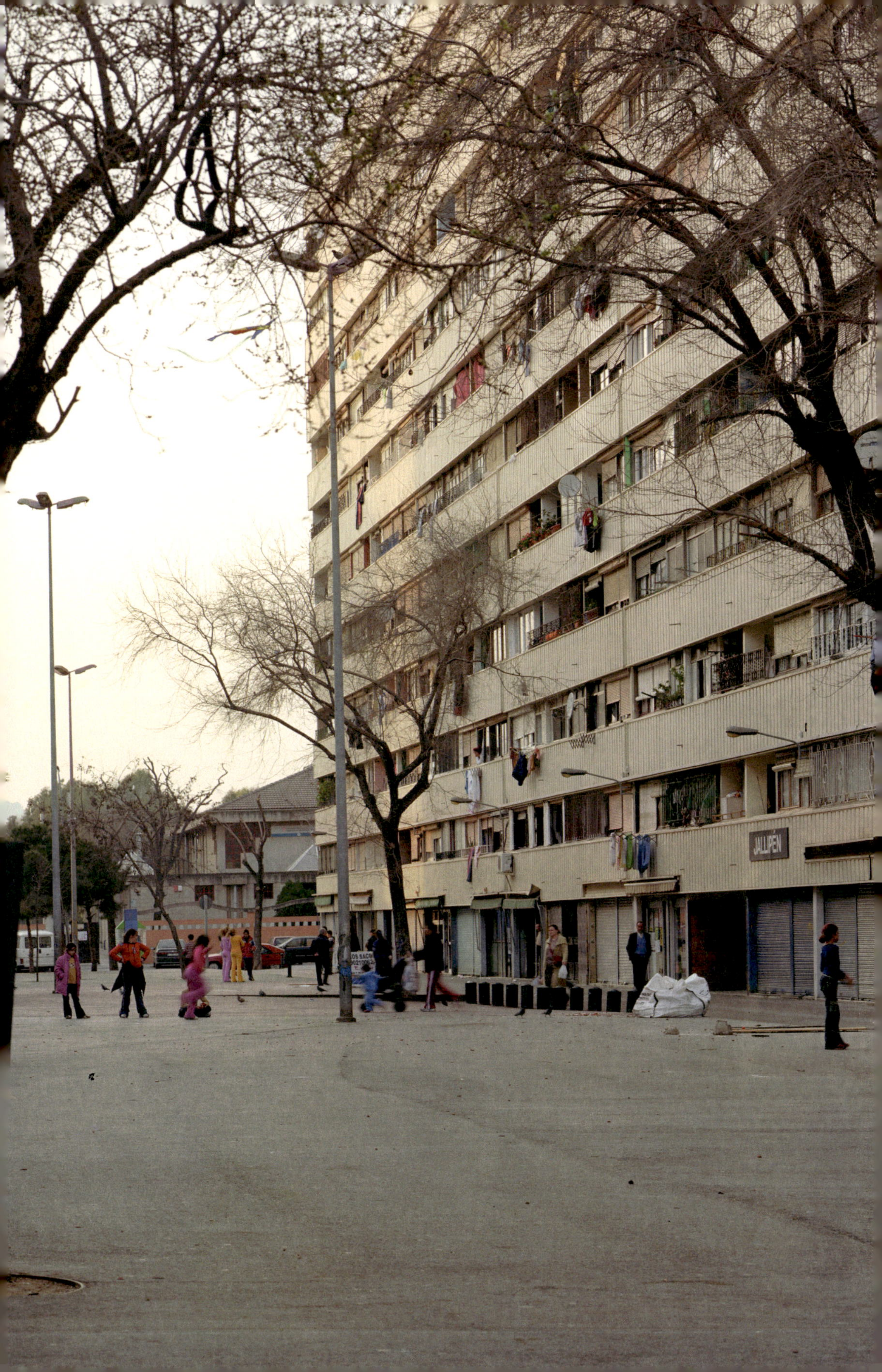
JALLIPEN

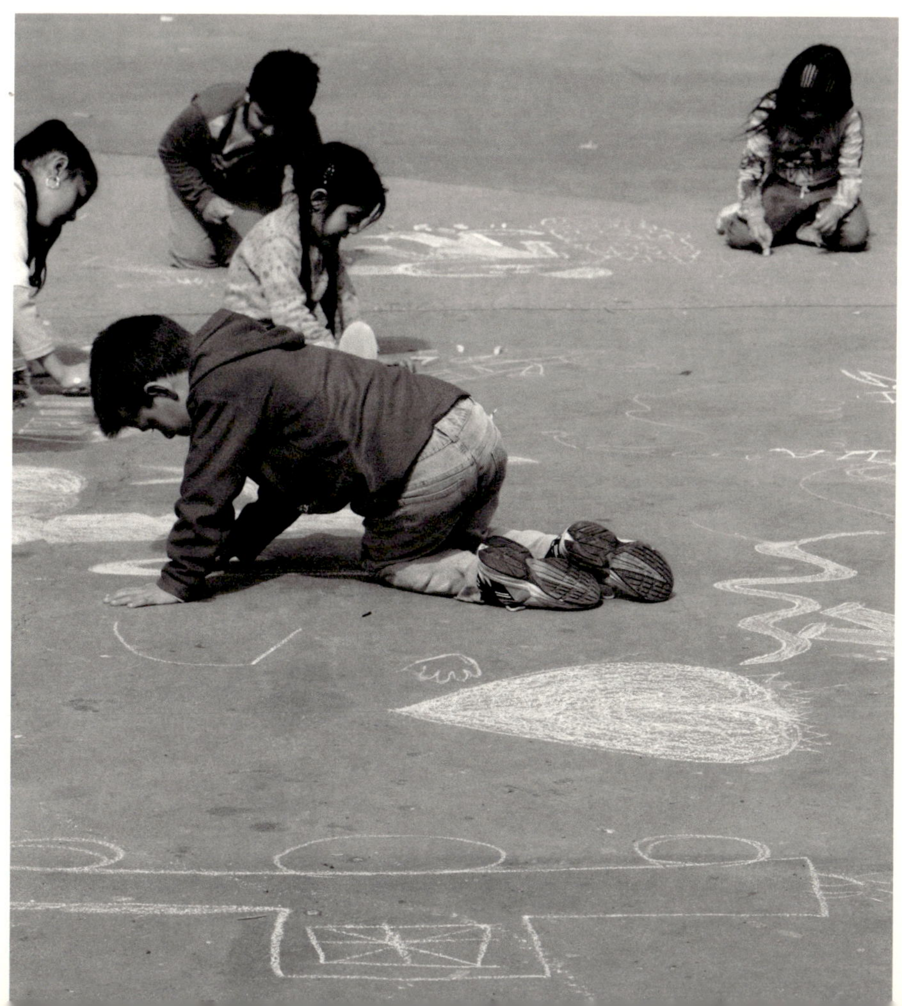

2.21

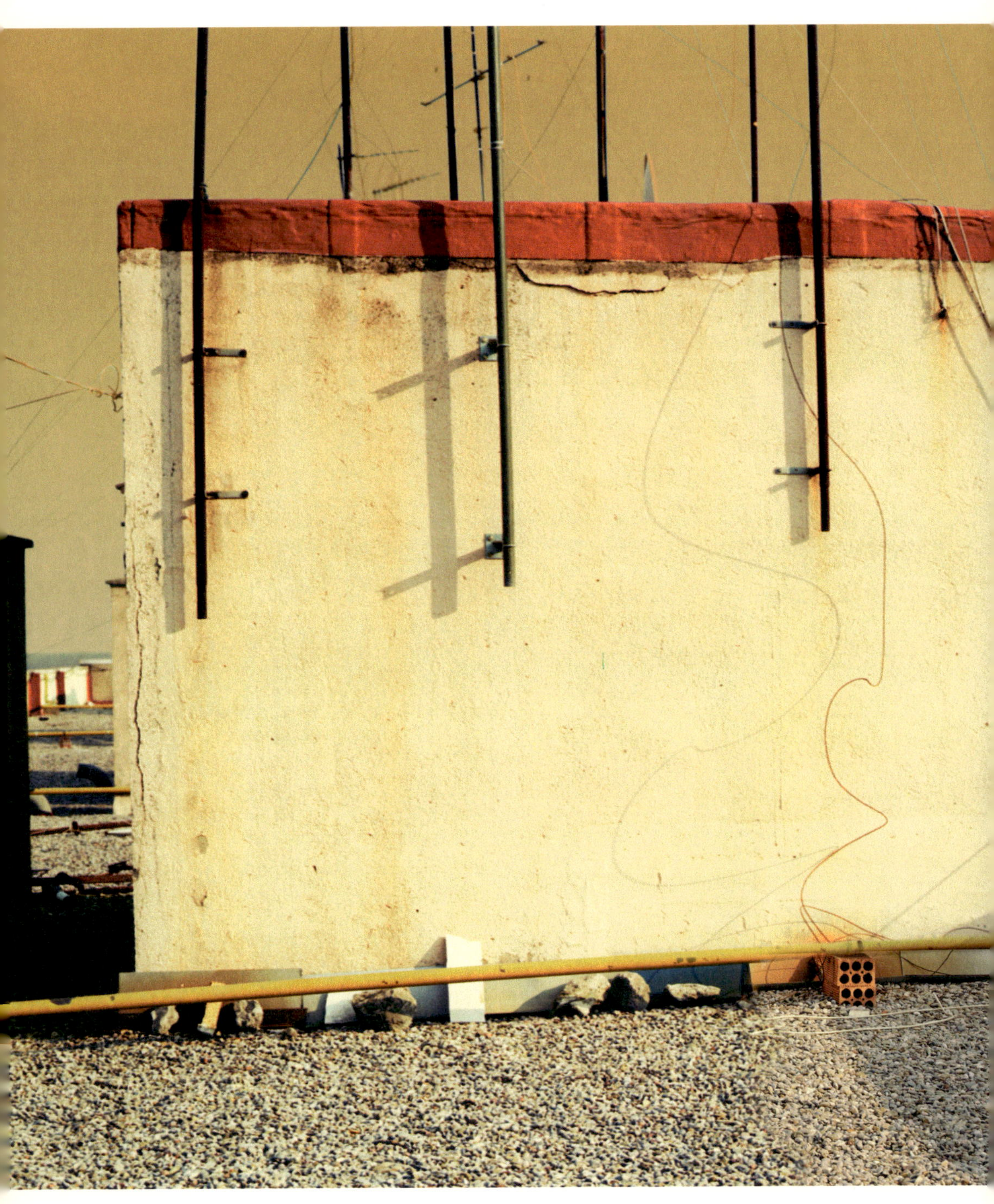

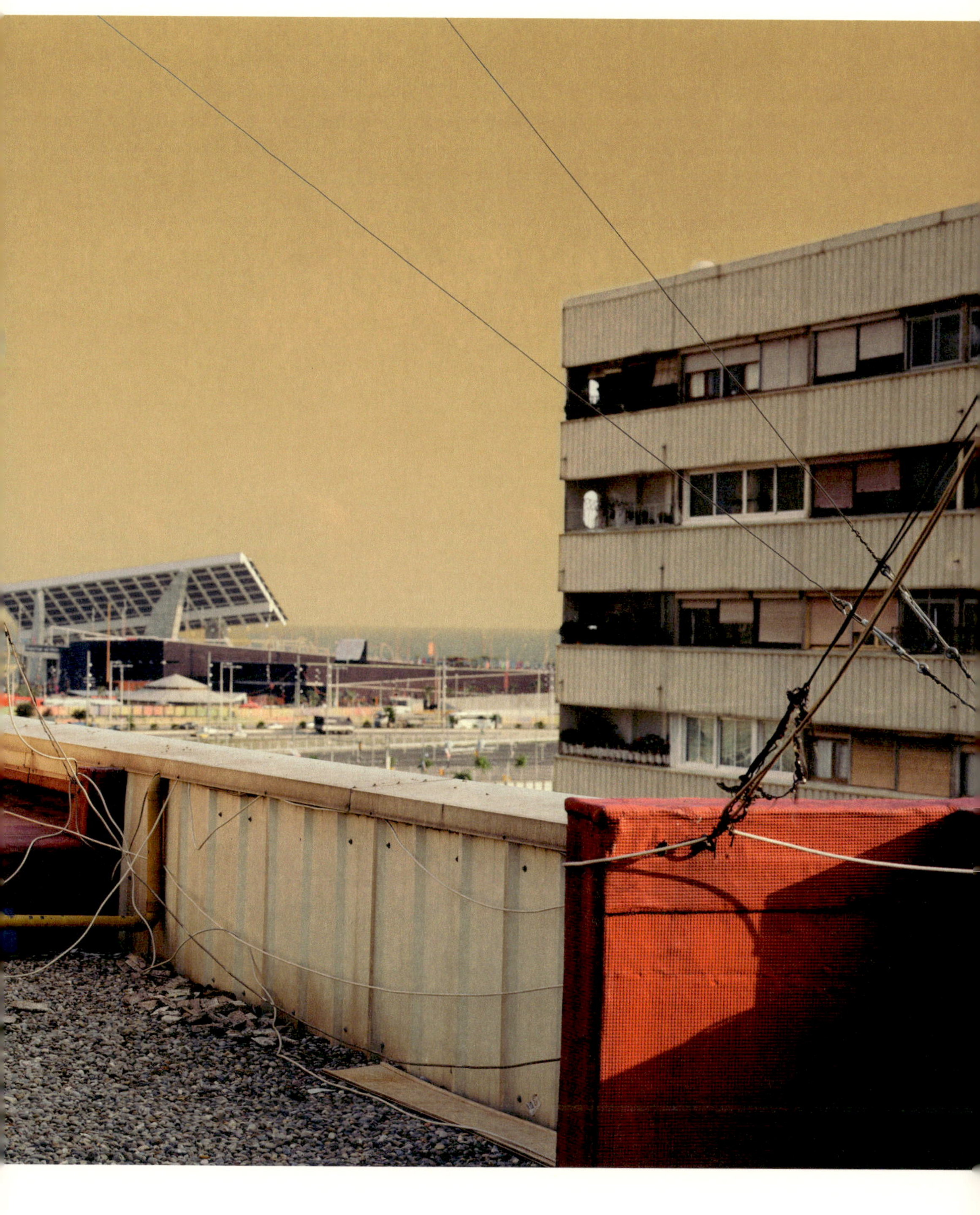

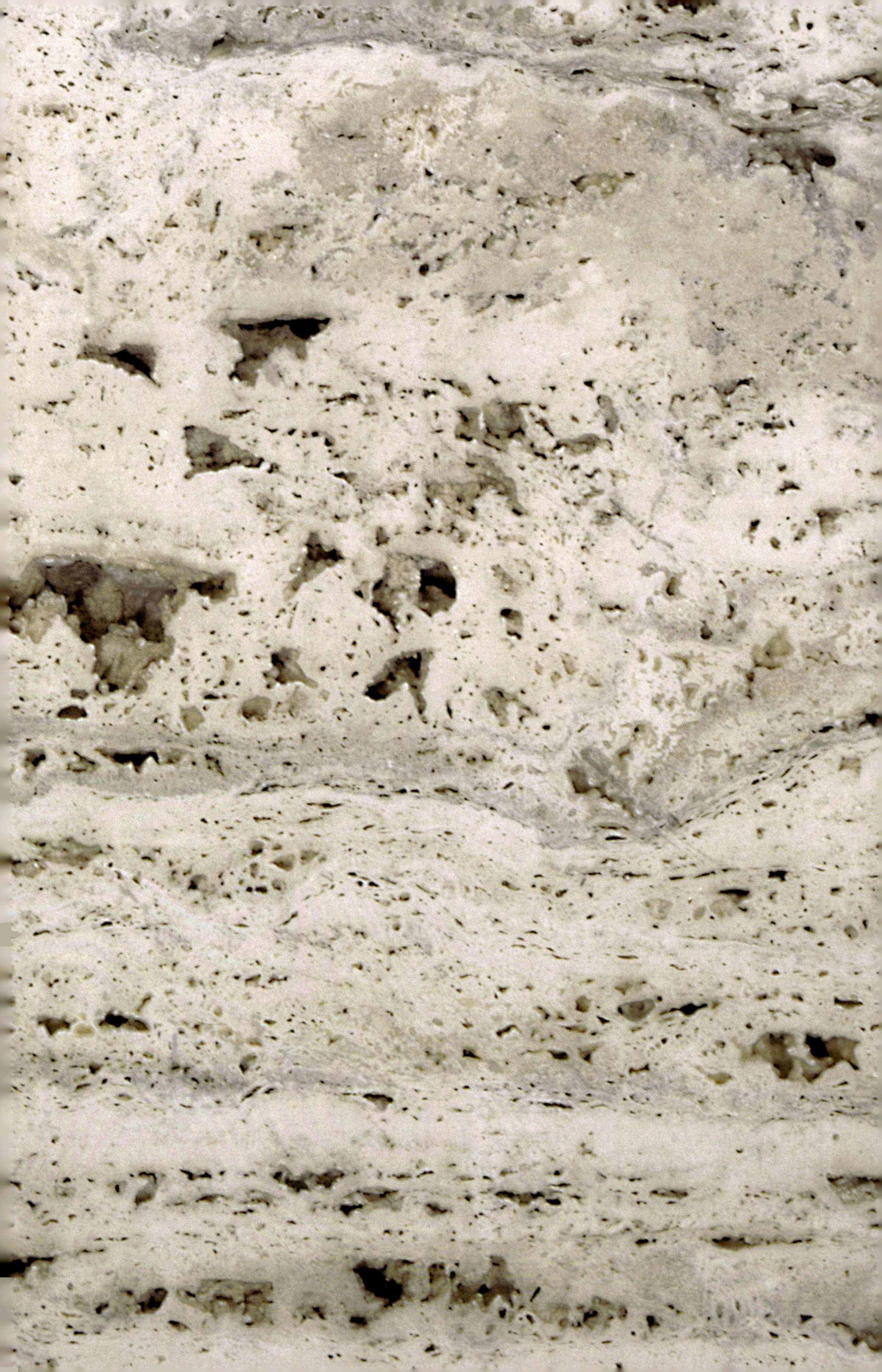

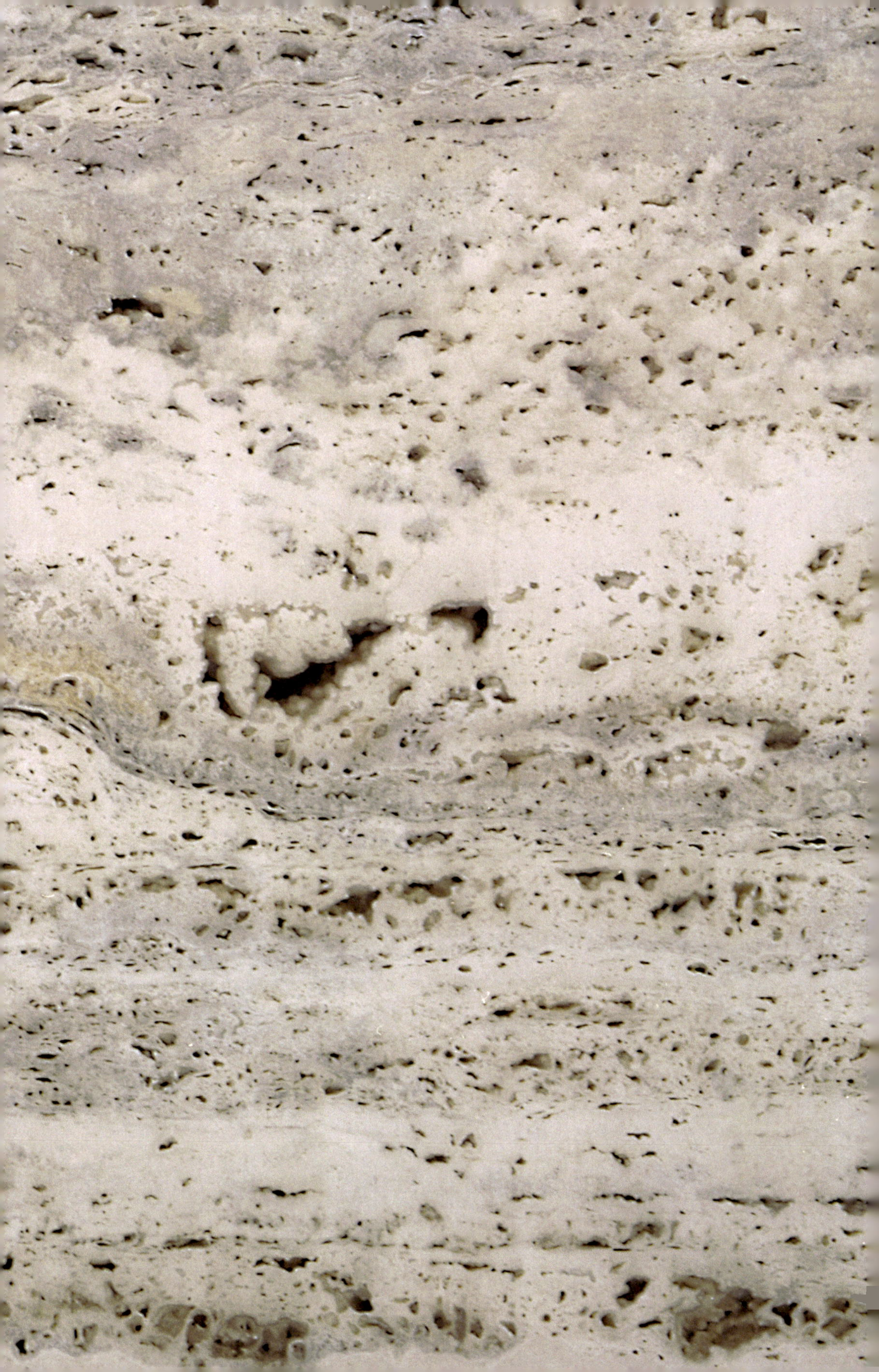

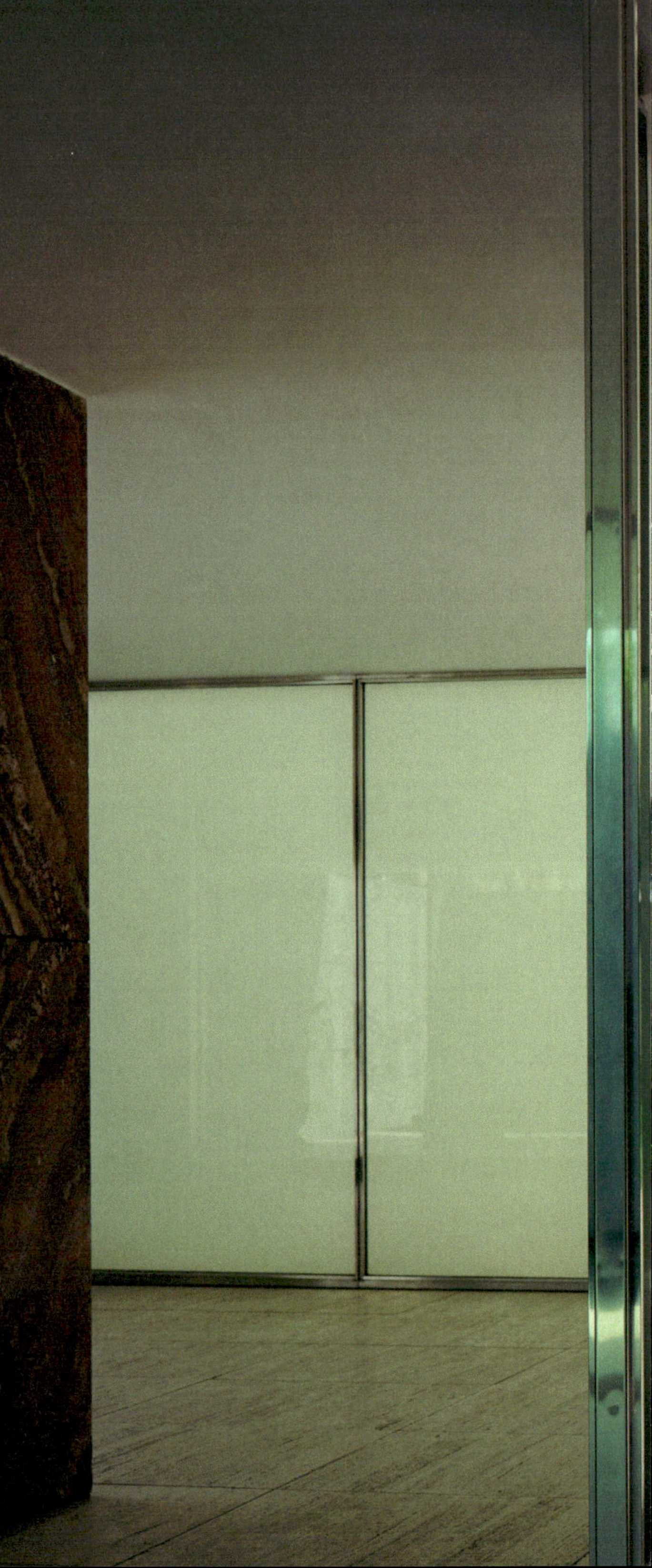

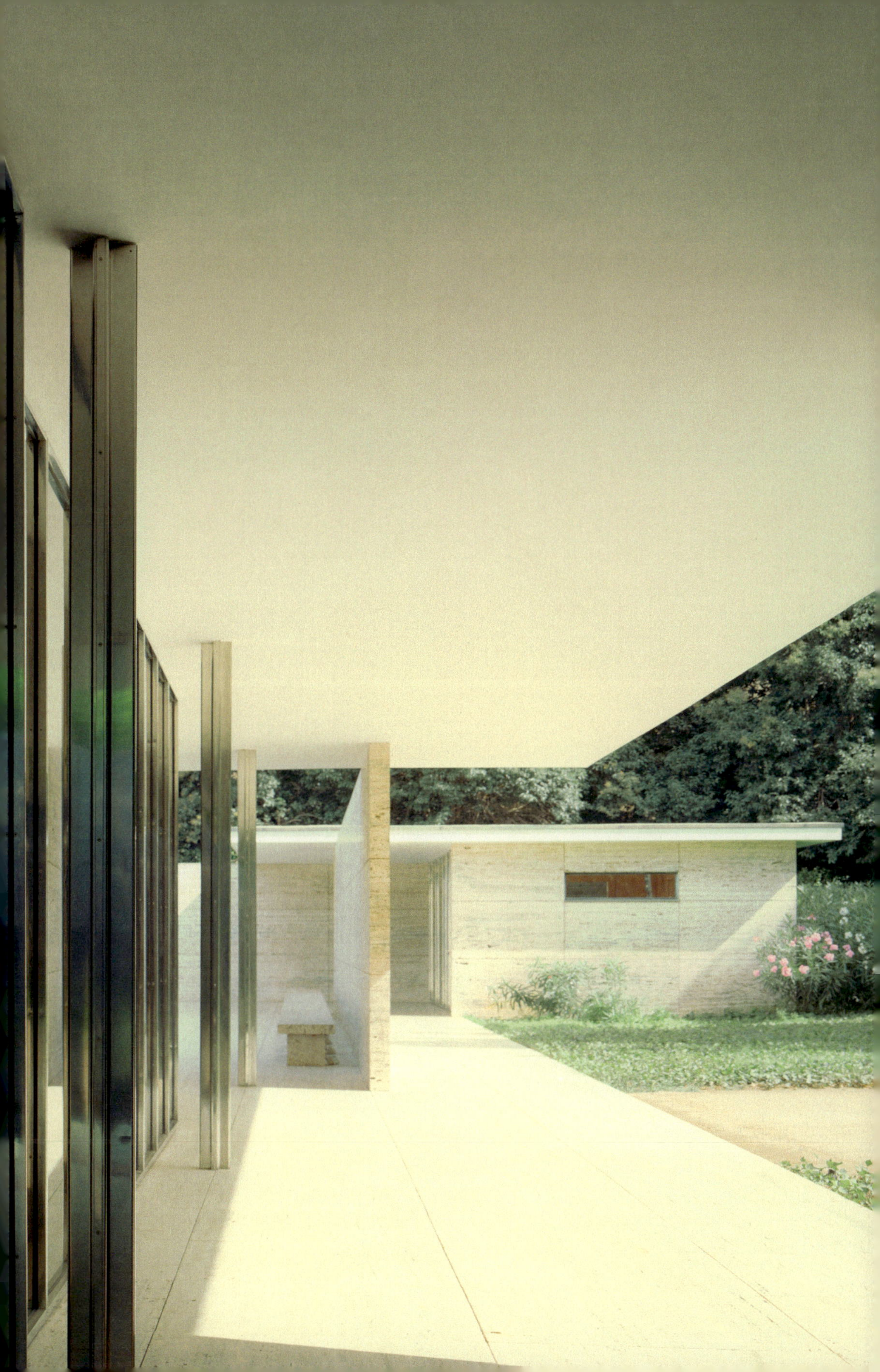

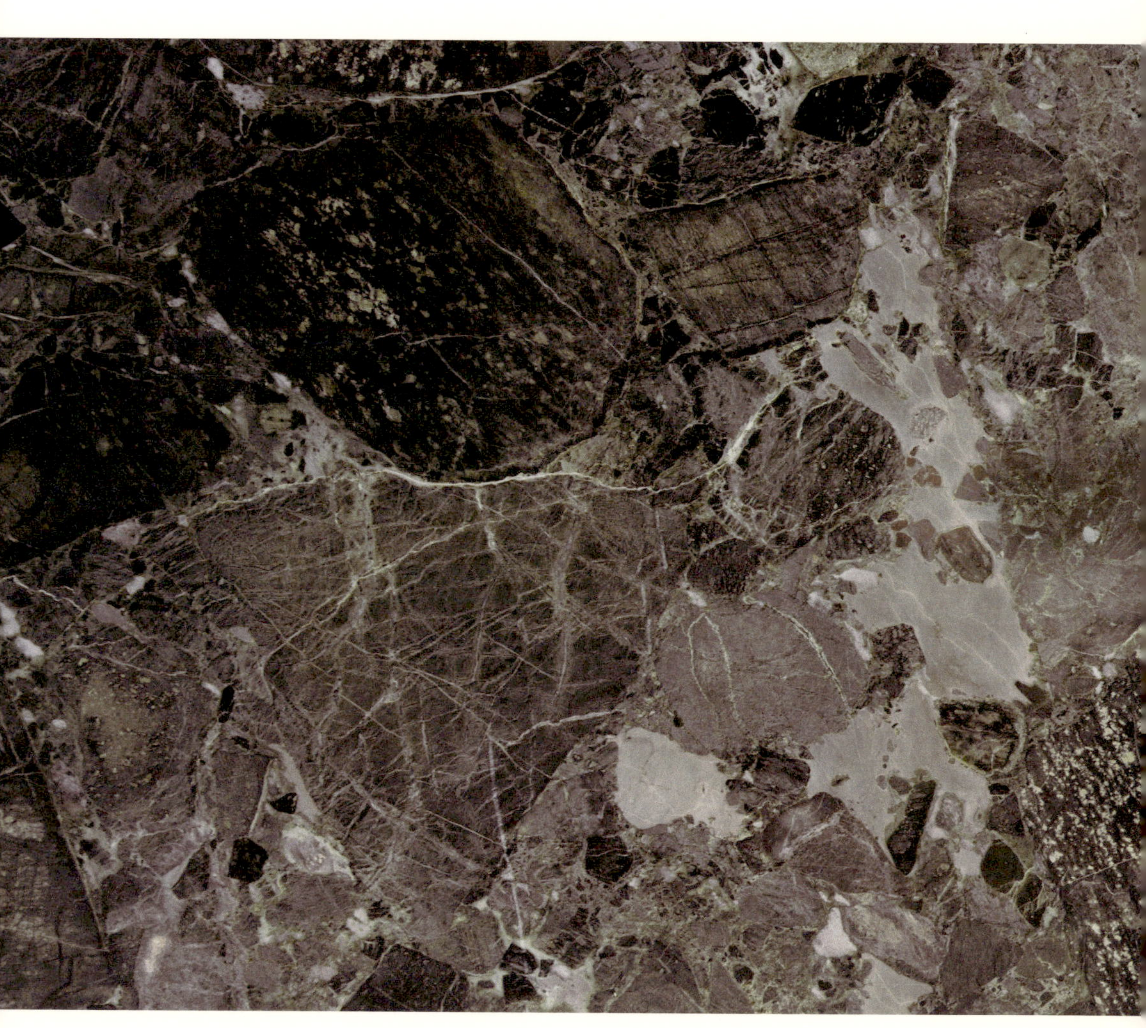

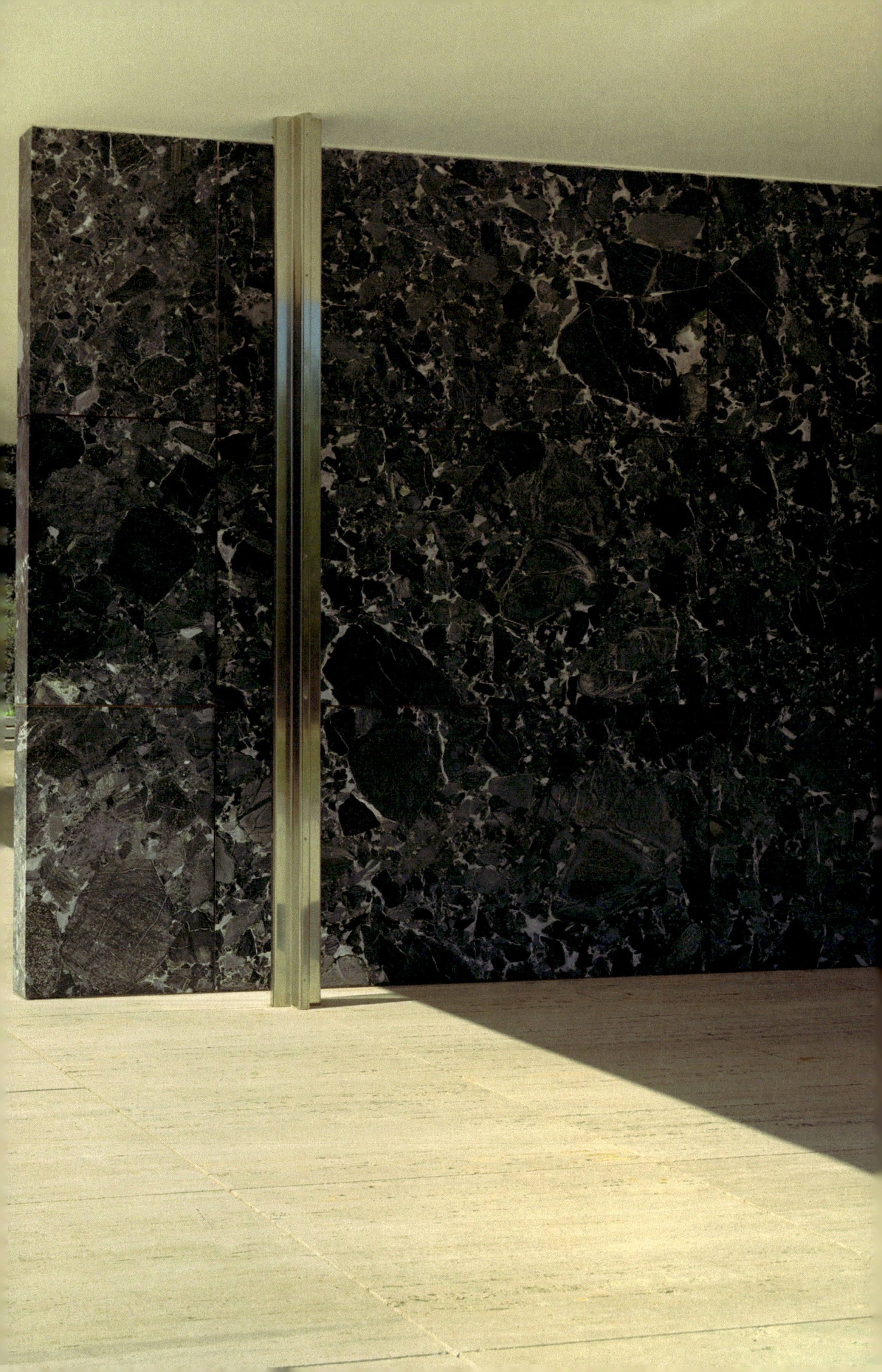

2.32

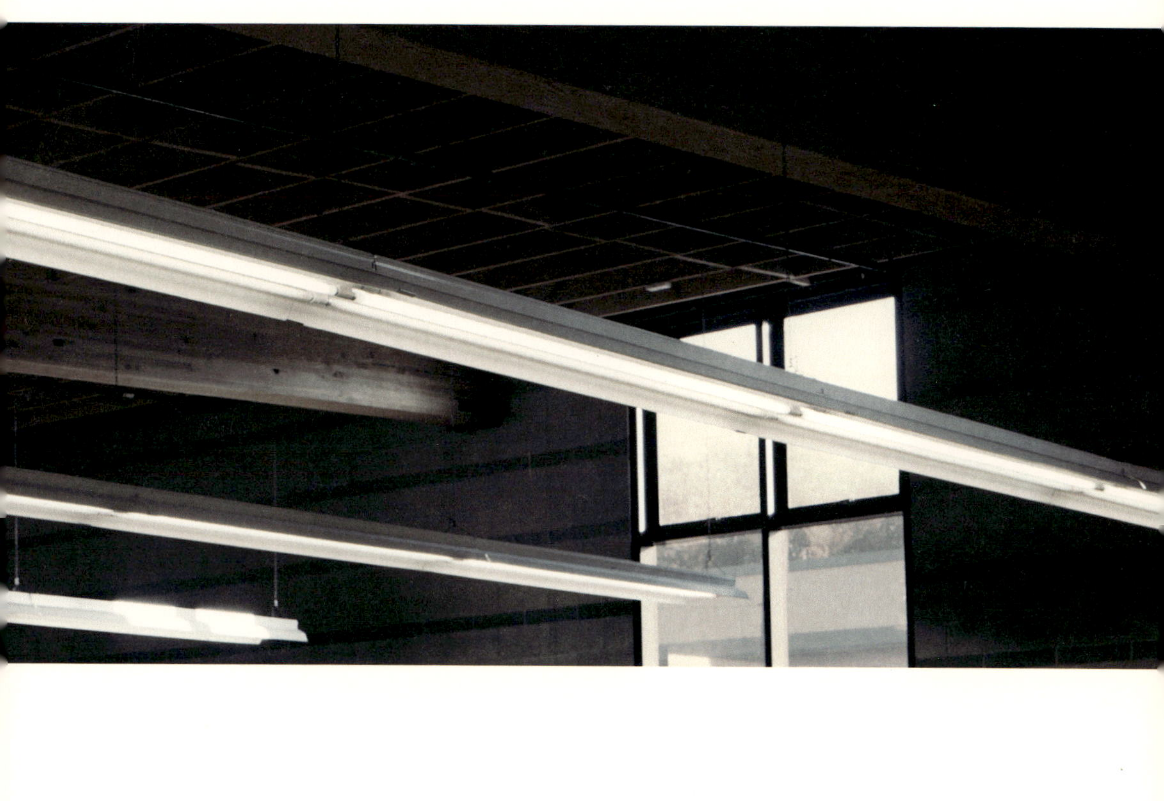

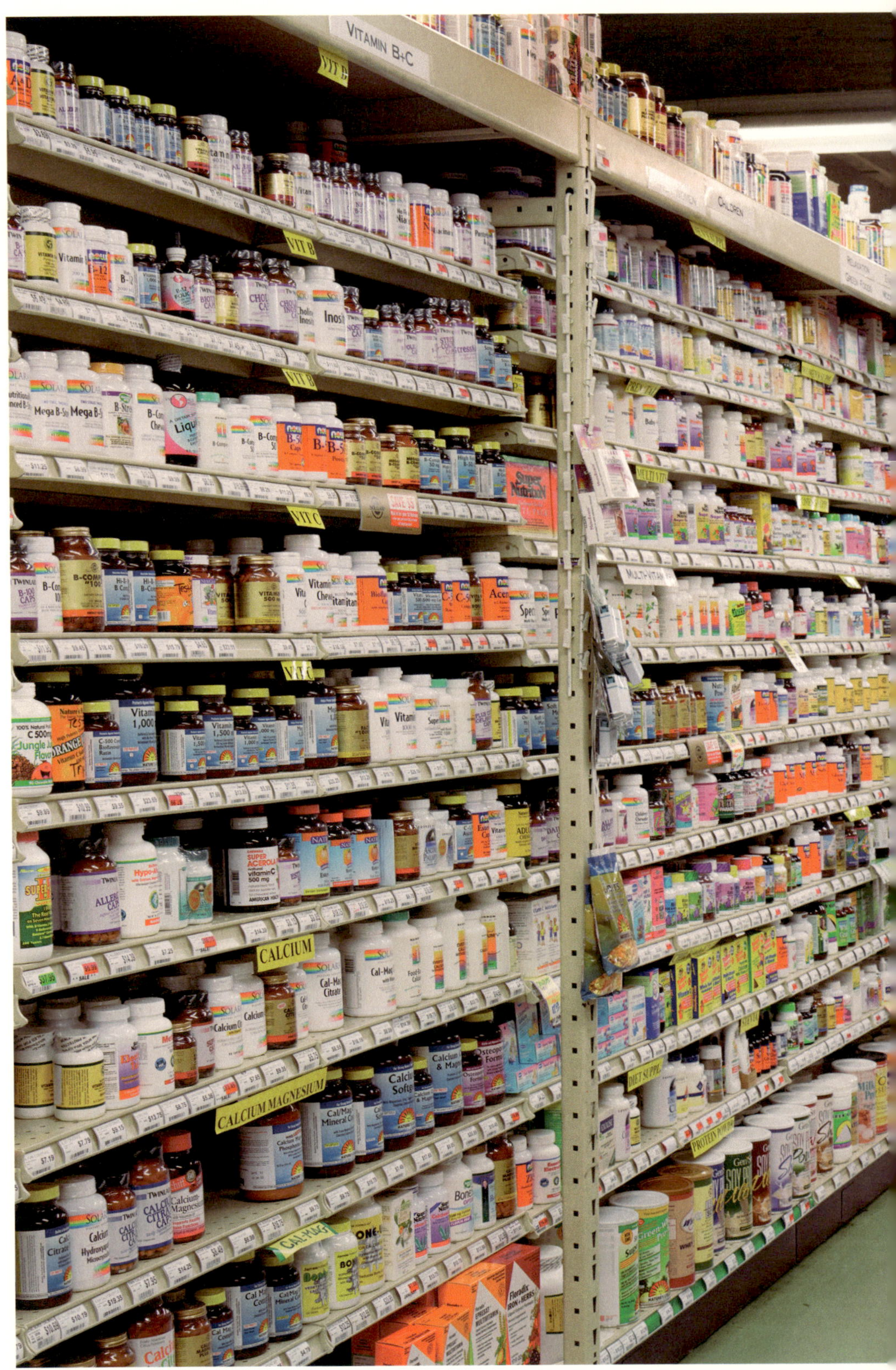

VITAMIN B+C
VIT B
VIT C
CALCIUM
CALCIUM MAGNESIUM
MULTI-VITAMIN
CHILDREN

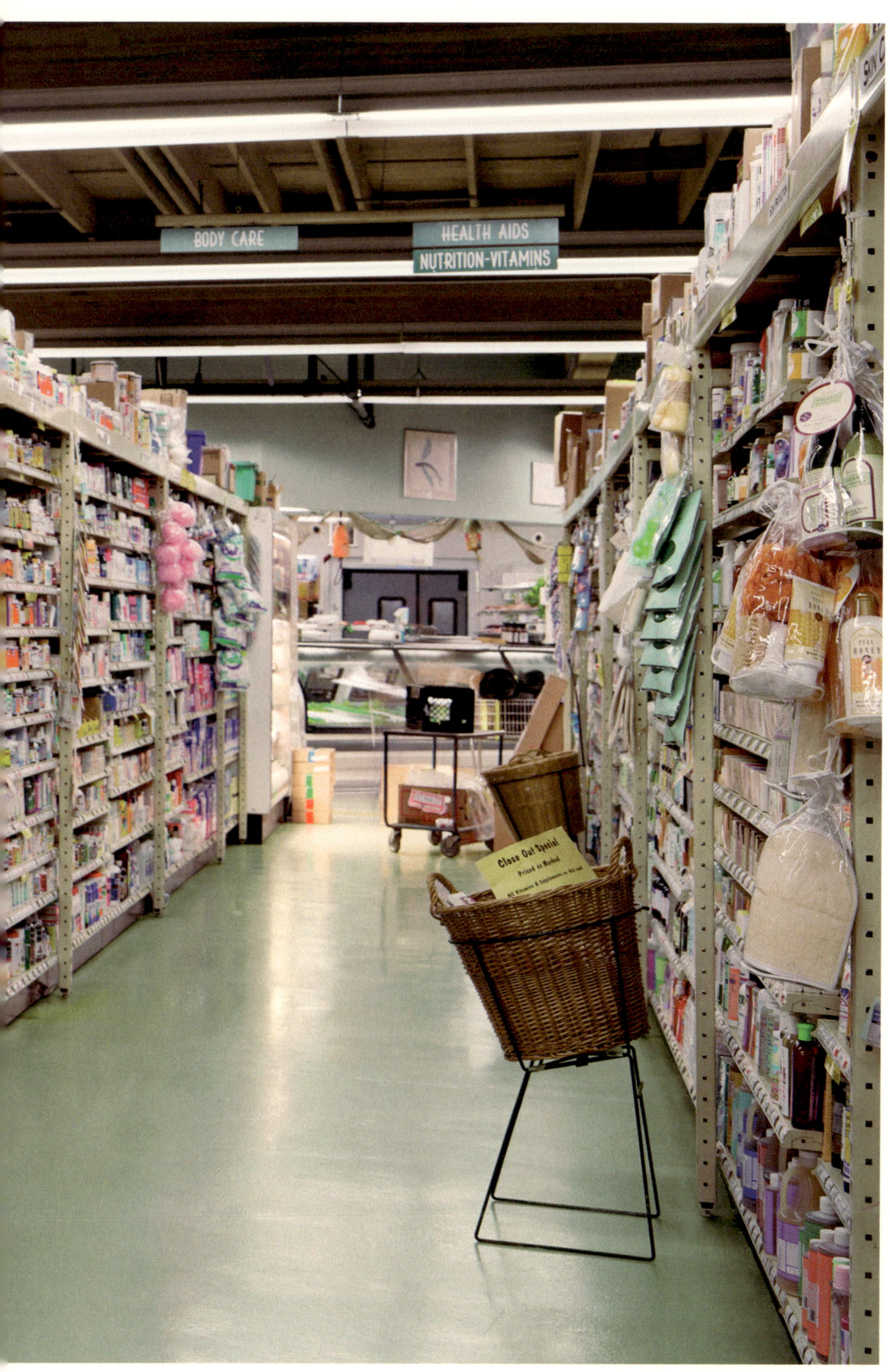

BODY CARE
HEALTH AIDS
NUTRITION-VITAMINS
Close Out Special
PURE HONEY

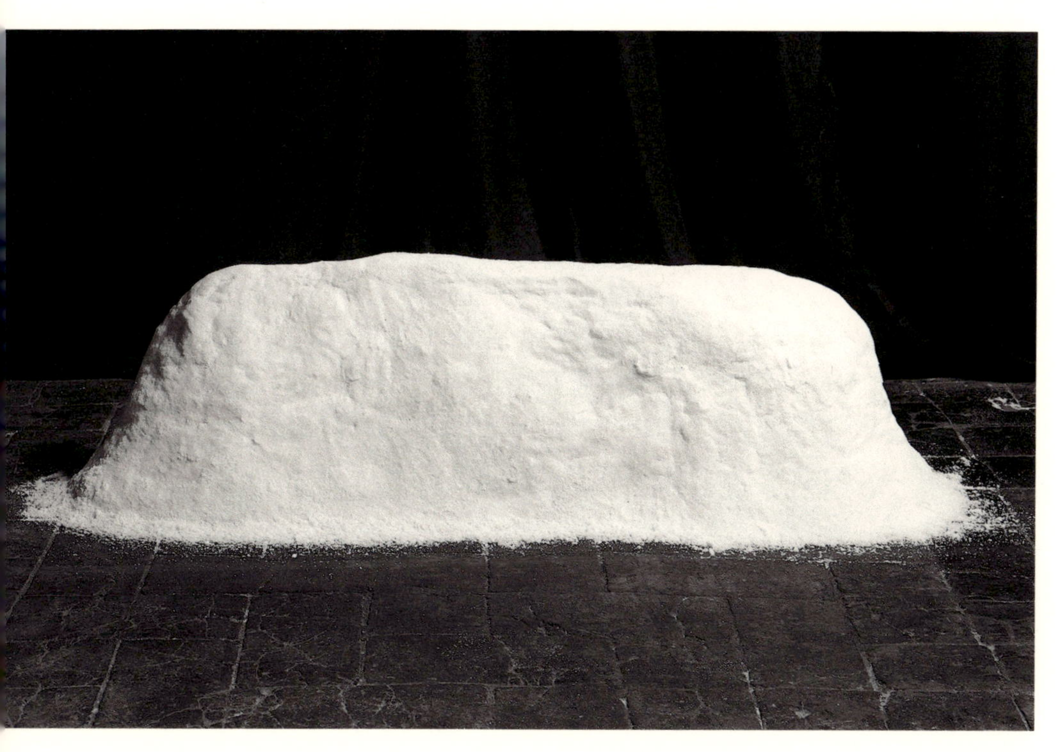

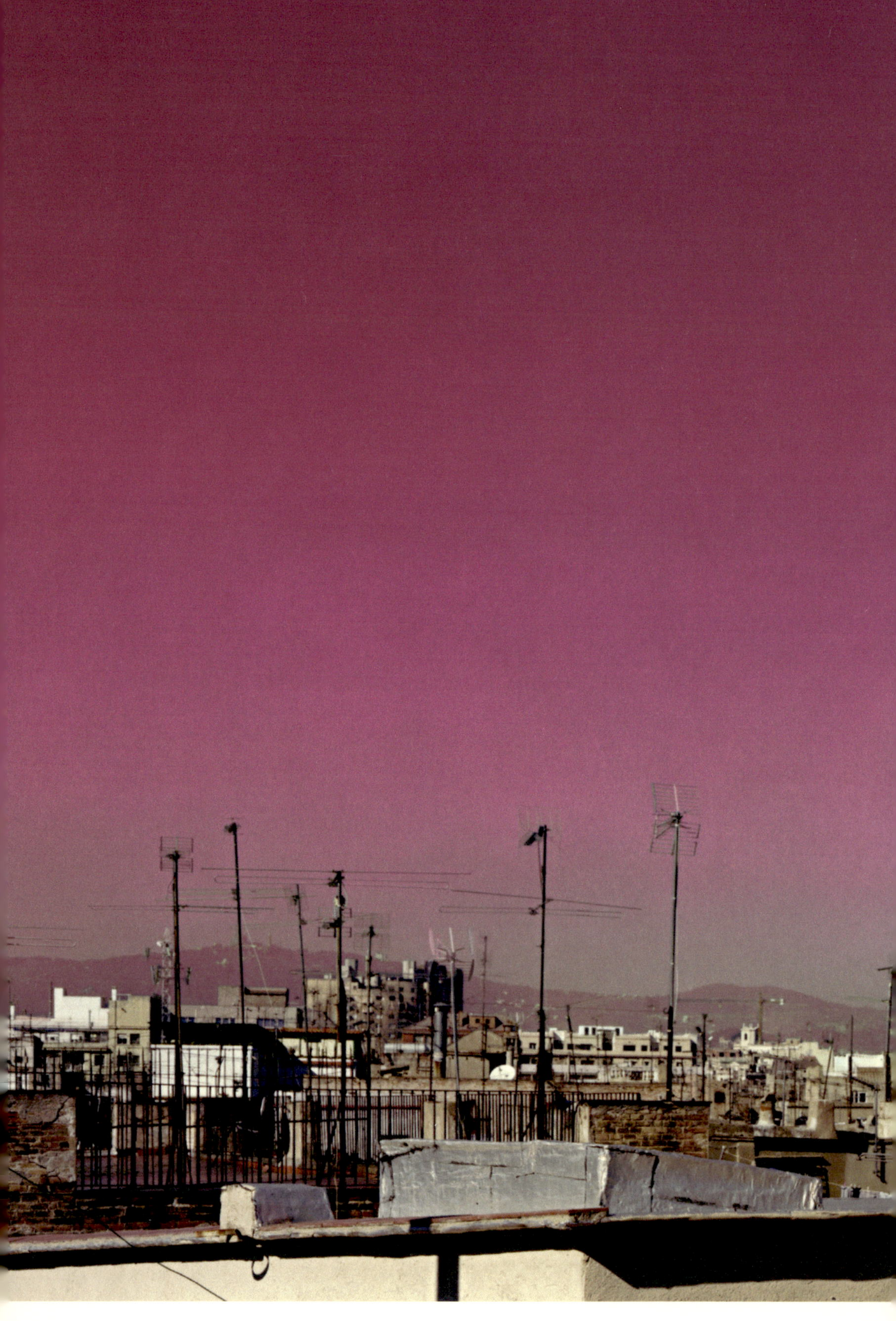

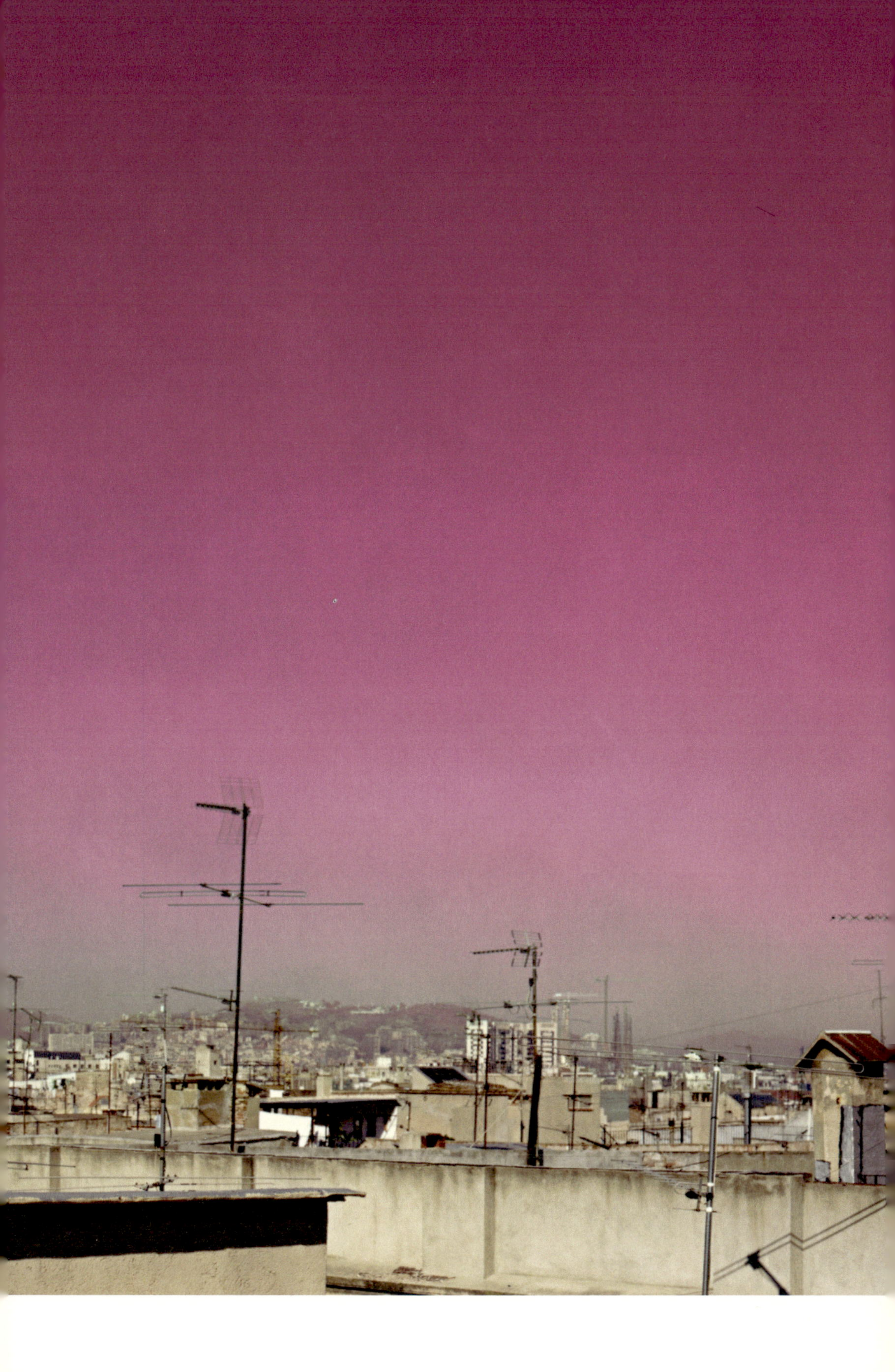

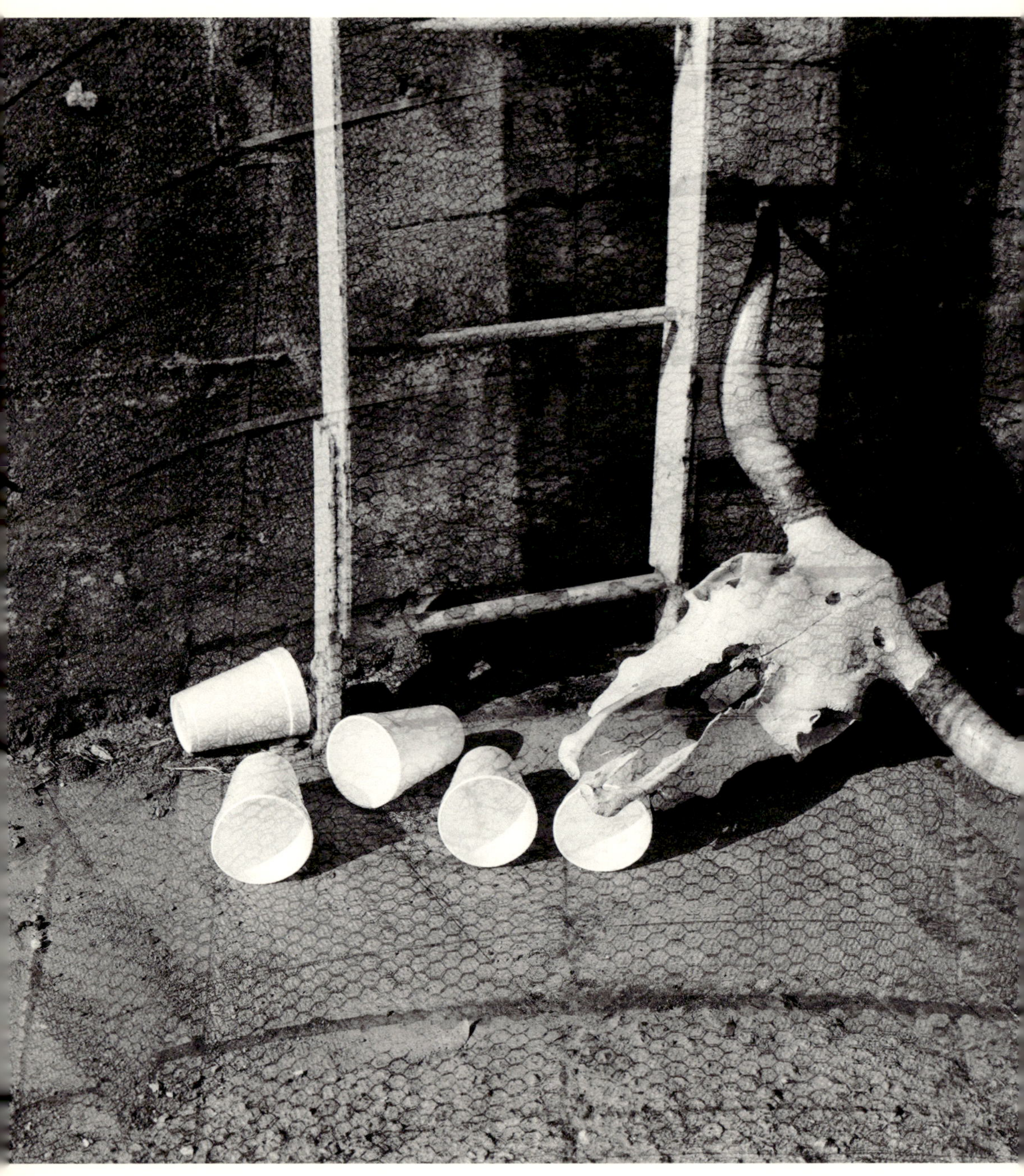

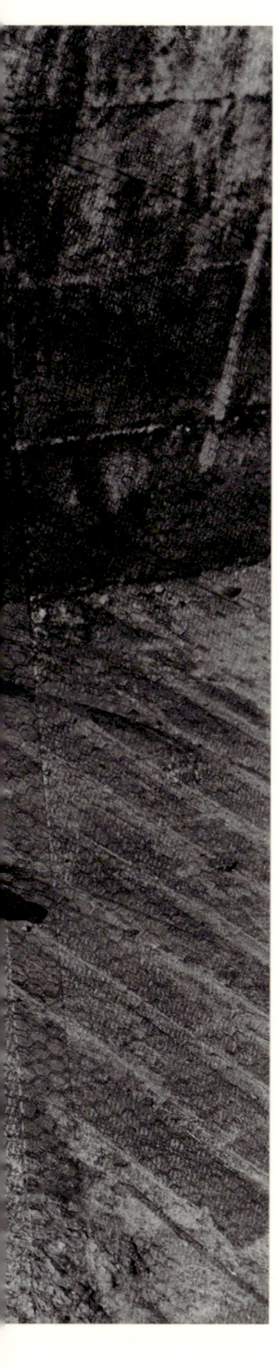

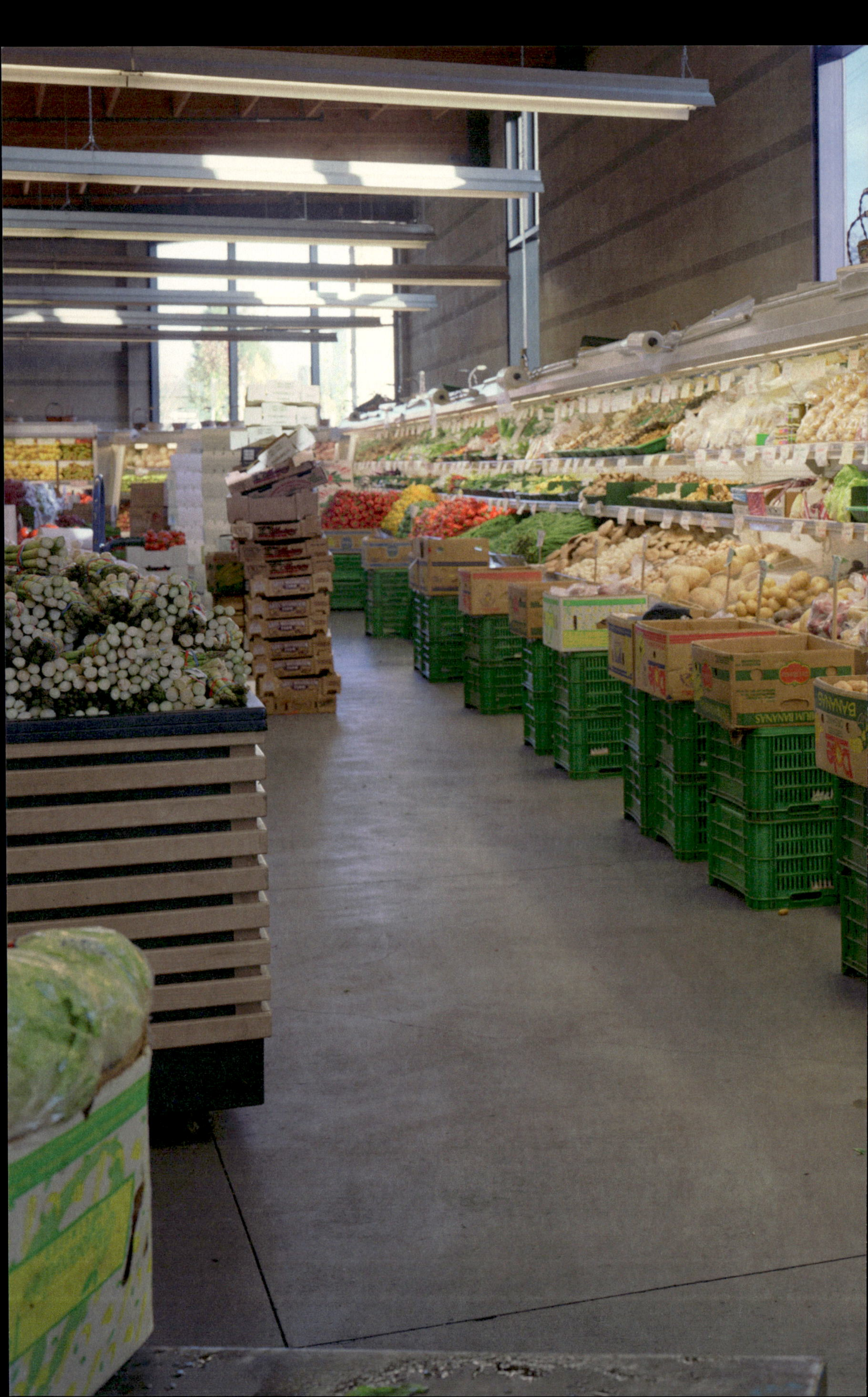

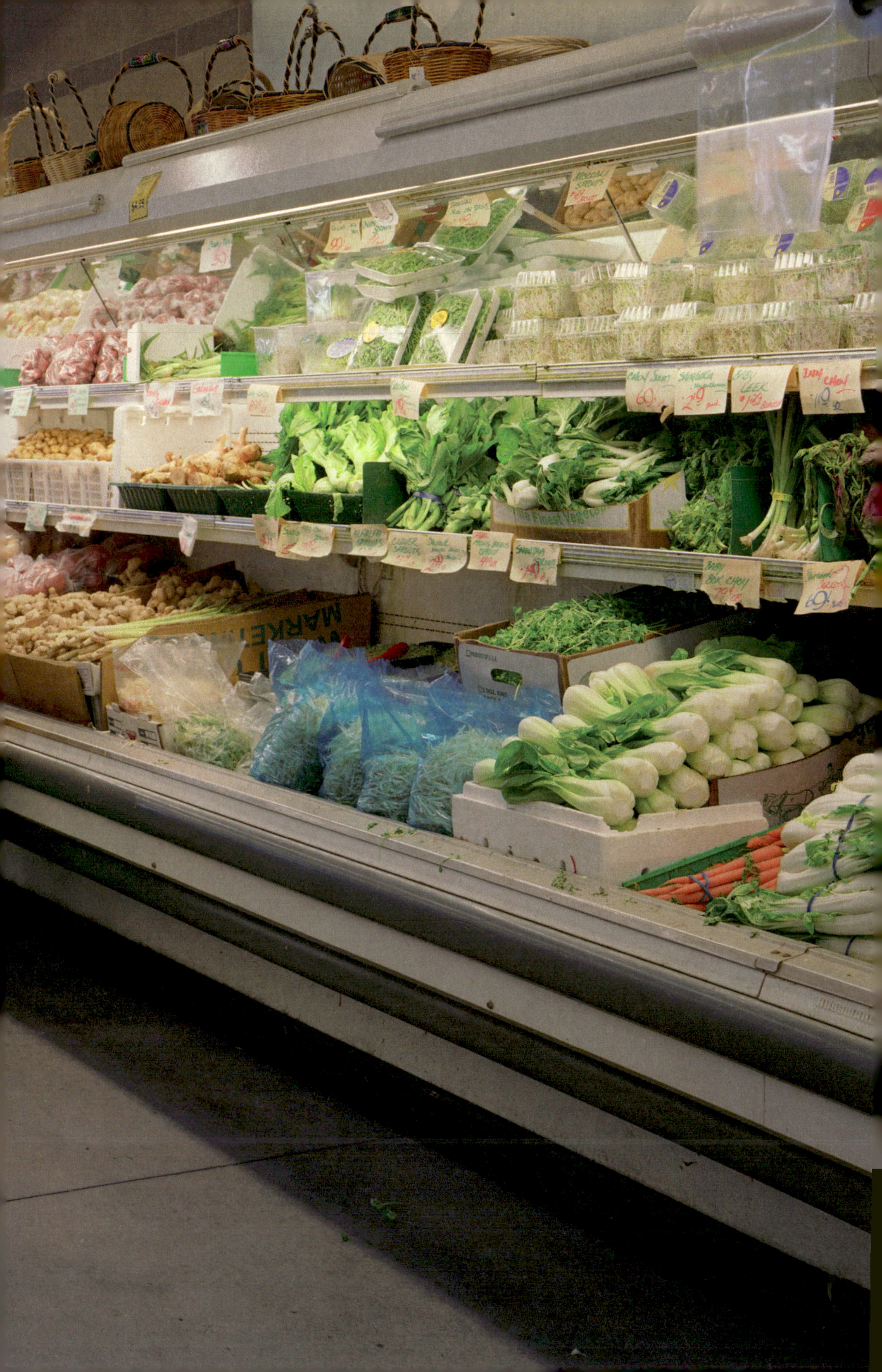

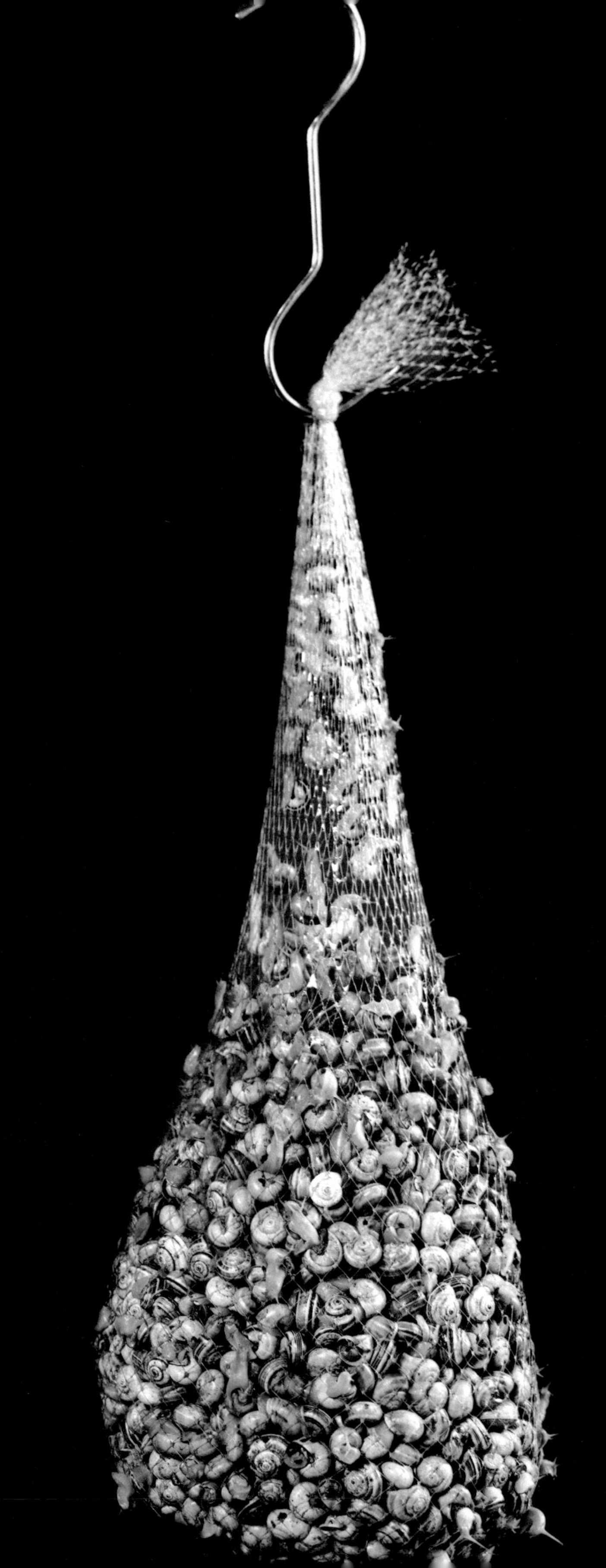

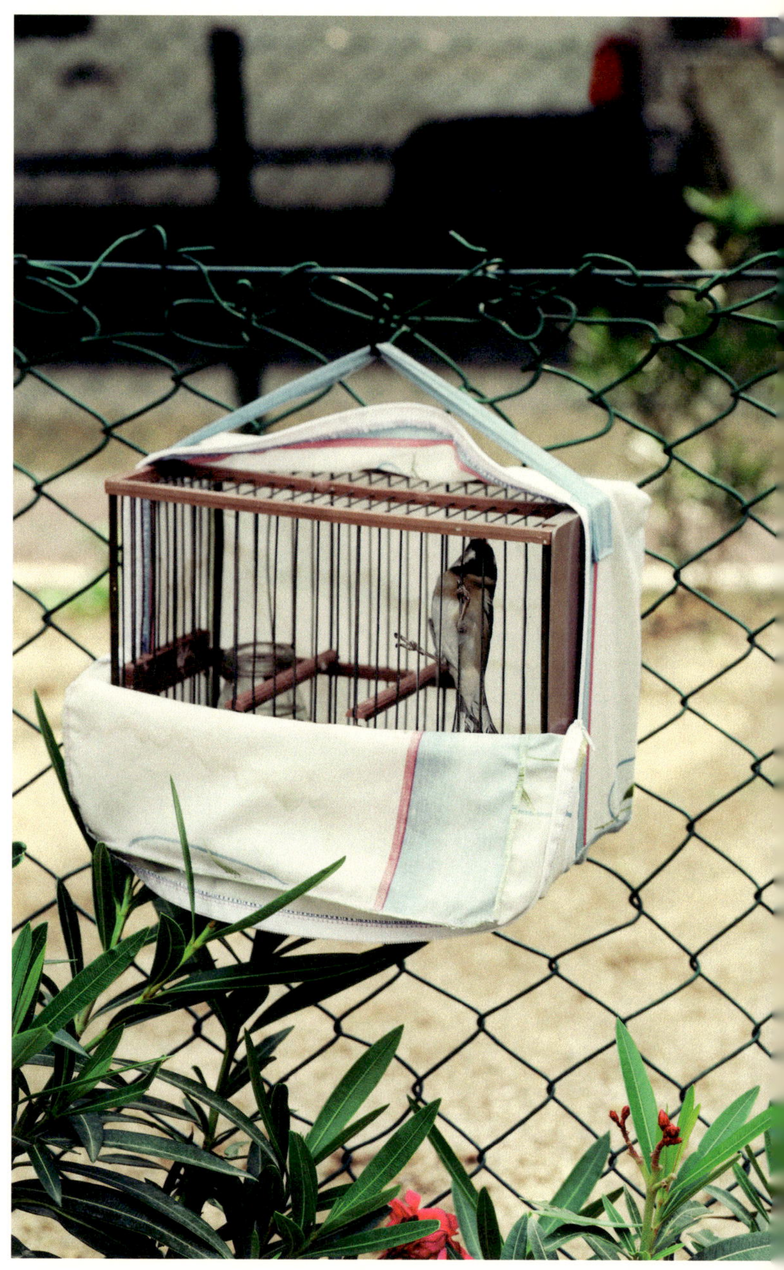

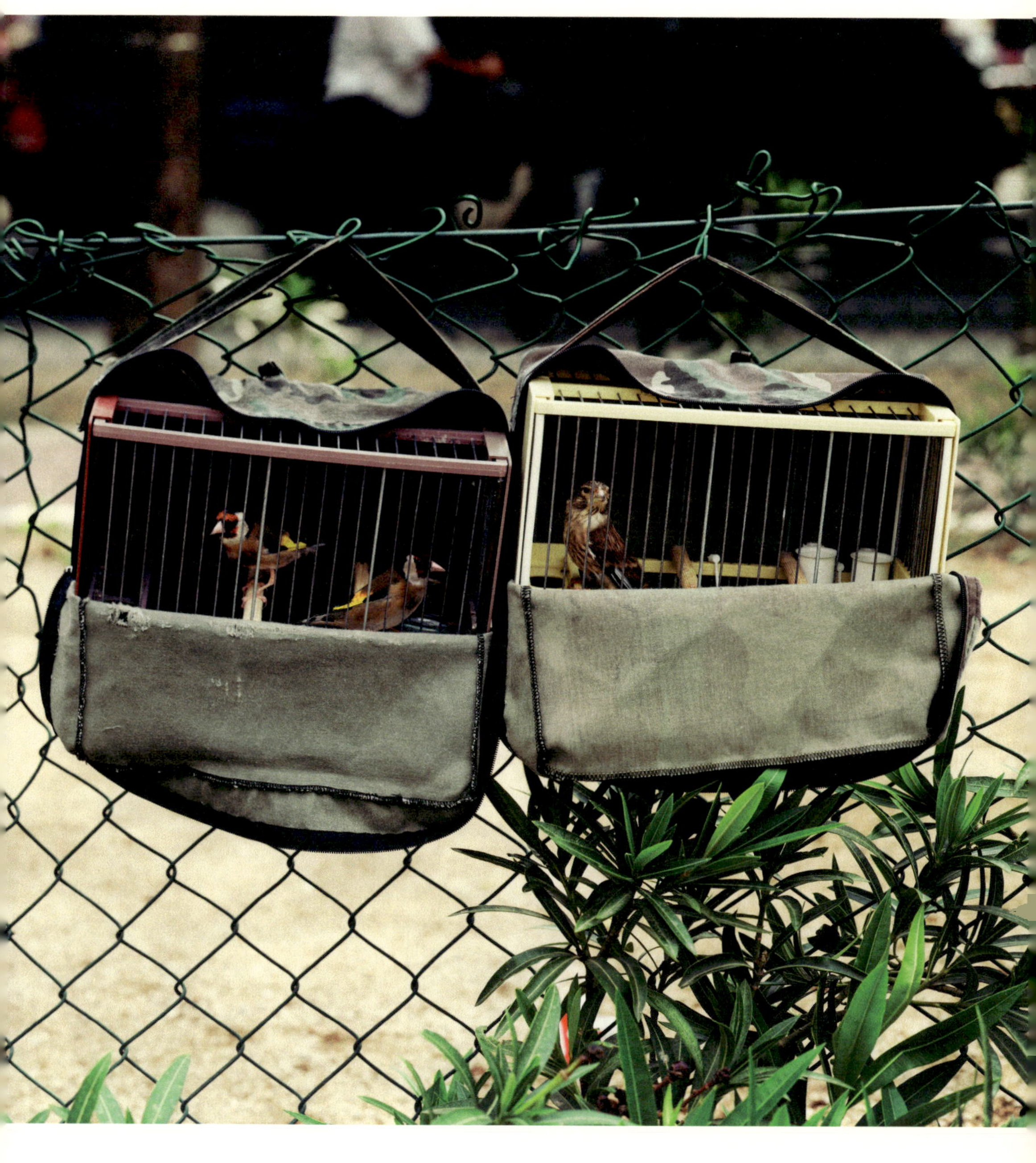

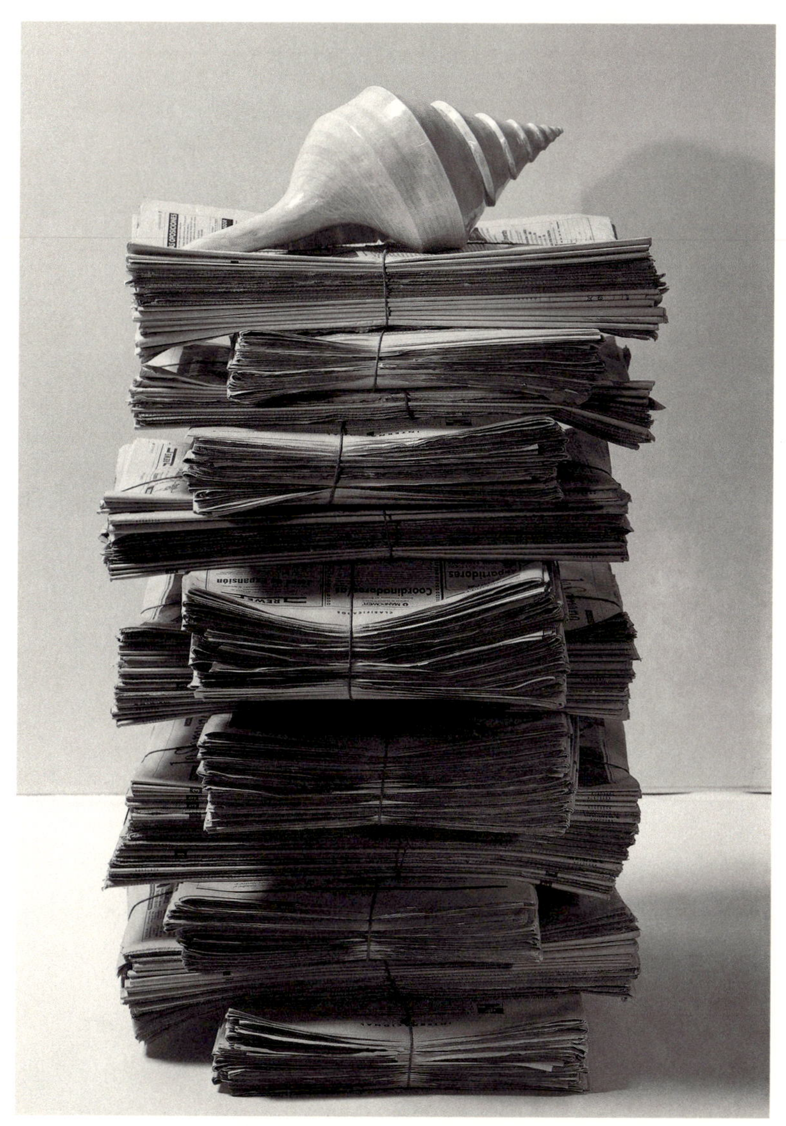

2.49

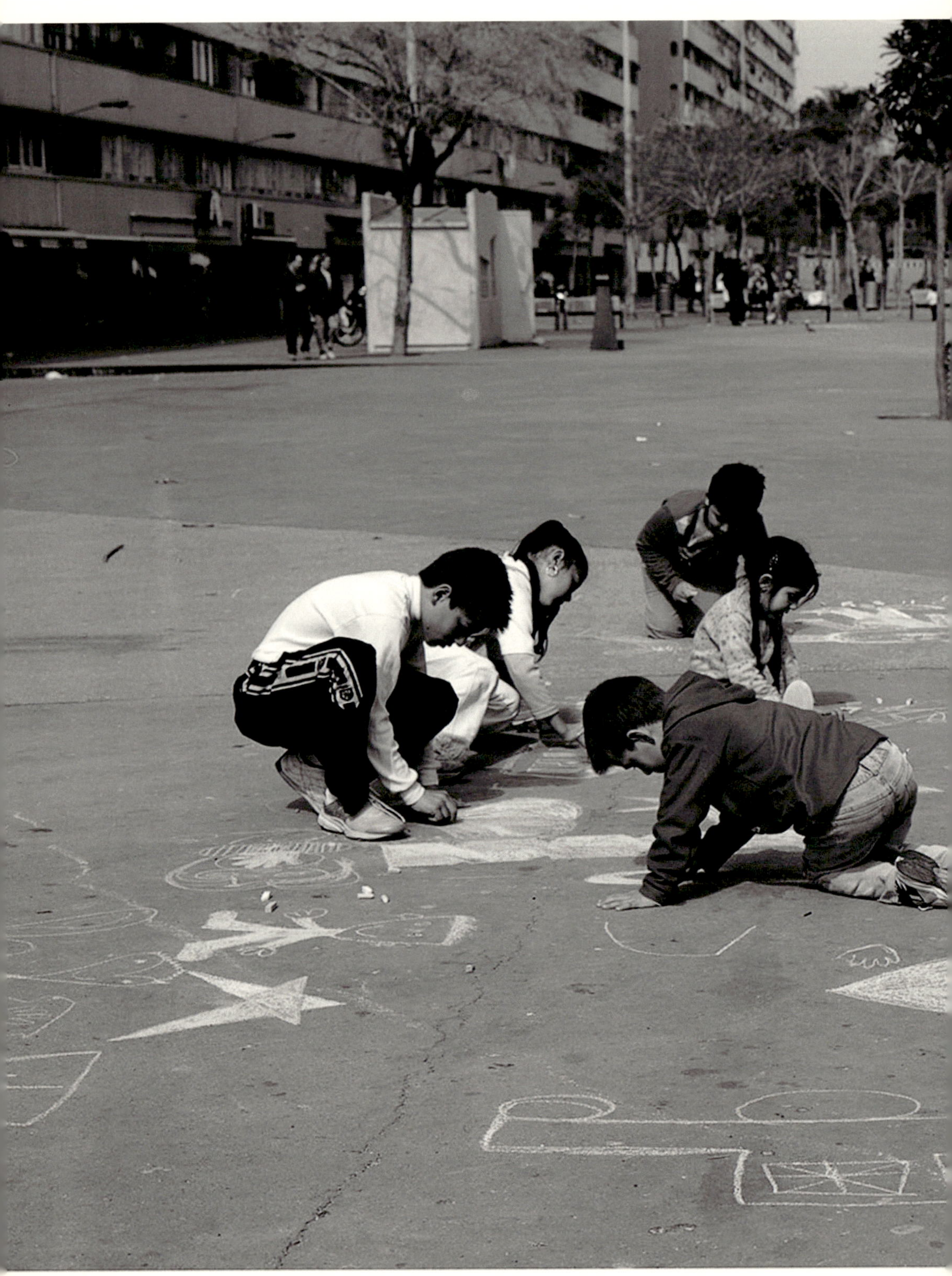

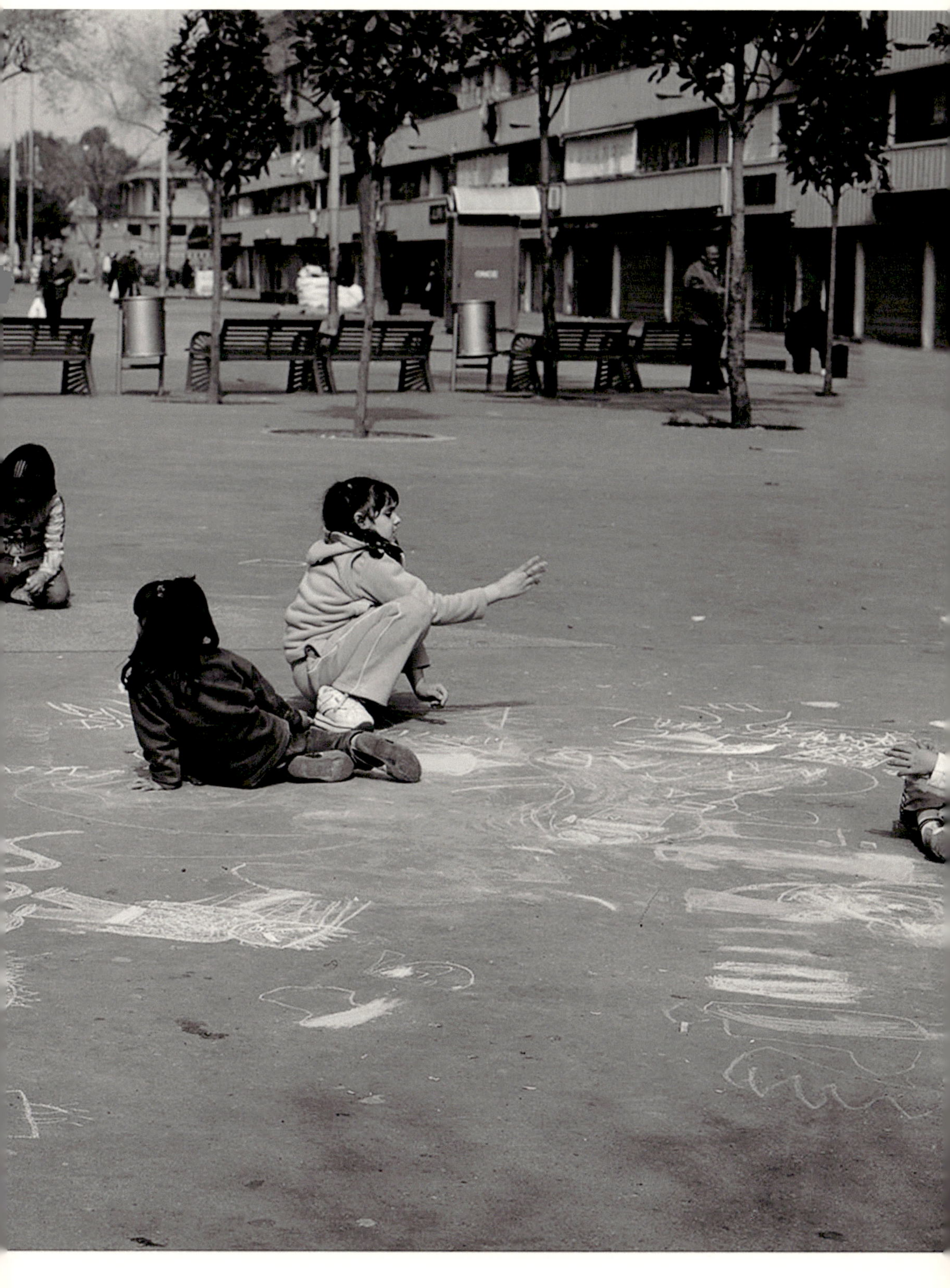

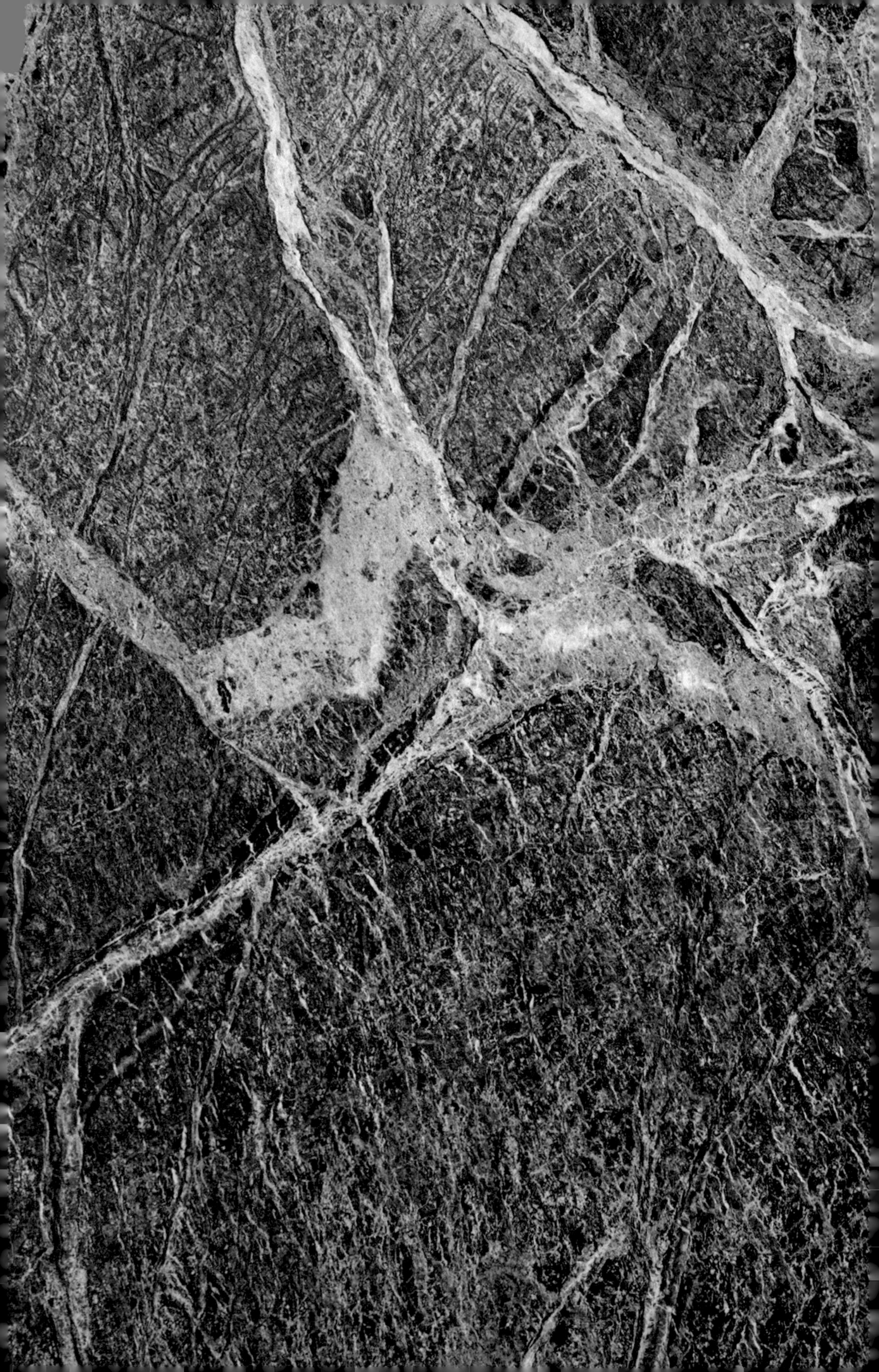

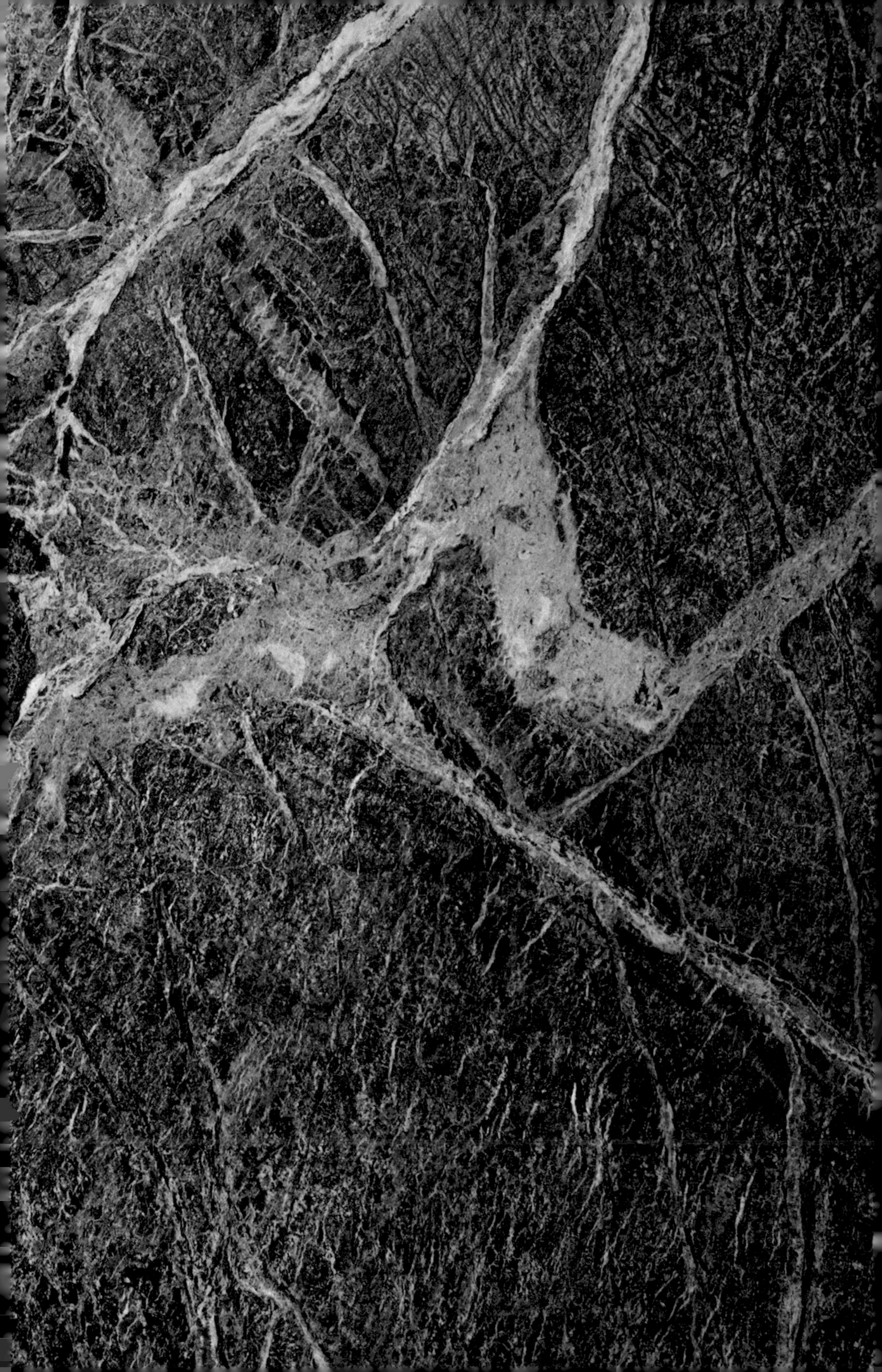

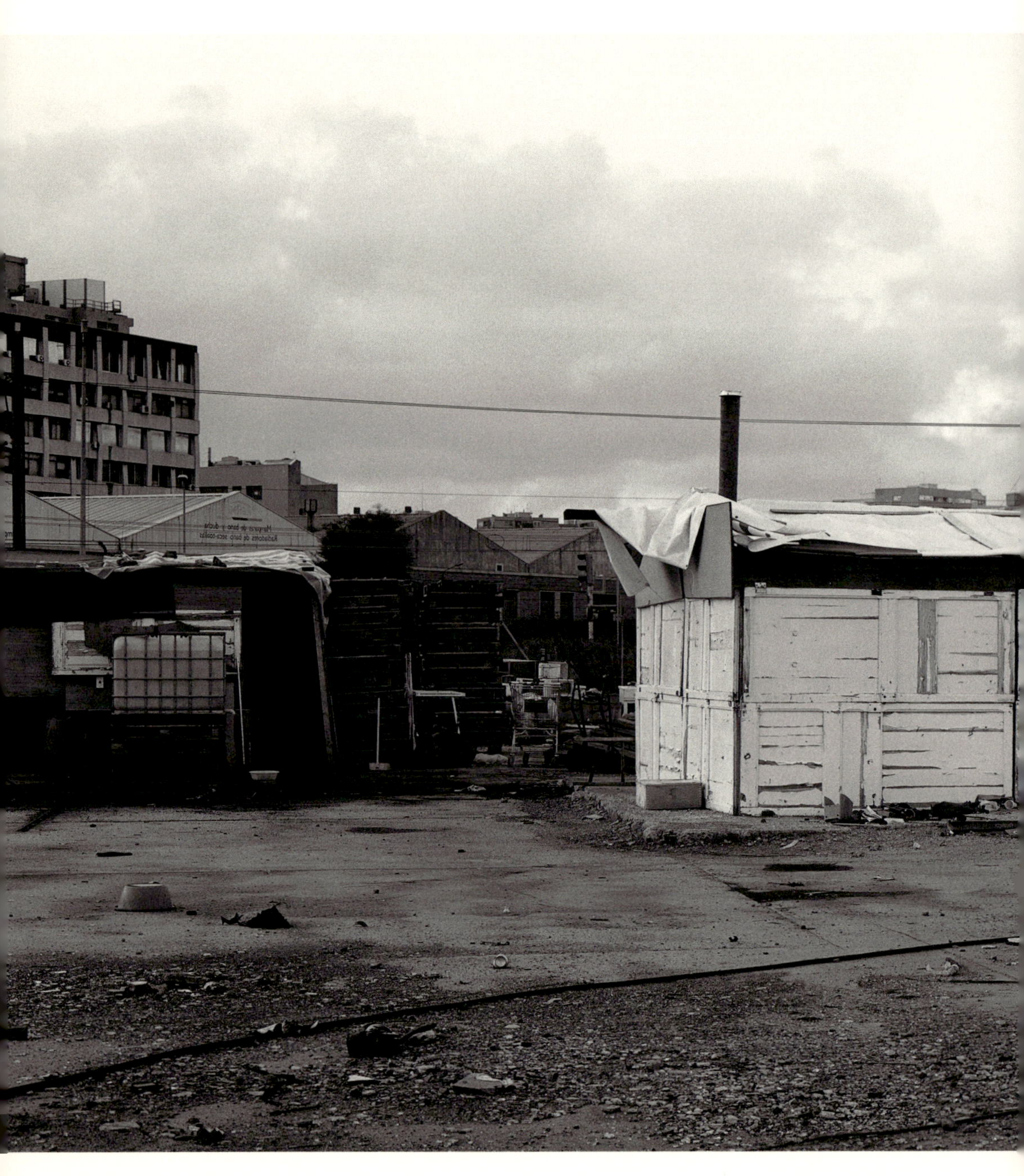

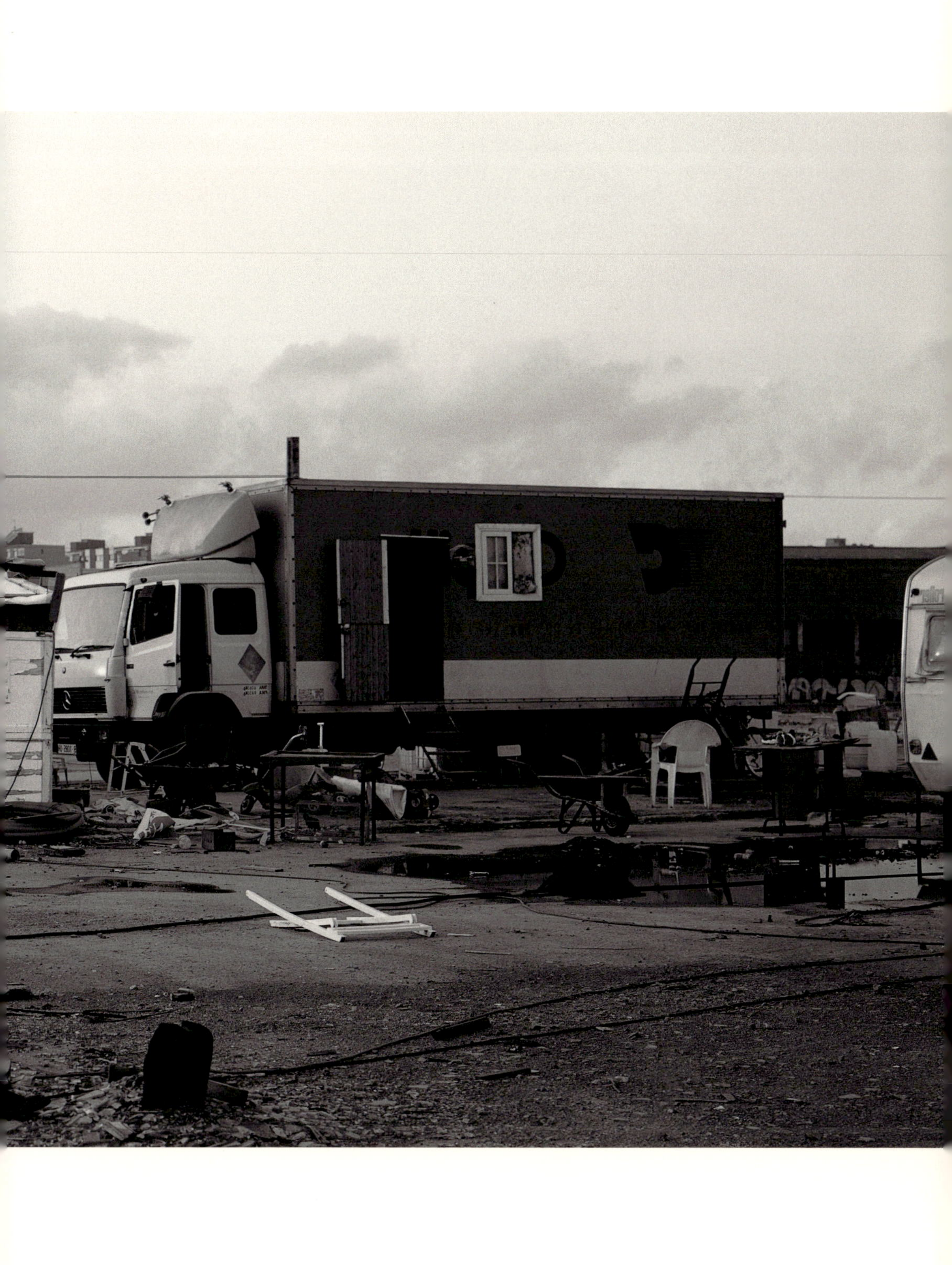

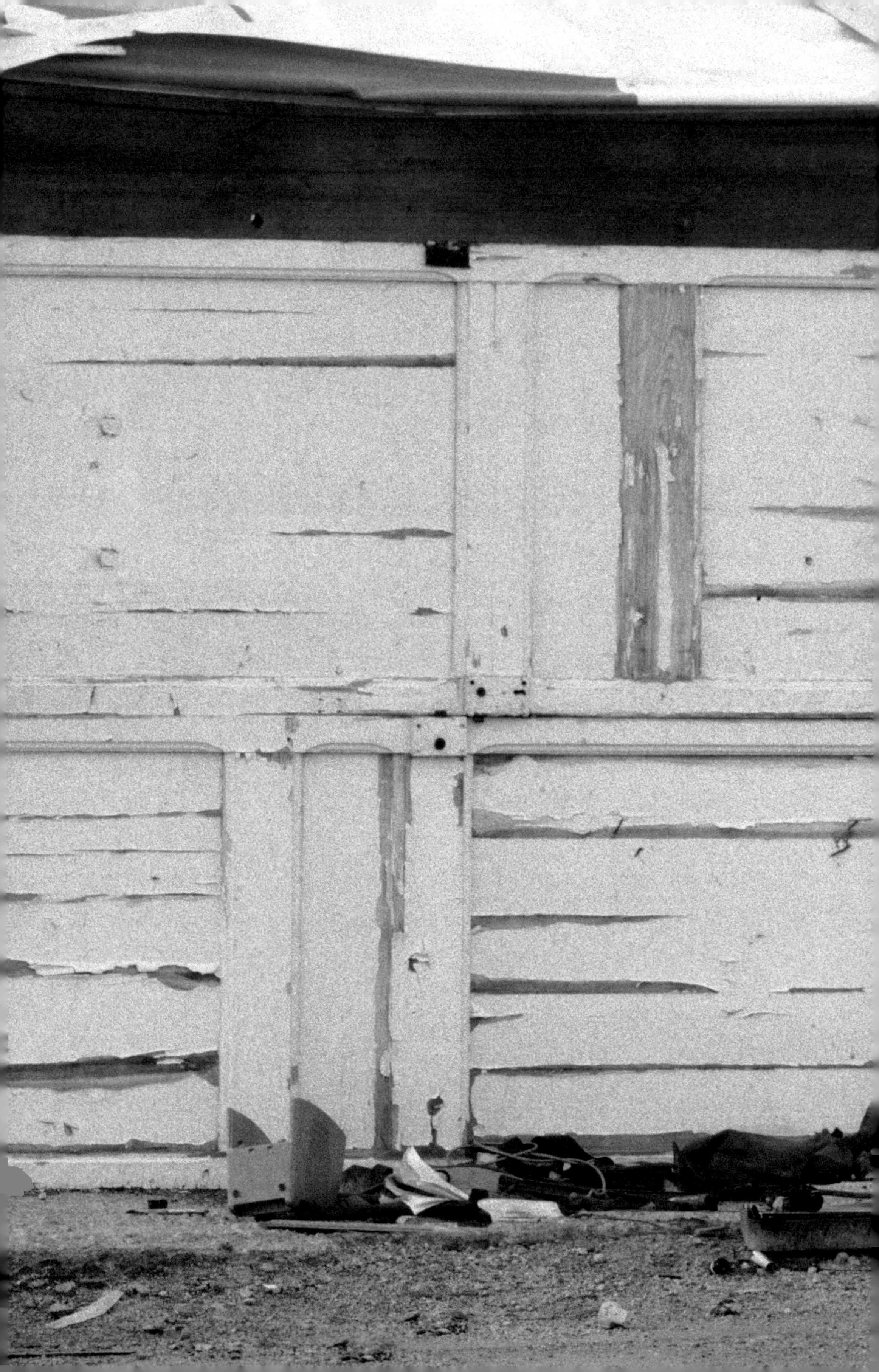

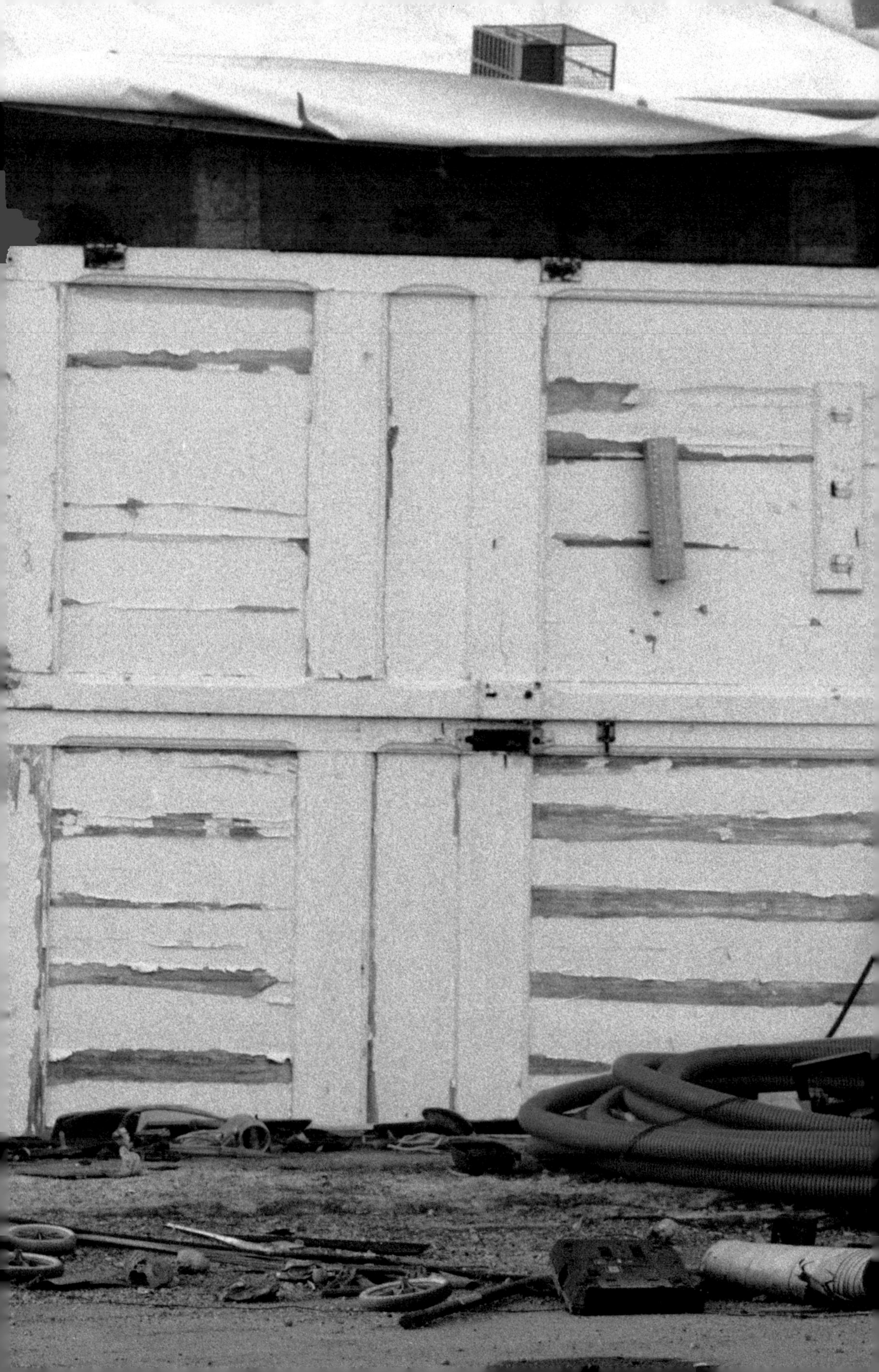

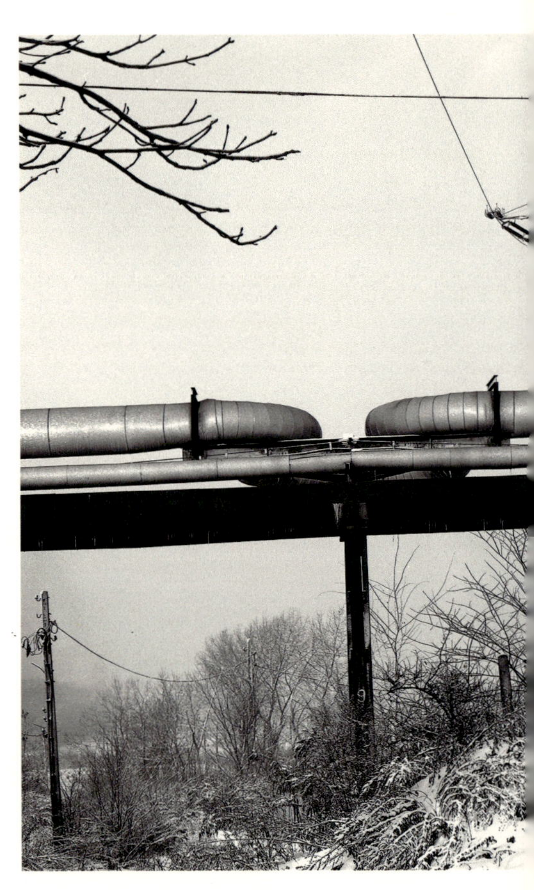

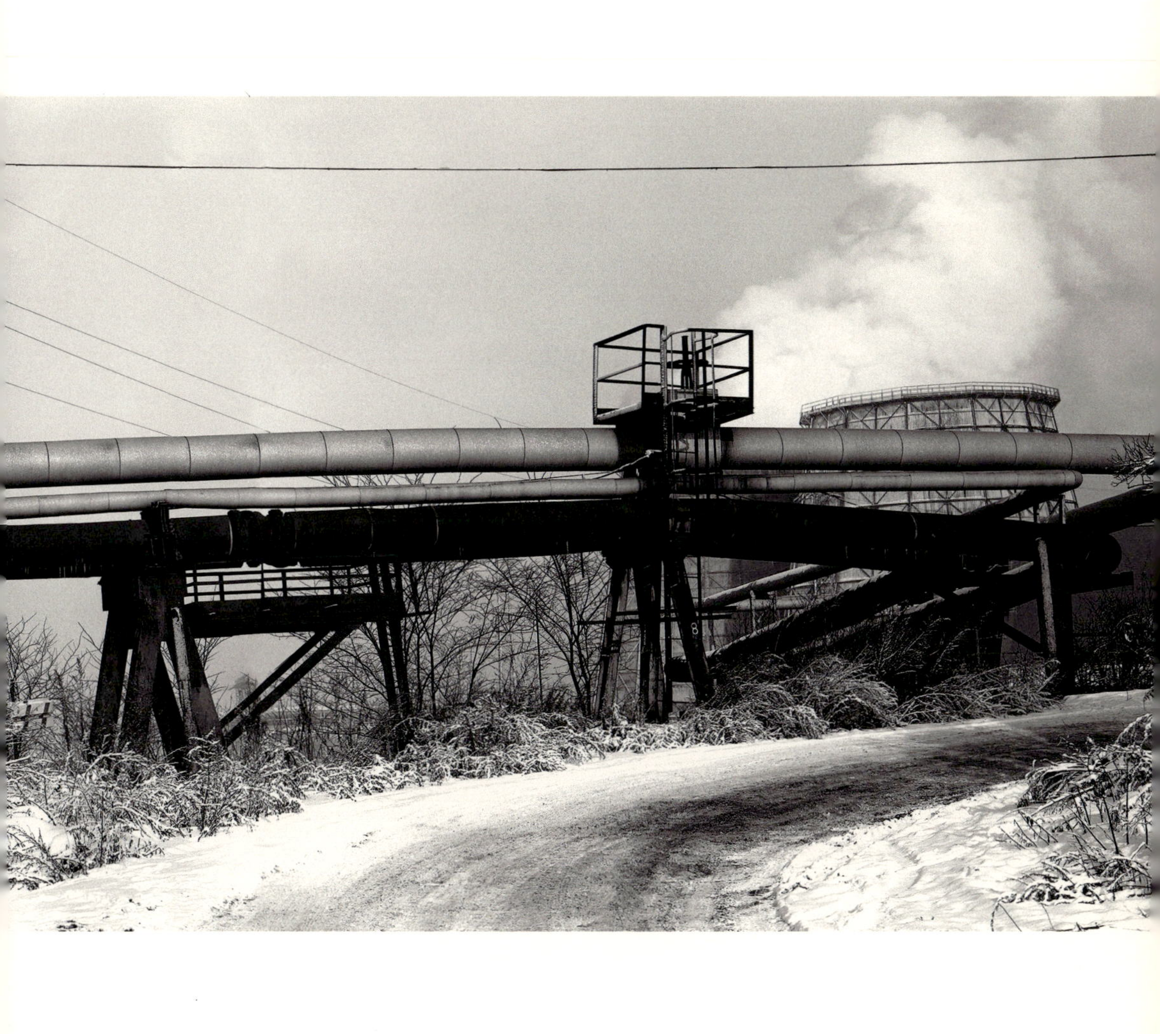

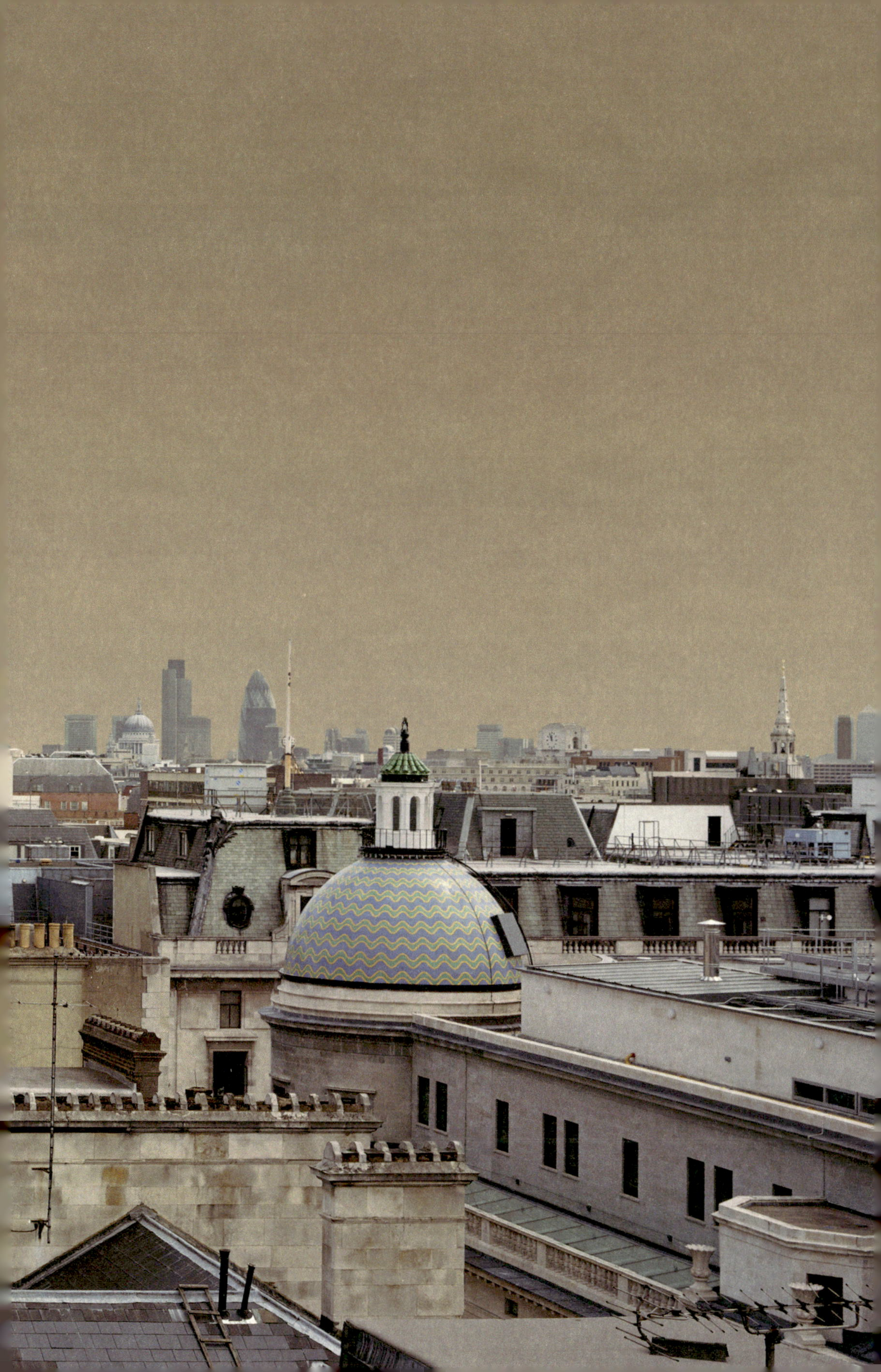

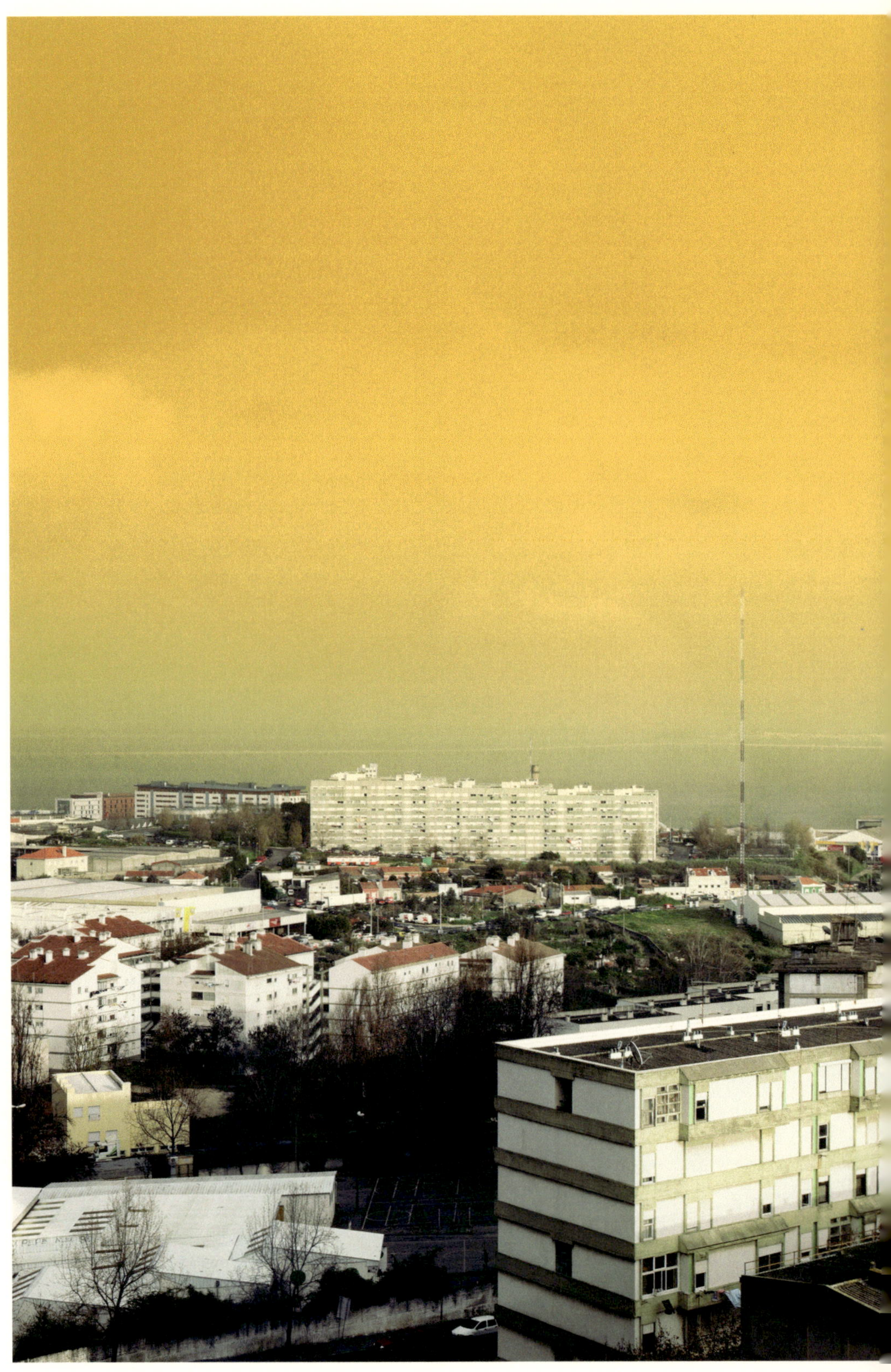

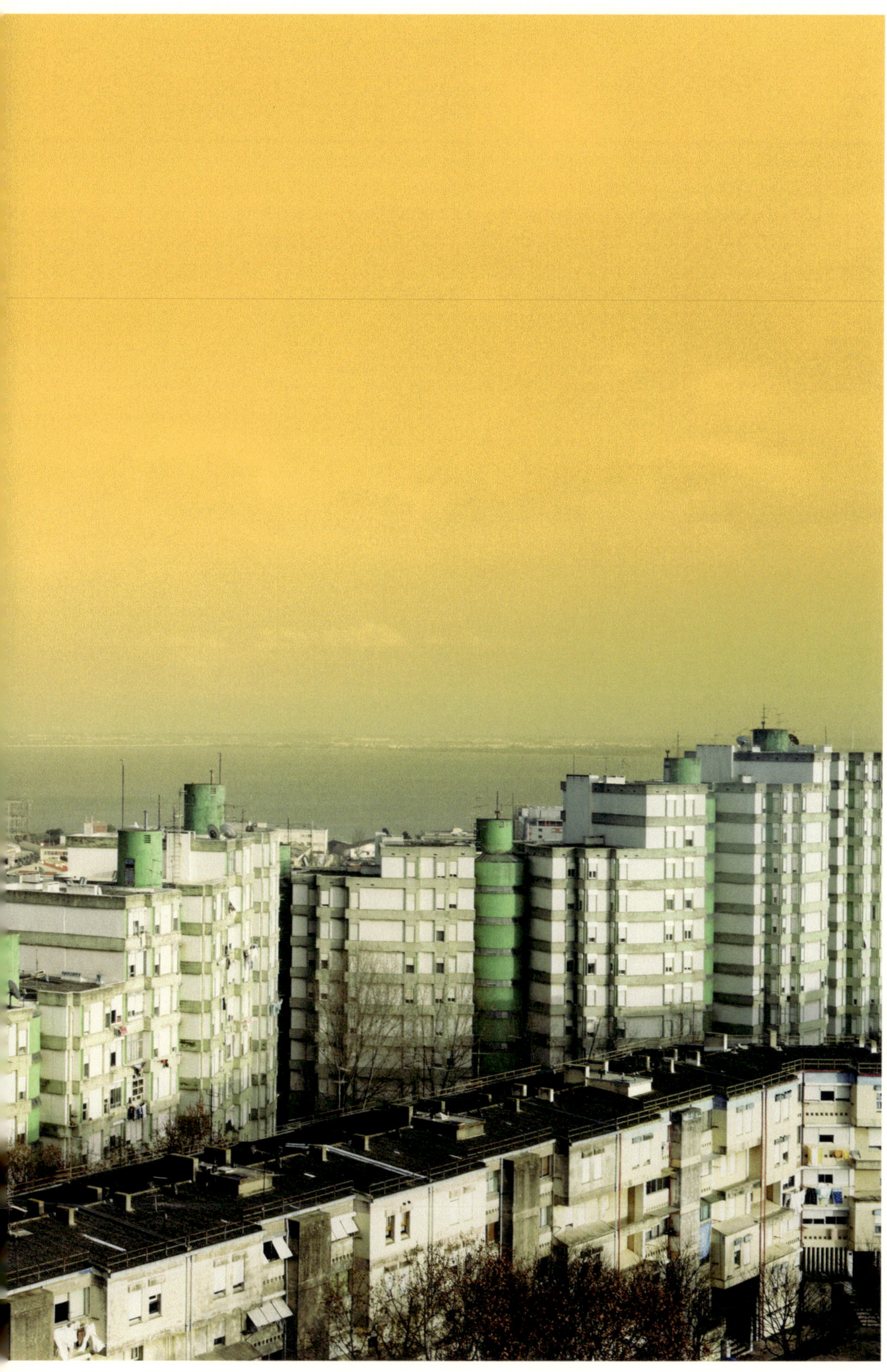

Ghosts

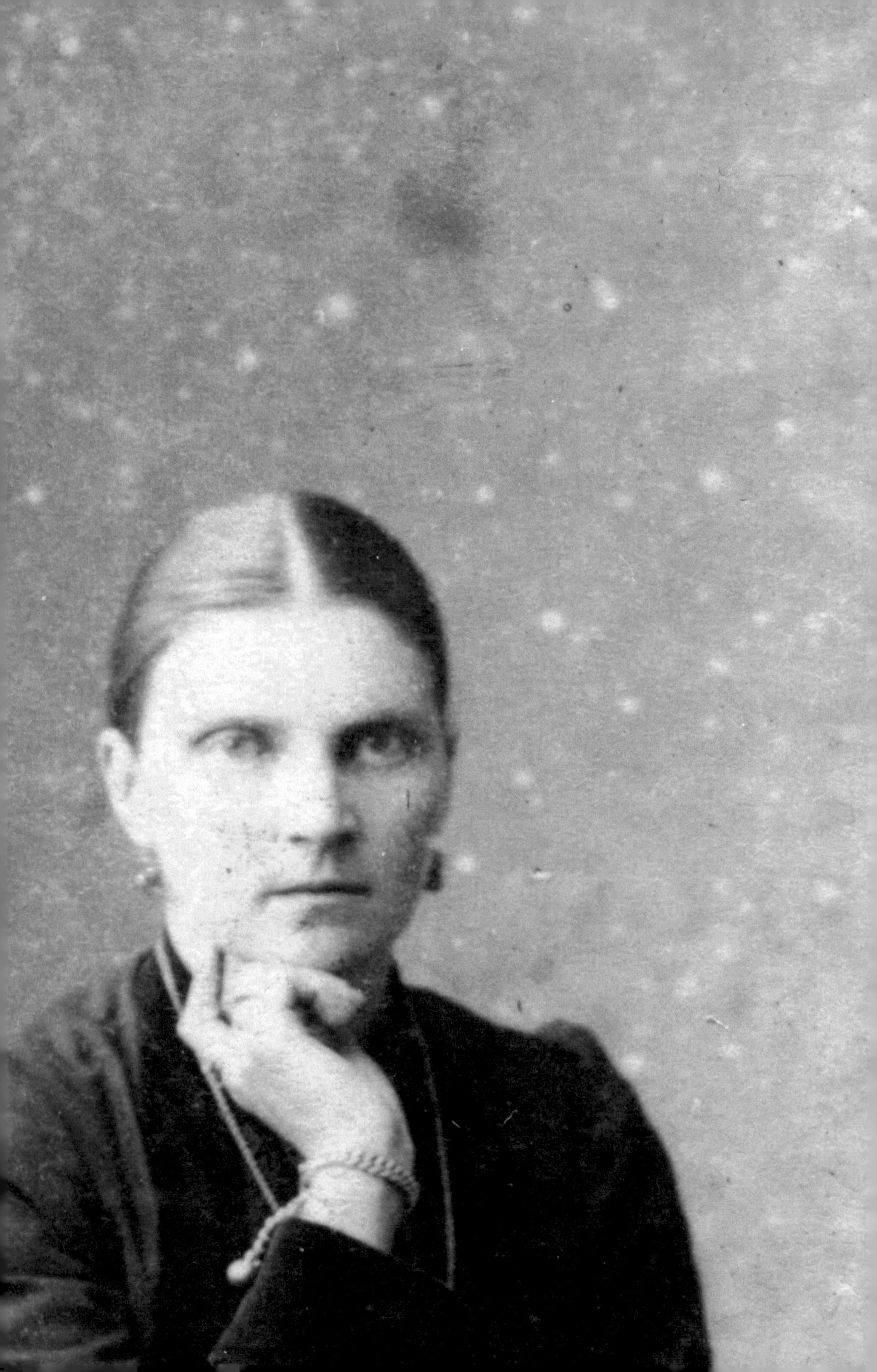

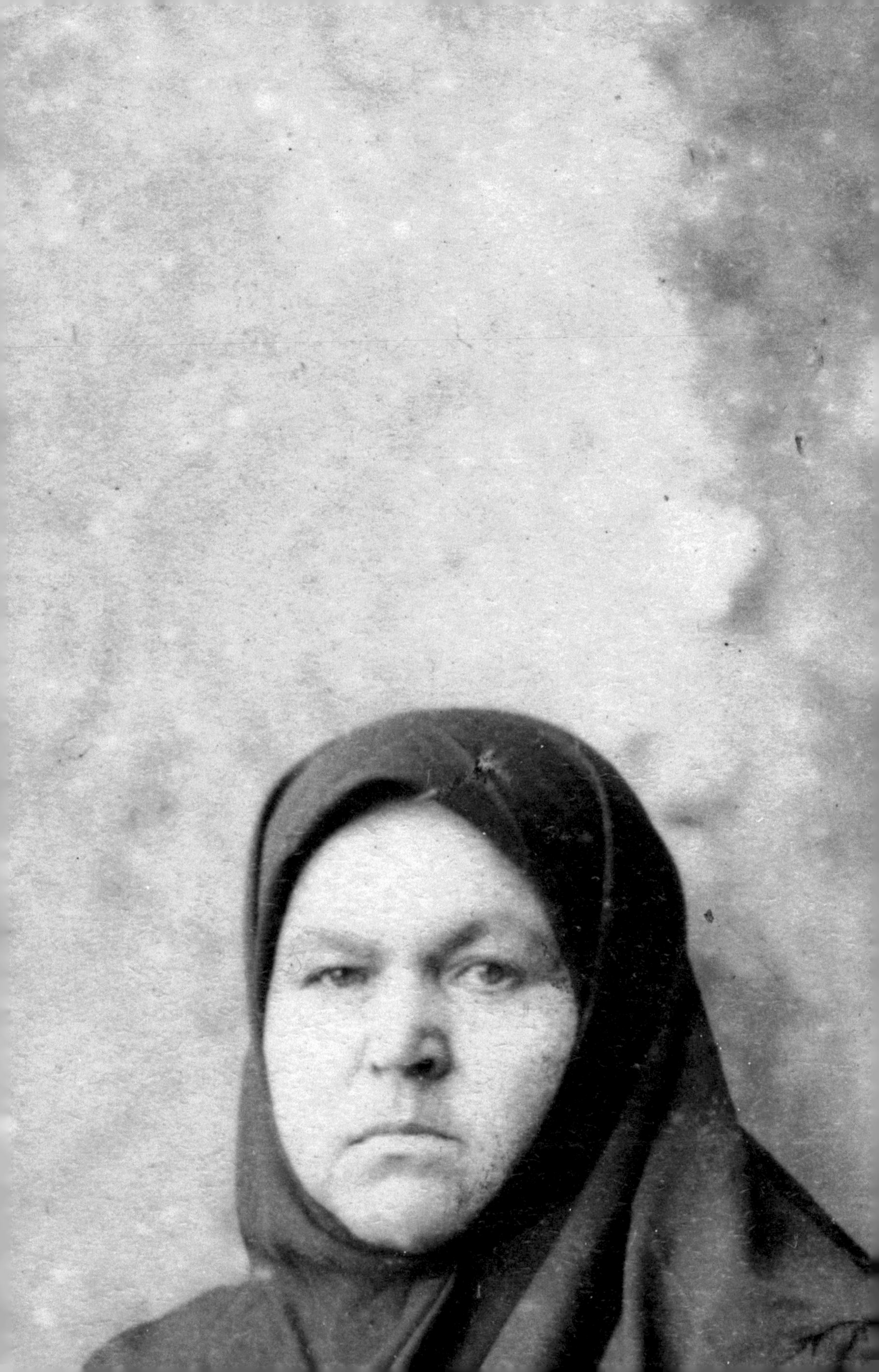

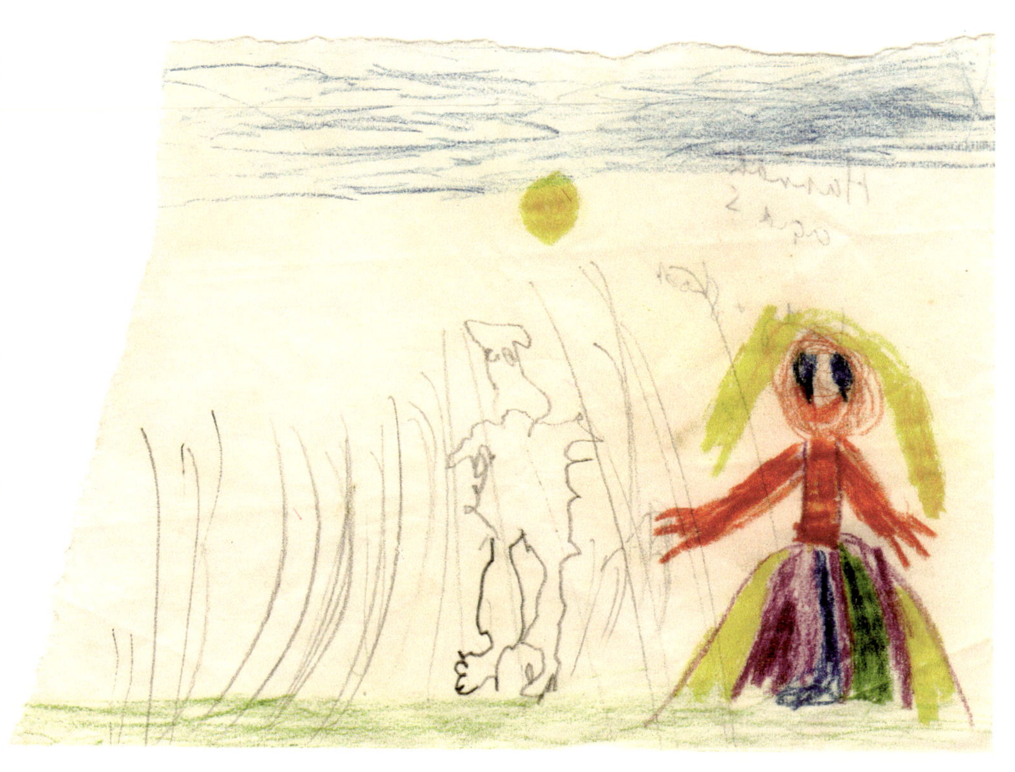

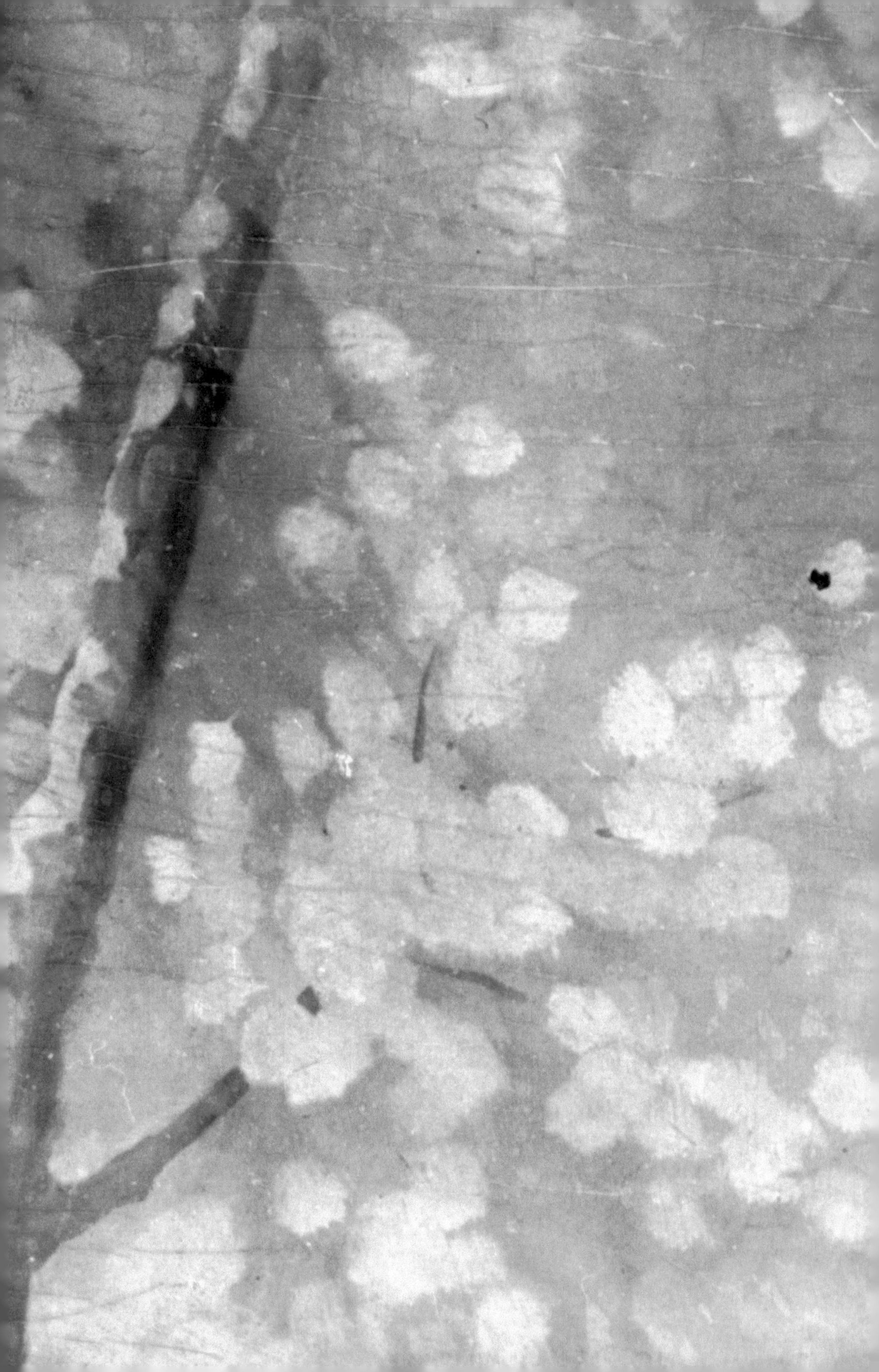

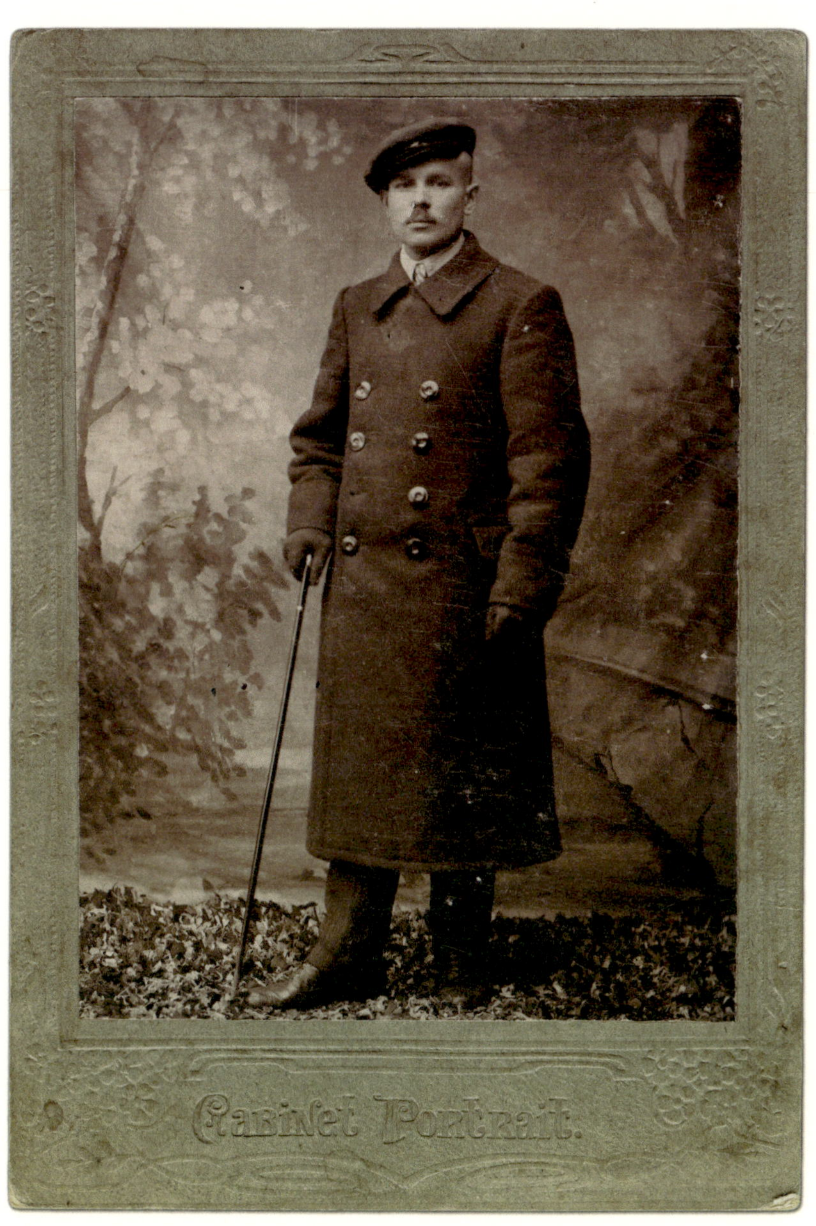

3.9

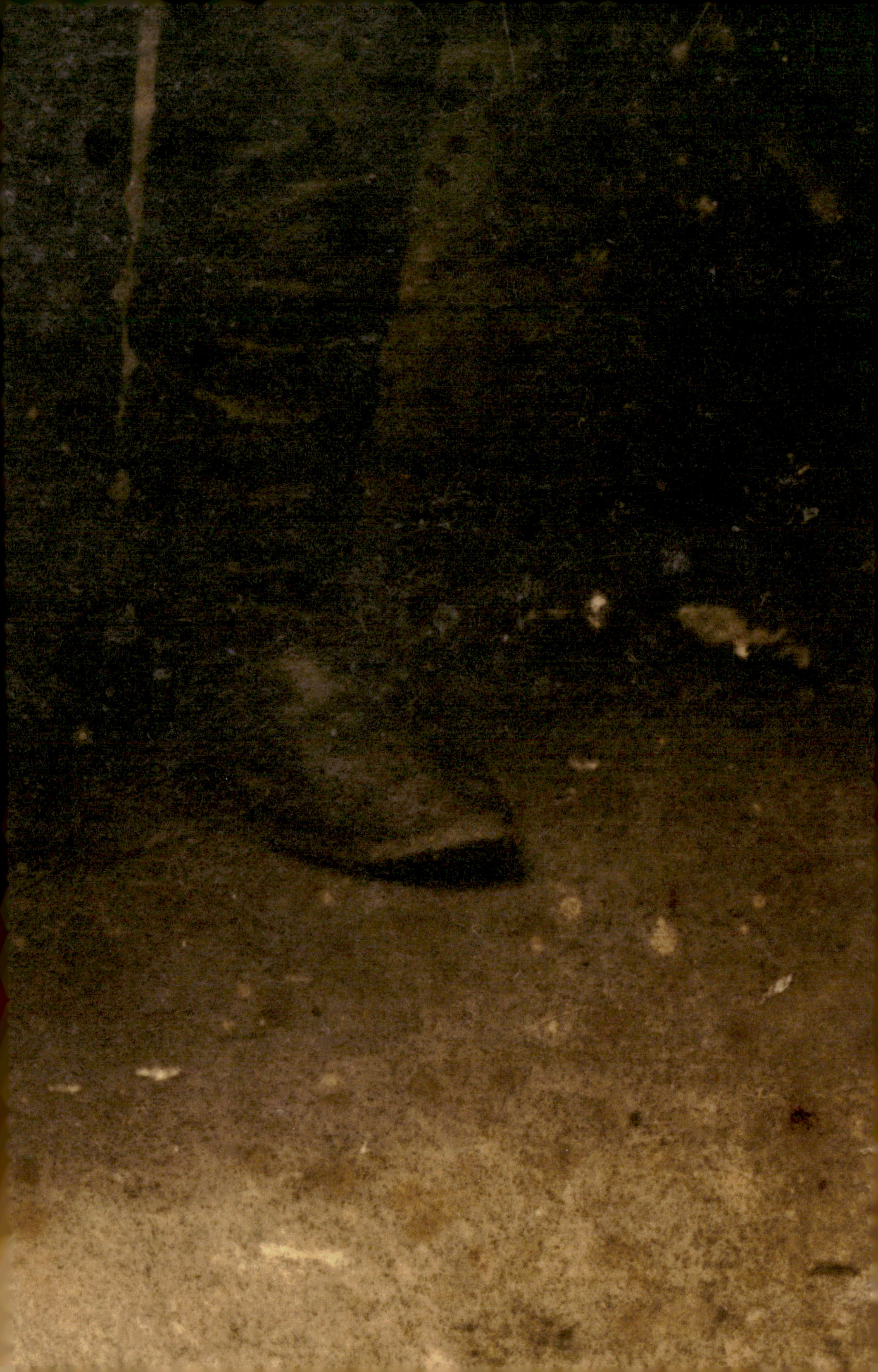

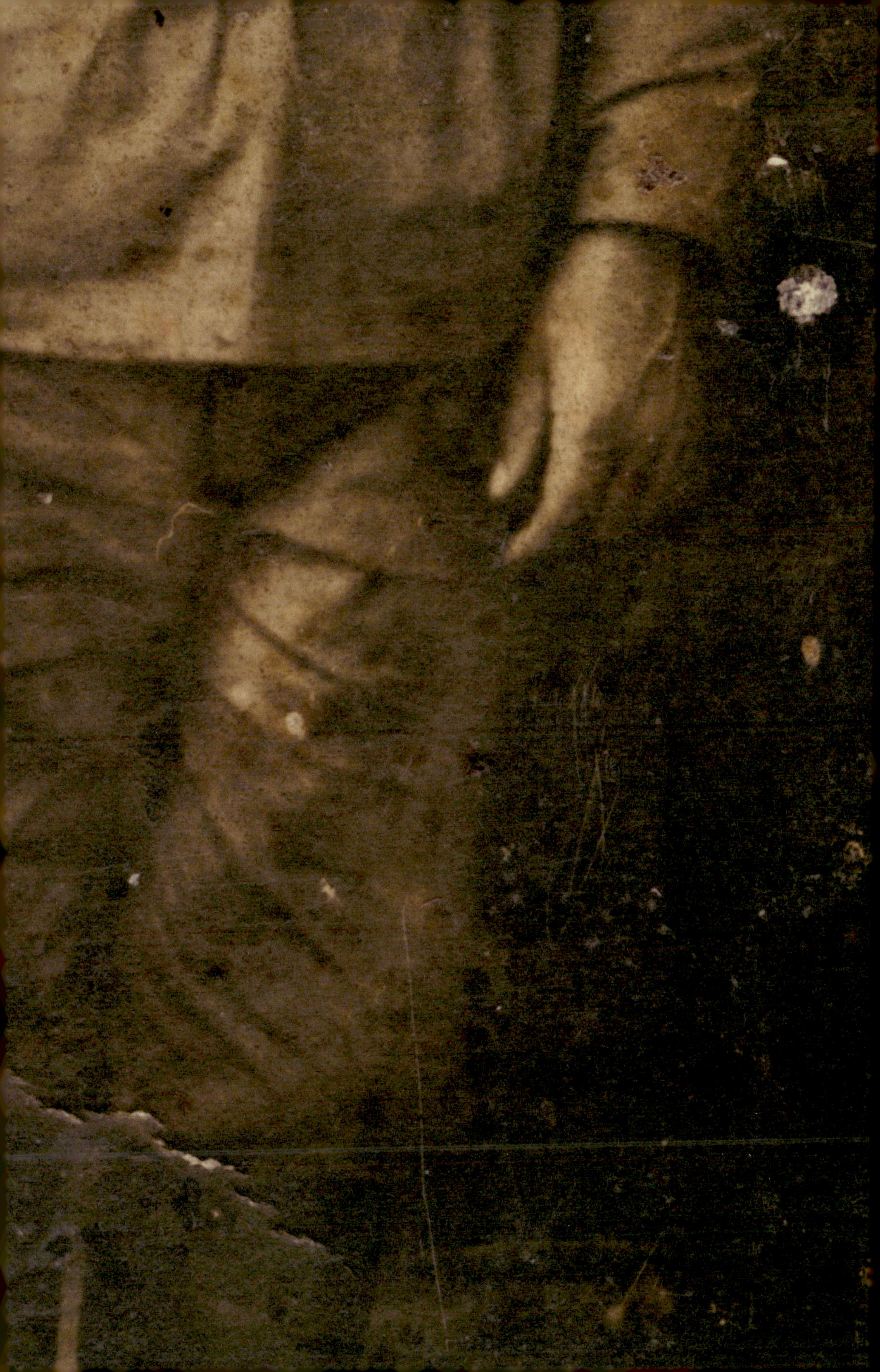

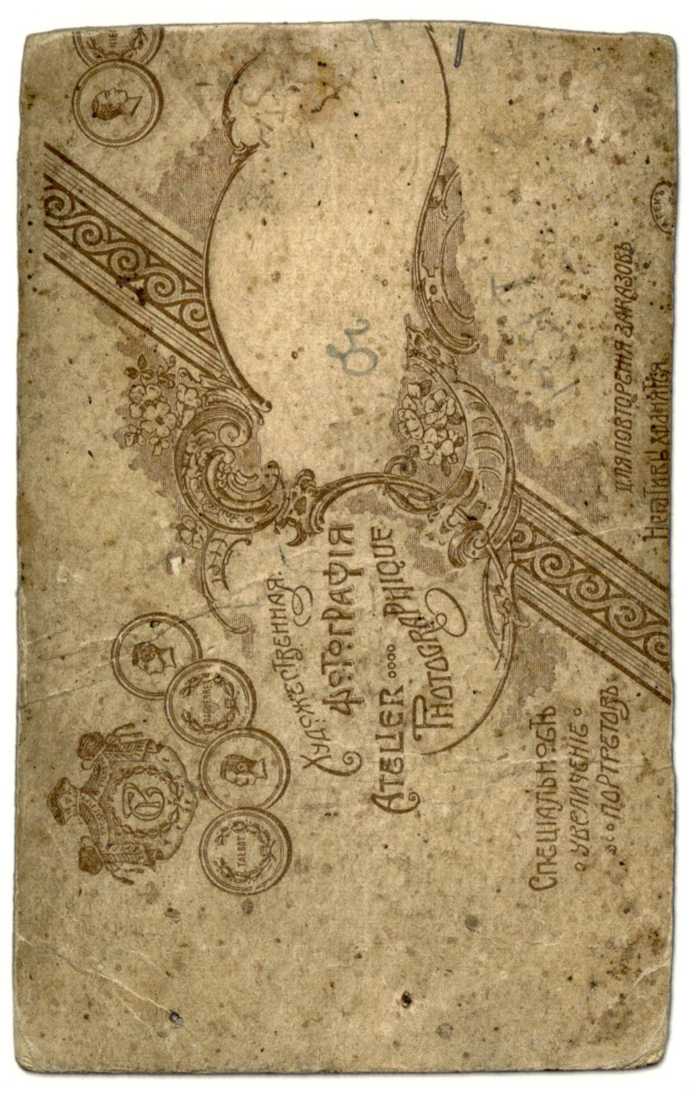

Художественная
Фотографія
Atelier oooo Photographique
Специальность
увеличеніе
Портретовъ
Для повторенія заказовъ
Негативы хранятся

3.12

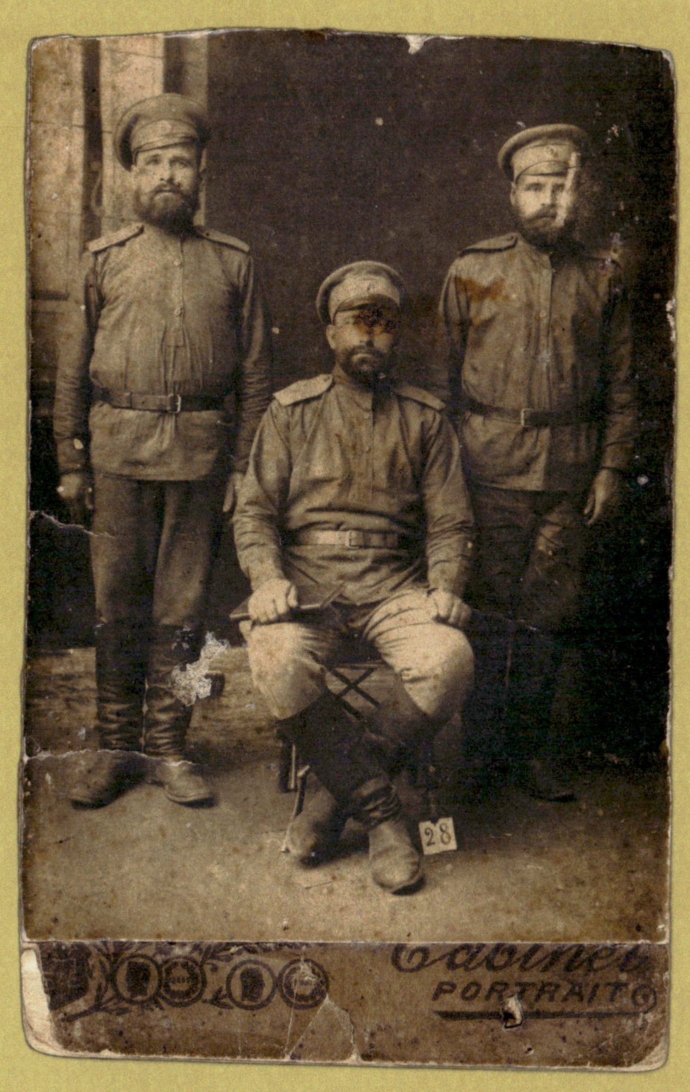
28
Cabinet
PORTRAIT

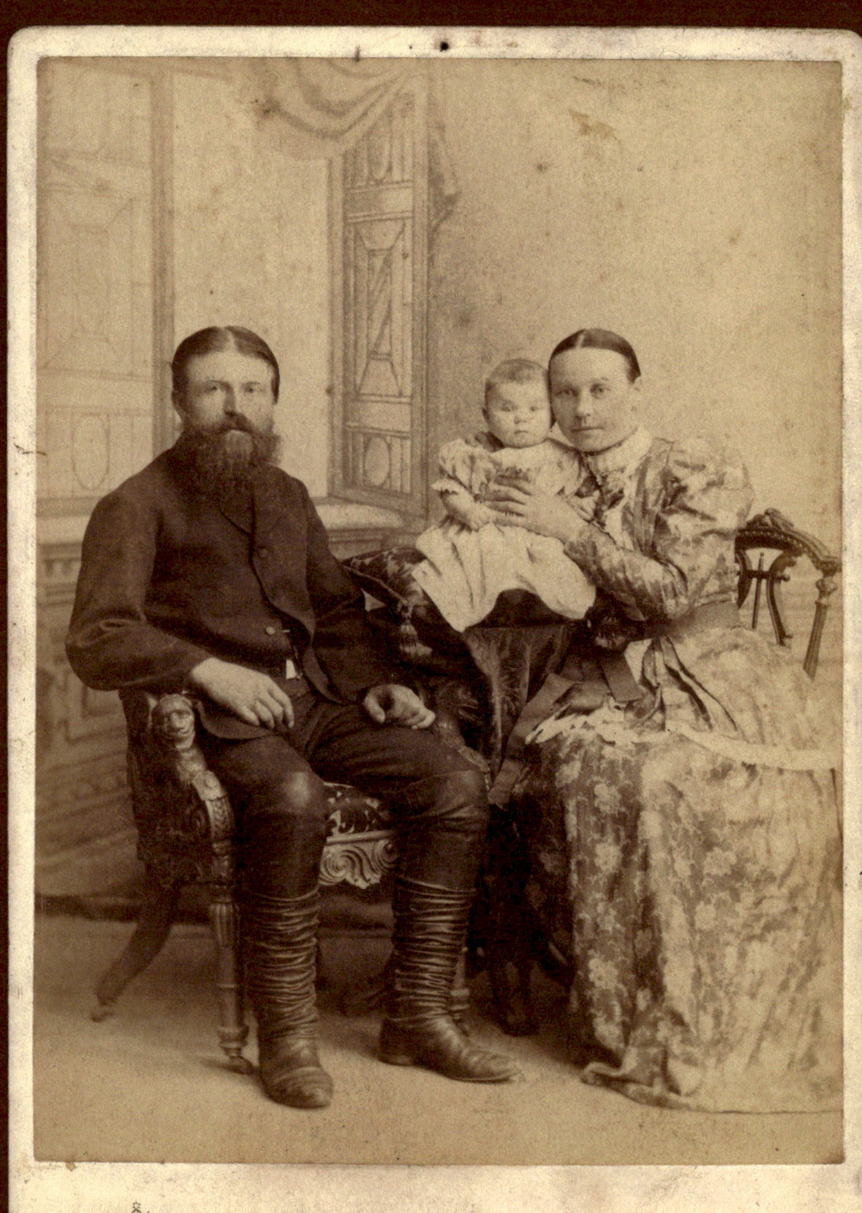
И. Львовъ
въ МОСКВѢ.

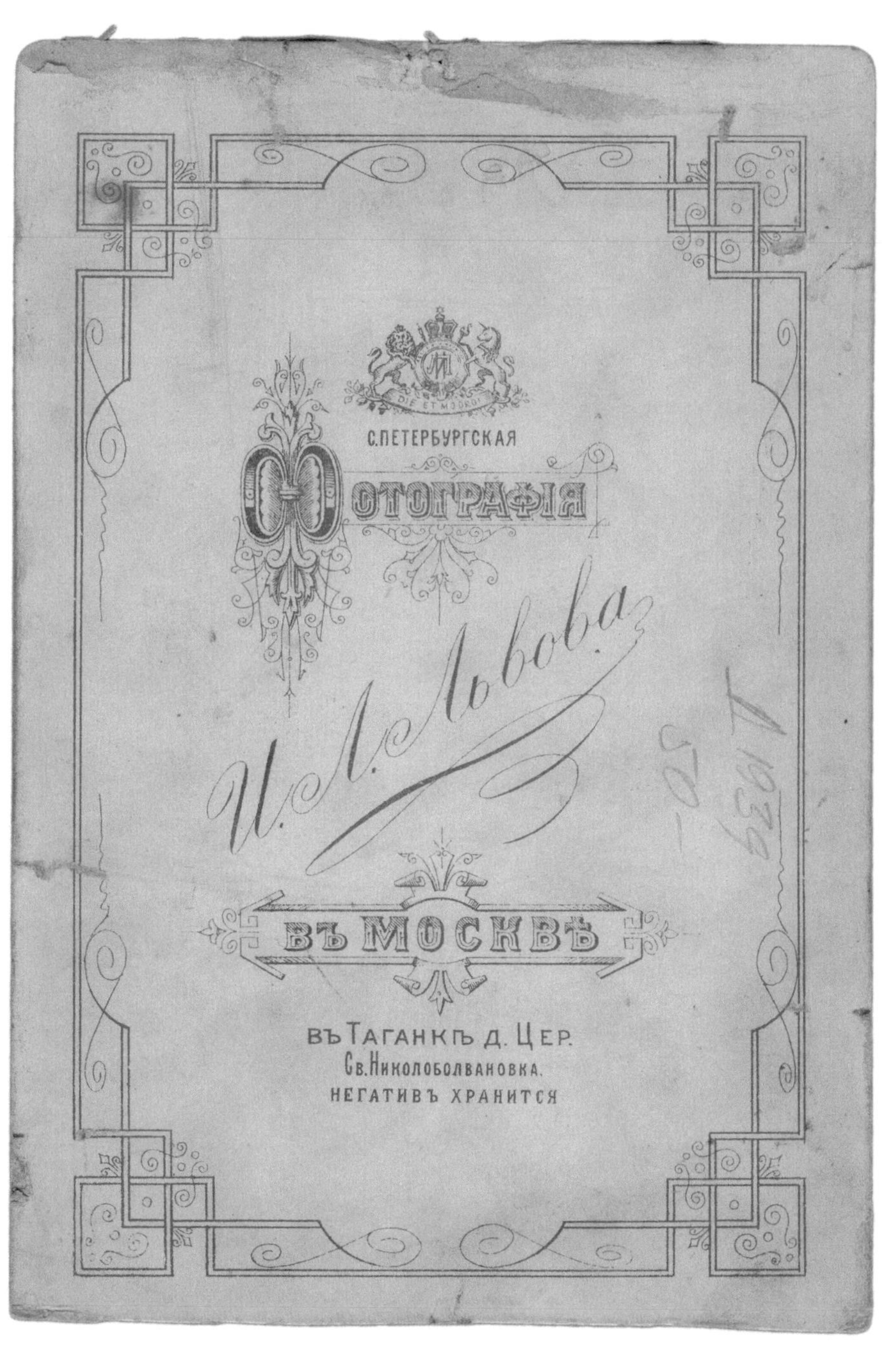

С.ПЕТЕРБУРГСКАЯ
ФОТОГРАФІЯ
DIE ET MODO
И.Л.Львова
ВЪ МОСКВѢ
ВЪ ТАГАНКѢ Д. ЦЕР.
Св. Николоболвановка.
НЕГАТИВЪ ХРАНИТСЯ

K 7 249/2

20 ->

K 7249/9

15

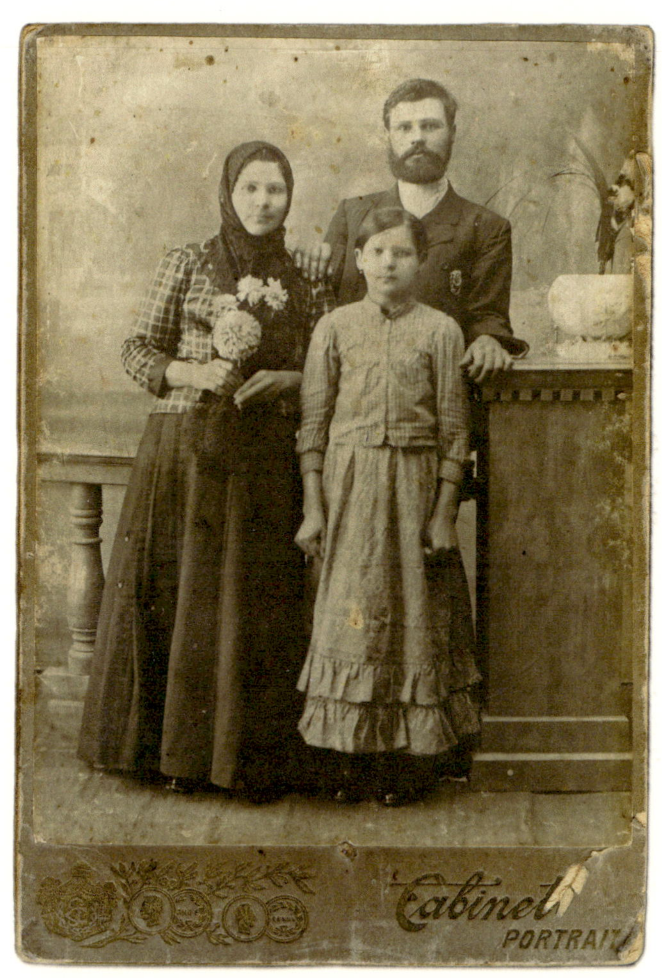

3.17

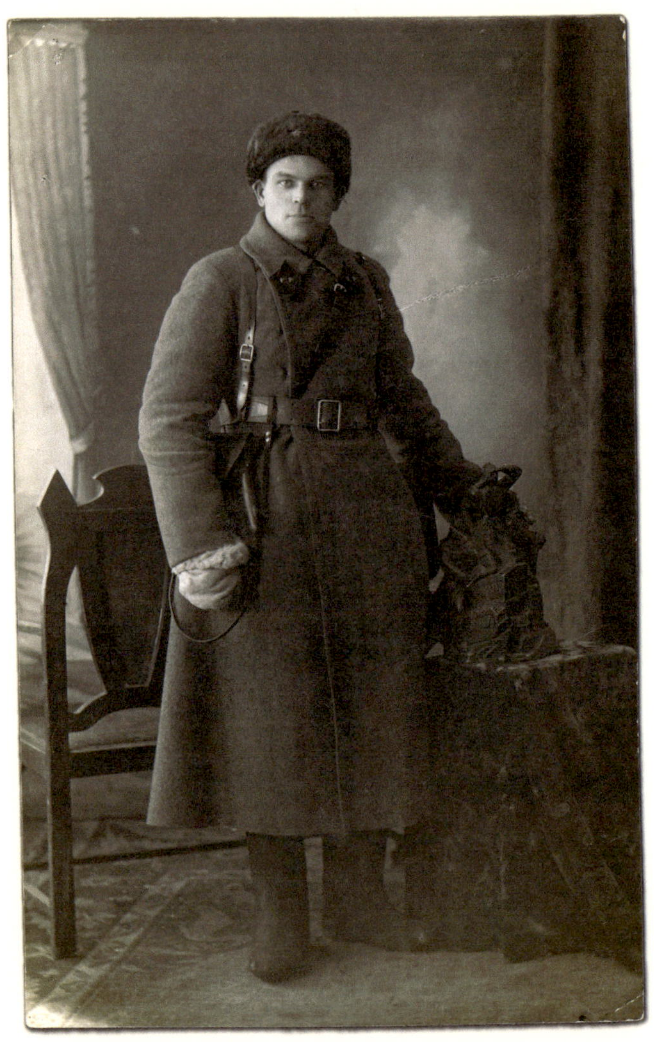

3.18

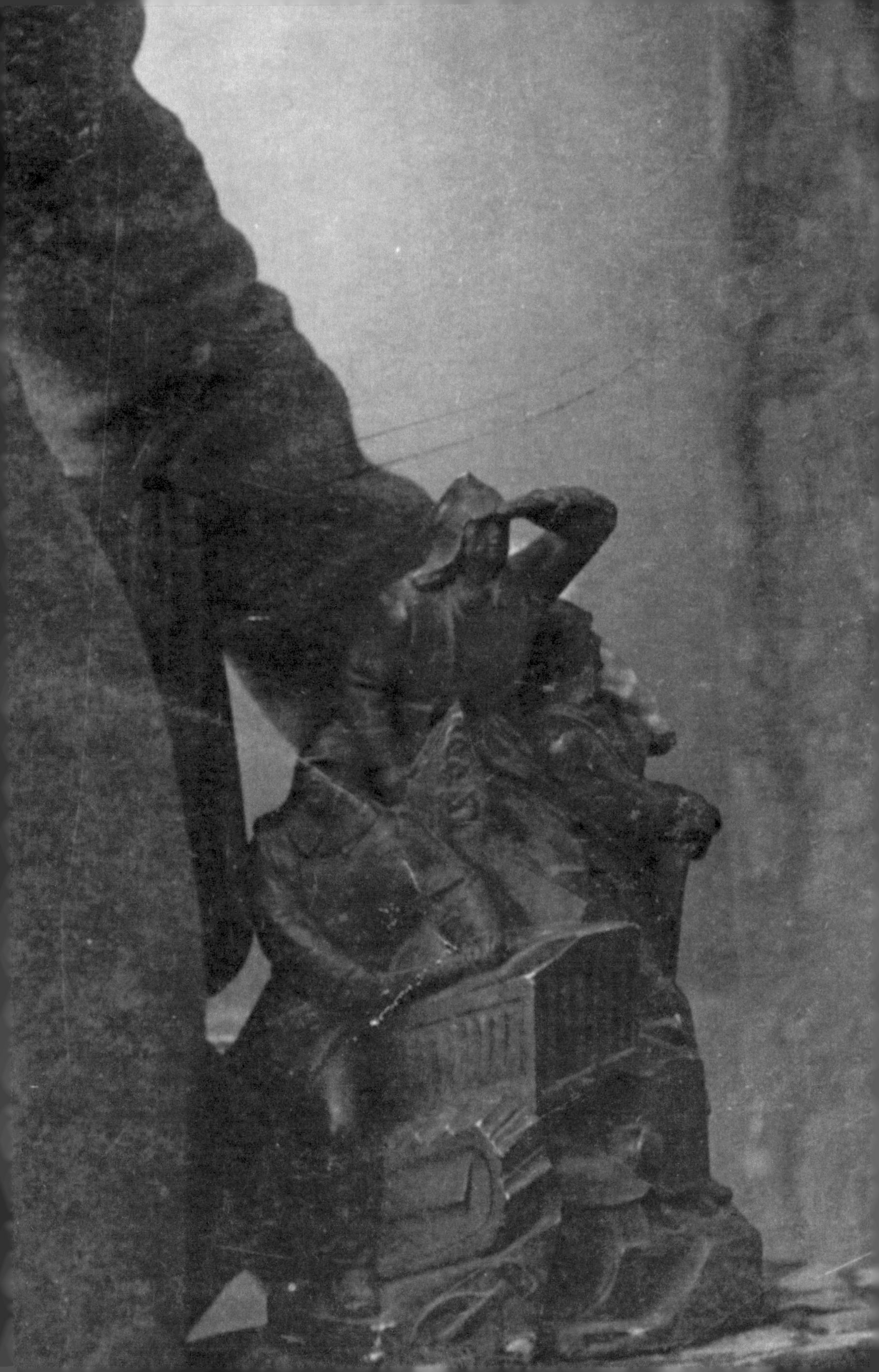

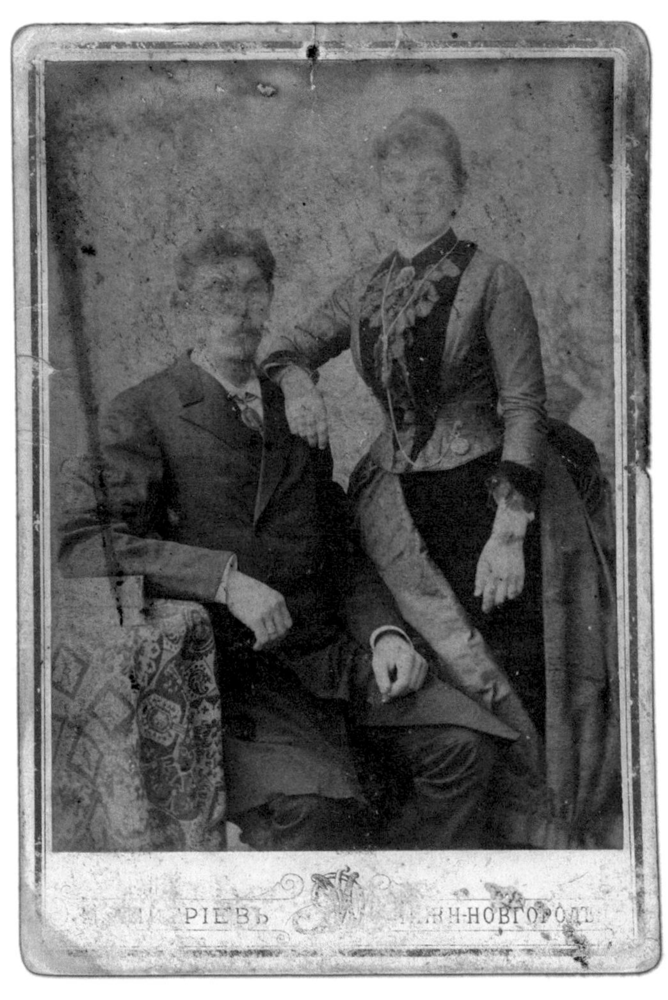

3.22

M. Dmitrieff
N. NOWGOROD.
ЗА ФОТОГРАФІЮ СЪ НАТУРЫ
ВТОРАЯ НАГРАДА

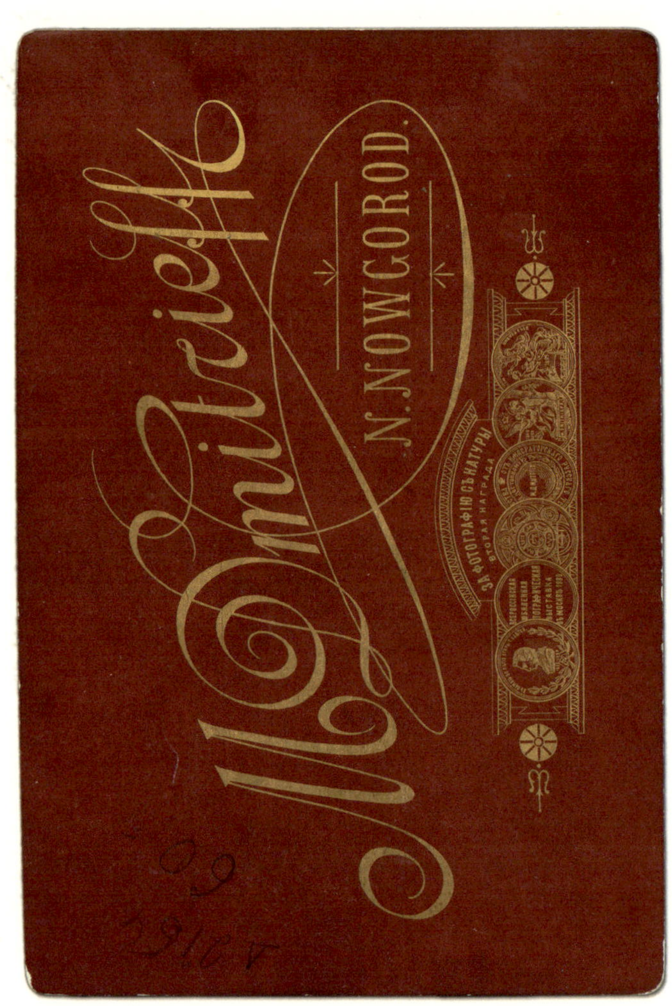

3.24

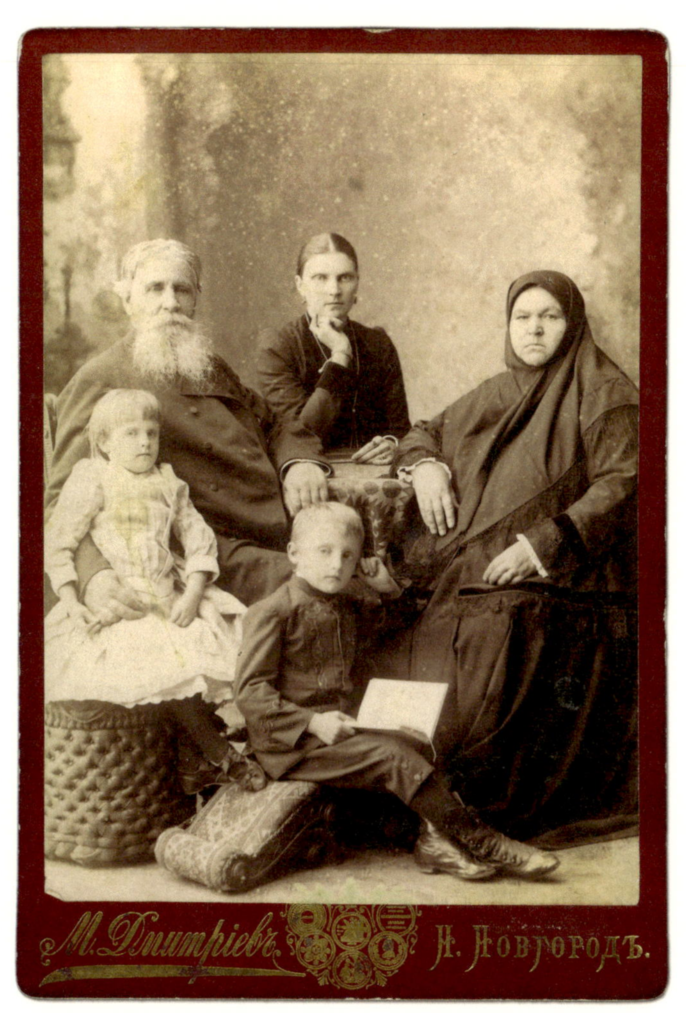

3.25

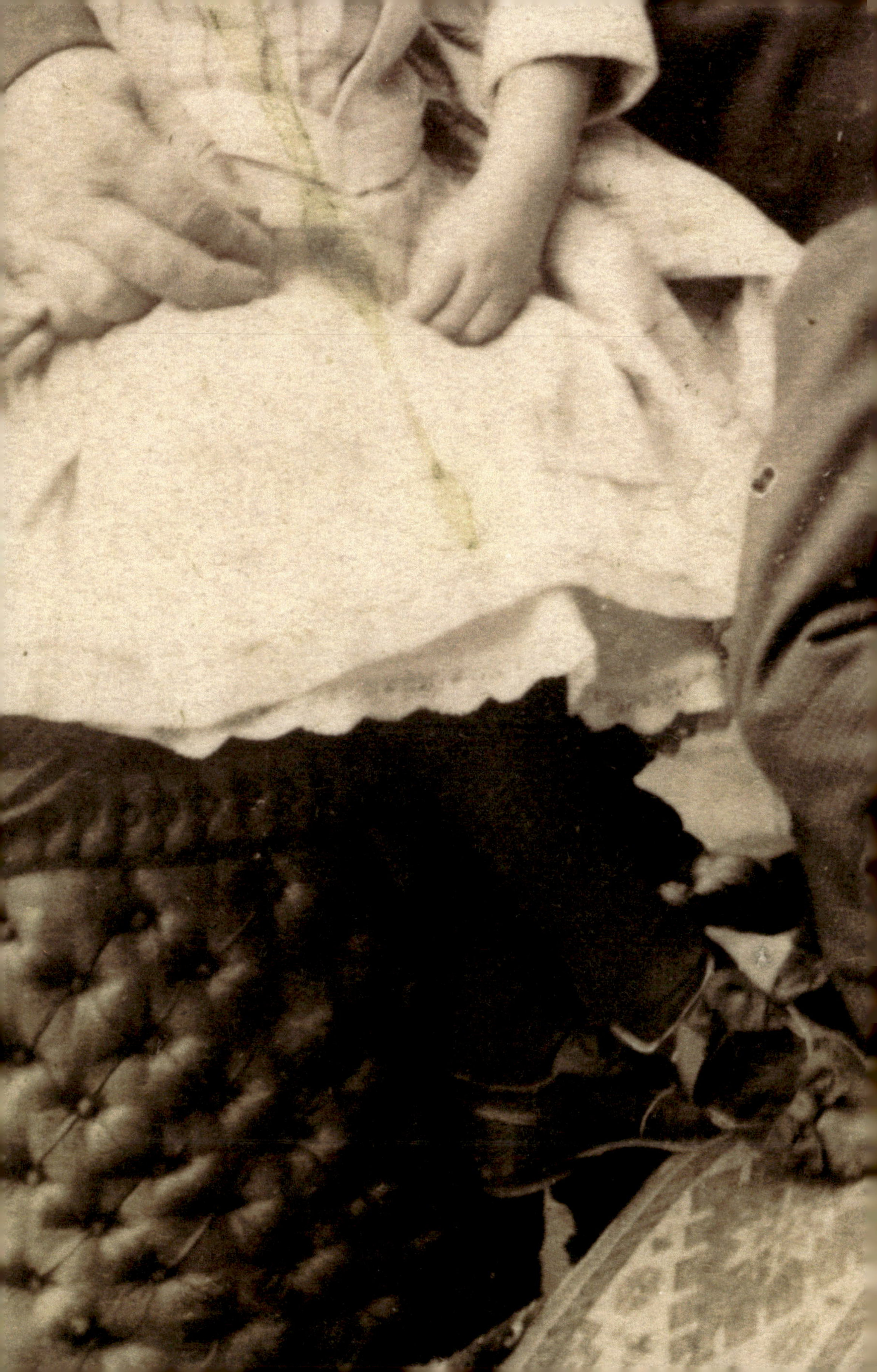

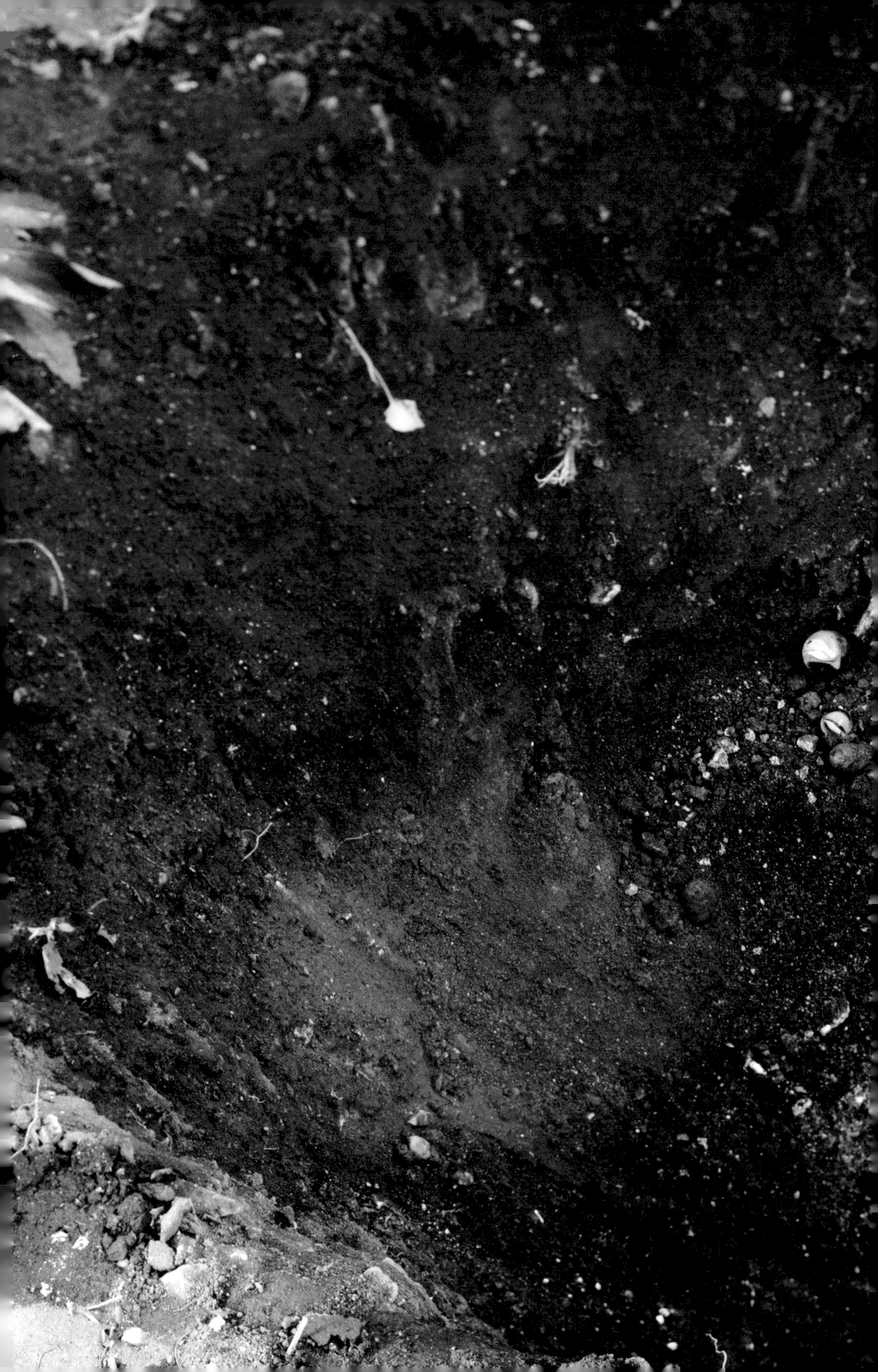

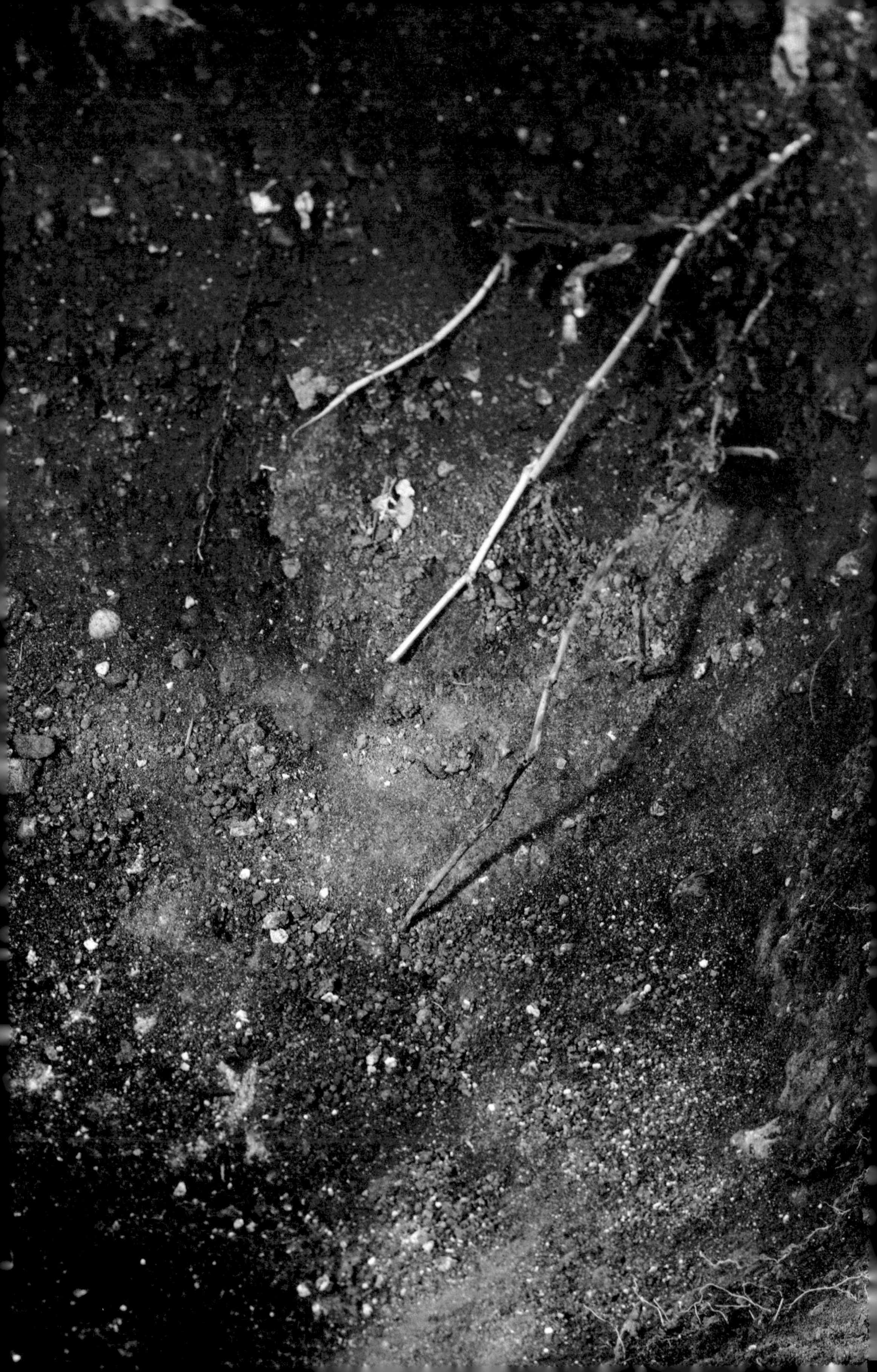

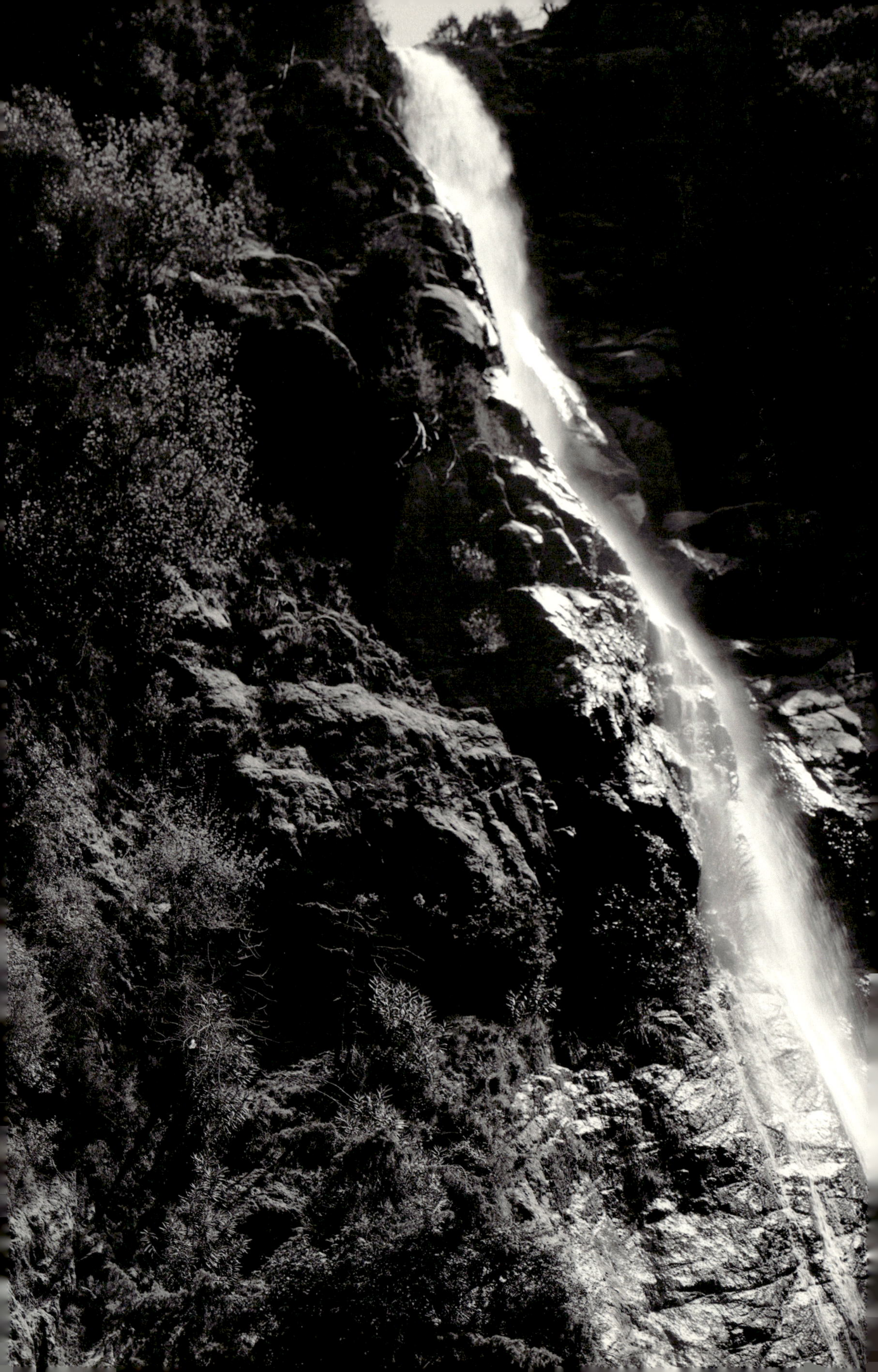

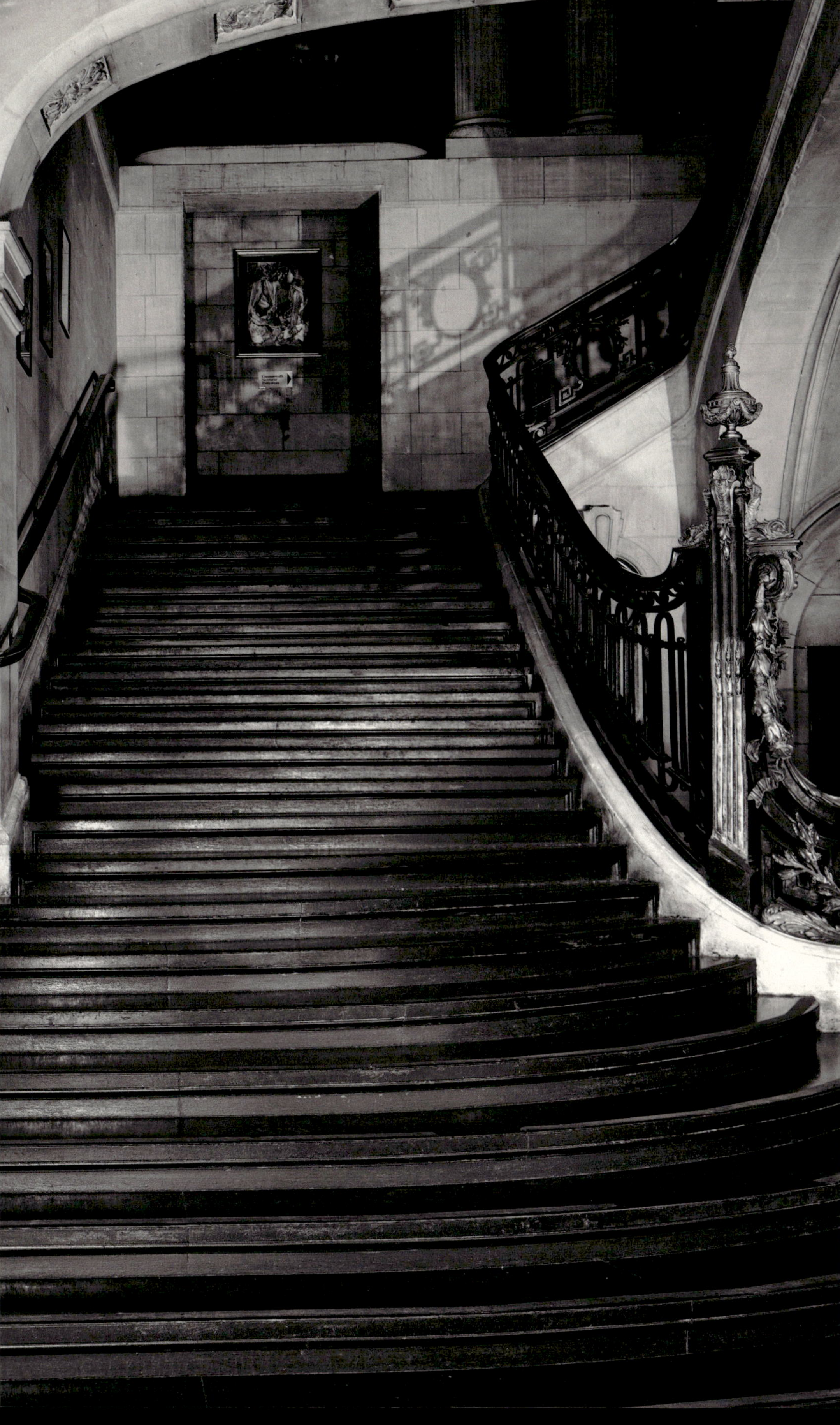

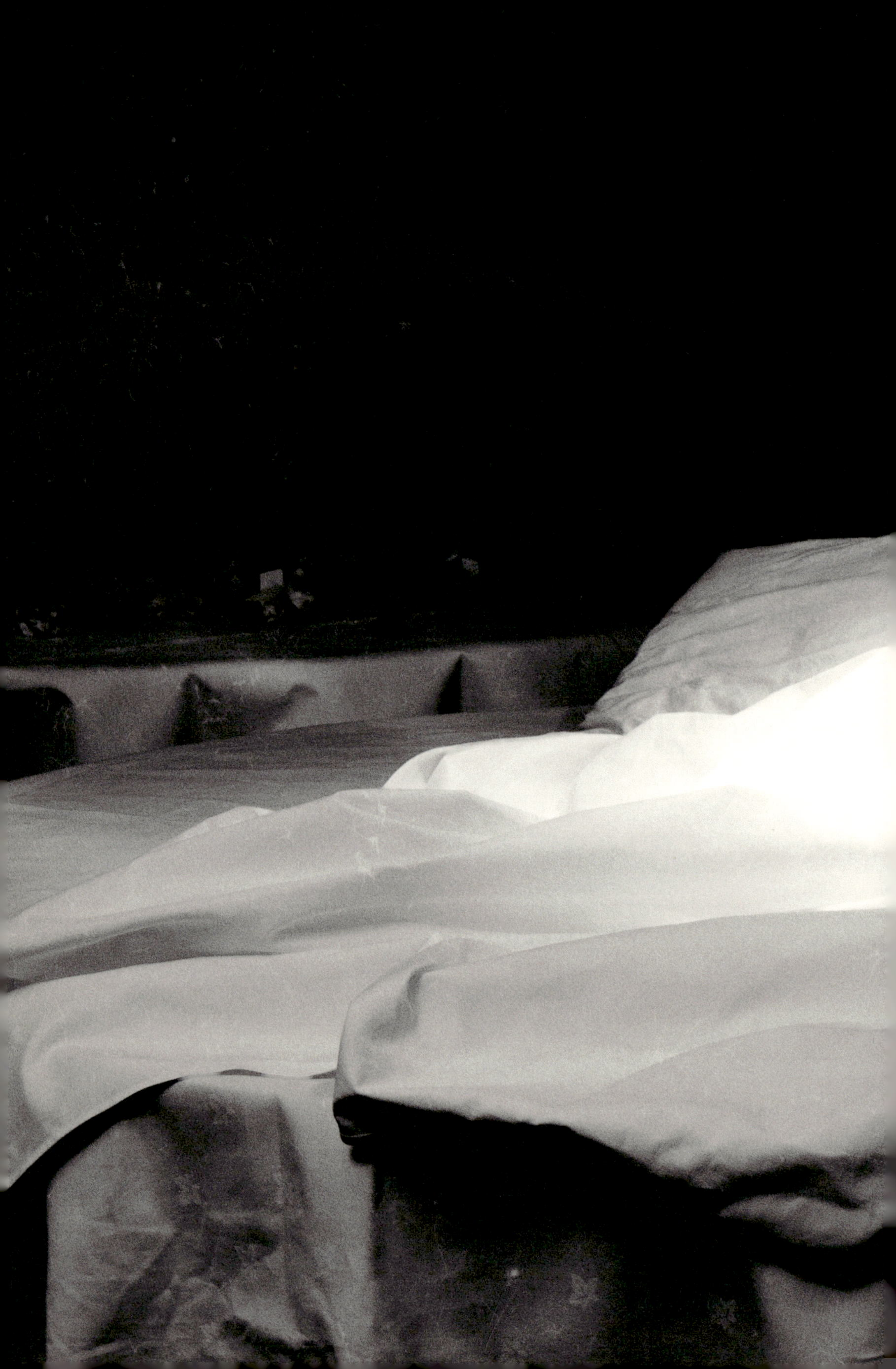

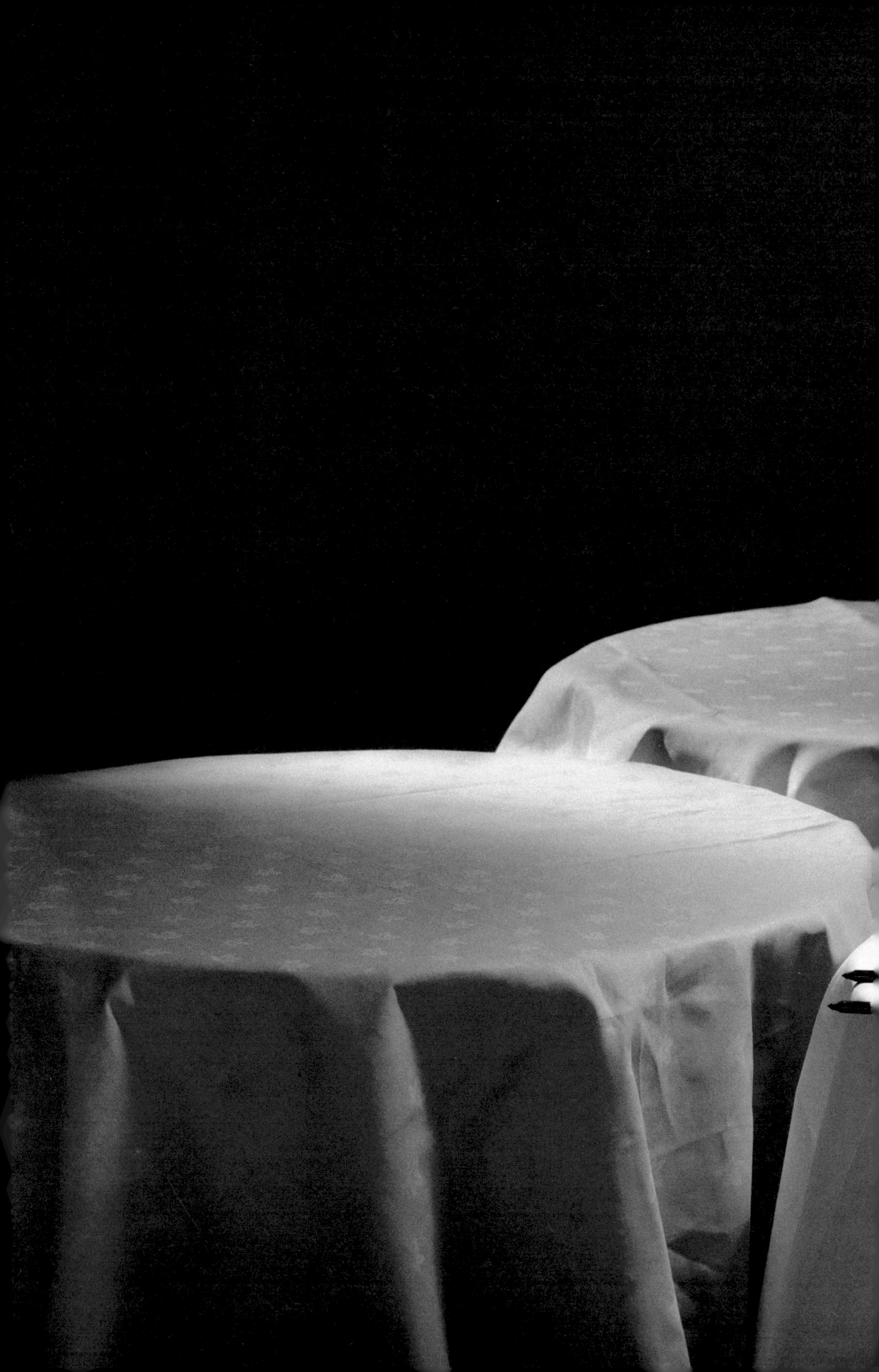

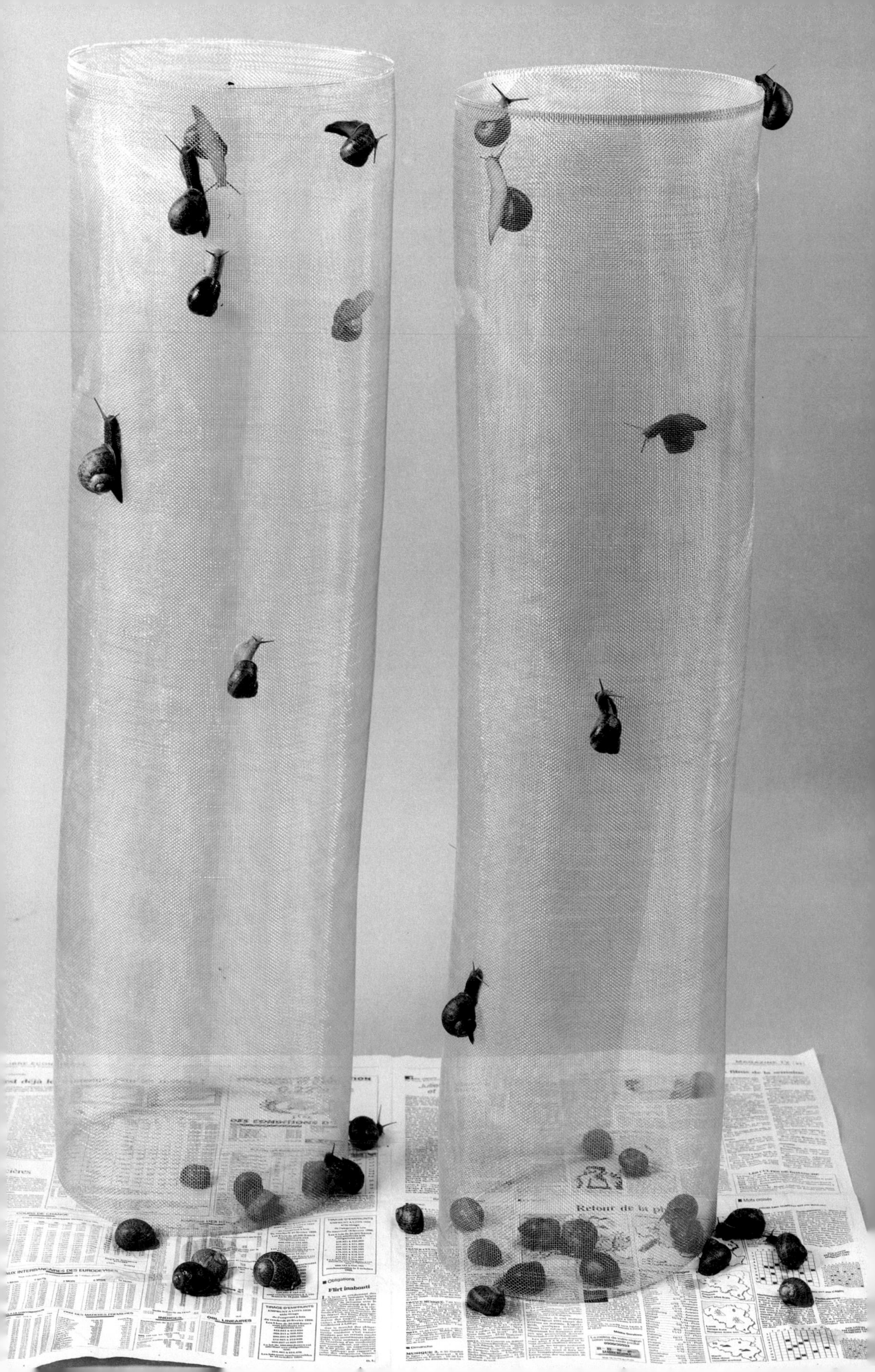

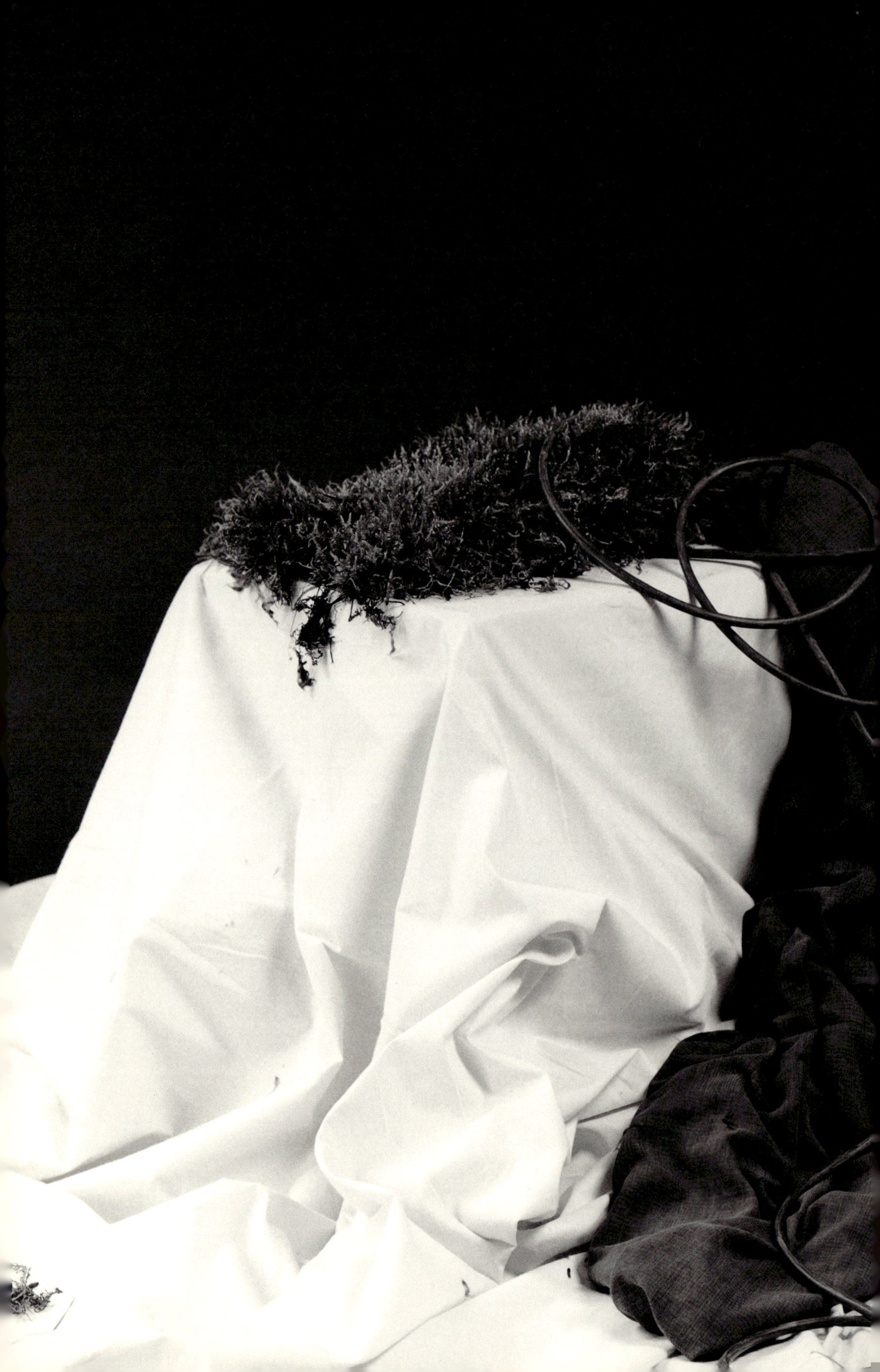

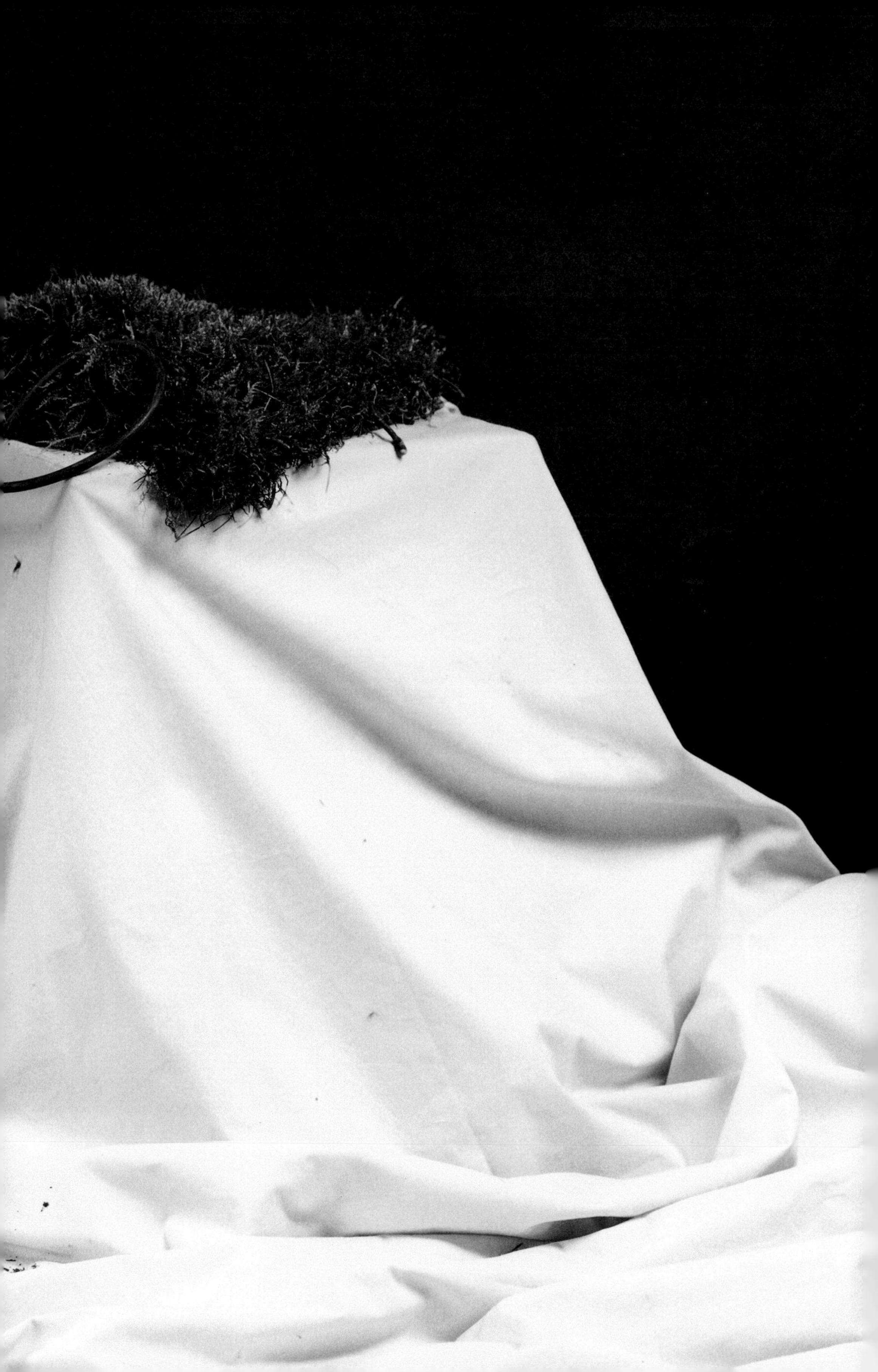

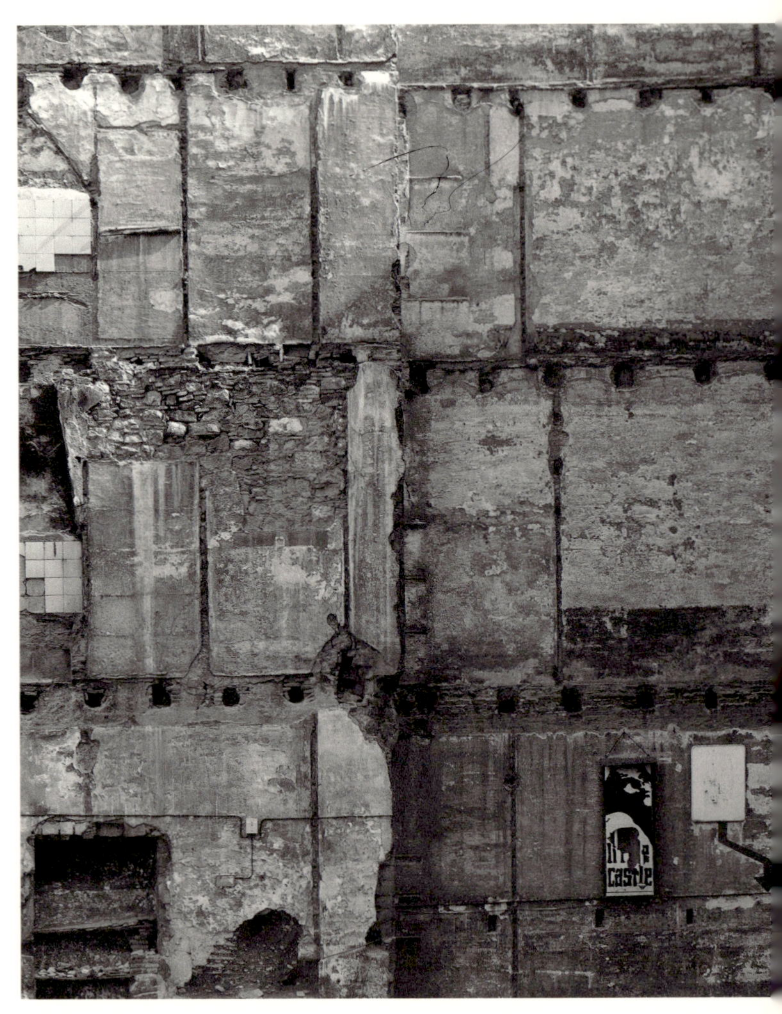

3.40

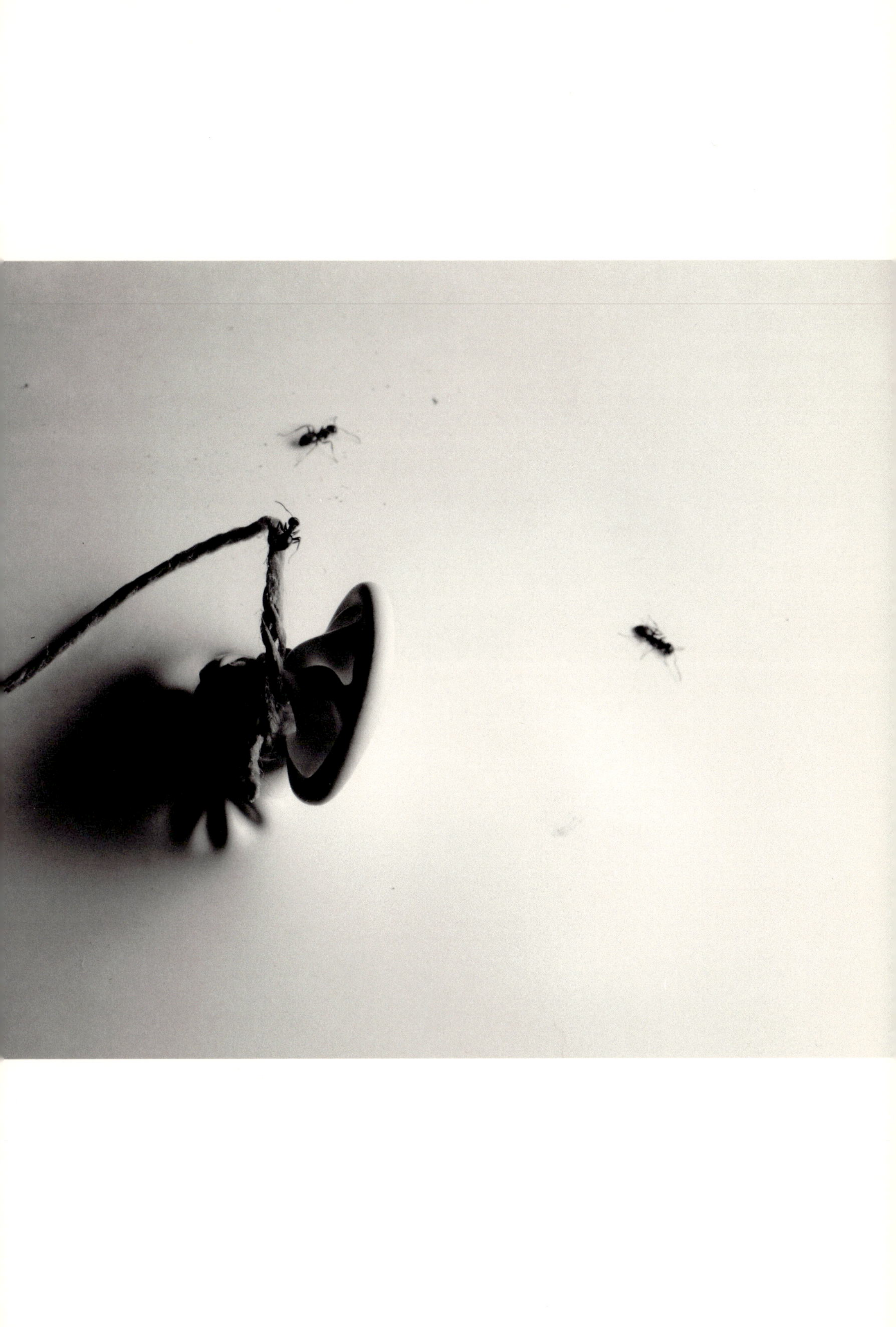

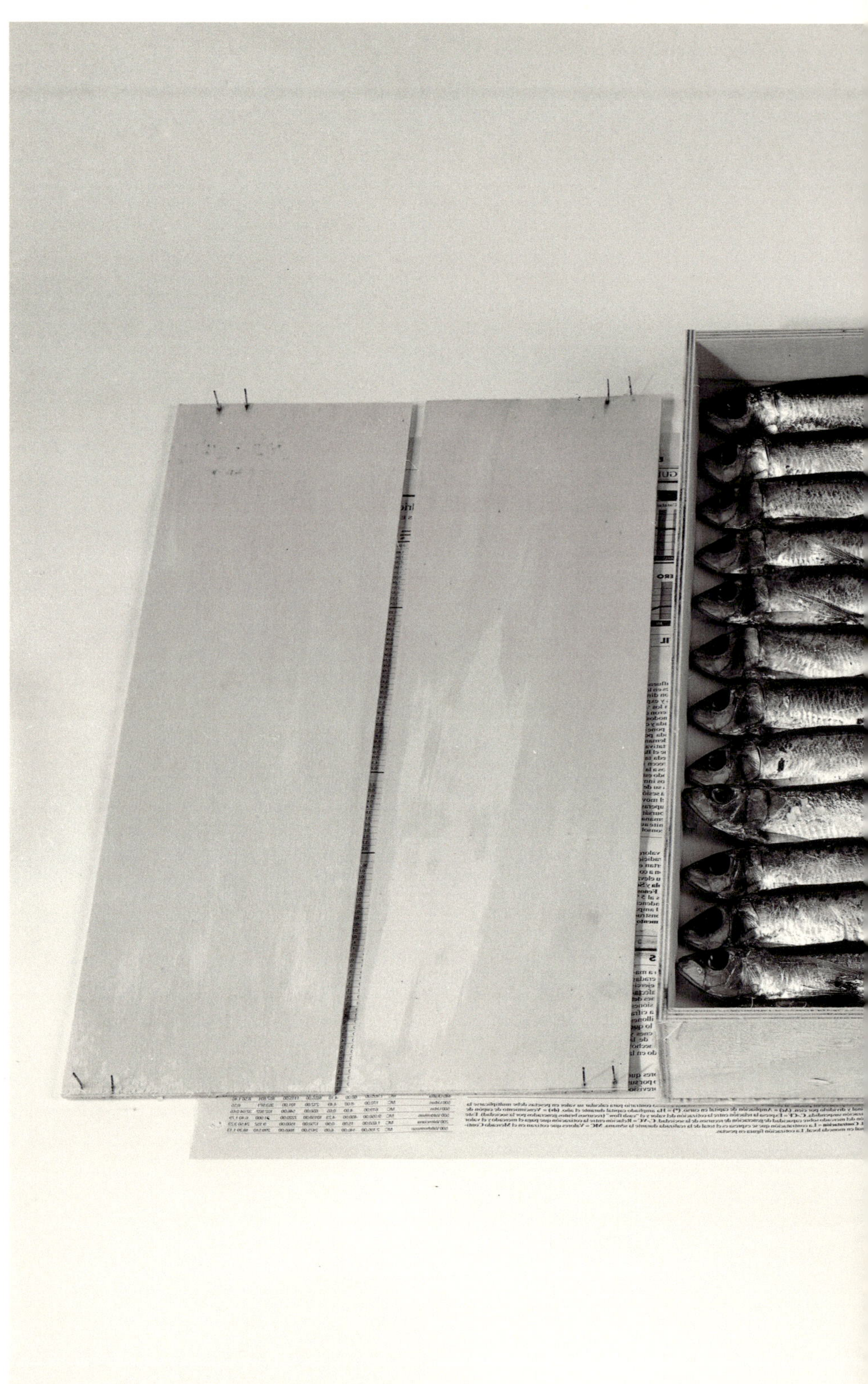

3.44

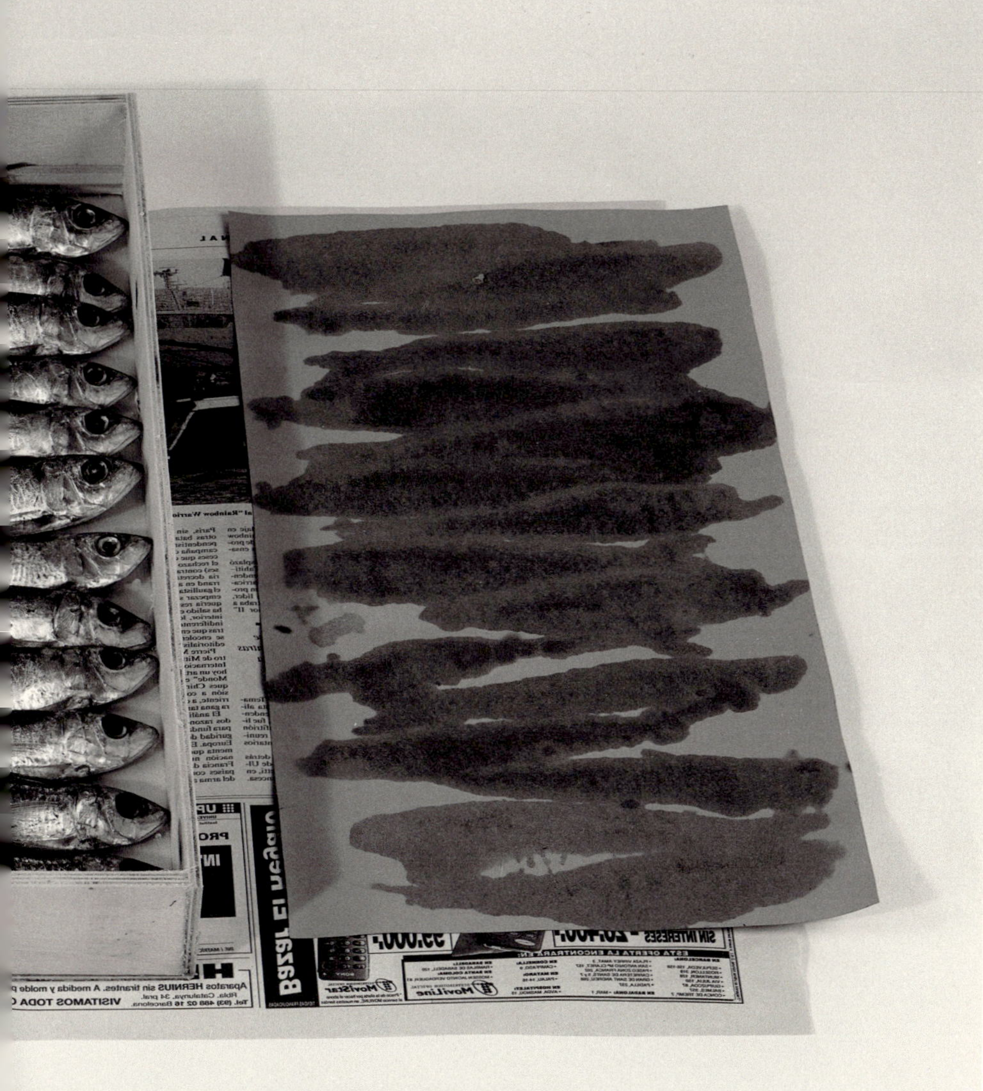

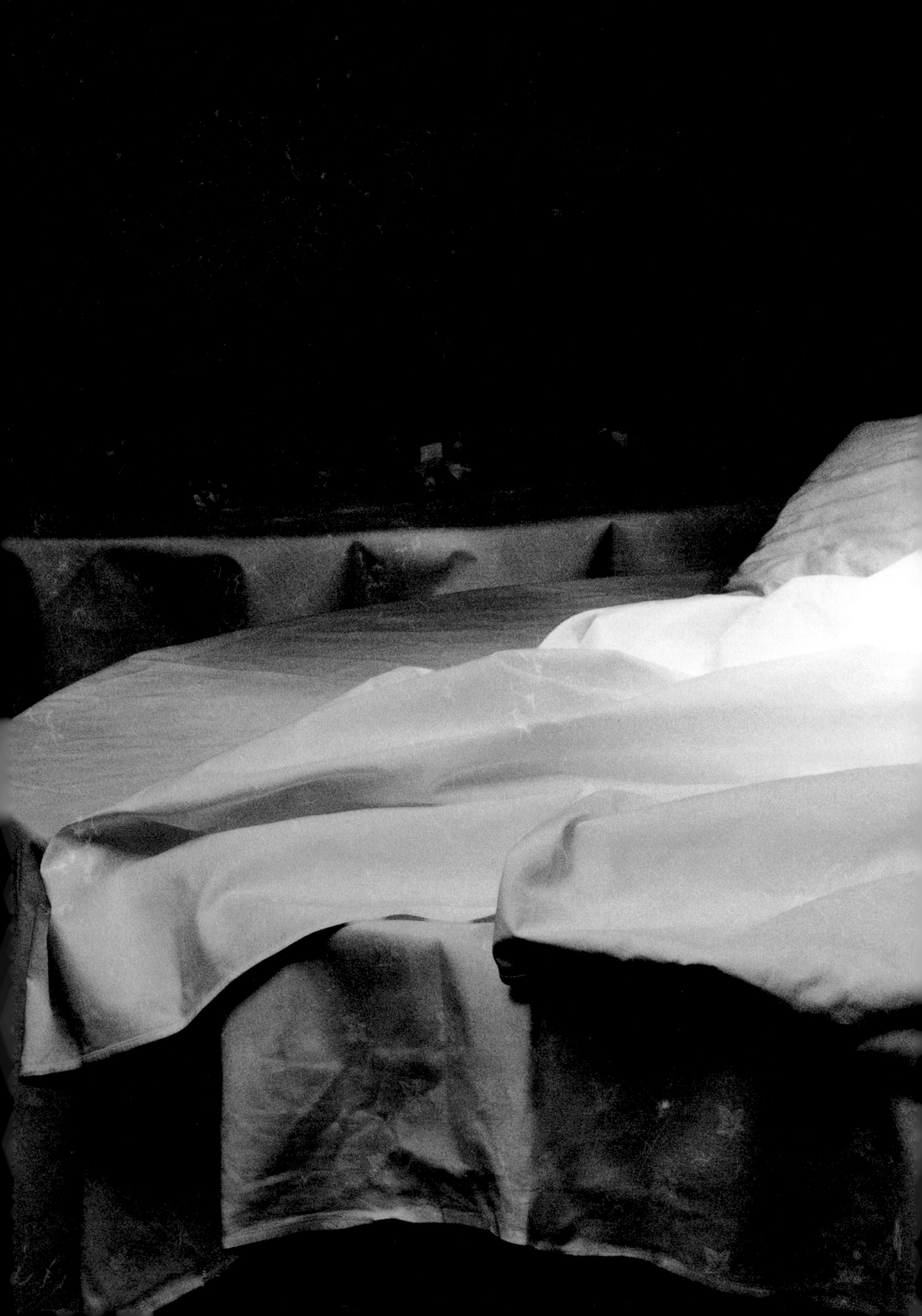

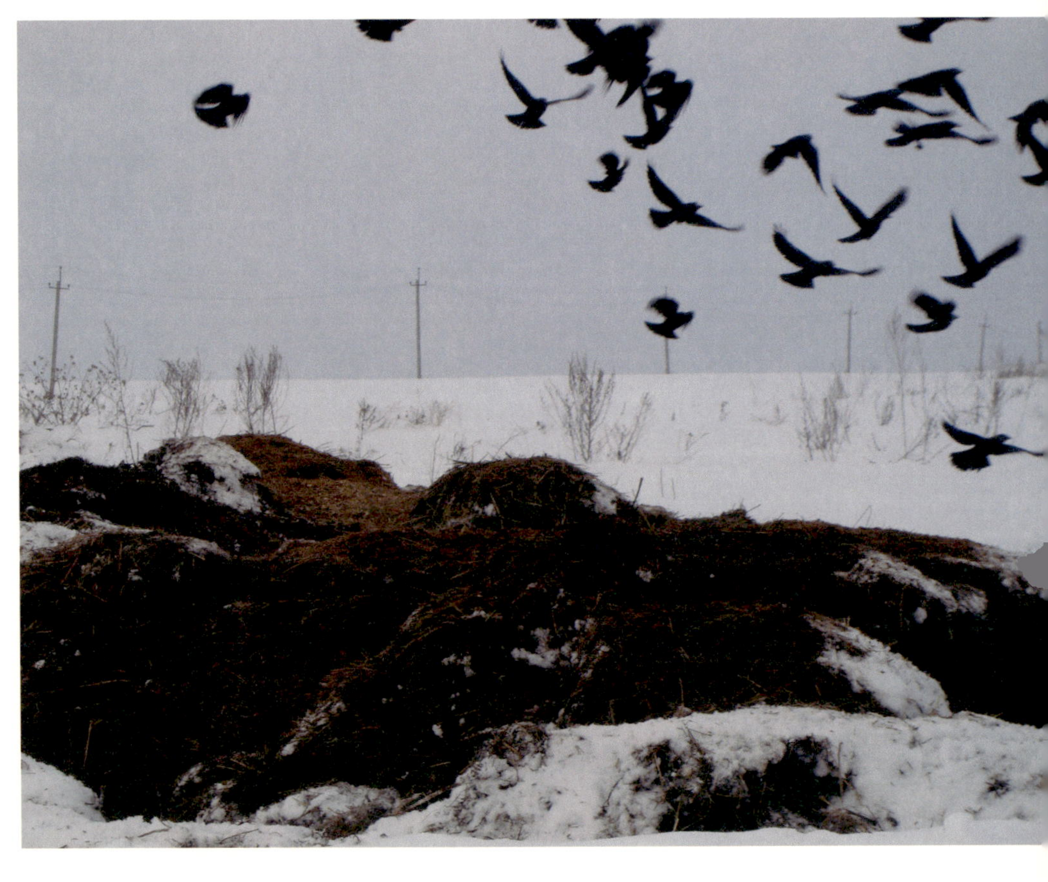

Scripts

SHOOTING SCRIPT
CONCEPT NOTE

Super 16mm, 30 minutes,
English subtitles

A   *The geese who are shut in the darkness of a wooden shed through the winter
will tolerate only one member of the family, they attack and hiss at all the rest.
Later it turns out that this is the person who will butcher one of them in the
snow for a special occasion.*

B   *A Romani mother has chosen a bride for her son. The girl moves to live with
her husband's family and has a child. When the child is four months old the girl
leaves and goes back to her family. The family of her husband is devastated. Family
discussions take place but eventually the girl decides to come back to her husband
and he goes to collect her.*

C   *An old style Russian intellectual, who lives alone and separately from his Romani
mother, eats daily with the family. He has been to the post office in the city and
believes they are not delivering his post and creates an angry drama. The postwoman
visits his wife. Reports of his scandalous behaviour lead to more traumas in the
household. However, the next day six letters arrive at his dilapidated house.*

D   *A girl has brought her mother the present of a black evening dress which she
acquired in the city market. The Romani mother wears the dress for many days
in a row day and night. Meals become ever more elaborate to justify the wearing
of the dress and stores are brought up from the freezing underground storeroom
– enormous bottled jars of vegetables, pickles and preserved fish take their place
on the table as the dress stays on.*

SETTINGS IN THE WORK

1.1 Camera/architecture

In each scene architecture is pitted against nature. We see the inhabitants of the village
in relation to nature and inside basic structures. We see Nizhny Novogorod in relation
to the immediate environment and inside the structures.

1.2 Camera/characters

We never see what is irrelevant to the characters we are with. We often see everything
from their point of view. Lots of hand held material. Mostly in really close to the
protagonists, lots of it shot from their points of view. Mostly from below the protagonists.
Scenes always have a point.

2. LANDSCAPE

Landscape plays a very important part in understanding the final two-channel exhibition
format. There are lots of long landscape shots and juxtapositions of the effects of Russian
history and its development on the landscape. (For a example the palaces of the new
Russian rich people in the field around Beshencevo and the old houses in the village.)
The relationship of nature and the gypsies is always present in this film. (Ljonchik and his
mother is the most important example in this case. By losing his money he is returned
to the forest.) The landscape is seen at all times of day and night – the early light in the
morning over the Volga, the moon at night over the road, etc..

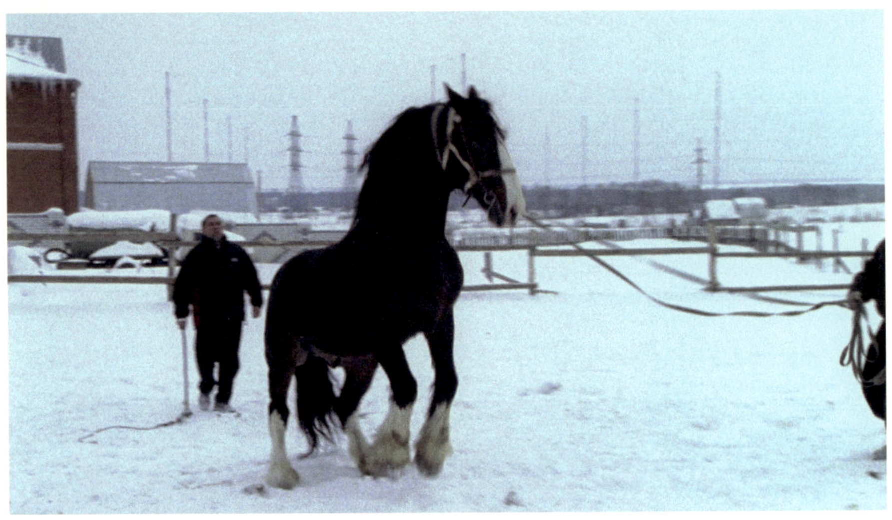

2.1 The city of Nizhny Novogorod

a. In the streets of Nizhny, distant shots as people go about their business. (Day)

b. Looking into peoples' flats as the light drops and the lights go on. (Night)

c. Above the city Kremlin, the soldiers as they walk about. (Day and night)

d. The decorative tree where people hang things from the branches. (Morning)

e. At the bus stop just outside the city. The motorway running from Nizhny Novogorod to the village. (From a car or a bus, various times of day)

f. At the market at the edge of the city as people go about their business buying and selling. (Early morning and evening)

g. In this case we have an opportunity of using the highest buildings in the city.

2.1/2 Car plant and the factory neighbourhood

a. Factory smoke, main car assembly buildings, pipes, water, broken glass, factories, delicate details on the buildings, cars. Trees, water, birds and any visible signs of life in the factory territory. (Like birds making nests, cats, etc..)

b. Different shots of the cinema, turned into a casino in the industrial area around the car factory.

c. Outside of the car factory, workers coming and going (morning and evening), both factory and office workers. Peoples' faces.

3.1 Volga and Oka Rivers

a. Looking down over the Volga River, looking into the distance, from down beside the river looking at the ice.

b. At night, up by the Kremlin, looking down over the Volga. Looking at the river terminal square with statue of the seamen in a group, the corner where the murals are, the river where there is an unfinished bridge, the river looking towards the area where the sun sets. (All day and night)

4.1 Train station

a. At the train station we see trains come and go. Station with people arriving and leaving from the main terminal. Close ups of the locomotives, wheels, women in uniform. Wide shots of railways and stoplights.

5.1. Beshencevo/Village (At as many times of day as possible)

Wide and close up shots of the forest (morning). Panoramic shots of the village from above. From the road looking towards the village with the name of the village visible. Panoramic shots from outside of the village towards Nizhny Novogorod (buildings on the horizon). In the village as dogs and people come and go, children as they leave school, cars drive through the village. Trees and nature in the village.

CHARACTERS

The main characters

Valentin – Father and husband to Edouard's family. Speaks many languages and now lives alone in a wreck of a house. He is very communicative and able to explain things around him, might act as a commentator for the village, still believing in the Communist way of life, Stalin, Lenin. etc.. Is a great lover of books and has a huge library in his small wooden house.

Zinaida Chiline – Roma mother, the centre of the family. Her life revolves around keeping the family together and making sure that the customs are maintained, hates books.

Natasha Chiline – Younger daughter of Valentin and Zinaida, lives at home with her Russian husband, very calm and gentle, peaceful, following the gypsy way with things.

Maxim Chiline – Natasha's husband, quite thick and occasionally rebellious but ultimately obeys the family orders and does what he is told.

Boris – Russian scientist, photographer and businessman living in Nizhny, part of the new generation of Russians making huge amount of money in short periods of time and believing in wild capitalism without doubt.

Ljonchik and his mother – A disastrous gypsy man who lives with his mother (Tamara), a wretched character. A couple of years ago he sold his house but spent all the money on the beautiful Russian girl who later dumped him. Nowadays he and his mother live on the village outskirts in a cheap and cold house.

Leonard Chiline – Edouard's brother – simple, strong, traditional character, able to carry out basic tasks. His Romani wife has run away but came back after a while.

People of Moscow, Nizhny Novogorod and Beshencevo.

SCENES DESTINED FOR THE LEFT SCREEN ARE IN BOLD

IN THE VILLAGE (Beshencevo) AND CITY (Nizhny Novogorod)

1.   INT / IN THE VILLAGE, BARN / EARLY MORNING

Mid shot, close up

1.1. *We are in the Chiline family's wooden shed. In the early morning light we can see the shadows of the animals. Hearing their sounds before we catch sight of them. We find geese, goats and pigs in the dark and beside them Zinaida is chopping*

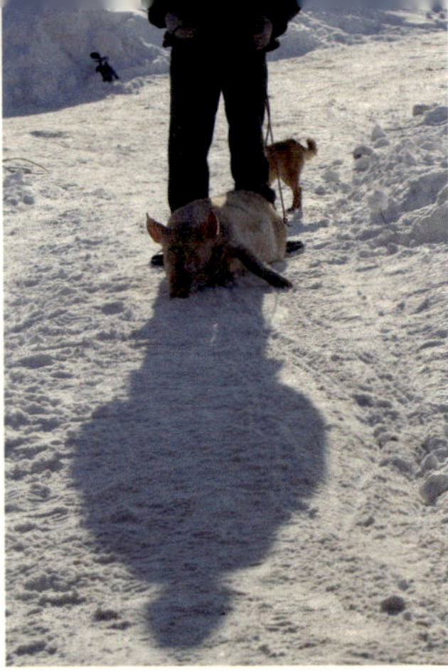

potatoes in the darkness. The place is lit with a small bulb light in the corner. To the side of the image light appears and the door opens. We see the texture of the wooden interior as the door opens. Old clothes hanging on the walls. Some posters with semi-naked models as well.

CUT TO

The path down to the garden from the shed. The geese are leaving the shed and move down the road towards us. They pass the camera in a hurry as a pan is banged in the background.

CUT TO

Inside the shed the pig and one of the geese are left behind. We barely see the pig routing around in the darkness.

CUT TO

1.2 *The animal is pulled through the darkness to the light outside by Leonard. Once outside the squealing animal is caught in the expert hands of the butcher.*

CUT TO

Close up

The wooden cross for hanging the pig.

Close up

A gleaming knife catches the light.

CUT TO

Close up

The pig's face and especially the eyes.

Mid-shot

The knife cuts clean across the pig's throat and red blood covers everything. The camera gradually pulls away to reveal bodies and hands covered in the pig's blood hauling the pig onto the roughly built cross outside. Suddenly what was filled with agonised sound is silent and barking slowly fills the air.

Left screen

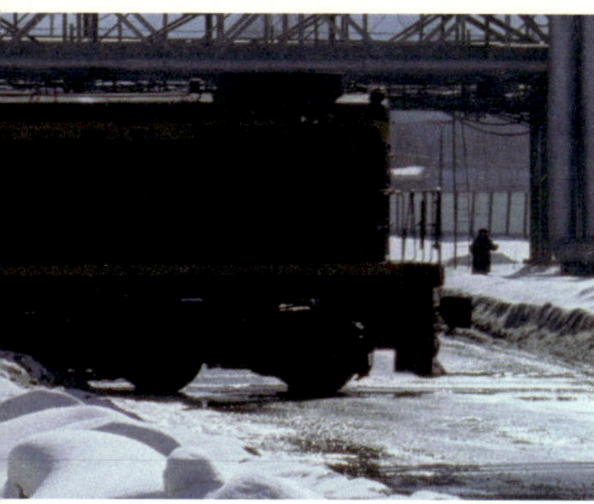

1.3

Throughout this sequence early morning in the city is going on with a very long shot of the bus stop in the square by the port and people getting off the train from Moscow. Tired and bedraggled from the night train people arrive on the platform at Nizhny. The city also seen from their anonymous eyes, general views. Early morning light, taxis and cars waiting....

CUT TO

2.   EXT AND CAR / VILLAGE / EARLY MORNING

MS, CU

From inside the car we can see Maxim is coming out of the front door of the building and heads towards the car. In the background, out of focus, the pig is hung up, and the blood. Maxim looks oblivious to the scene behind him. Later we watch him from a distance as he fiddles with the car and climbs in. His car is a dirty pale yellow Lada. He starts up noisily drowning out the dogs and people in the background.

CUT TO

We are behind Maxim in the car as he heads out of the village. He turns on the radio and Russian news mixed with pop music fills the car. We are aware of people passing the dirty windows, children running from their houses as the car passes. Maxim seems passive and oblivious to all, including the dead pig.

CUT TO

The camera swings dramatically between the dead pig and the car.

CUT TO

3.   INT CAR / ROAD TO NIZHNY / EARLY MORNING

Maxim's POV

On the main road between the village and Nizhny Maxim heads towards the city passing buses, walkers and trucks. The town starts to appear as massive blocks of flats.

Left screen

From Maxim's car we pass various blocks of flats, the bridge over the river which winds into the distance. There are many groups of people standing waiting around for buses, for the market. We pass the old part of town, the wooden houses looking

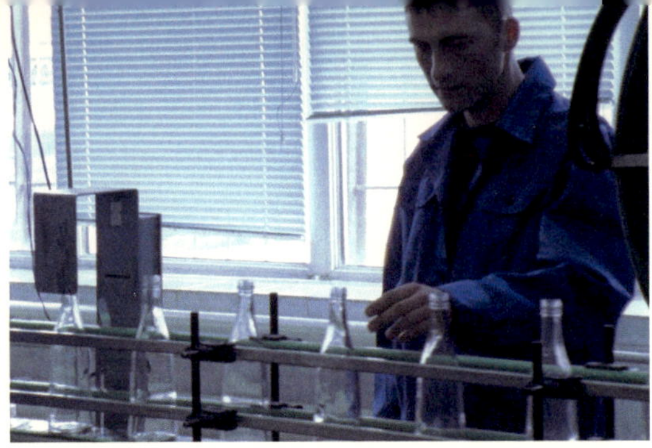

*dark after the concrete blocks. POV Maxim and behind Maxim looking to the left
side of the car.*

CUT TO

*Area by the old riverside factories. Maxim passes enormous gates, old granaries and we
are down beside the river. He stops the car by the riverbank and gets out to smoke
a cigarette. The factories are churning out smoke in the distance.*

Left screen

4.   INT/EXT / SUBURBS CAR / EARLY MORNING

*Boris is coming out of a large house in the suburbs, he is already talking on
his mobile, headphones on, and he climbs into his car. Boris is dressed in West
Coast American cool style although he personally is a large and typical Russian,
the clothes look out of place.*

POV Boris

*We see the road go by in the same way as Maxim, only the car interior is different.
The same music and the same news. As Maxim is already stopped and smoking
we don't compare them just appreciate the change of tone.*

CUT TO

(two shots matching for left and right screens)

*The river flowing past with ships coming and going. There is an unfinished bridge
in the river. To the right of the shot are trees and a long path. The river keeps flowing
past. On the right screen the old buildings behind show various signs of intervention,
a new pipe cuts across the architecture, an old entrance shows decayed courtyards
and crumbling doors. The shots match in the middle.*

CUT TO

*4.1 The camera closes in on Lenin's statue erected across the river way in the distance.
Smoke passes across the screen. We see industrial activity far into the vast distance;
there isn't an end to it.*

CUT TO

5.   INT / VODKA FACTORY BY THE CONVEYOR BELTS / MORNING

LS, MS, CU

*Vodka bottles are coming across the conveyor belt. They slide past the camera
and are sent on to further processes. Maxim is behind the conveyor belt. The camera*

looks patiently at what he is doing. The factory is out of focus behind. We hear the bottles and the machines noisy after the quiet of the cars. The camera spans the factory and concentrates periodically on various activities of the conveyor belts and workers. Maxim is more alone than some of the other workers who are joking around to one side of the space.

Camera concentrates as the vodka hits the bottle. Maxim picks up and holds the bottle on up to the light.

Close up

The snake in the bottle twirls around.

CUT TO

Left screen

5.1. At the same time on the left screen we are getting to know the city richer and poorer, different aspects of the day, people going to the factory, discussions in the street, beggars, business people, people at the bus stop. We leave the left screen with shots of the river flowing past and Lenin beyond. Shots often in conflict with each other. Sometimes abstraction, sky, river, trees moving in the wind, car wheels, occupy the screen...

Right Screen

6.   EXT/INT / VALENTIN'S HOUSE / EARLY MORNING

MS, CU

From the little distance we can see Valentin's house. Camera gently explores the carved wooden windows and the walls black with time.

CUT TO

Close up of Communist memorabilia (flags, posters, etc.) on Valentin's wooden walls, everything is in darkness and oldness. The flags stand out red and bright in contrast to the dusty environment. The lighting is a bare light bulb, which for the moment is off. We listen to the sounds of sleeping as we watch the detail of the wood on the walls and the spider's webs.

CUT TO

The camera sees old books piled up and clothes hung on a line. In the corner one can notice an old stove with different pots and pans sitting on it.

Close up

Different names of the books in many letter types. The camera gently explores them changing from Hebrew to English, Arabic to Russian.

CUT TO

Later we can see a jam jar left empty where some mice are trapped and struggling to get out, they are visible only by their out of focus forms and their struggle. The radio is blaring away with Russian Federation news and pop music.

CUT TO

In the darkness is the huddled form of a sleeping man. His grey hair is untidy; his bed

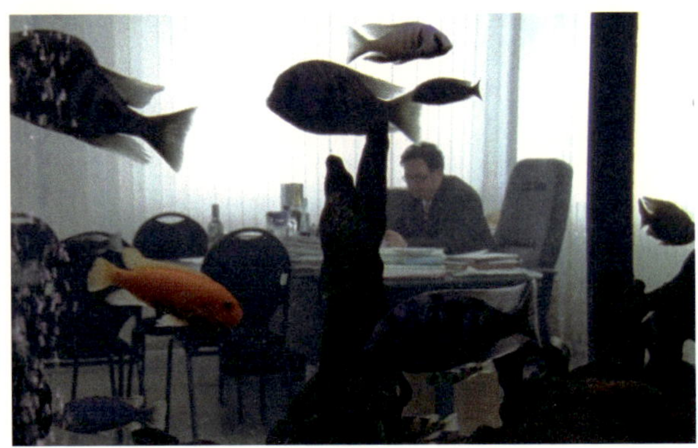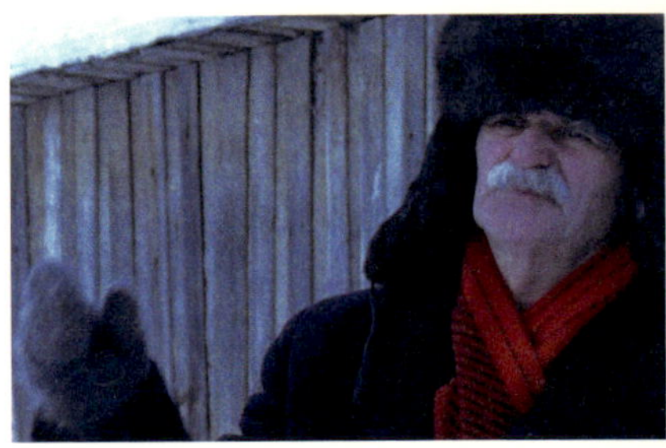

*is covered in old army coats. As he sits up he makes a comment to the camera. He slowly
sits on the edge of the bed deep in his own thoughts.*

Left screen

**6.1 Unfinished bits of Nizhny, apartment blocks which are slowly decaying, decorations
and window grills, details of Soviet ideology in the form of houses (what Valentin
would and does believe in).**

Both Screens

7.   EXT/INT / VALENTIN'S HOUSE / SLIGHTLY LATER

LS, MS, CU

*Valentin's house is a disordered wreck but originally a beautiful wooden house. From
the road it's impossible to see that anyone lives there. To one side of the house a man
is chopping wood. From the road we see the large and serious looking postwoman
approaching the house. She crosses the frame and approaches the house.*

Close Up

*We are close to her as she approaches and peers through the filthy window at the dark
interior and starts to knock on the window. A furious face appears on the other side
of the glass through the dirt.*

CUT TO

POV *postwoman.*

CUT TO

POV *Valentin.*

From the inside, the round face of the postwoman appears on the other side of the glass.

CUT TO

LS

7.1. *Outside we can see that there is a confrontation starting as Valentin appears, still
dressing himself. He looks furious but controlled and gestures wildly with his arms
to indicate a global situation. They have a face-to-face row about Valentin's mail.
The postwoman has brought him a newspaper but no mail; he says that they are keeping
his letters from him and that it is all a conspiracy against him. The row widens as he*

declares that she has never done her job properly and that people like her destroyed the Soviet Union.

CUT TO

Inside Valentin's house where the picture is the same except that the mouse has escaped. (Or dead?)

CUT TO

Valentin dressed. He talks to the camera giving us a short and precise account of his life and marriage.

"You see I was a technical translator, an intellectual man, I believed in the Soviet Union but I wanted an exotic wife so I married a gypsy woman, a woman very different to myself, and I gave up everything for that, but now she hates me and my books..."

CUT TO

The wooden walls and flags give us a rich, coloured environment. Sometimes they blur to abstraction.

8.   EXT / ROAD THROUGH THE VILLAGE / MORNING

LS

On the road through the village Valentin is now dressed and walking purposefully towards the other end of the village. He passes various houses, dogs come up to him and he talks to them. He has a long conversation with himself as he walks along. This is about history, the present diabolical state of Russia, disagreements in the village about the gas pipes running through the village and so on. Valentin refers to history as he walks along. Valentin comes to the place where the pig is already in the form of chunks of meat. He stops to congratulate his son on his strength, joking about his runaway wife. Leonard looks slowly into his father's face but says very little. They are very different, perhaps the father is a little jealous of the son.

CUT TO

Close up

Leonard's eyes.

CUT TO

His huge hands holding a knife.
(Valentin's POV and POV observer.)

9.   INT/EXT / SHED / A MINUTE LATER

Valentin is in the shed gathering grain for the geese. One goose left in the shed hisses at him as he goes about his business. He talks about his children as he continues. He talks to himself about his angry wife and his languages and practices his languages as he goes.

10. EXT / FIELD BEHIND THE HOUSE / SLIGHTLY LATER

Valentin brings grain in a bucket to the geese. He walks along carrying the family cat and stroking her as he goes. He doesn't stop talking about the family to himself. As he enters the field cautiously and approaches the geese, they hiss, flap their wings

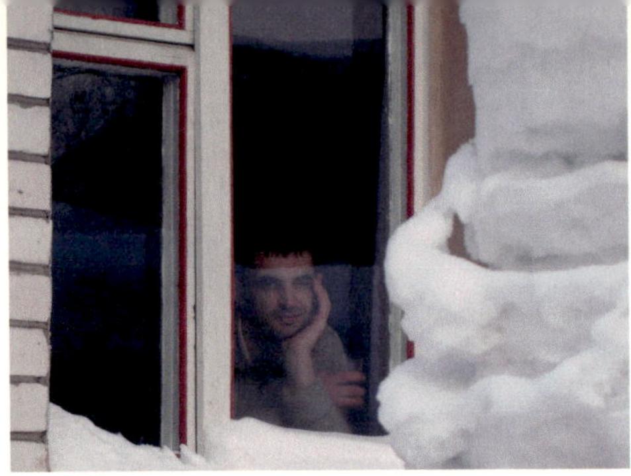

and chase him away. He scatters the grain and runs laughing from the field down towards the house. We leave Valentin passing the camera as the geese hiss and scream at him.

12. INT / FAMILY VILLAGE HOME / LATER MORNING

MS, CU

Inside Zinaida is organising her household of people. Natasha is making tea in the samovar (sound of samovar, crackling wood and steam hissing) whilst the postwoman is sitting fatly beside the table. She is explaining how Valentin has exploded at her and is dramatising the episode when in walks Valentin. There is an explosion and all three start to talk loudly at one another. Valentin continues to accuse the postwoman of treachery but his wife urgently recommends him to stop.

CUT TO

We are introduced to Natasha who calms everyone and is seen bringing food.

CUT TO

We are introduced to Ljonchik, another villager who sits down for tea.

CUT TO

Close up

Valentin talks to the camera.

CUT TO

Zinaida starts to sing lyrical Romani songs to the camera. We linger on each person as they speak and then the camera swings up and away often seeing the dark room with little to focus on, each person is seen very close, very sympathetically, very slowly as they talk. The scene establishes a community but at the same time provides only a brief look.

Left screen

12. INT/EXT / POST OFFICE / SAME MORNING

MS

In the post office letters and parcels are being sorted.

The village has one place for the letters and a hand is seen posting a few letters into the place for Valentin. It is a Soviet style place.

CU

Lights, lettering and posters, people in uniforms....

CU

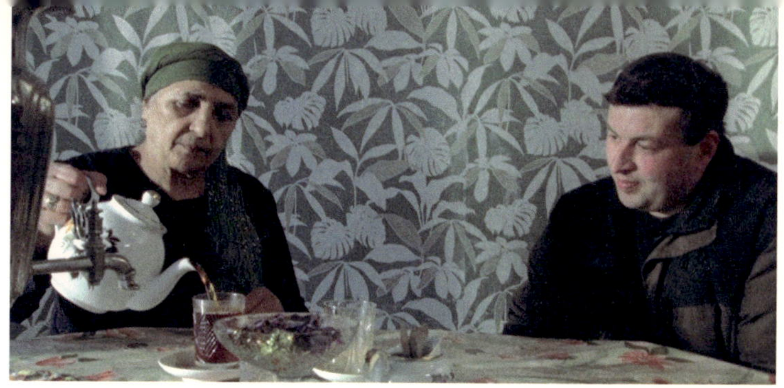

Letter with Valentin's name on it.

CUT TO

13. INT / VODKA FACTORY / SAME MORNING

MS

Boris is walking around the factory with a group of businessmen. There is a big difference between him and the workers. He looks affluent and modern.

14. INT / CAR FACTORY / SAME MORNING

LS, MS

There are a group of businessmen walking around the car factory, the scale is completely overbearing, the workers look tiny.

15. INT / CAR FACTORY / SAME TIME

LS, MS, CU

Valentin is walking through the factory as if he still works there, he is carrying a book and is visiting, he takes us through the vast spaces of the factory where cars are being put together. Valentin explains to the camera about the Ford factory, it was built by the Americans, it is a relic, it is a part of Soviet Russia, and it is surrounded by grimness, with no evidence of modernity. "But we believed in it, it gave us jobs."

Right screen

16. INT / SCHOOL ROOM / SAME MORNING

We are inside the village school. The classroom has windows all along one side and the children face the teacher who is writing on the board. She is like someone still in Soviet times. On the walls are pictures of animals and farmyard creatures. A blond boy is staring with despair out of the window. He doesn't concentrate on the class at all. He seems to be dreaming of something nice. The children are a mixture of Russian, Kurdish and Gipsy kids. They look completely different but share the room equally. Only the blond pale boy lacks attention. As he stares out of the window, he sees Ljonchik walking past the school windows towards the other side of the village with the slaughtered pig's head under his arm. The boy stares fixedly at the window.

POV

16.1 *Ljonchik looks at pig head under his arm and at the schoolhouse. His walk is plodding, the pig's head frightening. The other kids leave the classroom and the elderly teacher holds back the blond boy.*

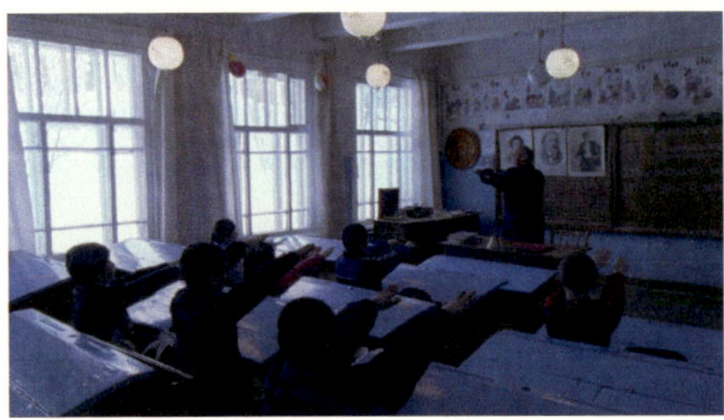

CUT TO

16.2 *The other children can be seen streaming past the window and spreading out in different directions as Ljonchik goes off into the distance. Some of the children walk with Ljonchik along the route as if the pig's head were the most natural companion.*

CUT TO

16.3 *Inside the teacher sits in front of the boy and helps him to count by holding up small wooden sticks. The boy's attention comes and goes.*

CUT TO

Left screen

**16.4 The children run off playing in the village. They throw stones trying to hit
an empty tin they have placed a distance away.**

Right screen

17. EXT / ROUTE THROUGH VILLAGE / LATE MORNING

Ljonchik is walking through the village. He carries the head of the pig under his arm. As he looks out through the village passing villagers greet him.

CUT TO

Close up of the Ljonchik house.

18. INT / YOSHA'S HOUSE / MID-DAY

MS, CU

We are inside Ljonchik house. He calls out to his mother who is sitting in her single, tidy and well kept but unmistakably gypsy room. Ljonchik takes the pig's head to show his mother. She begins to remember the time when she was in jail and she was forced to eat a part of the pig she didn't like. She dominates Ljonchik and demands more things from him. Ljonchik begins to explain to the camera his difficulties in life. He sadly talks to himself about his mother who continues to interrupt and gabble in the background.

Ljonchik talks about why he lives in a hovel, he talks about the beautiful woman who has stolen everything from him the poor and displaced gypsy man. Slowly he resolves to go and see the woman who has taken everything, his dominant mother screams at him that he is doing the wrong thing.

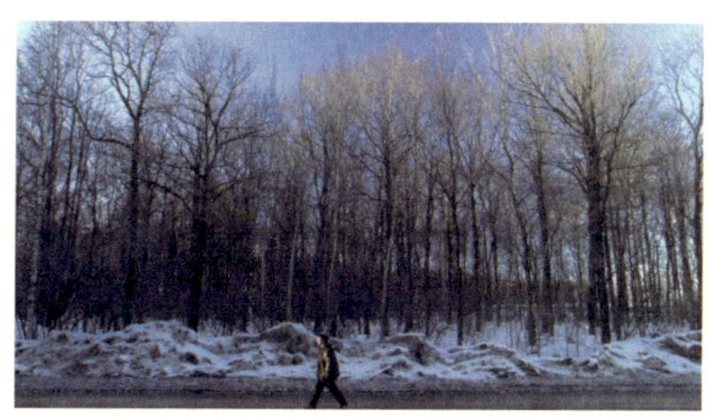

CUT TO

In the background Ljonchik's mother is turning on the small black and white TV and starts to watch Santa Barbara.

CUT TO

Close up of the TV screen.

CUT TO

Ljonchik walks away from the camera and appears on the left screen en route to the city.

CUT TO

19. EXT / ROUTE TO THE CITY / DAY

POV

We see the tall birch trees passing by. The fields are covered in snow, the factories in the background. Cars pass by, the odd person from the village waves at Ljonchik, nobody else is walking.

CUT TO

20. EXT/INT / HAIRDRESSER'S SHOP / EARLY AFTERNOON

POV

We are beside Ljonchik staring in at the interior of a brightly coloured, wealthy but tasteless hair salon. Inside two hairdressers, both blonde and hard looking, are doing the nails and hair of various clients. One of the hairdressers tidies the salon whilst the other rather brutally tends to the nails of a client under the dryer, her hair just done. We are not close to these people, they are just people doing things, their only interest is for Llonchik, we only examine them for him.

POV *Wife of Ljonchik.*

Ljonchik's ex-girlfriend is clearing up and looks up to see her ragged dirty husband staring in at the window. She calls the security guys. They urged him to disappear.

CUT TO

POV *Ljonchik and* POV *other person.*

CUT TO

POV *Ex-girlfriend.*

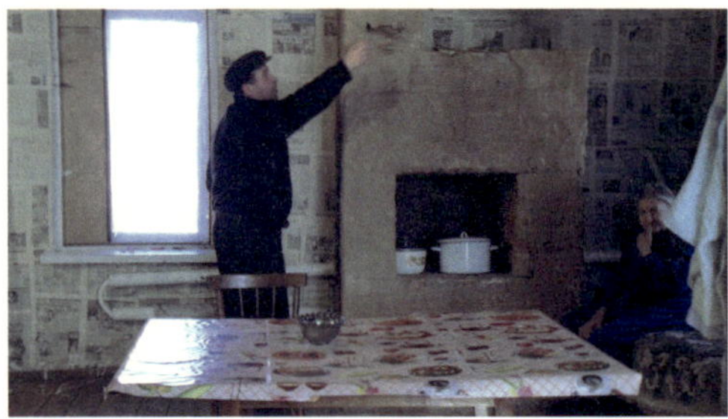

Left screen

CUT TO

21. EXT / STREET NIZHNY / LATER

Ljonchik is standing in a doorway down by the docks with a bottle in his hand. He's obviously been drinking heavily and is sadly cursing his wife, his mother and his village. The place is textured and dark. On the right screen the saloon is bright and ordered.

CUT TO

Right screen

22. INT / BUS NIZHNY / MID-DAY

CUT TO

Valentin is on the bus into the city. He softly sings to himself. He curses and swears against the new Russia. We can see he has no more context here than he had in the village. He talks to the Russian next to him telling him that he speaks ten languages and pulls out of his bag various books in different languages. We face him and the other man who looks a little sceptical at his claims until Valentin begins to read to him from a book in Urdu. The LS, MS, CU.

The man also looks sceptical when Valentin explains that his mail is being robbed and that he is on his way to re-claim his property. The man is pensive. We glimpse other people on the bus behind and around Valentin.

Left screen

The view out of the bus shows the two sides of the landscape as they pass alternately.

23. EXT / STREETS TO POST OFFICE / MID-DAY

MS

Valentin is alighting from the bus and heads towards the post office. He is brisk and happy looking – he enjoys a confrontation. He enters muttering about how useless Russia now is. People glance at him and go back to their work. He goes towards the counter and as he reaches it he starts to get angry, shouting and banging his hand to say that he wants his mail. The bland postwoman says that there is nothing for him and he accuses her of lying. People stare at him.

He leaves and walks alone and frustrated. Just as he reaches the bus a young post worker runs after him and presents him with at least six letters. He says nothing but looks

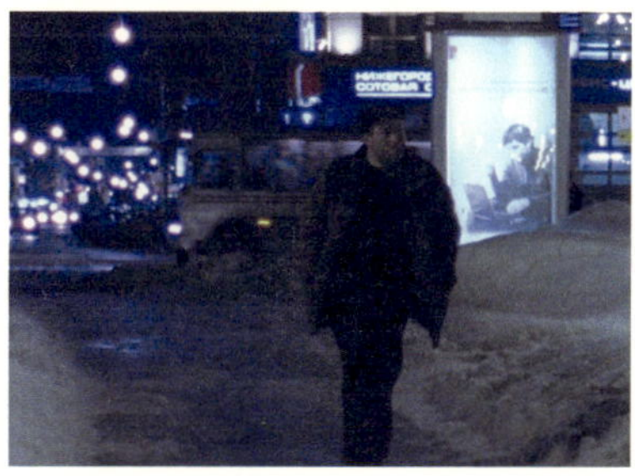

completely content at his rightness and his victory. He is seen climbing onto the bus.

CUT TO

24. INT / ZINAIDA'S HOME / LUNCHTIME

Main room, cellar, bedrooms.

MS, CU

Zinaida is moving around the house, she puts away bedding from all the rooms. Each blanket is piled in a spare room along with pillows in a large pile. Natasha enters carrying a bag in which she says she has a present for her mother. The present is a long black dress from the market. The brothers are close to the mother and laugh at her pleasure at the dress. She puts it on and parades around the room showing it off to the others…. She immediately opens a trap door and climbs downstairs to bring out bottles and jars of food to celebrate the dress and to have a family discussion. Leonard announces that he is going to ask his wife to come back.

Both screens used to look at the group interacting.

25. EXT / VILLAGE OF WIFE / AFTERNOON

LS, MS, CU

In the other village where Natasha, Leonard's wife has escaped, a crisis is also going on. She sits with her baby on a step outside a village home. The village children come and sit with her playing with the baby. Her mother comes to find her and brings Natasha to talk to her relatives. She says she is lonely, that she has missed her family and wants to come back to the village.

CUT TO

26. INT / ZINAIDA'S HOME / AFTERNOON

CU

Zinaida is trying to be cheerful in her dress. The brother is silent and walks quietly from room to room. The two brothers sit quietly together and talk to one another about the needs of Natasha, Leonard's wife. The brother in a gentle gesture brings a blanket for Natasha to sit on as if to prove that he can care for someone. We are seeing the other side of the man who killed the pig.

CUT TO

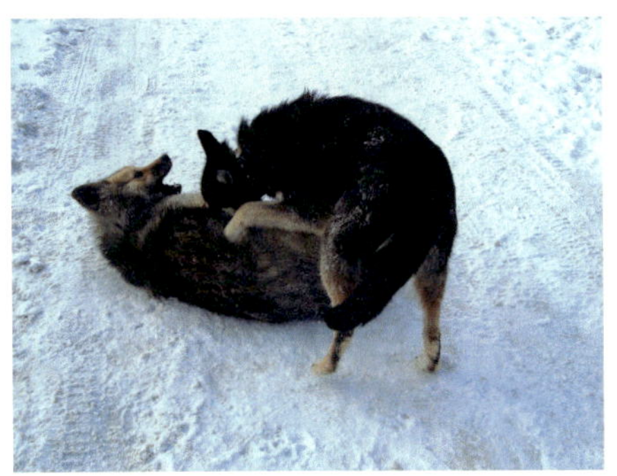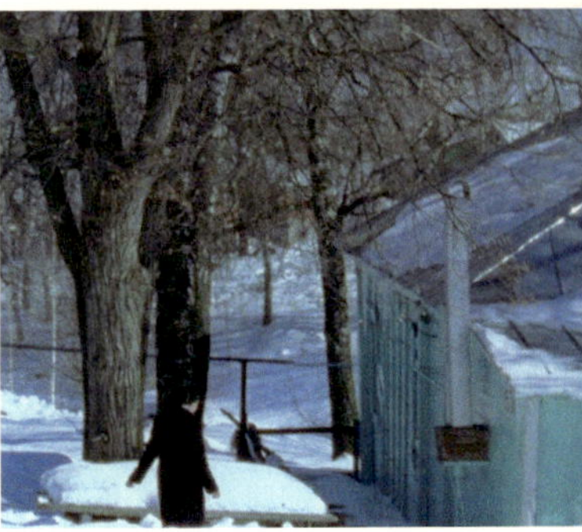

Left screen

27. INT/EXT / GIRL'S VILLAGE HOME / LATE AFTERNOON

CU

The girl is feeding her baby whilst the family members play instruments in the middle of their simple home. We follow the musicians outside and four or five musicians hang around the village street playing and singing.

CUT TO

Left and right screens

28. INT / GIRL'S VILLAGE HOME / FIVE MINUTES LATER

MS, CU

It is getting dark and in the house it is dim, very dim, we can barely see the figures. Zinaida dominates but it is her son who asks his wife to come home. A big discussion takes place, the baby with her wife in the centre of the room. Outside we can hear the village musicians.

CUT TO

On each screen we see the head of Zinaida and of the father of the girl. We watch as they discuss their children's future and each reacts to what the other has to say. An agreement is struck – the girl will come home with the child.

The screens are almost black as we see the building texture, the musicians are still playing under a light bulb, and the families are leaving and head out towards their car.

CUT TO

Left screen

Note: Music at the beginning of the second day, left and right screens somehow blend

29. EXT / KREMLIN / SAME TIME

MS

The boy climbs up the tree in order to tie the ribbon high in the branches. From his viewpoint he looks down on Ljonchik talking with a new girlfriend being bundled into the car. The day is bright and blue in the early light. The tree seems to hang above the river below in mid-air.

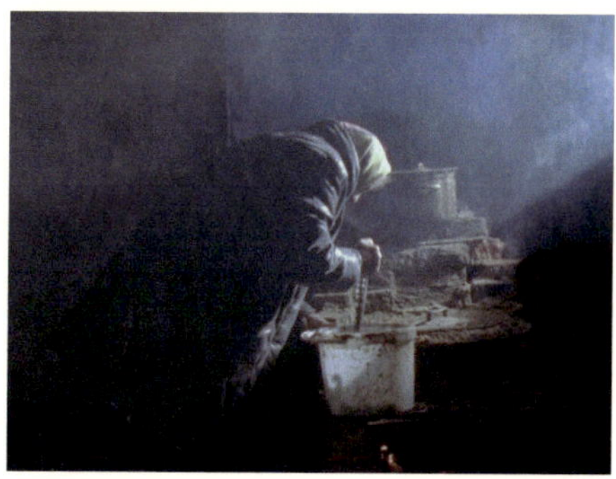

Right screen

CUT TO

30. EXT / LJONCHIK'S MOTHER'S HOUSE / EARLY MORNING

CU

Ljonchik's mother is in her wretched bed. She is getting up and dressing herself in layers of rags. She picks up and counts money and prepares to leave the house. Outside her dark window is a blossoming tree, she stares out at the tree in incomprehension, nature is obviously not her friend.

CUT TO

31. INT / SHED BY ZINAIDA'S HOUSE / EARLY MORNING

MS

Zinaida and Valentin are in the shed talking to the geese. Zinaida works hard chopping up potatoes for the animals, the geese hiss at Valentin, Zinaida sings. Valentin is obviously still in love. Zinaida is giving the geese food. They obviously trust and like her and loathe Valentin.

CUT TO

Darkness of a shut door and sounds of school starting.

CUT TO

32. INT / ZINAIDA'S HOUSE / DAY LATER

The wife is sitting with the baby enjoying her company. We are close to them and also see her unhappiness. She is beneath the image of the tree on the carpet.

CUT TO

Left screen

33. INT / SOVIET STYLE RESTAURANT / LUNCHTIME

LS, MS

Valentin is sitting having lunch. In the kitchen workers in uniform are shovelling plates of identical food out and the kitchen is bustling, there are lots of people helping in the kitchen. Soldiers and workers are lined up buying food. We pick up details of an old way of doing things from the bulbs and lighting to the plates, and tables and chairs — the people also look old fashioned from another era. Valentin sits down and addresses the camera whilst he talks about the changes around him to another man beside him, an old colleague of his. Valentin is talking about the former Soviet State and invites Valentin to go with him down to the port.

Right screen

34. INT / ZINAIDA'S HOUSE / AFTERNOON

CU

Zinaida is in the cellar down in the earth sorting out preserved fruits, sausages and salted food. We stay close to her as she sings to herself.

CUT TO

Left screen

35. EXT / OUTSIDE VODKA FACTORY / LATE AFTERNOON

Maxim is leaving the factory where Natasha is waiting for him. They walk towards the bus stop.

MS, CU

36. INT / INSIDE LOCAL SHOP / LATE AFTERNOON DARK

Maxim and Natasha are heading to the local store to buy a few things. They meet a local gypsy girl whose husband is in jail. They ask her how he is and she replies that perhaps he prefers to be there as he never is out or at home.

Epilogue

37. INT / LOCAL SHOP / EARLY EVENING

We see Valentin and a boy from the school sitting on the bench. While Valentin trys to read him a story of the THREE LITTLE PIGS in Norwegian.

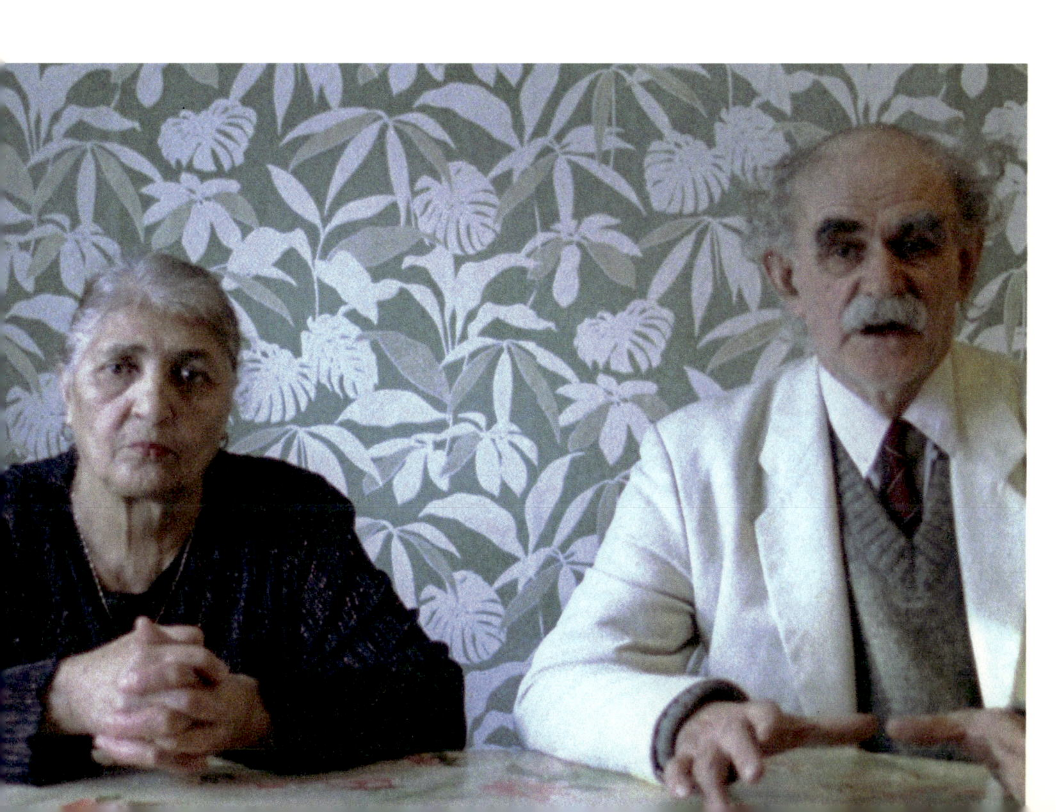

PARALLEL

Three films shot on Super 16mm
To be shown simultaneously

DEWA'S STORY
CONSTANTINE'S STORY
PAMELA'S STORY

DEWA'S STORY

The script has been written with Dewa and reflects his point of view. Each scene is based on his experiences, both after arriving in Spain and through his memories of Africa.

Dewa comes from Cameroon. His full name is Abdousalaam. He is 27 years old and came to Madrid two years ago. He does not have a community of people around him but has found a group of people in the park by the Palacio Real who he can sleep near to, they are all men from Cameroon.

Dewa speaks French and has been learning Spanish in the last few months. He speaks it well although sometimes complicated questions escape him and sometimes he fakes understanding.

He sleeps in the park and washes his clothes in a public washroom nearby. In Cameroon he comes from a village, the nearest big town being Garoua Boulat. The village he comes from is on the border with the Central African Republic, although he knows there are massive problems there he says they don't affect him. His mother died when he was 14 years old and he has three brothers and sisters whom he needs to look after, Usumano (boy 23 years old), Ouleah (girl 19 years old) Habsatu (girl 17 years old, she had polio at 12 years and cannot walk). Dewa had a girlfriend who was pregnant in his village but both she and the baby died (I don't know how).

The whole family stay in the village. His father Aasadoo (age 63) had a job running the postal service in the village but in a dispute lost the job and is relying on Dewa to support the family. Dewa's father is a figure of fear and respect. The average wage in Cameroon is 50 euros a month and so Dewa is able to send home enough from the job he has invented – parking cars in a public area.

Dewa was a footballer in Cameroon where he was contracted to play for local clubs. He started to play football in his village in normal shoes and with no equipment. He was then trained and has been playing around Cameroon. He had travelled in Cameroon quite a lot playing football where he was seen as a local talent.

From his village in Cameroon Dewa went to Yaounde. He took a plane from Yaounde to Douala. He arrived at the coast and then paid a security guard in the port to allow him onto a boat. He stayed throughout the voyage in the lowest part of the boat in the ballast and survived on two litres of water and a packet of biscuits for 17 days. He came up once during the voyage and saw the sea for the first time in his life.

On arrival in Portugal he came by bus to Madrid and seems to be delighted by Madrid as a city. He showed me a picture of the state he was in then, and he is still obviously very

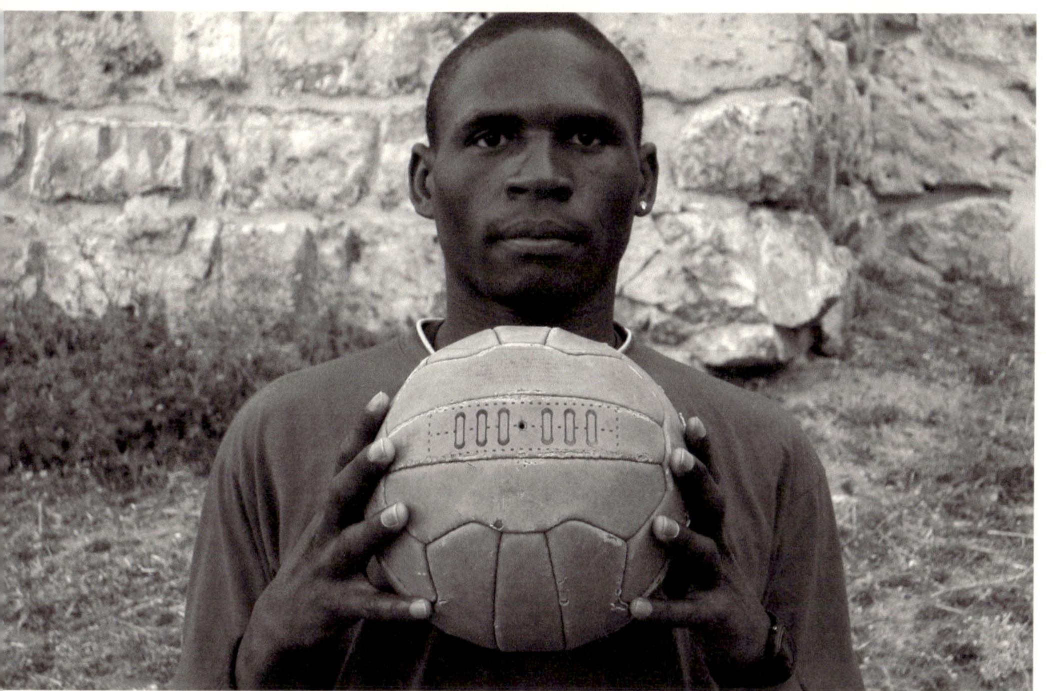

weakened by the journey to Spain. He is proud and tries not to show this. Dewa's only contact in Spain is with the Embassy where he has been able to obtain a passport since arriving in Madrid. He keeps this in the Embassy as he is not in a position to look after it.

Dewa is living in the park and looks after his things, which are few, as well as he can. Dewa is ambitious and is working to rebuild himself in order to move forward in his life and to support his family. He does not think about a partner or children, only about the money he needs to send his family in Cameroon. The cost of his present life is very high, he can trust no one and needs support. He is, however, talented and strong.

GENERAL SHOTS

1. Looking down over the park area from several points of view, from the road down, from the bridge, from the road behind.

2. The park at night, as it gets dark and in the morning, as it gets light, at all times of day.

3. Looking down from Las Vistillas towards the outskirts of the city in the morning and at night.

4. The groups of trees in the park. From above at all times of day. Particularly when they are silhouettes.

5. Details of the things Dewa looks at, for instance the trees in close up, the cars and the lights and doorways at night – all long takes.

6. Views of the sky and Madrid streets at various times of day.

7. Views of people in the park with animals. Views of people in the park sitting, walking, sleeping, etc..

8. Lots of material of the Cameroon park dwellers in their own company doing their daily tasks.

9.   Night time ambience shots of the park, Plaza Major and surroundings.

10. People parking and leaving with cars. Cars coming and going.

Note. We need to know we are in a Spanish city, maybe Madrid, possibly driving with Dewa through the city at night might work for this? General feel but not famous buildings.

MADRID

DEWA – Cameroon football player

MARC – Ghanaian musician with Liberian passport

OTHERS

Cameroon man in park as father

Cameroon girl as girlfriend

Trainer

Couple parking car

Racist girl parking car

People in bathhouse (five or six) including person in charge

Some Cameroon people from park to watch TV in bar

Camera

We only ever see the things relevant to Dewa. Sometimes we do not see whom he is talking to or what he has around, we are not distracted. Dewa is always taller than those around him so we always look up at him.

Sound Notes

Dewa's stories of what happened to him need to be concise and clear. We will need to work with him to create some consistency in this – to create a series of sound sequences that work independent of image for his memories as we may start a memory while something else is on the screen. This is his own story of himself.

We need to cover the following:

His going on board the boat with two bottles of water, etc.. Where he hid on a cargo boat containing hardwood – sounds of wood and boat.

His coming up and seeing the sea for the first time and being terrorised by the bright lights.

His escape from the boat in Portugal and his meeting someone who helped him.

His father's trying to stop him play football.

His mother's getting sick and dying.

His girlfriend's pregnancy and death.

His going to watch football games in a local home and paying to see TV videos of football.

The forest and the pygmies and animals at home.

Helicopters overhead.

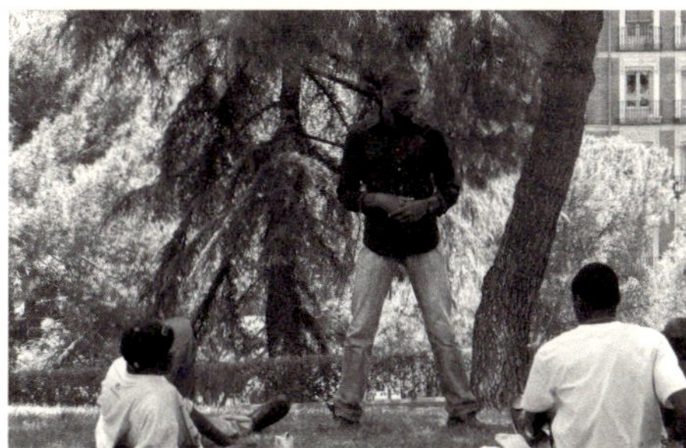

The first time Dewa saw his feet at night was in Europe. The night time city seems as bright as day after the blackness of night in Africa.

We also need lots of ambient sound for different times of day in order to capture the park, as that is mainly where we will be.

SEQUENCES RE-ENTERING PAST EVENTS ARE IN BOLD

1. EXT / PARK / AFTERNOON AROUND 5PM

Mid-shot, close up

Late afternoon light is still warm and bright.

The camera approaches in a car from above winding down the road from the street. To the right is the Cathedral and further away the Palacio Real. The streets are big and imposing but the road winds down into the park below which is green and lush.

A tall African man is parking cars; his manner is helpful but determined. The parking is public and there is no need for an attendant as the spaces are free, but his presence is so strong that he dominates the space.

As the passengers leave the car the man is courteous and polite. He is taller than the people who are paying him to look after their car.

He returns to his post sitting on the grass looking over the park beyond. People pass him by, older men in smart suits, runners, and people walking dogs. He could be in the desert or the country; his presence is that of a country person. (All mid-shot) People pass behind him, things are always moving around him, yet he is very much alone.

CUT TO

The African man moves towards a lower area with a central tree and other Africans resting beneath.

This part of the park is lower than the rest and contains ruins that have been excavated and restored. The place is protected and feels secure and apart from the route there we could be in Africa. We follow the man's route.

We notice the space around Dewa.

CUT TO

(MS)

He moves away from the group and begins to walk towards a street leading off to the right. Dewa sits down under a tree and surveys the ground below him in the park. He is thinking.

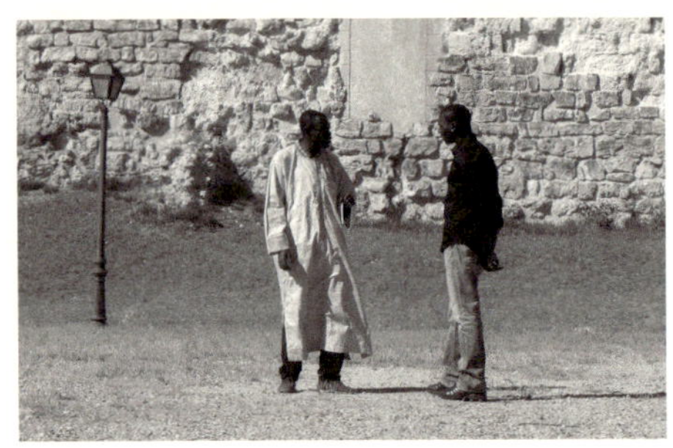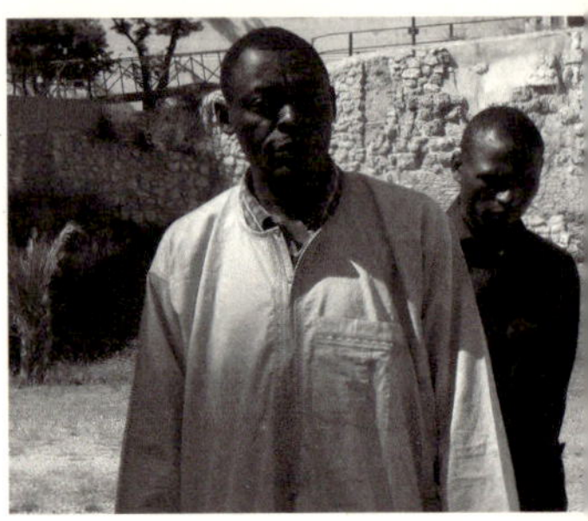

2.   EXT / LOWER IN THE PARK / AFTERNOON

LS, MS, CU

(DEWA'S ACTED SEQUENCES)

Mostly close up. We feel as Dewa is cramped and curled up unable to move, we see bits of body, the tree beside him, the water bottle.

Dewa is under the tree imagining he is on the boat to Spain, he is hidden in a tiny space for ballast in the boat, curled up and only able to move slightly. We know he is there because beside him he has two bottles of water and a half finished packet of biscuits. He takes sips of water every now and again we don't see him touch the biscuits. He remains curled up and furtive.

POV *Dewa.*

In front of him Dewa sees the park moving and people walking their dogs.

Note. Could be shot in extreme close up or out of focus as he is lying down and afraid, everything is very separate to himself. He will be very close to the tree, grass, and ground surfaces.

3.   EXT / PARK BY THE TREE / ONE HOUR LATER

LS

The park is getting dark and people drive away. Lights are beginning to go on. We look up at the bridge above. We have the feeling that Dewa is familiar with this scene of change. Dewa is seen with the other Cameroon people in a group.

It is getting darker, the park dwellers begin to be silhouettes.

Dewa crosses to a door in the wall of the park. He goes into the dark hole in the wall.

He takes out some bread and water in a bottle and begins to eat and to drink. His consumption is noticeably modest. He is always surrounded by space. He disappears again into the door in the wall and brings out a blanket. He crosses over to the tree area.

CUT TO

4.   EXT / UNDER THE TREES / AS IT GETS DARK

LS

Dewa lies down under the trees and goes to sleep. He is silhouetted in the dark space of the park. He is very calm and still. The camera moves around to see the park where people are walking amongst the trees and architecture above.

Close up

Dewa sleeping.

We move up to the trees above and dark night sky with stars.

*Dogs bark in the distance and people walk down the road by the sleepers.
Everything happens slowly.*

CUT TO

*Dewa wakes up during the night, a dog is barking, a couple argue nearby. He sits in
the dark looking out over the park. We realise he is completely alone. He looks at his
hands and examines them, he has his plastic bag beside him, he holds the water
in the bottle but does not drink from it, and we know this is all he has.*

Dark silhouettes, dark shapes and shadows, everything happens slowly.

CUT TO

MS

*A man and woman return to the car Dewa is guarding, they have obviously been out
and had a good time and look over to the place where Dewa is sleeping, they get into
their car and go leaving the place fairly empty of cars, now only the dog walkers are
around and a few couples heading towards the park. Dewa remains asleep.*

CUT TO

5.   EXT / UNDER THE TREES / STILL NIGHT TIME

MS, CU

(DEWA'S ACTED SEQUENCES) (Light from above in Las Vistillas.)

**Dewa wakes up imagining another time. He is hidden in the boat and is coming
up for air. He is where we have seen him before beside the tree on the slope in the
park. He crawls up out of his position leaving his bottle of water and bag of biscuits.**

**He gets up and moves crawling towards the edge of the cars. He gets up holding
onto the handrail of the boat which is tipping with the waves. He looks out and
above him sees a big light beaming down on him. He is terrified and thinks the bad
spirits have finally come to take him away. He quickly ducks and crawls back down,
nobody has seen him and he feels completely alone. He hides again.**

Note. The light is a light from above shining down, placed on the bridge above.

Close up

Dewa's body as he crawls back down from the deck.

It is still dark.

CUT TO

6.   EXT / PARK SLEEPING AREA / VERY EARLY MORNING

*Dewa is already up. He is doing press-ups in an empty space. In his actions one senses
a strictness behind him which is his backbone and strength. As he does them he counts
the number he has done. He goes through a series of routines for training, it is barely*

light. As he finishes he moves upwards along the road and up over the bridge.

POV Dewa as it gets light over the city.

CUT TO

7.   EXT / CENTRE OF THE PLAZA MAJOR / MORNING 6AM

Dewa is seated in the Plaza under the statue in the centre. He is just waiting. Beside him is a carrier bag with his washing things in it. He seems to be in a completely different timeframe to the space around him, the Plaza is completely empty. He takes some bread from his bag and feeds the birds which are gathered there.

(Close up of Dewa throwing the food to the birds.)

Dewa gives all the food to the birds leaving nothing for himself. Why doesn't he keep more for himself?

Dewa closes his eyes and appears to be thinking about his home in Africa.

He talks to himself in his own language, listing the animals in his home, village and the surrounding area.

"If my father hadn't insisted on my getting up so early everyday for 27 years I would still be asleep."

Goats, monkeys, cows, gorillas, lions.

(DEWA'S ACTED SEQUENCES)

Dewa acts out throwing food to the birds as if they were animals in Africa. He has a favourite with a local name and imagines he is there talking to his favourite bird. He uses the empty square as his theatre and gives away all the food he has in his hand.

CUT TO

8.   EXT / STREET TO BATHHOUSE / EARLY MORNING

Dewa turns a corner and descends some steps into a dark doorway.

CUT TO

9.   INT / BATHHOUSE / LATER, STILL EARLY 10AM

Dewa crosses in front of a metal open door. Dewa could not be more different or more separate yet the man who runs the bathhouse greets him with fondness and offers him anything he needs. He obviously has a routine here.

CUT TO

Close up

Dewa is in the shower; he carefully places the soap and towel and washes. He then wraps the towel around himself and begins to wash his clothes. We follow his hands as he crosses his body and as he washes the clothes. Almost black and dim in the shadows, very little light. Dewa is immaculate, careful, clean, meticulous, distanced.

CUT TO

Mid-shot

Camera swings around to the other older Spanish men who look curiously at Dewa.

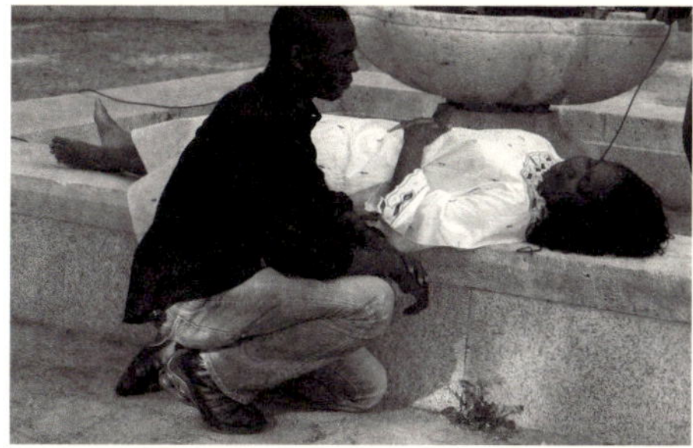

*They are anxious to talk to him but his height and strength make them seem small.
You can see they are wondering about him.*

Podemos audarte en algo?

No gracias, estoy bien.

*One of the men offers him a cigarette but Dewa refuses. He is polite and has obviously
caught the sympathy of the other men there. As he is dressing one of the old men starts
to talk to a friend.*

He venido en barco.

CUT TO

*Dewa is washing his clothes carefully whilst being stared at by the older men.
He has a few things in the bag that he has with him.*

CUT TO

10. EXT / PARK BACK AREA / SLIGHTLY LATER

CU, MS

Dewa is carefully laying out his clothes to dry on the bushes. He has few things and they
are left in the sun to dry.

Note. Shoot as if this were Cameroon.

CUT TO

11. EXT / PARKING CARS / MID-DAY

POV Dewa

*A man gets out of a car that Dewa is assisting in parking. He asks Dewa to look after
his car. He asks him where he is from. Dewa replies – "Cameroon".*

Brief conversation.

CUT TO

POV Dewa

*A woman is parking her car, again Dewa pockets a few coins from the woman and
return to his place watching the cars. As she leaves the woman shouts an insult –*

"Black bastard, you shouldn't be here".

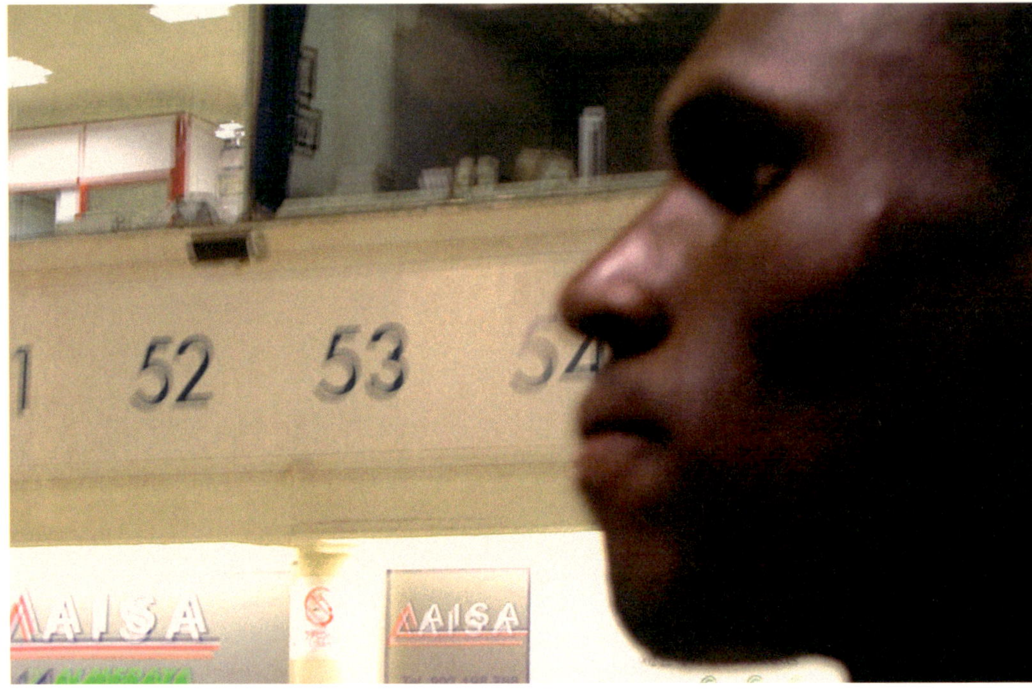

Dewa shrugs his shoulders and fails to react.

CUT TO

A third man holding a sports bag parks his car, Dewa assists him and the man asks him where he is from. He repeats Cameroon and the man says how good the football players are from Cameroon. Dewa's face lights up. He tells him that he used to play football in Cameroon. Note. The flat Plaza is in the background, connects to next scene.

CUT TO

12. EXT / PARK PLAZA / DAY

(DEWA'S ACTED SEQUENCES)

MS, CU, LS

Dewa is standing in the flat Plaza with an older man (representing his father) who wears Cameroon dress. The man tells Dewa he needs to do a normal job, that football is a route to nowhere that he needs to behave better; he pretends to beat him with a stick. Dewa is clear and defiant but says little.

A conversation is recorded as they face one another in confrontation.

CUT TO

13. EXT / OUTSIDE CAMEROON EMBASSY / DAY

Dewa is standing around outside the embassy. He goes inside and emerges carrying a new Cameroon passport. He stops outside and looks at his new passport. This is very obviously the first time he has held a passport.

CUT TO

14. EXT / PARK BY TREES / MID-DAY

(DEWA'S ACTED SEQUENCES)

Dewa says to himself that his father is far away.

Dewa creeps to the edge of the boat that is a car. He looks around and feels his way. He looks around and jumps to the other side of the road as if it were water. He hurts himself in the jump and hobbles away to hide behind another car. We leave him hiding behind a boat(car) as he creeps from one hiding place to the next.

Note. Sound recording of Dewa describing his escape from the boat.

CUT TO

15. EXT / LOCUTORIO / MID-DAY

Dewa takes the money from his pocket and carefully fills in a Western Union form. He counts out 50 euros in change. The woman behind the glass, an African, takes the 200 coins and carefully counts them. Dewa casually mentions that this will keep his family for a month.

The woman behind the desk shows little interest but carries out the order and gives the paper to Dewa.

Close up

Paper showing the address and Dewa's writing.

CUT TO

16. EXT/INT / ESTACION DEL SUR, MADRID / NIGHT TIME 11PM

(DEWA'S ACTED SEQUENCES) MS

Dewa with only a small plastic bag is standing in the bus station. He looks stunned and obviously doesn't know where he is. He sits down on a bench in the bus station for a while. Another African man carrying a drum is passing by. Dewa tries to stop him. The man brushes him off but eventually takes notice of him and stops. He asks the man in French where the park is, the man answers him in Spanish and asks him where he has come from.

Dewa explains that he has got off a boat. He takes out a scrap of paper and draws the boat. He draws the bottom of the boat and himself down in the bottom. The other man introduces himself, his name is Marc and he is from Ghana.

MS *continues*

Marc tells Dewa something of his situation. He was in a military band in Ghana and wanted to be a musician. He escaped from the band and has now bought a Liberian passport of 200 euros. He shows it to Dewa. Dewa seems fresh and innocent. He looks with wonder at this old hand.

Marc helps Dewa with money to aid his trip.

Dewa asks directions to the park and Marc tells him how to get there.

Dewa walks away into the night.

CUT TO

17. EXT / THE PARK / EARLY MORNING

Close up

Dewa wakes up and stretches his aching limbs.

CUT TO

18. EXT / PARK AREA / LATE AFTERNOON

Dewa is exchanging money (15 euros) for a mobile phone. We never see the person who sells it to him, he is irrelevant. Dewa now has a mobile.

He calls to his village after talking to a friend and leaves the number for his father. We never see the transactions, just Dewa and his phone. We realise he is very lonely. His loneliness is obvious.

CUT TO

19. EXT / PARK BY STEPS / EARLY EVENING

(DEWA'S ACTED SEQUENCES)

Dewa becomes his mother. She becomes ill, she is walking and gradually begins to hold her stomach and to talk in her local tongue of being ill.

Dewa's mother is in Dewa's arms. She is very ill.

Another person has taken the place of Dewa as his mother and this time he is nursing the other Cameroon man who seems to be the same person as Dewa and as his mother. Dewa is nursing the man and is talking to his mother. He tells her in his local language that he will take care of his family, that they are his responsibility, that he loves her. She gradually dies.

He tries to wake her; he repeatedly shakes her and tries to give her water from a bowl.

As she dies Dewa gets up and walks out of his imaginary room with his arms above his head. (Cameroon sign of death.)

20. EXT / STREET BY PARK / EARLY EVENING

CU, MS

Dewa sits alone in the park on some steps. He is feeling the loss of his mother he imagines his girlfriend.

CUT TO

21. EXT / PARK SAME PLACE / AS IT GETS DARK

MS, CU

(DEWA'S ACTED SEQUENCES)

Dewa imagines his girlfriend who is pregnant with his baby, She is also in his arms, and this time he imagines her without another person present. She is a reality and she is dying in his arms. He whispers words to her imaginary head and when she dies in his arms he is calm and tranquil. He once again leaves the space with his arms above his head.

This time we leave with him.

Note. He was 14 when he got his girlfriend pregnant so he needs to somehow seem younger in this sequence.

CUT TO

22. EXT / THE PARK / MORNING

The trainer from the day before is getting out of the car (POV man). He looks over at Dewa who is resting under a tree in the middle distance. He goes over and wakes up Dewa who stumbles, awake. The two talk standing. The man offers to take Dewa to play football. Dewa is overcome with emotion and has difficulty understanding the offer.

CUT TO

23. EXT/INT / IN THE CAR THROUGH MADRID / DAY

(Music) POV Dewa

We are in the car behind Dewa who is looking out at Madrid as they drive past government buildings. Dewa looks out through the window and Madrid passes behind him. We look only at Dewa as we listen to the questions that the other man asks him.... The camera doesn't move and stays on Dewa's face as he listens to questions and watches the road. The traffic passes behind; a policeman waves them on, various sites pass behind.

De donde vienes?

Dewa describes his home in the village which is on the border of Cameroon and the Central African Republic. Dewa brings out of his bag a crumpled Cameroon map. He points to the area he came from.

Vienes del lado de CAF, que desastre!

Como sabes los equipos?

Dewa describes going to the village and one person has a TV, the rest pay to enter the hut and watch the matches.

24. INT / FOOTBALL BAR / NIGHT

(DEWA'S ACTED SEQUENCES)

Dewa is in a bar with other park people. They are completely enthusiastic about football. In one moment the men in the bar change to a more innocent stance and as Dewa remembers watching football on video one of them takes on the role of taking money and they all close in together and begin to respond to the football on the TV as if in their village.

Note. This is a mixture of present and past, we will need to improvise.

CUT TO

25. EXT / ENTRANCE METRO WITH ESCALATOR / EARLY EVENING

MS, CU

Dewa is seen coming out of the club and walking away. His appearance is still that of someone in Africa, he is in the street with space around him. As the light goes down he is seen descending an escalator into the Metro in a mixture of artificial and daylight haze.

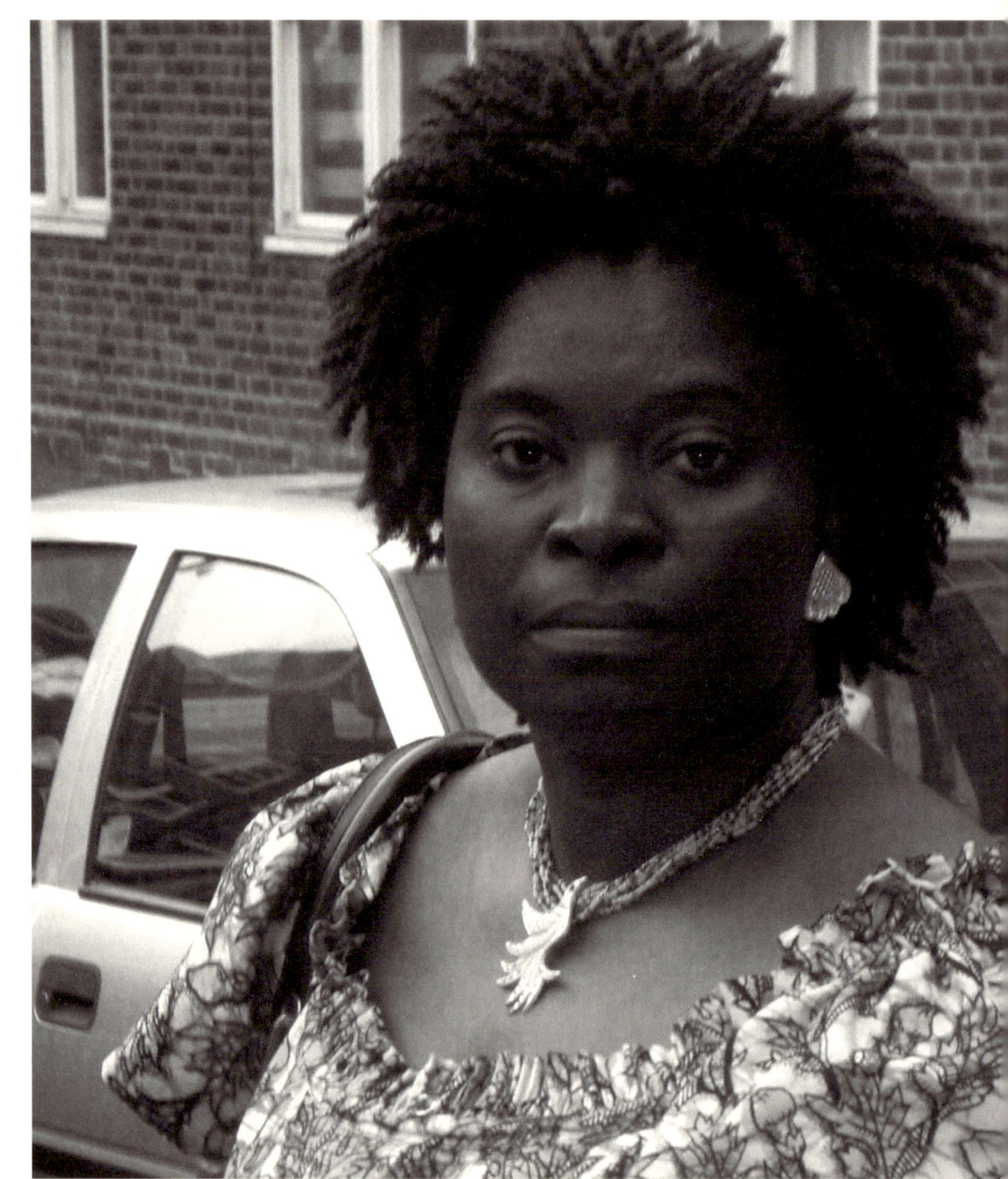

CONSTANTINE'S STORY

The script has been written with Constantine and reflects her experiences; each scene is based on an experience in London. I am the first Caucasian person she has known.

To emphasise in filming.

Constantine's relationship to nature and Africa is through videos and film, Dewa is closer to nature and a sense of time and weather, etc., even washing is a closer experience for him.

Dewa's anxiety is his present, Constantine is answering to a higher order, religion and the preacher.

Dewa is still surrounded by nature in the park, washing and hanging out clothes, sleeping outside, running and feeding the birds....

Dewa's remoteness and distance is like the place he comes from, Constantine's bustling marketplace life is like the place she comes from too....

Dewa regresses into his experiences on the boat, Constantine thinks about her experience of marriage and love, (what is love to Constantine? for Dewa love is his mother).

While Dewa remembers his boat experiences, Constantine lies in bed thinking.

Dewa's personal stuff is his papers, Constantine's personal stuff is her handbag and its contents.

NOTE. LIVES NOT TO BE SEEN ONLY IN SOCIAL TERMS, HUMAN BEINGS DEALING WITH THEIR CONDITION BOTH LOCAL AND GLOBAL

CONSTANTINE'S STORY

Video shop on Ball's Pond Road as it runs into Hackney. The video shop is a dingy store renting and selling African videos of film from all over Africa. The store is run by Magnus a Nigerian who left Nigeria many years ago where he worked as a broadcaster. The video store rents out all kinds of films, from African porno through to comedies and romantic stories made in different African countries. It also has critically acclaimed African films distributed by Magnus to experts in World Cinema. Magnus listens to stories from all kinds of Africans coming into the store, so he is aware of many different aspects of the characters who are his clients. The store is on a busy road where buses going east pass by. There are many abandoned shops around but the area is the centre of vibrant African shops and culture that exist alongside the heavier and less legal storefronts. Magnus is always found in the same place beside his old computer in the back of his dingy store where people come to him. Two young attractive African women help Magnus in the store.

Shots

General – outside shop from other side of the street as cars and buses pass, inside the back of the shop (TV on, rows of videos).

Close ups of rows of evangelical, political, romantic, pornographic, music and art house films.

Magnus' Rolodex of customer names as he flicks through.

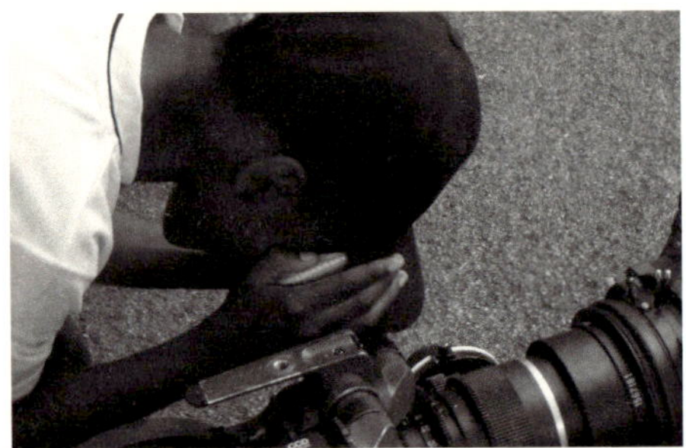

Church is the spiritual centre for Ivory Coast people in London. Preacher Vincent runs it. It is situated on the edge of a small industrial area at the back of Hackney Road. The church has a blue sign outside telling the seemingly empty surrounding that it is "The Place of Victory". A canal runs nearby. The church is in the basement of the building. The space is white; the lectern the preacher uses is made of modern Perspex with red lettering. There are about 120 seats and the space is packed during the meetings, lighting is fluorescent tubing.

Shots

Close ups of trailing plastic flowers, the Perspex lectern, in service angles of bodies, hands raised, bibles with notations, clothing of pastor and women, people in relation to one another.

Market seen from the entrance and once entered is a vibrant, busy and a culturally diverse place. Goods are displayed as they would be in their countries of origin creating a collage effect through the market. There are items that seem completely foreign and strange for instance a cardboard box of live snails each snail being around nine inches long. Clothing stores from Ghana are filled with Dutch fabric in strong patterns. There are exotic and multicoloured fish on stalls; smaller rather empty stalls contain plantain, whitish grains, and tinned foods. Small stalls do complicated African hairstyles; others sell music from diverse sources. Lots of the stalls have evangelical religious messages and banners. There is a stall run by another man from the Ivory Coast selling hundreds of different phone cards giving different rates for African calls.

Shots

General – texture of people and the market from above, individual stalls and their music, clothes, each is a territory.

Close Up – food (fish, plantain, white grains, tins, snails, hair, music stall, African calling cards).

Cafe is a small African cafe hidden in a side street in Dalston. The food is heavy solid food served in big quantities. The people going there eat as if at home in Africa, they choose particularly tasty bits of animal intestine and big amounts of rice or other grains. Lines form during busy times of the day whilst the market is going on.

Shots

General – line of men waiting to be served in conversation, the kitchen, the back room.

Close ups of food being served.

Apartment where Constantine lives with her family in Hackney. She lives in a series of small inter-connected rooms. The flat is heavily barred from the outside with a narrow open balcony running from the corridor and staircase to the apartment door. The inside is cheerful and bright with a few objects and images.

Shots

The pink sofa, the balcony and flats beyond, the situation of the flat in general,
from the outside.

ONE WEEKEND...

1.   INT / VIDEO SHOP / FRIDAY MID-DAY

*The camera sees a woman looking intently at the videos on sale. With her another
younger woman is also staring at the videos on sale. We are so close to the women
and the videos that we don't notice anything but the atmosphere around them.
They are talking in French and the camera circles the women, they move towards
the lines of videos.*

*The camera, hand held, follows Constantine as she selects the videos and carries them
to the desk to pay.*

*The shop looks dark and the titles are dull until we read them, … Martin Luther King,
Love Stories from Africa, Nelson Mandela, Malo Sago, …*

*All kinds of religious stuff. Several people pass her in the background, glimpses
of them before her.*

*At the desk Magnus, the video shop owner, takes the videos and the camera follows
him as he moves into the back room to get the copies and returns them to Constantine.
While he is getting them, her eyes stray to the pornographic videos on the shelf beside
the counter. We don't have any idea what she thinks of them. POV Constantine.*

We are always very close to her so just her head and a bit of clothing are visible.

*No real conversation takes place but she is friendly with the video store owner who
greets her and asks her how she is doing. They chat about the films for a while.*

CUT TO

2.   EXT / BLOCK OF FLATS / 7.30PM

*Constantine walks across the courtyard of her block of flats. We are aware of the fading
light and the architecture. The architecture is shadowy and not really distinct.*

*We watch her pass as she heads into the block, the bricks forming a backdrop to her.
She looks like an exotic butterfly in the dull surroundings or a woman in a village
in Africa, her walk is slow and considered. She is carrying the videos.*

3.   INT / CONSTANTINE'S FLAT / EVENING

*A film passes before Constantine's eyes. Constantine and her son are watching
an African film − both are silent. We are only aware of Constantine and her son
and the film, the room is only a shadowy presence. Constantine is wearing another
dress, 'a relaxed at home' but very traditional African dress. She talks to her son
in French explaining to him things about the film. She never mentions either her
husband or family only her country. The camera circles around them refusing to
be still. In the film we see African stories and an African landscape. It is a complete
contrast to where we are.*

POV *Constantine,* POV *Brian to mother.*

FADE TO

<u>**4.** INT / BEDROOM / NIGHT</u>

*Constantine is lying in bed preparing to sleep. She is thinking about things.
Her eyes are open.*

CUT TO

<u>**5.** INT / BATHROOM / NIGHT TIME</u>

*Constantine is sitting on the loo. She is thinking. She is praying for the safe return
of her husband. She is missing him. Her prayers are in French.*

CUT TO

<u>**6.** INT / SITTING ROOM / EARLY MORNING</u>

*There is a knock on the door of the flat. Constantine is dressed in her best clothes
for church and getting herself looking good. Her son too is dressed up. She looks
nervous and worried but she goes to answer the door. A man stands there with two
big boxes for her. They are full of African food, he brings them in and she begins to open
them. For a minute it might be her husband but it isn't. We are in the middle of the
corridor looking out at the man and then he walks past us through the tiny space
into the kitchen.*

Camera follows Constantine as a piece of Africa has just arrived on her doorstep.

CUT TO

<u>**7.** EXT / CHURCH BUILDING AND OVAL / 10AM</u>

LS

*Constantine, her son and sister are in the street. They walk towards the church and greet
others as they walk in. Other family groups include men, Constantine is proud and her
clothing is magnificent as she moves towards the inside. She is with her son and sister
as they greet people.*

CUT TO

<u>**8.** INT / CHURCH SPACE / 10.30AM</u>

*People are close together, they sing and dance moving rhythmically, they pray together
and the service really takes off, it's more like a party, the preacher leads the service,
he has a strong male presence. The whole event is really loud.*

The camera concentrates on Constantine's prayers.

*Texture of bodies, hair and actions. The room marks the space, a white box. Constantine
prays for the safe return of her husband. The preacher prays for problems with the home,
office, for the queen, princes....*

POV Constantine, POV Vincent.

CUT TO

<u>**9.** INT/EXT / BUS / LATE AFTERNOON SUNDAY</u>

Close up

*Constantine sits on the bus looking out of the window, we don't know anything about
what is going on in her head, and she looks lonely but not unhappy.*

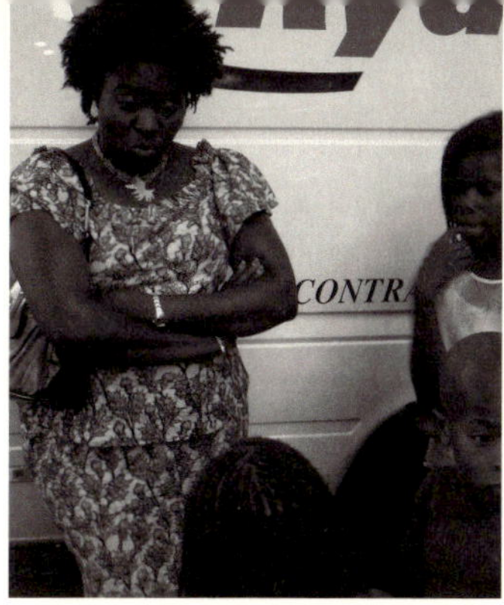

The surroundings pass behind her giving constant movement to the screen. We never see any of the other people on the bus. Constantine takes a mirror and looks in it, she checks the time on her watch, she gazes to the outside, she checks an address in her address book.

CUT TO

10. INT / PREACHER'S FLAT AND CORRIDOR / 6PM

There is an amazing long corridor off which lies the entrance to the flat where the preacher lives. We watch as Constantine walks away from us silhouetted against the corridor that seems to swallow her up.

CUT TO

A conversation is in progress in Vincent's flat. Constantine prays first with the preacher for the solution to her problems. Next there is a conversation between Vincent and Constantine.

Constantine explains her problems, that her husband has not called, that he is away on a course, that she is worried about him. Vincent is calm and refers to sentences in the bible....

Each question that the preacher asks, Constantine answers. We see that she is straightforward, forceful, a match for anyone.

Constantine says:

"He's due back tonight...."

Plano contra plano.

CUT TO

11. EXT / CONSTANTINE'S FLAT / AS IT GETS DARK

Constantine is standing looking out over the blocks of flats. She leans on her balcony. She is watching for figures in the semi-darkness. We are aware both of her figure and her awareness as she looks around her, but we don't know exactly what for. The other flats are a patterned background behind her. We understand this is her home; Africa seems a long way away.

Camera follows her gaze.

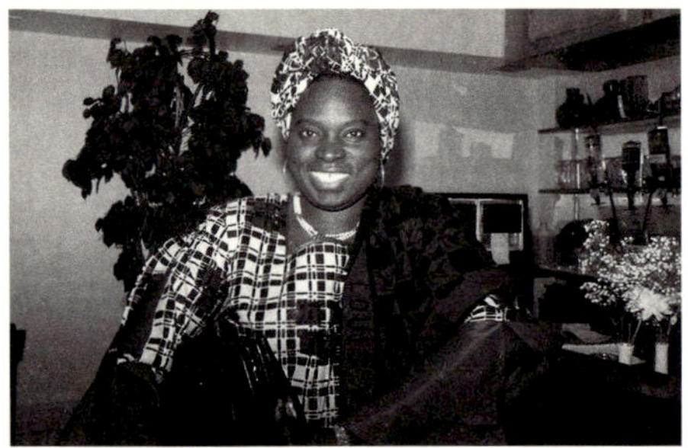

12. INT / CONSTANTINE'S FLAT / NIGHT

Mid-shot, close up

We view the chaos of the small room.

We follow the actions of the two sisters as they pack and unpack clothes.

A suitcase lies open and the bright colours of clothes are strewn around.

Constantine and her sister are packing things to take back to Africa and piling up clothes to sell. A knock on the door brings another man with shoes to bring back to Africa. Constantine crosses and re-crosses the space as she goes in and out of the room.

As she crosses the room she picks up a small torn piece of paper, on it is written her name. She puts it to one side.

As they sort the clothes Constantine finds another small piece of paper with a word on it.

CUT TO

13. INT / FLAT SITTING ROOM / EVENING

Constantine and her sister are putting together the puzzle of the piece of paper. The finished paper reads as an unfinished letter.

Constantine's husband is leaving her for a woman who lives in New York.

All close up

CUT TO

DREAM SEQUENCE

14. INT AND FILM / BEDROOM / NIGHT

Constantine is in bed in her blue room. We see her eyes shut, crumpled clothes and bed linen.

FADE TO

We are looking at a sequence from one of Constantine's films. In the film a woman is forced to betray the man she loves for the man's father. African landscape fills the screen.

FADE TO

During the night Constantine gets up, goes to the kitchen pours herself a glass of water and drinks it. We leave her before she gets back into bed.

She passes the camera, which stays close to her as she drinks and returns to bed.

CUT TO

15. INT / SITTING ROOM / EARLY MORNING

We are close to Constantine as she is on the phone.

*She is calling her husband's boss's office. She speaks to the receptionist first.
The receptionist tells Constantine that her husband is not there, he is on holiday.
She puts down the phone. She picks it up again, she waits and asks to speak to her
husband's boss, Mr Wright. Mr Wright comes on the phone and she asks him very
correctly where is her husband.*

*(Slightly wider shot) We barely see Constantine's face throughout this, just her body
as she moves around and its as if she is confronting something but at the same time
avoiding being seen doing so.*

He went on holiday Mrs Diomade.

(Voice while we look at the wall, POV Constantine.)

But he can't have done that, he was on a course.

You know me; you can tell me if you needed him to go somewhere.

*But Mrs Diomade this is what he told me. He is due back in the morning. I hope there
isn't a problem.*

She puts the phone down.

CUT TO

16. EXT / MARKET / A LITTLE LATER

*We have picked Constantine out in the crowd. She is shopping for food in the market.
We have our eyes on her face as she scans the food. Her hands skillfully handle snails,
plantain, African sorghum.*

*Her face tells us nothing about her. We see her framed against various small shops,
for fabric, for clothes, for food, for music.*

*She calmly shops for a phone card from a small stall. The countries where she might
call are outlined around her head on the posters as she purchases the card. She has
a conversation with the guy who sells phone cards. Both are from the Ivory Coast, they
talk as if in a village, each asks about the other, their kids their marriages. Constantine
replies guardedly to each question. A solid conversation takes place where each tells
their story. Suddenly Constantine is angry and out of control, it's the first time we see
the effect of the last 24 hours on her.*

MUSIC FROM THE MARKET STALLS

CUT TO

17. INT / THE VIDEO STORE / AFTERNOON

*Constantine confesses her home situation to Magnus. She is tense and open.
She speaks in English. Magnus listens and tells her he can help.*

Mid-shot, not too intimate

CUT TO

18. INT / THE RESTAURANT / AFTERNOON

Constantine looks at the videos with her son. They choose piles of meat; intestines and thick sauces fill their plates. Constantine's son says nothing about the father, they eat together. He stares at the men in the shop and the way they eat their food. The men are full of camaraderie.

Constantine's son talks to his mother as if he is the man of the house. Constantine confesses to her son that her own father had four wives and that her mother was not happy about it. She also shows her son his father's passport that she says she now will look after.

Camera looks at them face on together, one shot as they talk.

CUT TO

19. EXT / BALCONY FLATS / EVENING

LS

Constantine is looking down over the square of grass below where her son is playing football with loads of kids from the surrounding blocks. There are only two white kids in a sea of children from lots of different places (clothes, hair, etc.). Constantine scans the scene looking also at the windows beyond where there are a few signs of different people occupying the flats.

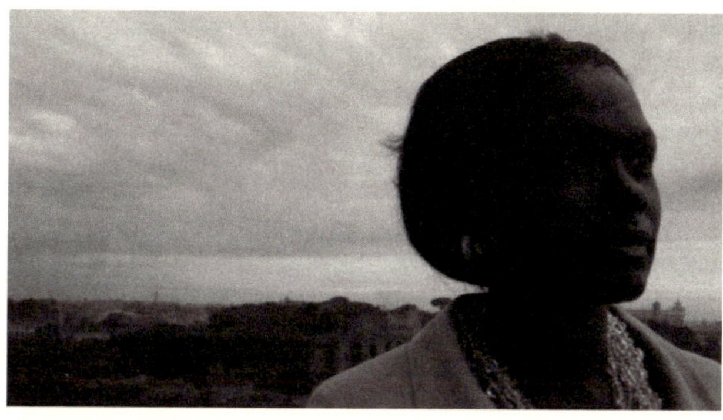

PAMELA'S STORY

BACKGROUND

Pamela comes from a large Ugandan family. She is in her early to mid-30s. She is married to an Italian diplomat and has three children, all quite young, and has lived in Japan, Italy and Paris.

Pamela grew up in Uganda in an educated family, her father was persecuted by the regime of Amin and during that time she lived in the family home in the village of Lale in the district of Soroti in Uganda. Later she was sent to a boarding school where she says she learnt to manage the social side of the world. She is consequently polite, careful and well organised in her life. Her family is extensive, her father had several wives of whom her mother was the second, the later wives did not remain part of the family and her relationship with her mother is distant and formal. She says this is because she spent much of her childhood in boarding school. Her many brothers and sisters live at different economic levels, from some living in the village and remaining fairly poor to diplomats living in the United States. Pamela studied social sciences at university in Uganda where she was crowned Miss Uganda University. Through her title she was introduced to her Italian husband Marco Sylvia who was working at the Italian University. She married him in Italy and says that at her wedding were the whole Italian side of the family, maybe 50 people and just her and one of her sisters from her African family.

Because of her very extensive family in Uganda, with many brothers and sisters from different mothers, she is expert at managing these different levels of social intercourse.

Pamela has three children Matteo (Okedi), Guido (Obyara) and Glulia (Lyudu).

Pamela's relationship with her Italian family is complex. Her husband's parents are separated and her mother in law, Luciana, remains distant and she feels she is a disappointment to her, she rarely visits them and does not take on a strong family role. Pamela believes this is because she is African and her children are therefore part African. Her father in law, Hugo, has quite a different attitude, they pass their holidays in Italy with Hugo who works in the Italian courts as a conciliator. Pamela feels she can talk to him about anything.

Pamela works for the Food and Agriculture Organisation (FAO, part of the UN) as a Junior Program Officer in Rome and has been travelling back and forth between Paris and Rome during the week taking her baby with her and leaving her other children in Paris with their father where he has been posted in the diplomatic service. She is completely dedicated to the idea of working and can imagine nothing worse than her role as a purely

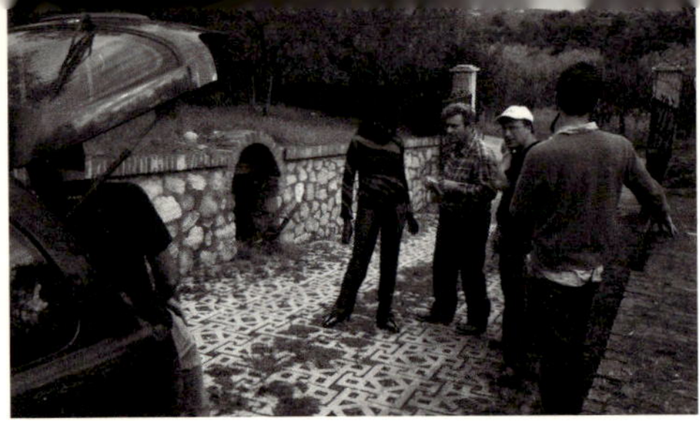

diplomatic wife. She says that she would not be taken seriously in her husband's social world unless she had a job and that socially she is completely passed over unless she works and can be seen to have a function outside the home. Her husband seems to support her in this.

She has worked hard to remain true to her ideas about how her life should remain, for instance when she was in Japan she raised $70,000 US and built a school for her village (including houses and a structure for this to operate with future planning – animals, provision to feed the students, house staff and so on). She traces her dedication back to the memory of her time in the village when her life there gave her stability.

She also admits to an enormous level of discipline, determination and ambition and has embraced this project with enthusiasm.

During their time in the village the family would listen for the sound of cars, any cars entering the village would mean the presence of army people who often came to search for her father. At the sound of cars her father would run into the bush to hide and would remain there hours, days, weeks or months depending on the danger level. Pamela also admits she is excessively careful for her own children, not liking to let them out of her sight and always being excessively aware of their safety. When her father could not earn money because of the situation her mother often lamented the fact that she did not work and had given up everything because they had no way of getting money. Her mother now manages village properties and a cinema which they own and she has as a way of getting money. Her father died some years ago.

Because through tradition her father had several families Pamela was born only when he was 50 years old and is probably one of the last to have had the benefit of a strong relationship with him.

Pamela is now building a house in the village to enable her to take her family to visit her own country. She discusses the way she is doing this with her father in law who advises her about how to avoid conflict with her past, for instance by giving the work not to her family but to contractors. Pamela is also very aware that she is the potential source of money for her whole family, she says that any African living in Europe has this problem and that it is part of her identity. She has strict guidelines for the way she spends money, for instance never giving money for luxuries such as radios but only if the money will help to make her family more self-sufficient. Whilst I was in her house she had a row with her younger sister, who lives in Rome and depends on her, about the phone bills she was running up. She also lamented the fact that her sister has many friends and she had few because she has also worked so hard to keep her situation together that she has little time for them.

NOTES FOR FILMING

We will always film Pamela in relation to her environment, including her in each shot with the exception of places where everything works from her POV and the flashbacks where she sees shadow images and night time shots. We often see particular parts of her body, her hair and hands are expressive, her body is long and she is tall. We look slightly up at her much of the time. The flashback scenes where she looks back at her childhood are hand held and often seen as shadowy and quite impressionistic.

ARCHITECTURE

Whereas Dewa is seen in relation to nature and he lives close to it, Constantine in relation to the decayed modernism we associate with much of the inner city, Pamela is living and working in the structures that control today. She walks through modern spaces, she eats in a UN canteen, she moves through the world. Although as is obvious in the video she made herself of her village it is as primitive and basic as the other two protagonists'. Her memories also include conflict and loss that in some way needs to be portrayed through the architecture. Ironically, through distance from her background, she has regained a controlling attitude to nature and is contributing to change.

CONNECTIONS TO DEWA AND CONSTANTINE

Flashback night time scenes with car coming towards us and away connect to Dewa's climbing onto the deck of the boat.

Connection to Sc 8

Looking at Pamela's hands as she thinks about things connects to Dewa as he sits and thinks in various places, Pamela is sitting at a desk, eating, holding papers in a strong bureaucratic environment, Dewa is in the park holding papers, thinking about his predicament as he sits in the station, Constantine as she talks to the preacher about her problems.

Connection to Sc 4

Pamela takes a shower, this is where she thinks about her life. This is also where Dewa thinks about his life.

Connection to Sc 14

Constantine reads and refers to the bible, this is her written material and the reference she has to written language. She also shows a photo to her son in the restaurant.

Dewa reads his birth certificate and paperwork that he always keeps with him.

Pamela reads in the newspaper in the canteen at work. She also reads official papers with stamps and signatures and tends to emails.

Connection to Sc 5

Dewa watches football on TV in the bar.

Constantine watches a film on TV showing the street life of Africa and a boy the age of her son.

Pamela watches a video of her family in the village. This is her brother who lives

in a round grass roofed house set on bare earth. It is Pamela's mother who is opening the school building in the country village, that Pamela funded with external support. The method for watching the material is the same, what Pamela is watching is more basic and nearer to nature than the others, she re-connects to her roots.

Connection to Sc 10.1

Pamela drives a car in the city, Dewa walks, Constantine takes the bus.

Connection to Sc 15

Dewa carries a bottle of water with him and sips it with caution. Constantine drinks at night in her kitchen. Pamela also carries water but with a different connotation.

Connection to Sc 4, 5

Dewa looks at the trees and wood during his flashback as they pass before his eyes. Constantine looks at moving water which moves below her as the Thames tide ebbs and flows. Pamela watches the sky as planes fly across.

Connection to Sc 17

Constantine shops in the market, Dewa looks at people buying water, Pamela buys things at the local store and converses with Italian shopkeepers.

Connection to Sc 11

CAST

Pamela – central protagonist

Pamela's sister Sylvia – 25 year old pretty, playful, also plays Pamela as a child in the bush when her father has to hide, Pamela preparing for boarding school

Pamela's boss – white male? Or white female?

Pamela's father – (appears as a shadow but in traditional dress)

Hugo – Pamela's father in law

Pamela's children as voices – **Matteo, Guido, Glulia**

Others – security guard FAO

– people in lift FAO

– people in canteen FAO

LOCATIONS

1. Food and Agriculture Organisation, Rome.
   The building is a big serious Italian piece of modern architecture, full of open spaces and vistas. It has the 'UN' look of officialdom and stature. There are desks and security, various floors with open vistas and plenty of glass and dark stone.

2. Country house of Hugo. Very informal place with messy garden one hour out of Rome. Hugo is a senior figure who is very accepting of his daughter in law

and this is where we will shoot the scenes outside the city. His house is basic
and not luxurious.

3.   Fields and open space near to Hugo's house. (Scenes for Pamela's father's escape.)

4.   Stairwell of Pamela's apartment building. A modern 1960s designed wide stairwell,
very light and pleasurable to look at.

5.   Where Pamela is staying.

1.   INT/EXT / STREET BY FAO / EARLY MORNING

Mid-shot, close up

*We are following Pamela as she approaches the Food and Agriculture Organisation
building in Rome. A landmark modern building. We look at her from behind as she
walks towards the building and enters through the main door immediately preparing
to pass through security. We are close to her and have no distance from her body
just watching her head as the different backgrounds pass behind her.*

CUT TO

2.   INT / FAO MAIN HALL SECURITY / MORNING A FEW MOMENTS LATER

CU

All staying very close to Pamela we don't see her yet from a distance.

*Pamela greets the security guards with familiarity and we watch as she puts her bag
on the belt to go through the machine. She deals with each person formally and with
politeness. We watch as she passes through various aggressively swinging doors.*

She is dressed prettily and adventurously but not expensively.

CUT TO

*She walks across the huge hallway eventually she walks into the distance and we see her
silhouetted against the large modern interior space. This is the first time she appears in
silhouette against the large space.*

CUT TO

3.   INT / LIFT / MORNING A FEW MOMENTS LATER

CU

*Pamela is entering the lift moving with care and precision. We are back in close to her
as the lift doors open and she enters then turns around to face the door where she will
exit. She keeps her official work face clearly there as she greets a colleague and
goes up to the floor on which she works. We are aware of each person in the lift.
Pamela is polite but distant to each who comes in.*

CUT TO

4.   INT / PAMELA'S OFFICE / LATER IN THE MORNING

MS, CU

*Pamela is at her desk working at papers. She has a glass and bottle of water next to her.
We look with her at the detailed plans for African development, very much the official
vision of the needs of rural communities.*

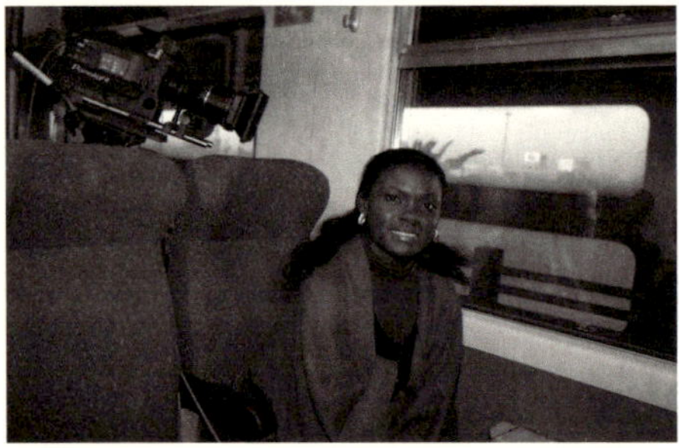

Pamela

"If they would just give me the money I could do the whole project in a year and save them money. I built the school in my village for $70,000 US, classrooms, houses for the teachers, animals...."

We concentrate on the papers and on the voices coming at her about all the different things she needs to do.

POV *Pamela*

The papers include the heading of the FAO and any number of stamps.

A white colleague enters the office with another batch of papers and coolly observes her as they communicate formally face to face about the job in hand. We are aware that Pamela both commands respect and has to earn more each time. She is sitting down at her desk, he is standing beside the desk looking down at her.

The white colleague is clear and also very polite in their slightly surreal interchange. He requests various things and then walks away. As he walks away she gets up and walks over to a printer away from us. She walks away and out of the room.

(Note. Look at barmaid in *Fear Eats the Soul.)*

CUT TO

5.   INT / CANTEEN / LUNCHTIME

MS, CU

Pamela is walking towards us across the canteen. On her tray are a big plate of rice and a salad and water, nothing else.

We see her in silhouette against the canteen space and the others sitting there, they are distant and out of focus. She takes a place beside the window and takes a newspaper from her bag. She props this up on the table in front of her and prepares to read and eat at the same time.

We focus on her intake of the news. POV *Pamela.*

She looks at the economic pages and at the African news pages. We zero in on the words and images she is looking at.

CUT TO

*We look out across Rome taking in details, we move back and forward across the paper and out into the room and looking down onto Rome slowly the scene loses focus until it is just landscape shapes (*POV *Pamela).*

CUT TO

FLASHBACK

NOTE. Pamela plays her mother and her sister plays Pamela.

6.   EXT / COUNTRY ROAD / AFTERNOON

There is the sound of cars in the distance. The sound of a mother calling to her children and shadows on the wall.

The shadow of a woman pushing people out of the way moves across the picture. The wall is a white flat wall we could be anywhere.

"Look for your father, run and find him he has to go, quickly....

I think he went over to the school.

Well go and find him there and tell him to go into the bush Pamela...."

The shadows show a woman in traditional dress and a young girl.

There are more shadows on the wall and a loud knock on a wooden door. We see textures and shadows and the profile of an African woman slowly moving across in the shadows.

African woman in traditional dress – Pamela.

Pamela as teenager – Sylvia.

Woman's African dress, teenager's clothes 80s Africa style.

CUT TO

7.   EXT / IN THE MIDDLE OF THE FIELDS / LATE AFTERNOON LIGHT IS GOING

LS, MS, CU

We listen to heavy breathing and rustling on the ground and a distant view of the road and sound of cars. As the light disappears we just see the lights of the cars coming towards us. POV Pamela's father. We see the lights and outlines of buildings. All happening in very slow motion, the car slowly moving away along the dark road.

Pamela's father – clothes, trousers and shirt and shoes.

Cars in the distance.

Possible outside lighting.

CUT TO

8.   EXT / ROUGH ROAD AS THE LIGHT DROPS / EARLY EVENING

LS, MS

We watch the shadow of a man as he walks along a rough road, he is furtive and careful, and we can see this from the shadow we don't need to see the man. We observe the scene carefully and slowly, we are in another time.

Pamela

"I must be aware somehow of what my father went through."

CUT TO

9. INT / PAMELA'S OFFICE / AFTERNOON

MS, CU

Pamela is sitting in her office moving papers around.

Pamela files papers and listens to her answer phone, messages are left by her children, by her mother, by her husband each with a report on their part of the world, the weather, the politics, the jobs. Pamela listens whilst filing pieces of paper as she goes. The tools of her trade seem to be the computer, the filing cabinet, the telephone, the paper pile, a large map behind her reminds us that her job is in relation to Africa and African issues. At one moment we see the cabinet, the computer, the map and the phone surrounding Pamela as she works.

CUT TO

10. EXT / CAFE BY RUINS / EVENING LOW DAYLIGHT

MS, CU

Sylvia's phone is sitting in the middle of the table, it goes off several times but no one answers it.

Pamela is having a strong conversation with her sister; we break into the middle of the conversation where Pamela's sister is sulkily stirring her drink whilst Pamela gives her a dressing down. Pamela says that she unable to keep paying the bills for her sister, the mobile phone bill is too much for her and she needs to save money. She says that she does not have the kind of life of leisure that her sister has, she has not saved money and she is working at a useless job.

Pamela goes on to tell her sister that she went through her whole life to create a good future for her whole family and she needs to get a sense of reality. Her sister just sits and listens, she fiddles with things, she looks around mainly she looks at Pamela.

Both women play with their hands. Pamela drinks water while her sister drinks Coca-Cola. All Pamela's pent up feelings of injustice and her clarity are present, she is powerful and the parent to her sister.

Pamela

"I have never had the kind of social life you had, I have always had to work, to make our father proud of us, the trouble was that he was too old by the time you were born...."

"You know I never give money for luxury things. In the village I do not pay for radios or things like that but if my brother has a plan to make money then I will help."

"And even when I was Miss Uganda University I worked hard in the University on my degree in order to make progress and not to stay in one place."

The camera looks back at Sylvia who looks at the camera. Rome is behind her.

CUT TO

FLASHBACK

Filmed from the TV of video footage shot by Pamela in her village.

PAMELA IS IN HER VILLAGE. THE CAMERA IS UNSTEADY, FOLLOWING CHILDREN AROUND ON THE GROUND AS THEY STAND AND LOOK AT THE CAMERA.
Her brother is there too dressed in traditional clothing and looking at the camera.

The film shows round traditional huts and children running free.

We see the outline of the television but not the room or the context, it could be either Pamela or her sister watching.

11. INT / SMALL GROCERY SHOP / EVENING

Pamela stops by a small and old-fashioned grocery store to buy groceries looking along the shelves for simple healthy things to eat. She enters the shop, looks around, the man in the grocery store stares a little and treats her politely. As she stares at the goods she looks along the shelves. There is only a very polite connection between them. The shop is the most traditional thing we have seen in Rome. Pamela comments on her husband's latest posting abroad to the shopkeeper. We look with Pamela at the food on the shelves. She pays with a credit card and leaves keeping her distance and a space around her.

CUT TO

12. EXT / ROME STREET NEAR APARTMENT / EVENING

LS, MS

We see Pamela walking towards her apartment. She looks busy even at night but she walks in a relaxed and confident way as if she knows the city well. She carries a small bag of groceries through the gathering darkness.

13. INT / INTERIOR APARTMENT SPACE / EVENING

CU

We are beside Pamela as she stands by the window talking to her children on the phone. They are elsewhere in Belgium where her husband has been posted. We see her at an angle, not directly, and she looks emotional as she asks them about their day and talks to them about what she is doing. The camera stays fixed on her a long time before moving off to look at the sky outside which is almost black.

CUT TO

13.1 INT / PAMELA'S BEDROOM / EVENING

FLASHBACK

Her sister for this flashback plays Pamela.

A shadow of a young girl beside a bed is seen putting things into a suitcase in an institutional setting. Just the bed head and the shadow of the girl piling things into a suitcase, all are shadowy and we are sure that the girl is Pamela but see no features. She picks up a glass of water, drinks from it, and continues to pack, then heaves the suitcase off the bed, climbs into bed and settles down to sleep.

The camera moves little, just following the shadows.

Voice-over Pamela

"My relationship with my mother is formal, I was sent to boarding school in Kampala and so I didn't see my mother often."

CUT TO

14. INT / DOMESTIC SPACE / MORNING

CU

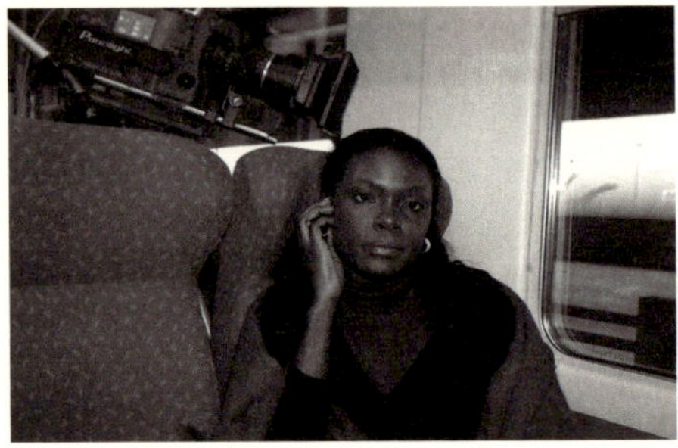

Pamela takes off her clothes and moves into the shower. She is behind a glass screen as she washes thoroughly keeping her hair dry. She talks and sings to herself as she washes, we see her from the shoulders up as she steps out wrapped in a towel framed in the doorway she is distantly organising her day.

CUT TO

Pamela is leaving the flat in a different outfit to the previous day. We see her as she descends the modern 60s Italian designed apartment staircase. The staircase winds downward and Pamela is carrying her travel bag as she leaves the door.

CUT TO

15. EXT / CAR / MORNING

CU, MS

Pamela is arriving at Hugo's house.

Through the car window we see Hugo come out of his house to greet her as climbs out of the car. We are in the countryside and away from Rome, the space reminds us of Africa.

Pamela's head outlined against a country background of soft brown colours.

CUT TO

16. EXT / GARDEN OF HUGO'S HOUSE / LATE AFTERNOON

CU, MS

Pamela's head outlined against kitchen wall in the background. Hugo faces her in the kitchen of his messy house. The scene is intimate but bare.

Pamela talks to Hugo about her children and marriage, her need to return to Africa, the way the whole family need money over there. She talks to Hugo about her plan to build a house in the village. He tells her to keep the project away from her family, to employ a contractor. She wonders if her absent husband will ever come there. Hugo acts as parental figure. The main thing is their enjoyment of the relationship.

She shows Hugo pictures of the school that she has built and of her mother at the opening of the school. She mentions her hiding during the time she was in the village; she says that she doesn't have a picture of her father.

17. EXT / FIELDS / LATE AFTERNOON

LS

Pamela and Hugo are walking in the fields around his house. Pamela looks at home.

We see them only in the distance, earth surrounding them.

CUT TO

18. EXT / SPECIAL OUTSIDE SPACE / A FEW MINUTES LATER

MS

Pamela is saying goodbye.

*She leaves the scene by telling Hugo she is off to Brussels to spend time with
her children and her husband.*

19. INT/EXT / RAILWAY TO AIRPORT / EARLY EVENING

LS,MS,CU

*Pamela is seated in an empty railway carriage on her way to the airport. She looks out at the
Rome signage and the crossing and uncrossing railway tracks, she is almost black against the
darkening outside which passes through the industrial suburbs of Rome and we get the clear
feeling she is tired of the effort she is making.*

SHOOTING SCRIPT FOR SHOOT WITH
GYPSY COMMUNITY IN LA MINA

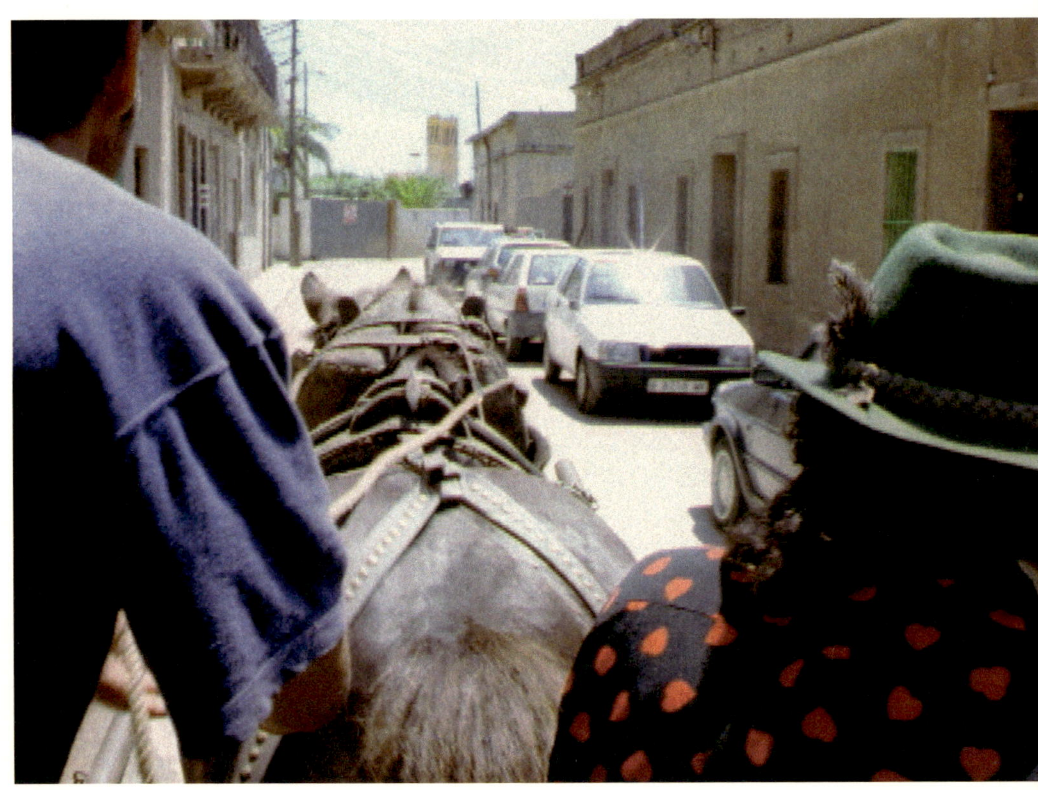

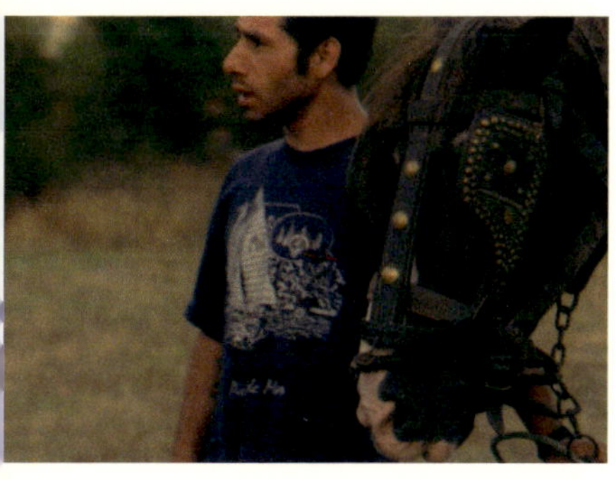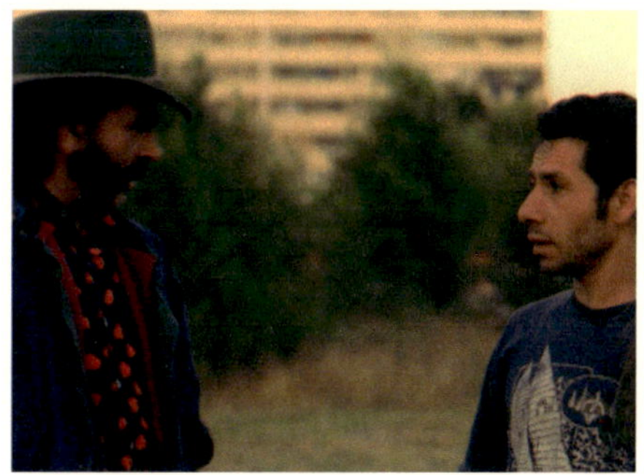

GENERAL

How stories are told/relationship of gypsies to architecture/structures

Script is made up of events which are half fiction/half real. All the characters throughout are gypsies, playing themselves; some characters play a combination of several other characters or are in situations that have happened to someone else.

There are very few pre-planned speeches, mainly overheard conversation and scenes where a room is left for improvisation. (Example: where Tio Emilio talks to the camera about why a gypsy will rip his shirt at the sight of the traditional stained sheet during a wedding.) There are six films each ten minutes, total time around one hour.

The stories told are real things that happen to the gypsies in their lives which I have witnessed or which they have told me about. As gypsies can be very dramatic in real life, these things affect their lives absolutely in the moment. (Example: when Antonio's horse is stolen, he becomes hunched, moody, distraught, drunk and stays alone.) There is also the possibility of exploring possibilities dramatically as filming takes place and therefore script is an outline to be filled in at times by the characters.

The most important aspect of the way the scenes take place will be the atmosphere, feeling and look which each situation has. The placement of the camera in each scene will be very important in establishing the look of the gypsies outlined against their architectural environment.

Filming will always centre on real experience of gypsies' community, using the structures of their own events to order the stories.

Example: gypsies smoking poros and guarding the tiny birds in cages which they have caught in the wild, sit in an abandoned concrete plaza behind Miraille's theatre which they have made a meeting place, their caged birds are hung in neat rows on the walls behind them. In close up the faces of these men are expressive, animated, humourous and individual, words are thrown back and forth between them, the filmed action is in their bodily relationship to the architecture and to one another rather than in purposeful performed actions. Each confronts the camera with the confidence of people accustomed to living in a tight group away from values or approval of an outside world, at the same time they like and respond to the idea of performing. The sense of time within which they operate is immediate, but also slow and 'timeless'.

Each film shows one aspect of life in la Mina. The gypsies in each film section have different occupations, social positions and lifestyles which interact constantly often

connected by the architecture: Bernardo the gypsy elder who makes bastons lives
in the same staircase as the mechanic; Frasco who collects thrown away metal using his
bike for transport hangs around with the men who keep birds and smoke poros and so
on. The films show the agile way that the gypsies adapt to their unsympathetic environment.

Gypsy Point of View

In the films we see the urban scene through the actions and eyes of the gypsies.
Some of the time the camera's point of view is that of the gypsies gathered, or of the boy,
occasionally the camera steps outside to observe the whole scene. Through the actions
and eyes of the gypsies the open harsh concrete plaza of Tio Emilio becomes a courthouse.
The abandoned ground beside the autopista is the territory of Antonio used for ordering
and recycling the materials he collects in the streets and for tethering his horse under the
advertising hoardings. Los Hungaros create the space of an open theatre as they park
their caravans in a semi-circle allowing action to happen in the centre area. Rafael who
sings powerfully and alone in the centre of the vast plaza of la Mina has created an opera
house where he is centre stage to the balconies of the high-rise blocks around him.

There is almost no reference to the future or past throughout the shoot, seen in 'present'
attitudes of characters with the possible exception of Tio Emilio, both in his own territory
and when he talks with Los Hungaros, when he may talk about a lost past.

Situations take place at different times of day with one day sometimes flowing into the
next. The time of day is marked less by meals, school or jobs but by the light, day of the
week and the possibility of coming across others in the street. Phones are mobile or irrelevant.
Characters improvise constantly and do things when they feel like it in gypsy society.
A gypsy may appear suddenly having disappeared for a while (maybe a day, three days,
a month, a year…). Fiestas and events are organised in a short space of time whilst events
a long distance away often seem to be about to happen. (Example: a flamenco festival
planned for a year's time is spoken about as if it is about to take place immediately.)

Spaces for improvisation will allow gypsies to describe aspects of their culture by acting
them out. (Example: the dancer is allowed to be very expressive when dancing where
her level of self-expression is respected whilst in other parts of her life she is modest
and remains in the background whilst her husband expresses her needs and desires.)

Camera

Long takes throughout the shoot to include beginning and end of actions un-interrupted.
Lots of takes where little happens and the camera concentrates on expressions and body
language of the main characters in relation to their environment and architecture. Camera
positions will always be slightly below the figures or at the same height and not from above
except for some long shots or journeys. (Example: when the gypsies cross the bridge
to go to the market.)

Perspectives going back in space as figures recede behind one another to be used when
there are groups of people. When characters are talking to one another there are lots of
close ups to emphasise body language and communication especially against the texture
of the architecture and space.

During the filming we avoid scenes which are purely ethnographic in interest and we concentrate on getting much more deeply involved and physically close to the people we are filming.

In each place we are introduced to the space and architecture in relation to the people who occupy spaces by extended walks through streets, plazas, waste ground, etc.. Long takes look at faces and bodies in relation to the activities happening and to the place.

To end each story long takes with a different rhythm and theatrical placing of characters is used. These vary in each story but will connect by use of exterior/interior shots and contrasting/similar set-ups and figures; movement left to right is followed by next shot same direction.

When the characters speak a few scripted lines they are obviously given to the characters but reflect a memory or duplication of words spoken before.

Eventual form of the films will be a mixture of storytelling and continuity editing with direct to the camera interviews and statements.

Portraits

Main characters are often seen in close up, singled out and catching their expressions at odd moments as we look from one to another to get confirmation of the mood and feeling of the people we are with. Using zoom and hand held where necessary. In order not to disturb the everyday goings on of the plazas (conversations, judgements, deals, fights, etc.). Zoom can be used to see the actions and relationships of far away groups and individuals as if we are looking through binoculars at scenes happening a long way off. Each character, whether major or minor will appear at least once in close up which will act as a portrait and memory for us as we see the characters appear and re-appear through the films.

Sound

Sound is almost always recorded at time of action with lots of wild-track. Contrast between times where more rural sounds present (around horses, caravans and sea) and urban daytime sound (around Plaza, market, autopista, etc.) and dancing and music. The only time outside music is used is when El Coto is listening to music through his headphones.

Relationship child to Tio Emilio – Film presence

The son of gypsies with three wheel car (Manolo) is almost always present and a conductor hilo) throughout and also Tio Emilio, they represent age extremes. Manolo is the most mobile of all the characters. These two characters will form the link that is dramatic but can also be visible between scenes and between films.

General shots

Looking down on the plaza from the rooftop of one of the buildings.
Looking towards the sea from the rooftop of one of the buildings.
Roof of worst block looking in another direction.
In the abandoned area of La catalana looking towards the power plant.

From the worst block of flats looking outwards to the street.
Looking out at the plaza from statue of Camaron de la Isla looking past the statue
to activities in the plaza.
On the street corner where older men sit at the community centre.
Looking into the Plaza of Mirailles.
The area around the sea and power plant.
At the market, under and beside the autopista, activities of the market.
Looking up into the staircase of one of the blocks of flats.
Looking into the main plaza of La Mina where bars are operating, women sell clothing,
old men stand with formal clothes, drug deals take place, etc..

Shooting order

Determined by how easy it will be to shoot in each place and by how many problems might
be created by gypsy community leaving most difficult scenes until last and Fiesta to the
end where we want everyone to be present if possible.

1. Tio Emilio
2. Hungaros
3. Mecanico and Pajaros (three or four)
4. Antonio (three or four) (Frasco works at night can arrive early in the morning)
    (the people pass through the area on their way to market on Tuesday)
5. Bailadora (market and fiesta) (could be split)
6. Musicos and fiesta

Final Order (possible)

Antonio, Frasco and his cart (seen still dark, early morning to mid-day, time jumps)
Tio Emilio (afternoon to dusk)
Hungaros (afternoon to early evening to darkness)
Mecanico, pajaros, etc.. (afternoon)
Bailadora (morning, evening, night)
Musicos (evening, night, late)

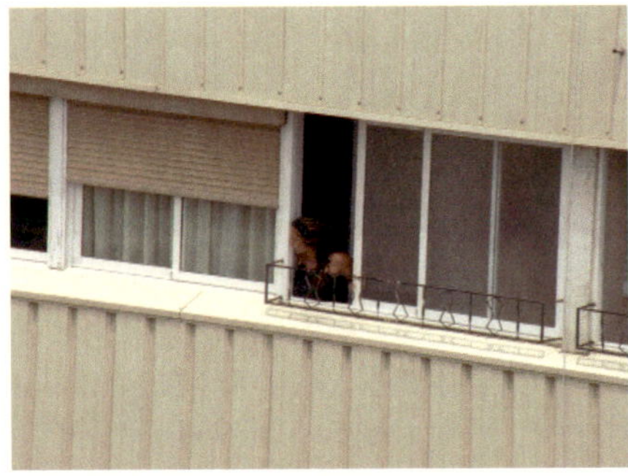

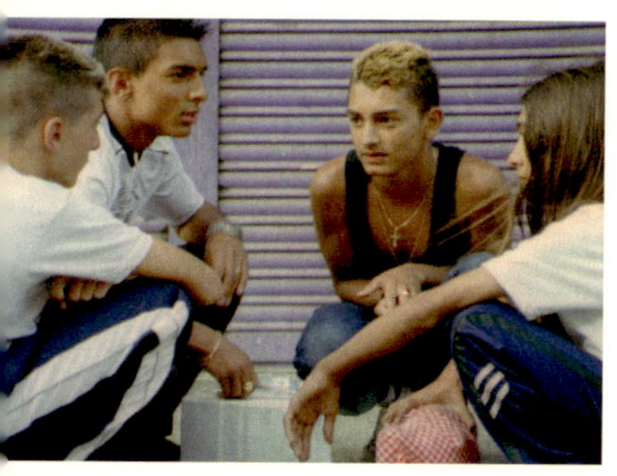

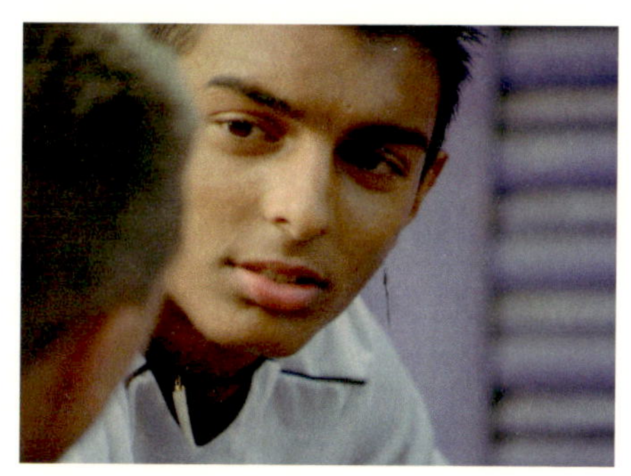

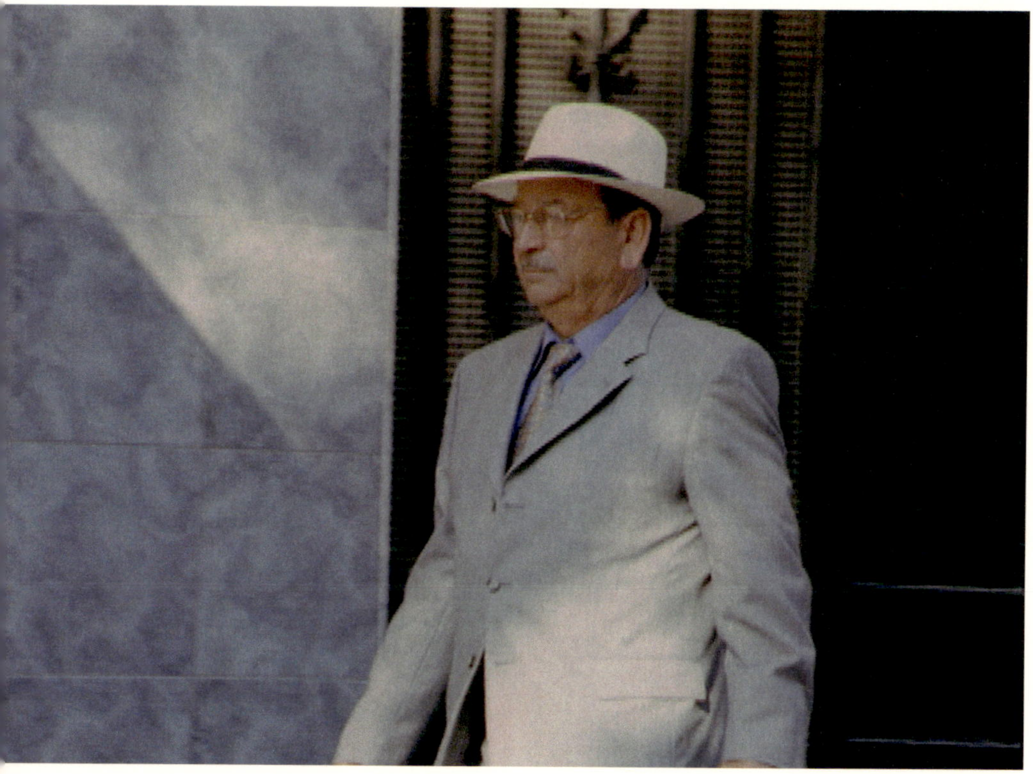

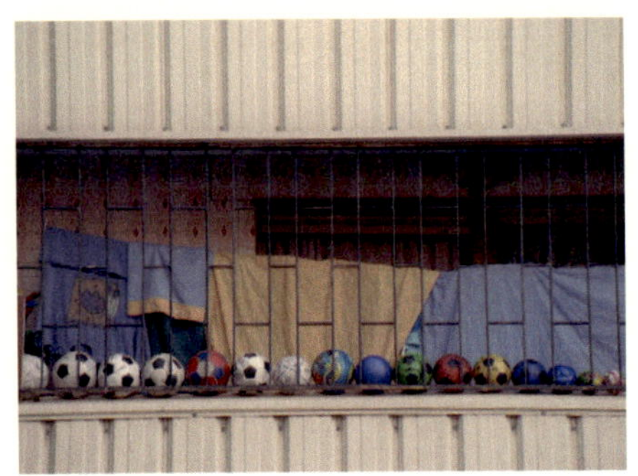 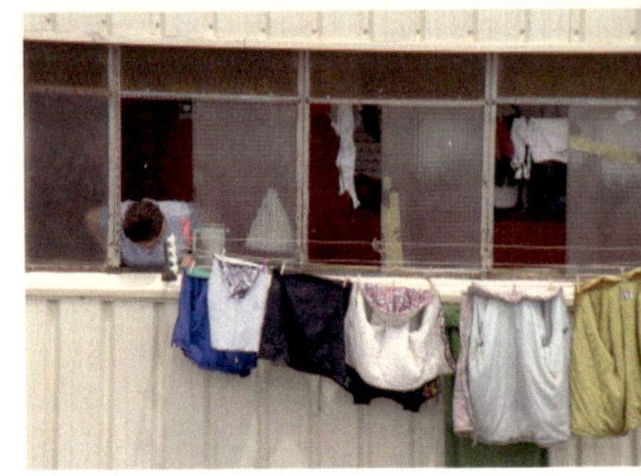

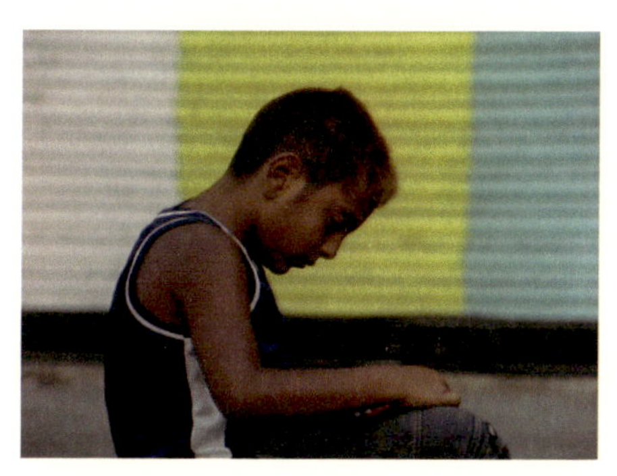

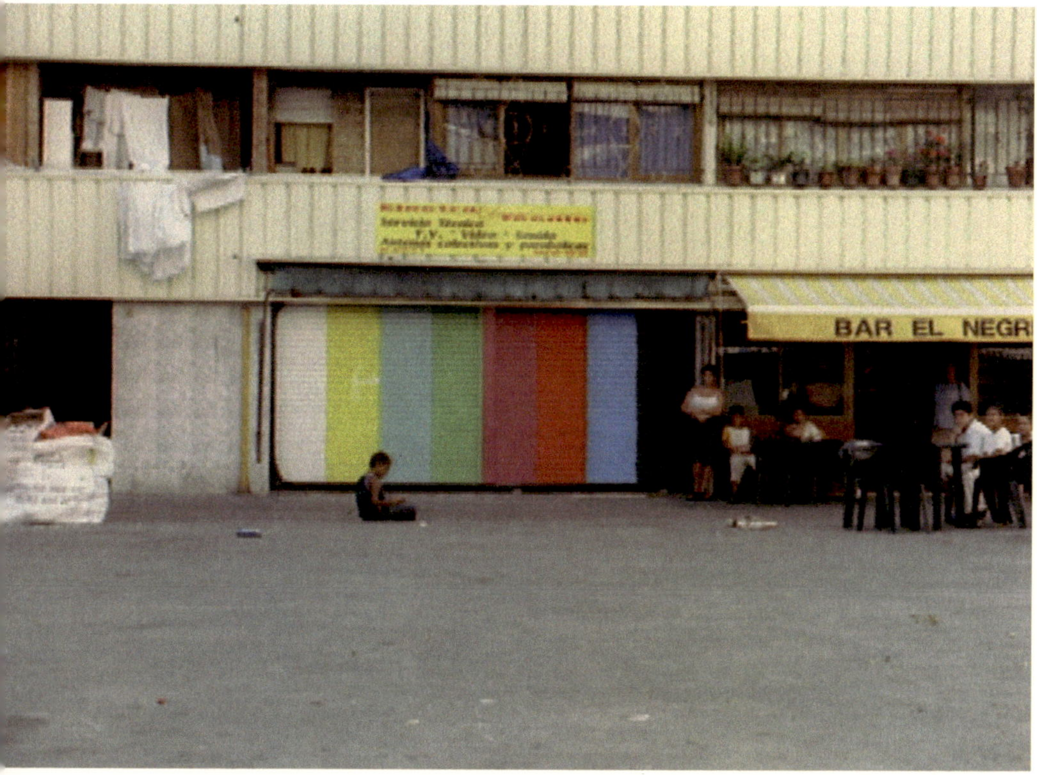

BAR EL NEGR

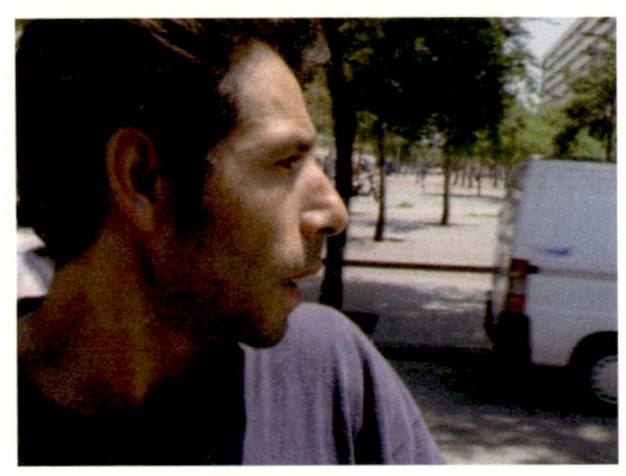

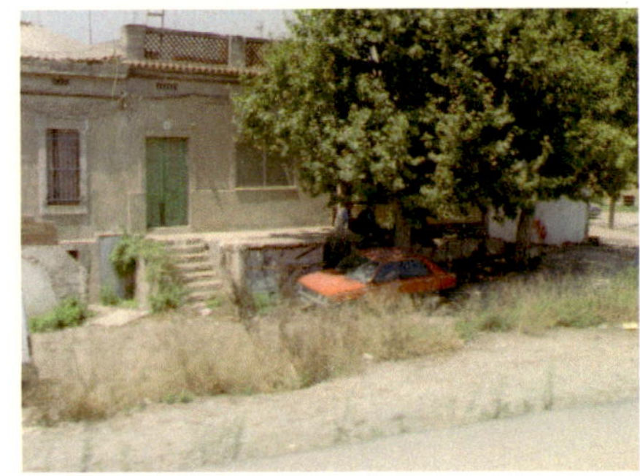

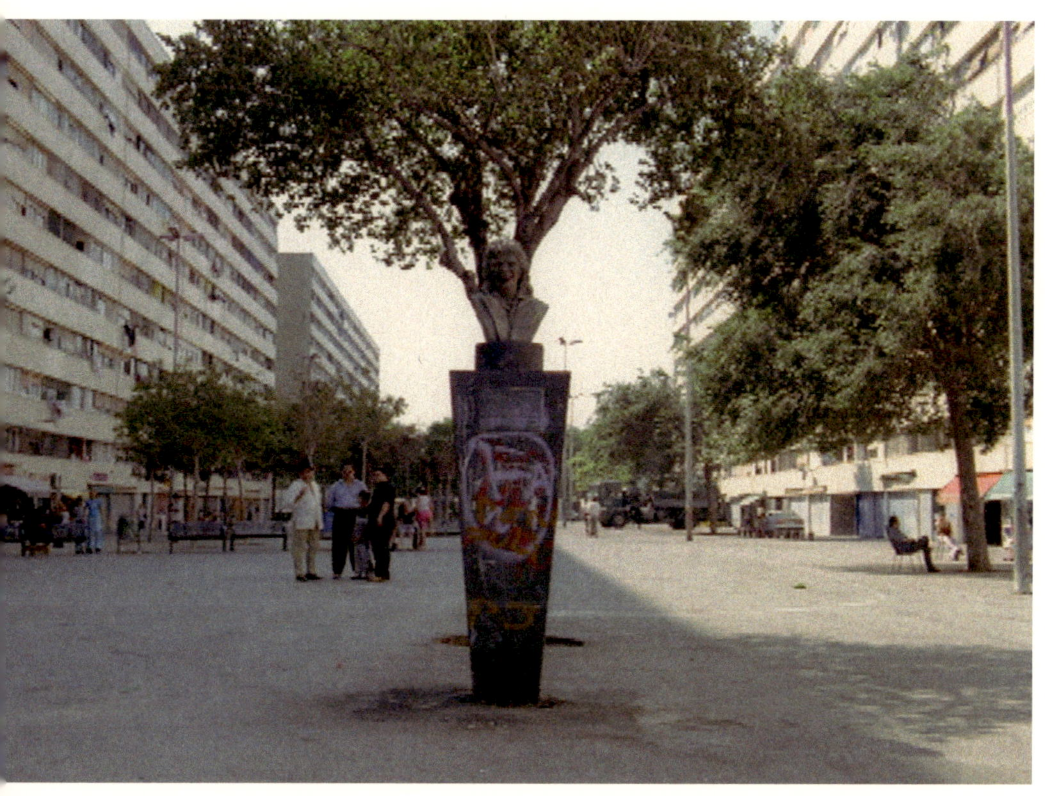

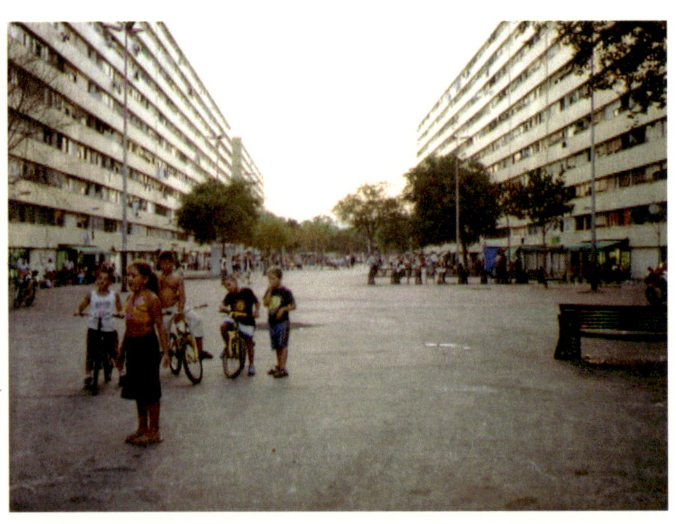

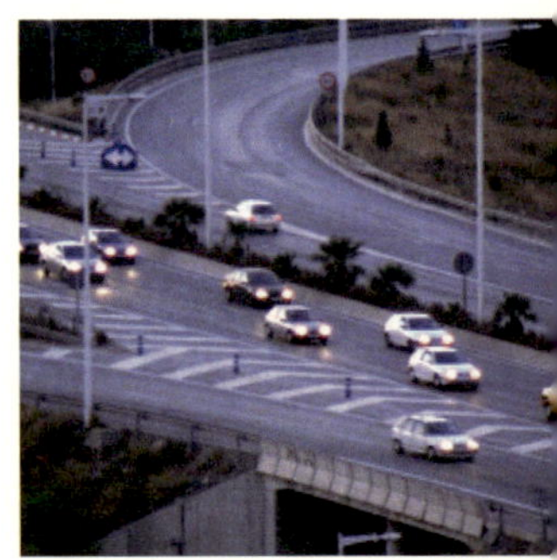

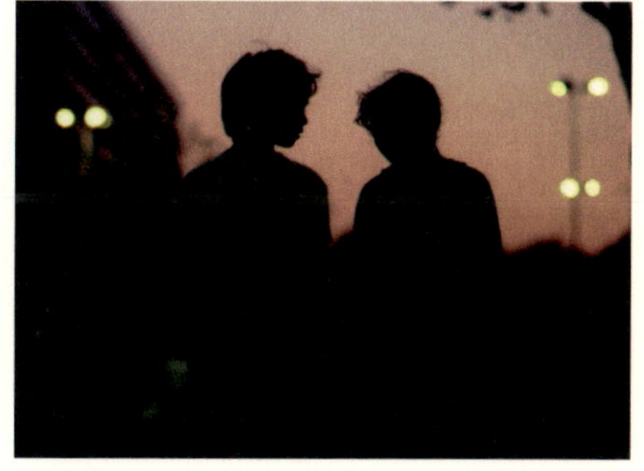

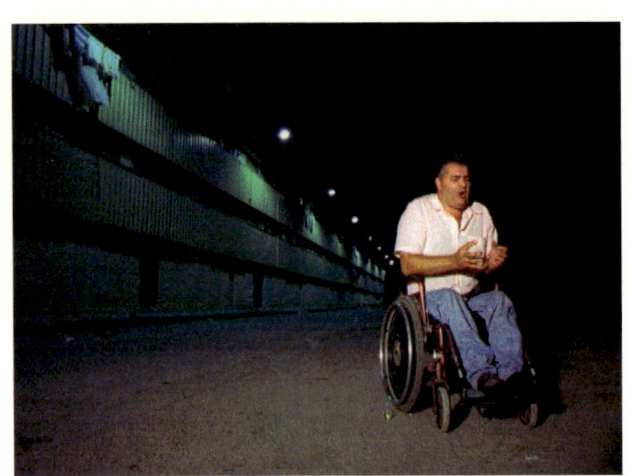

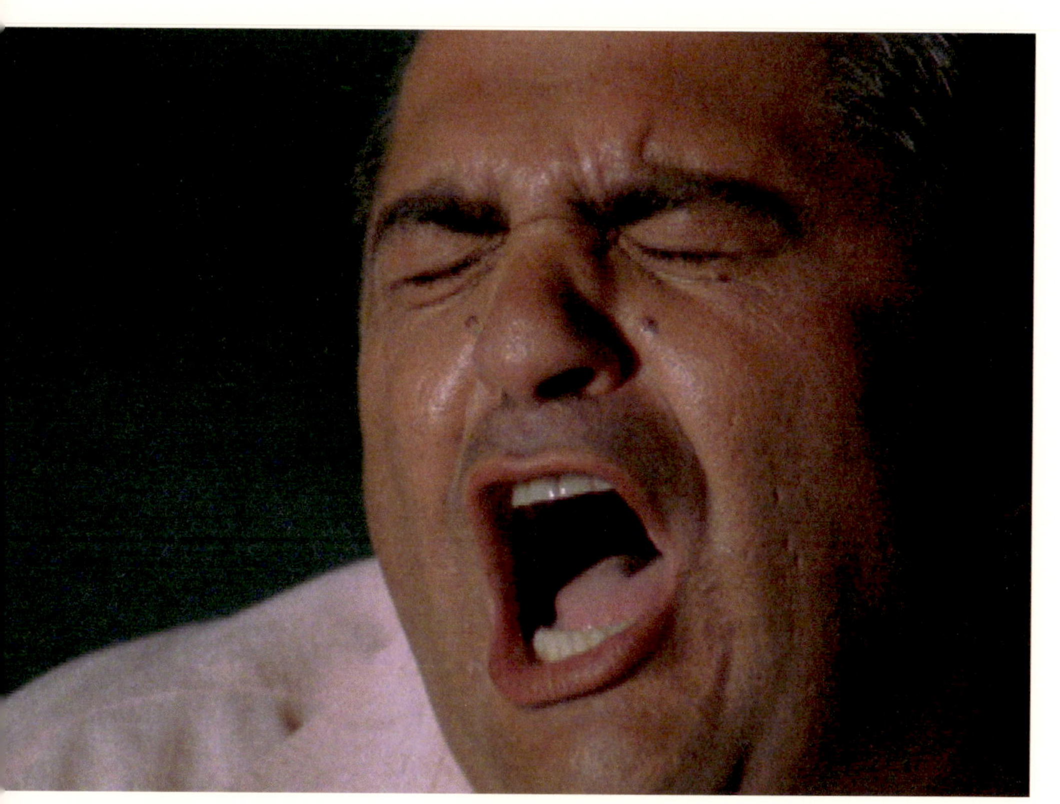

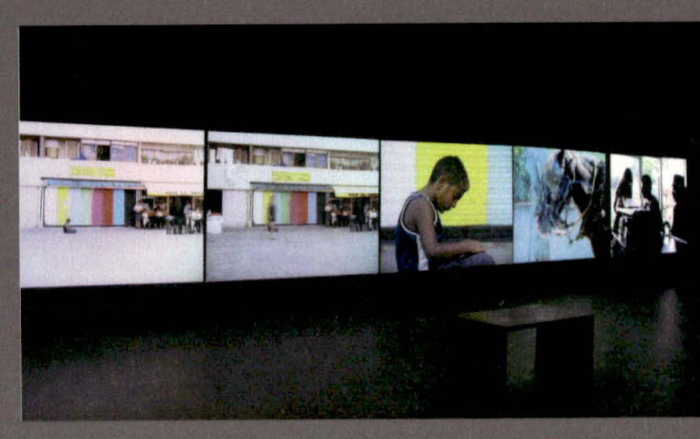

Pavilions

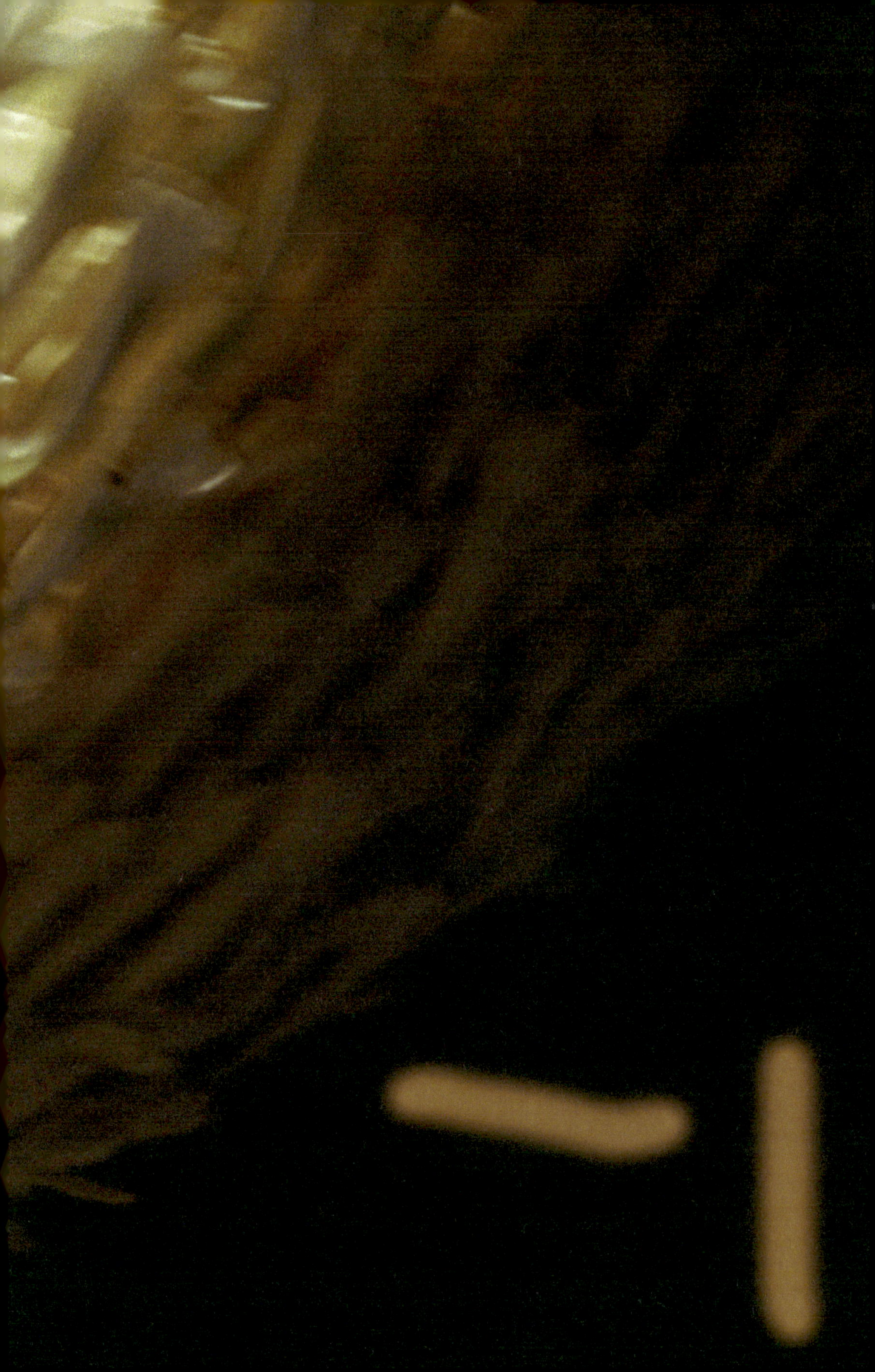

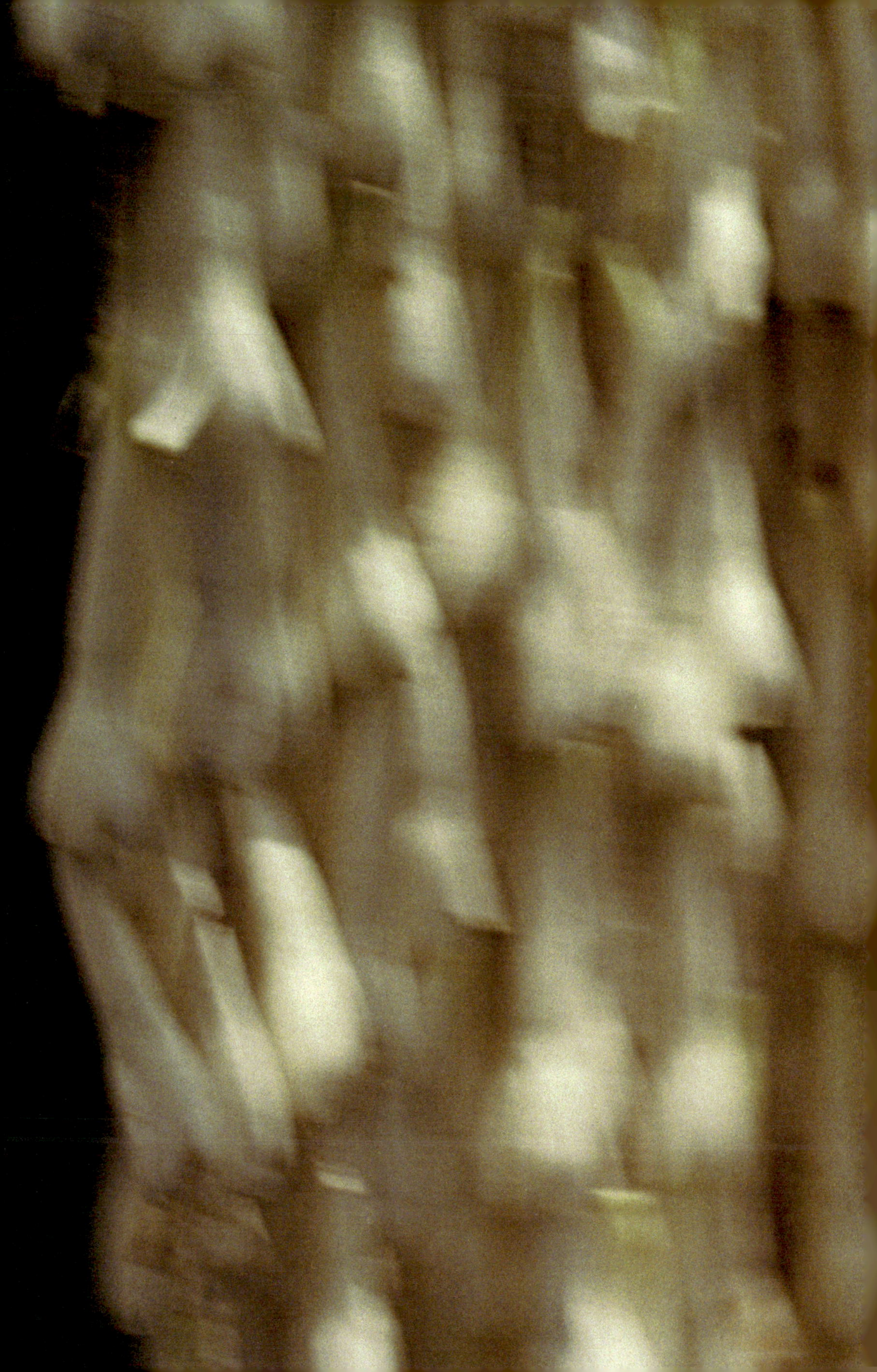

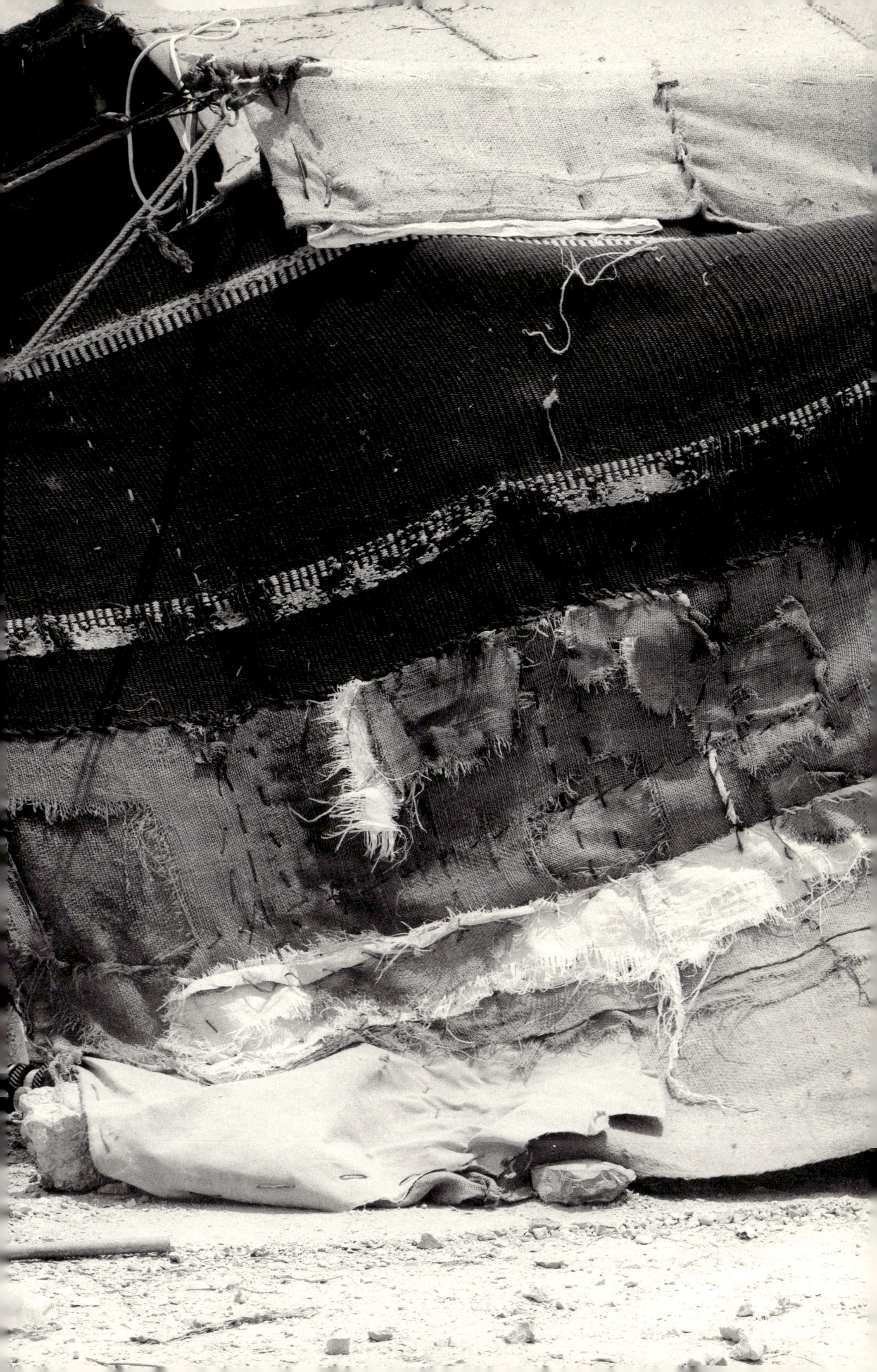

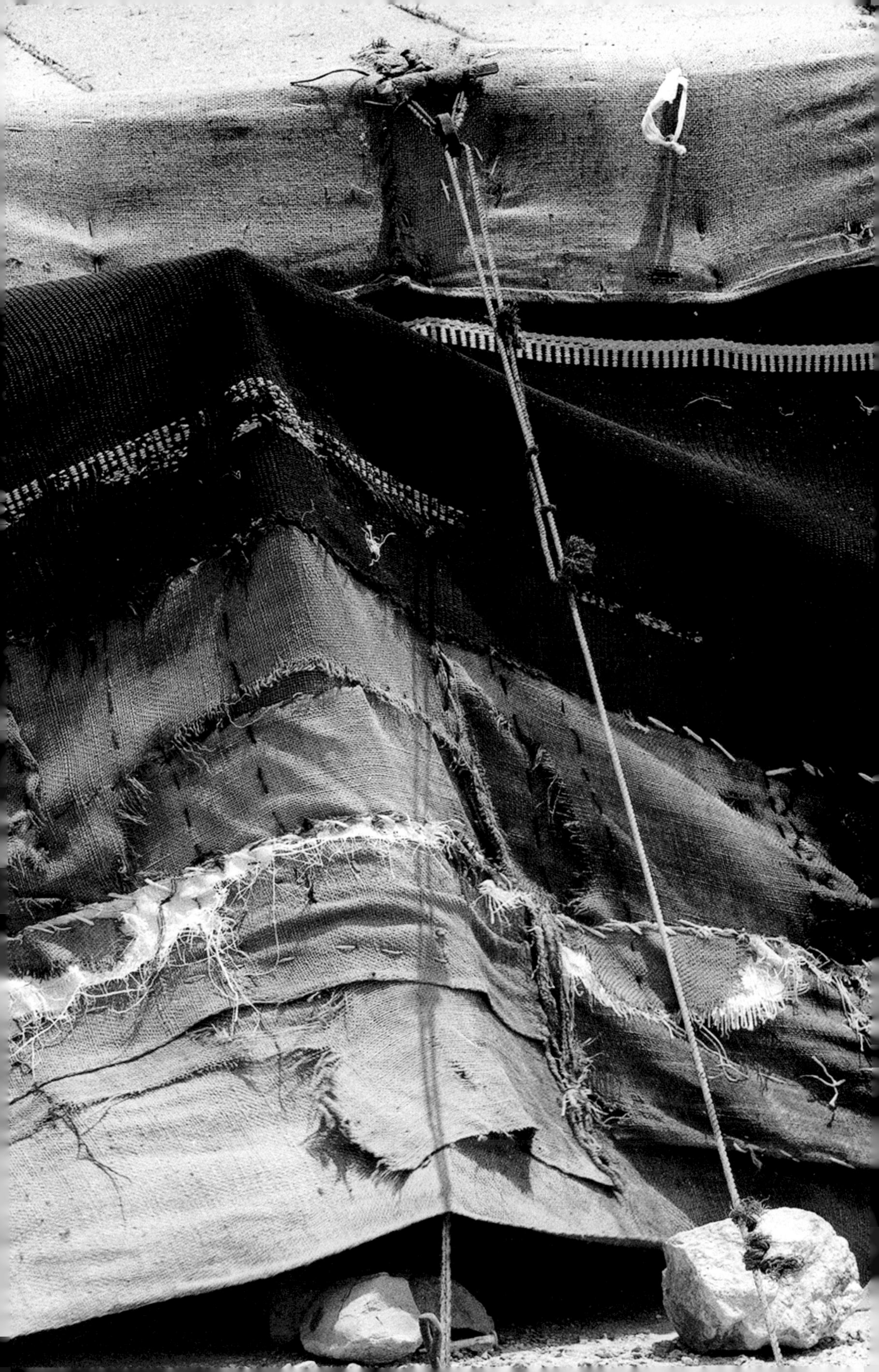

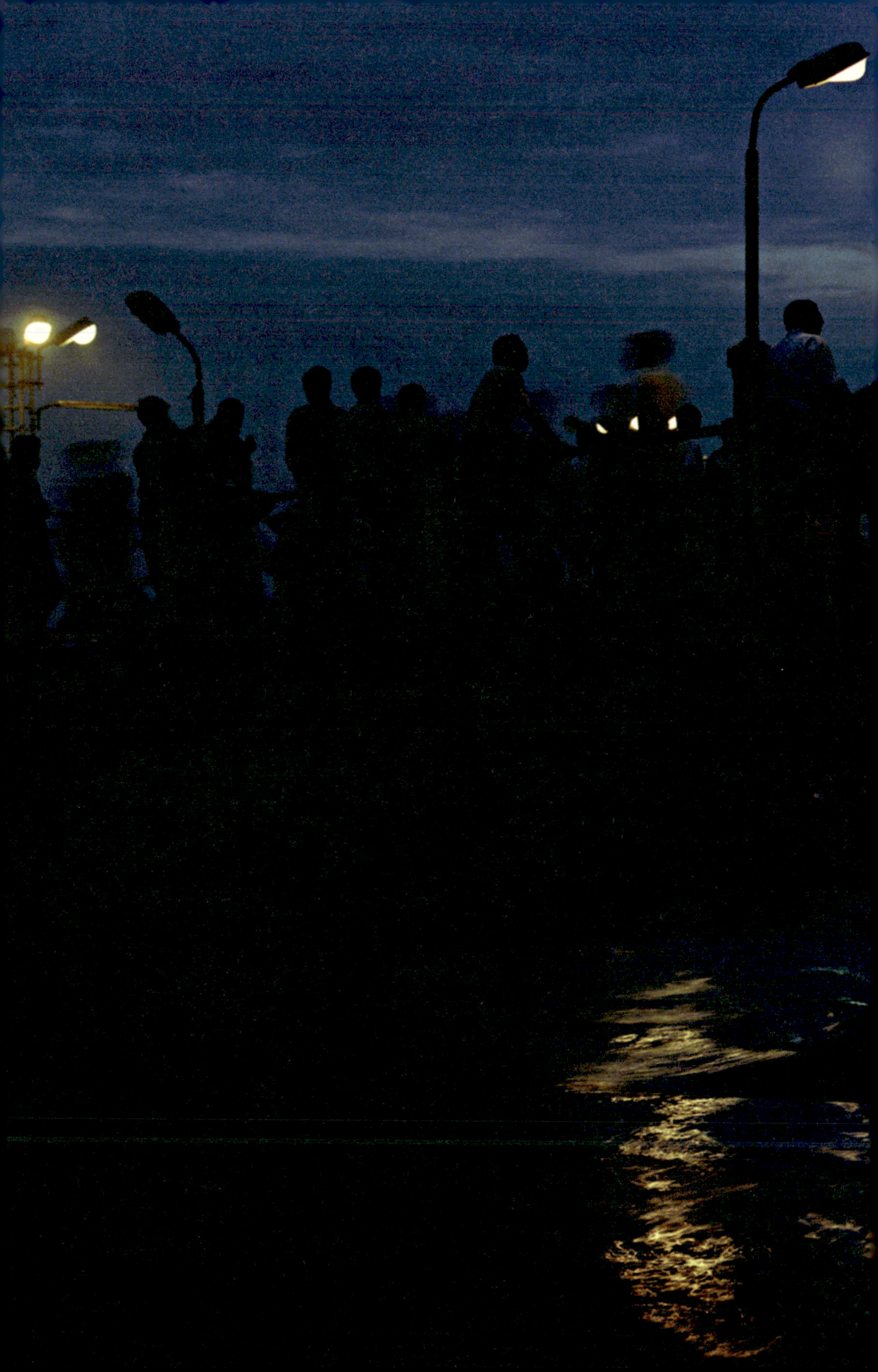

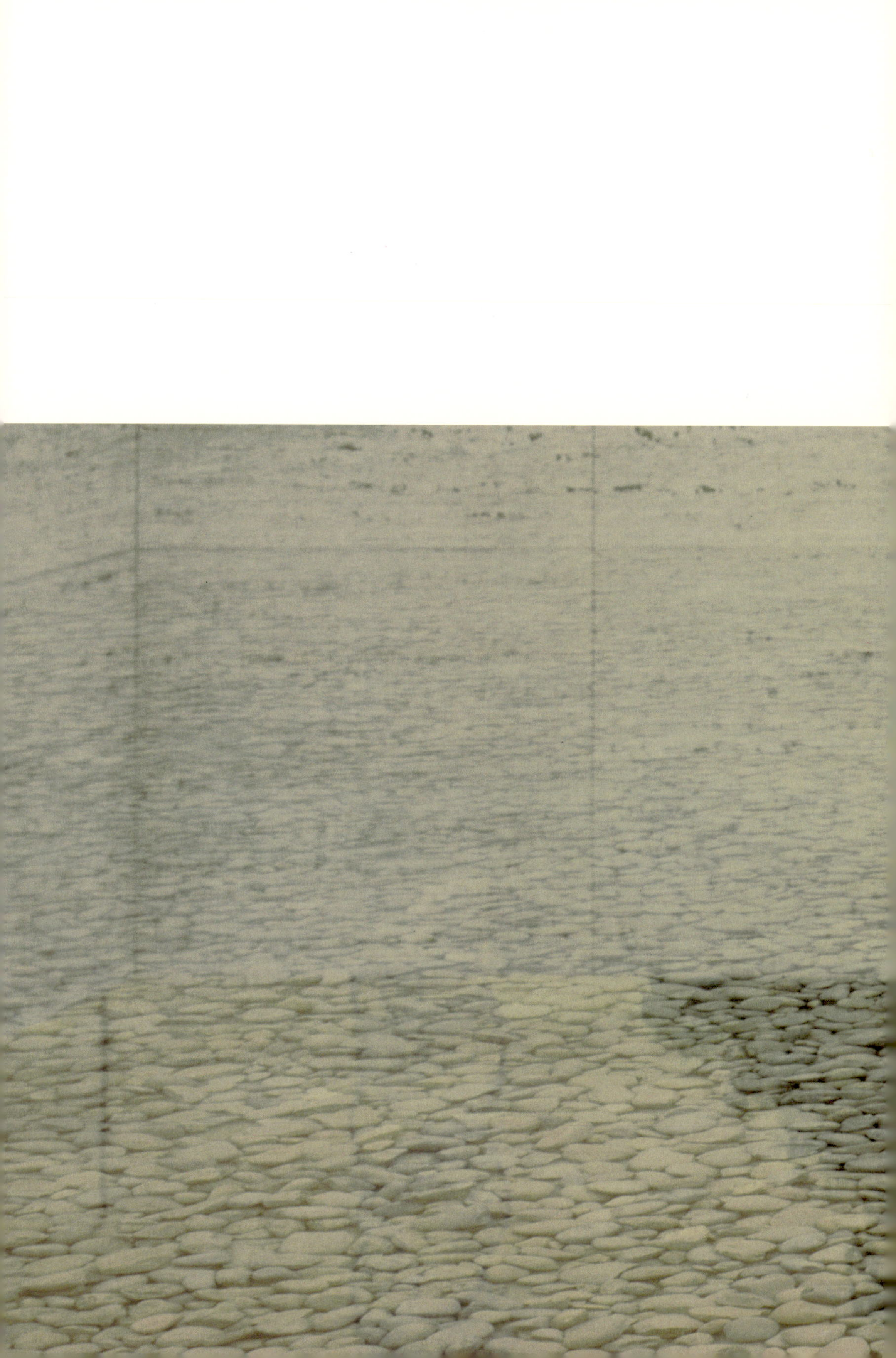

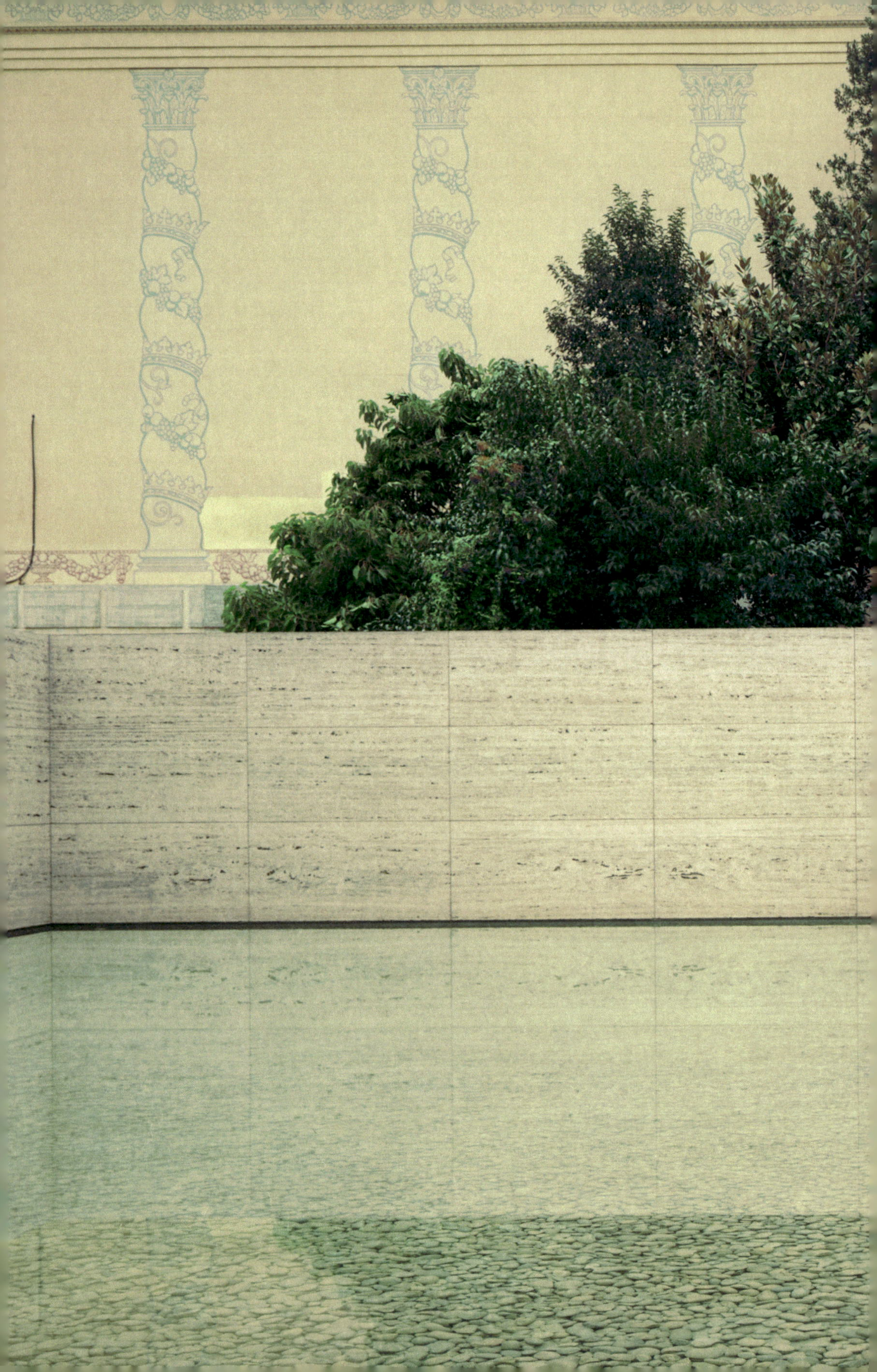

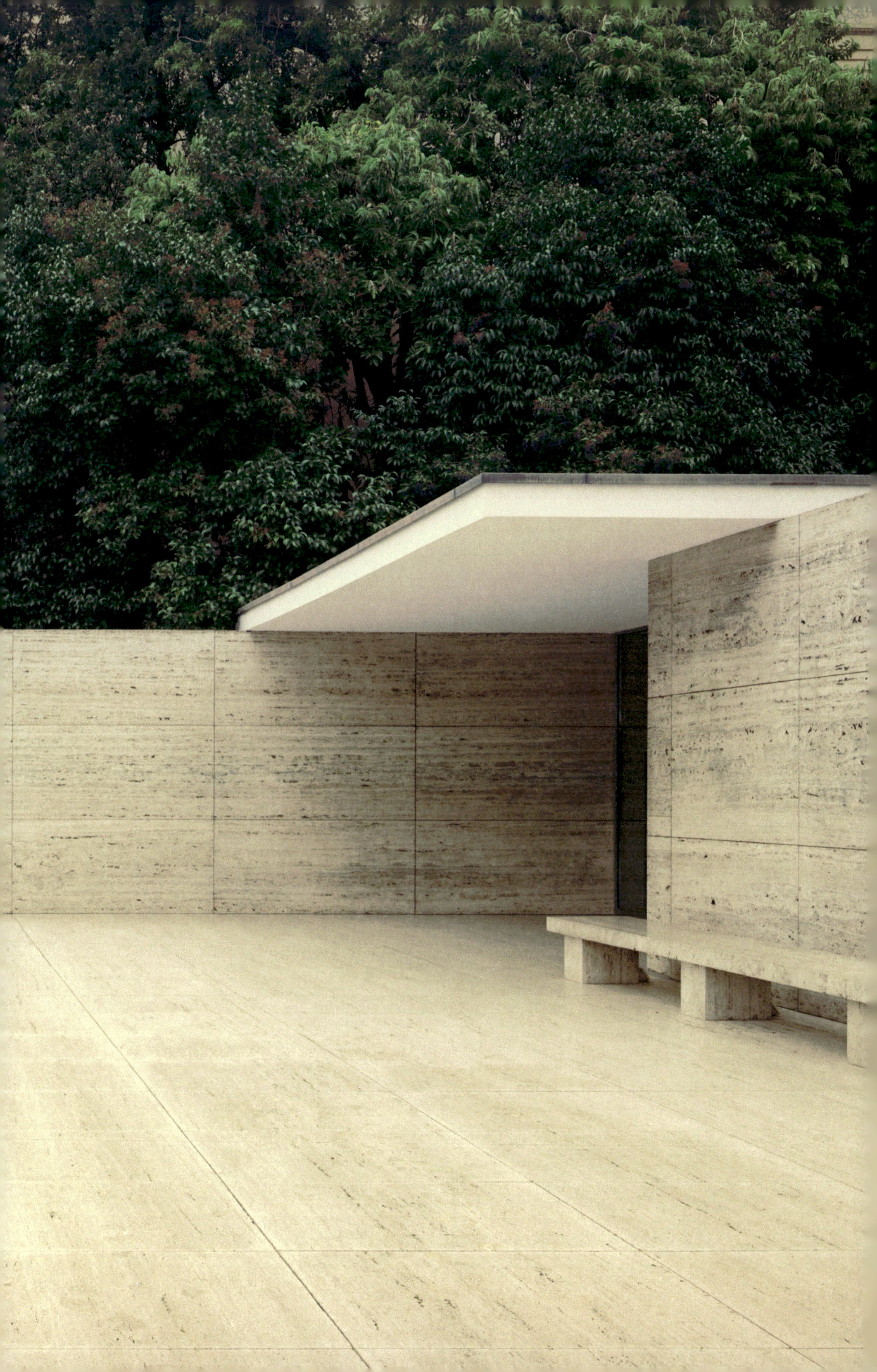

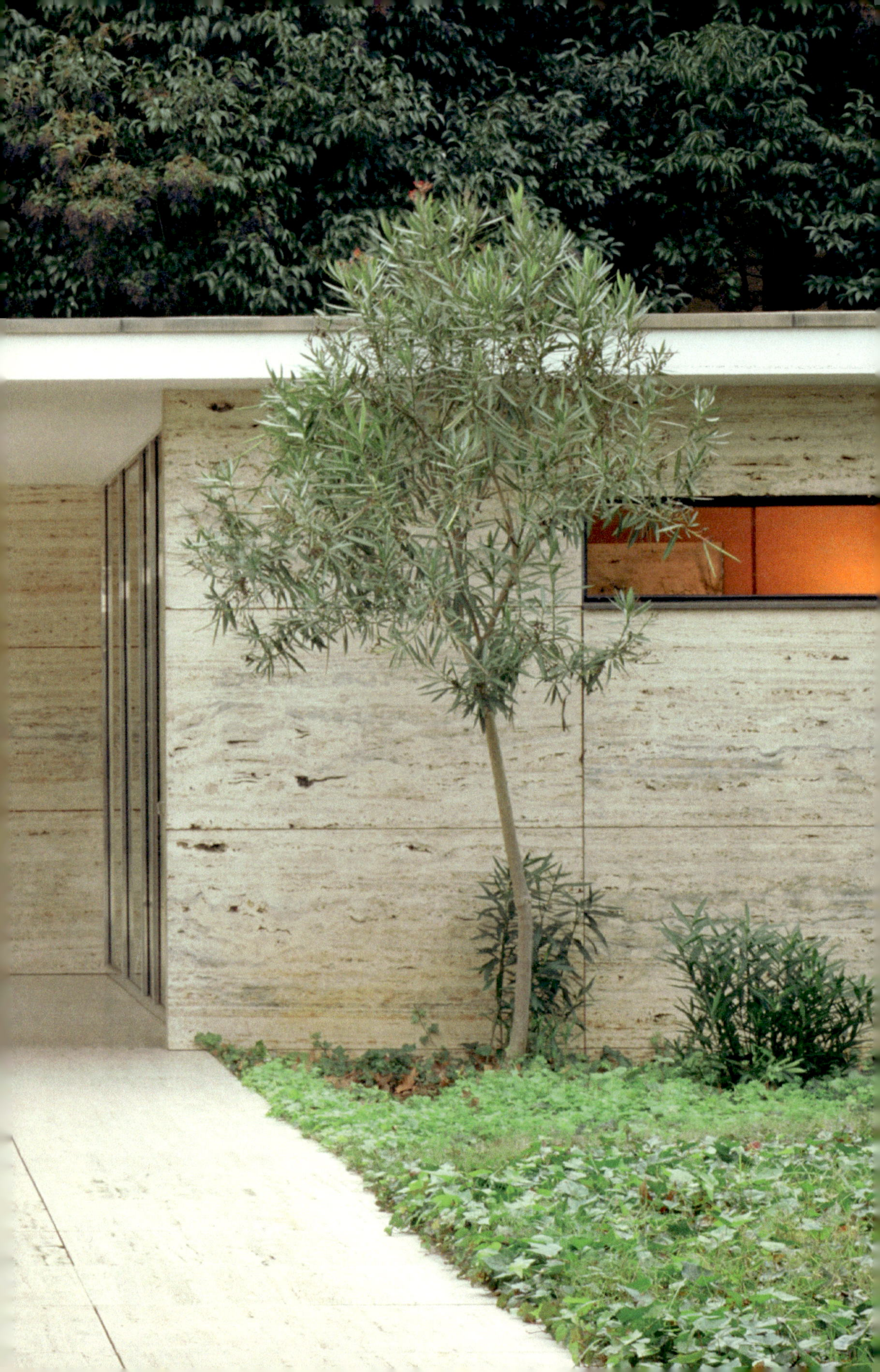

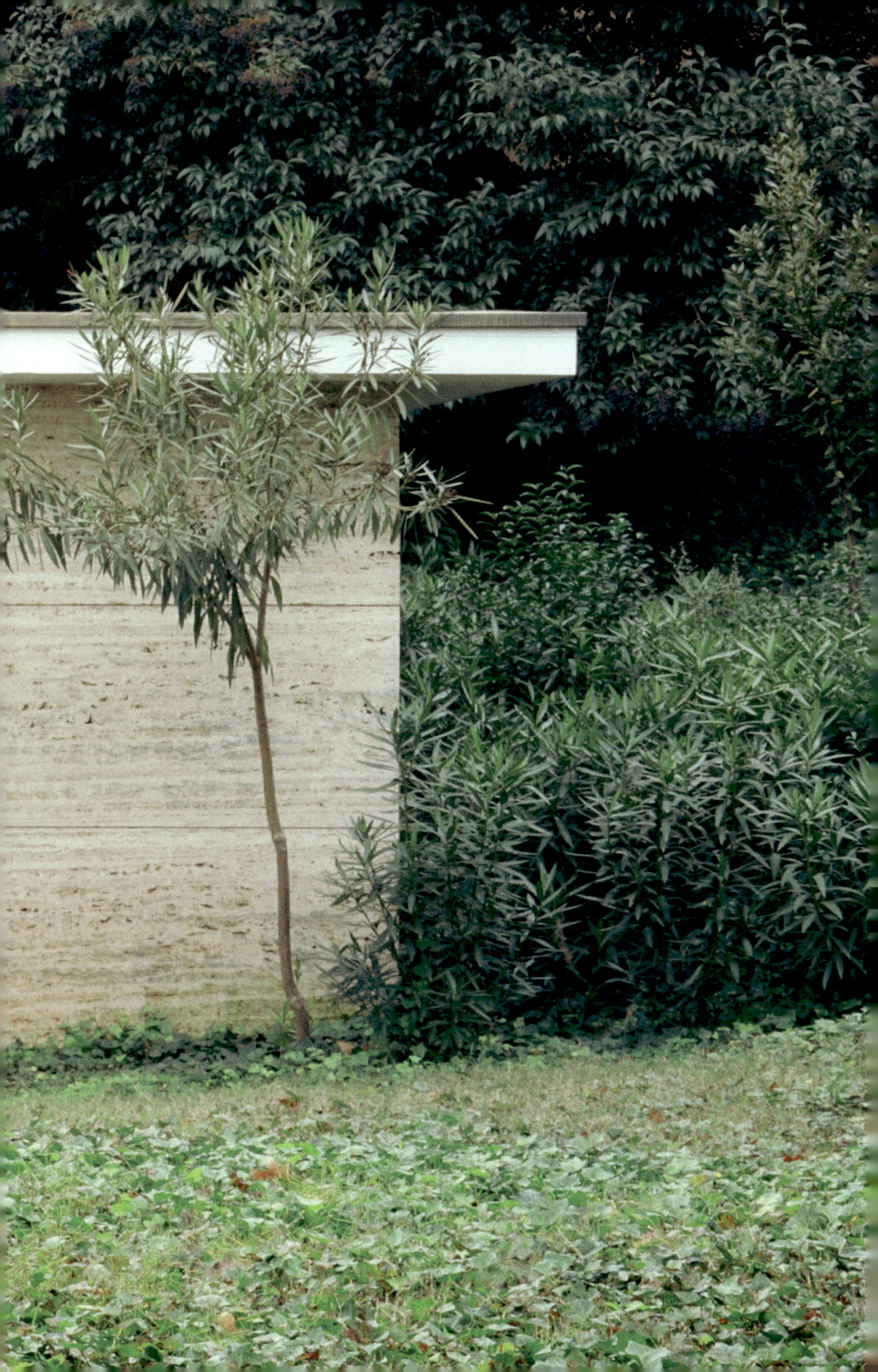

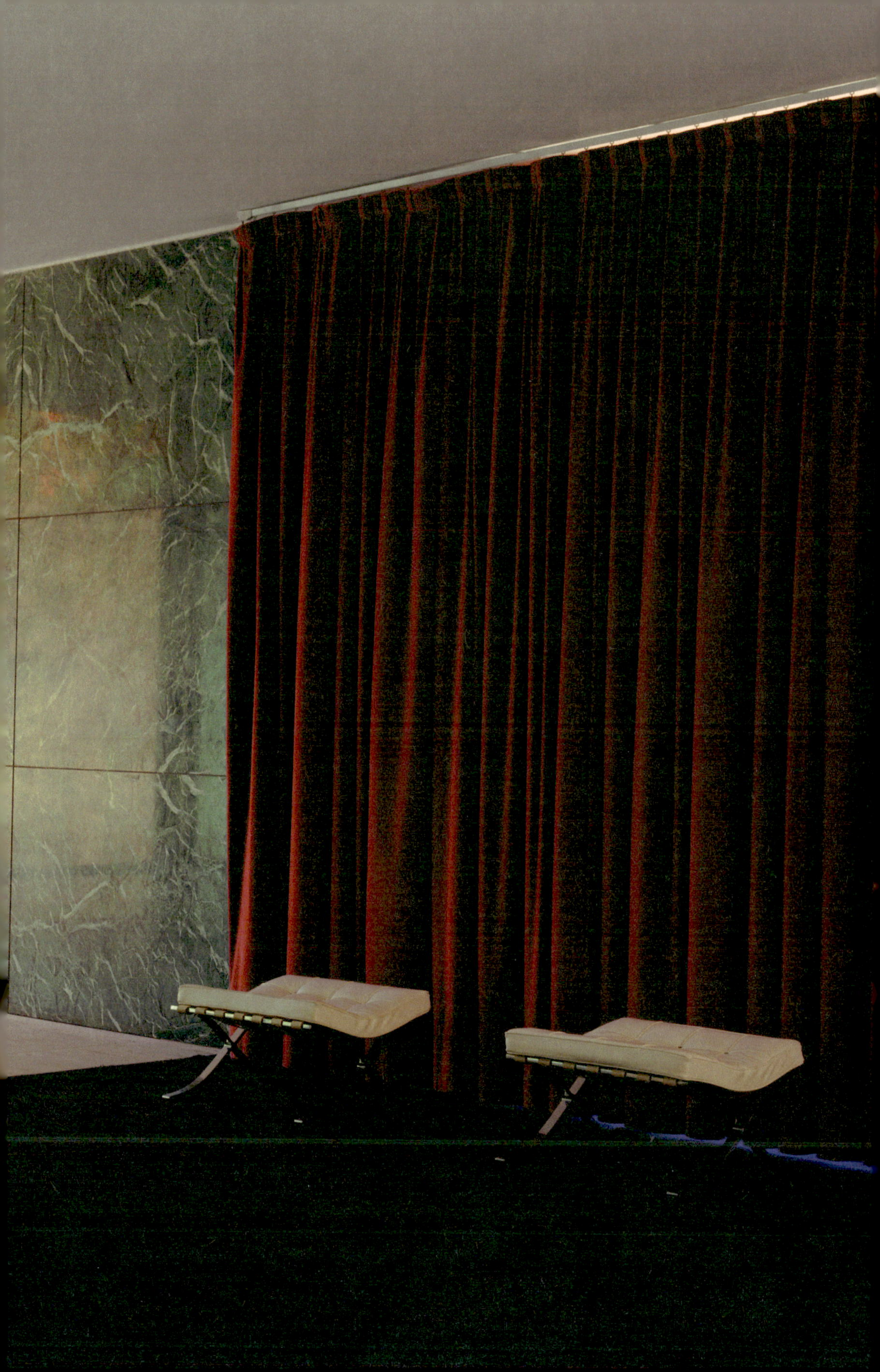

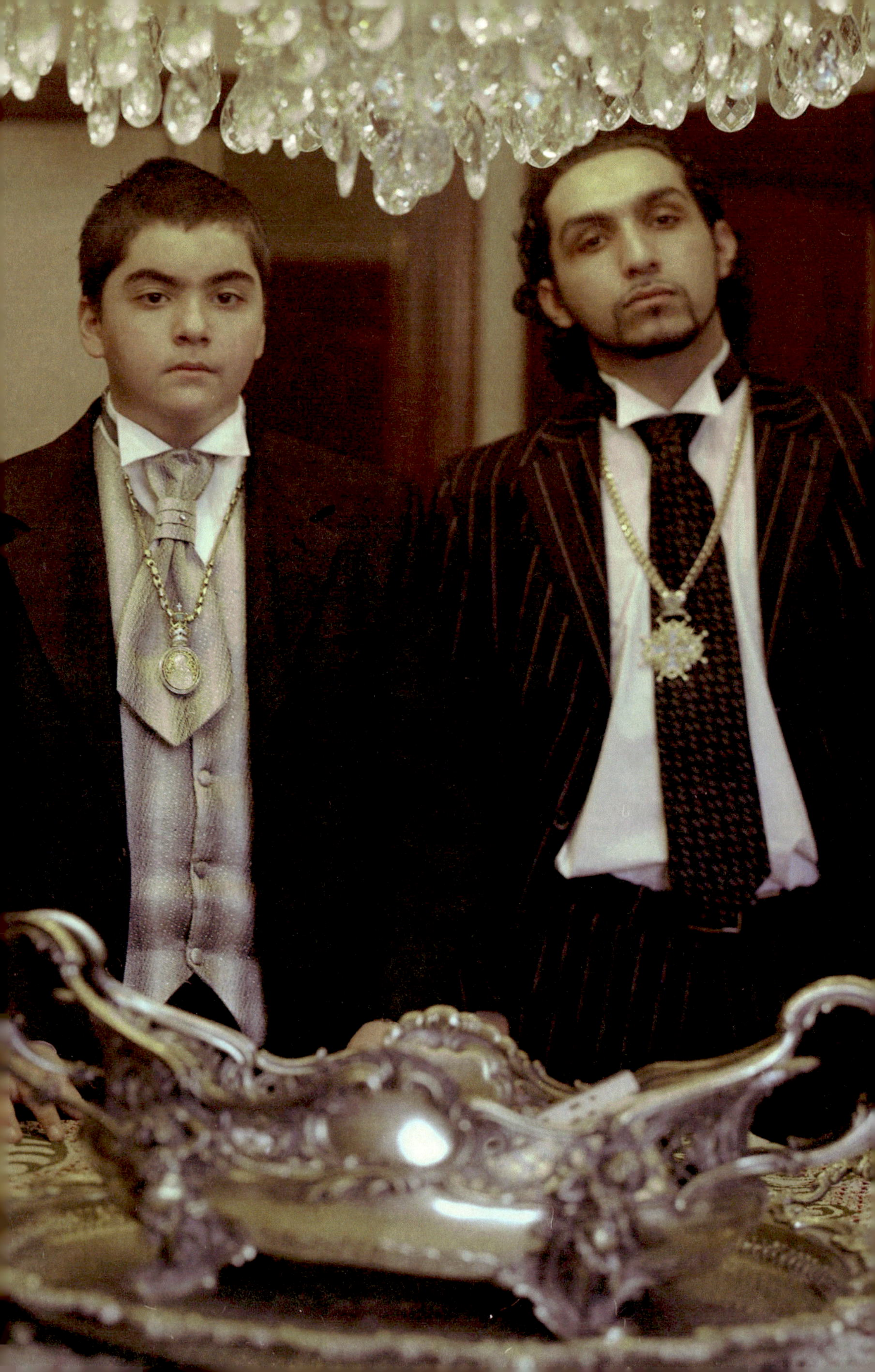

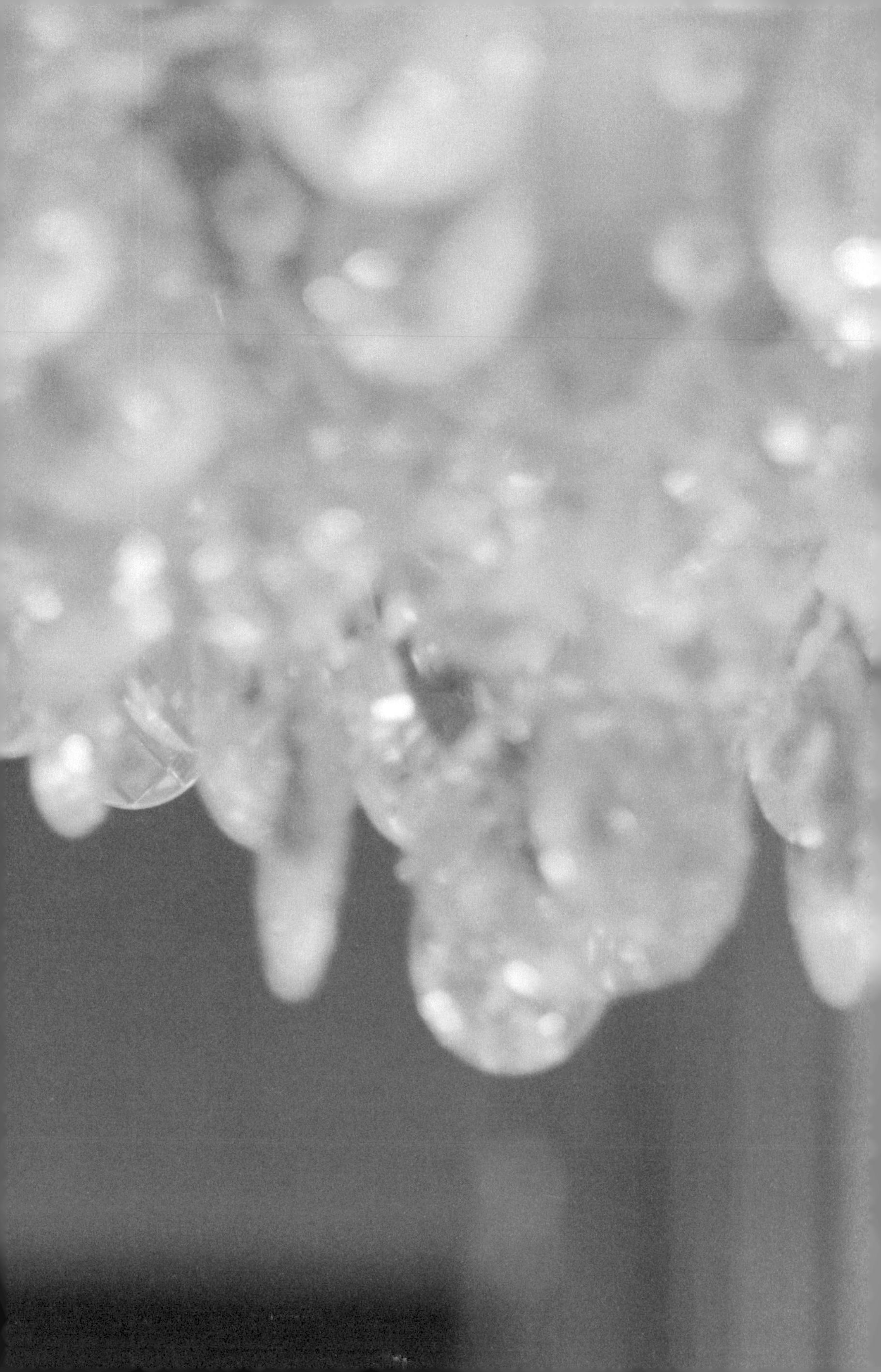

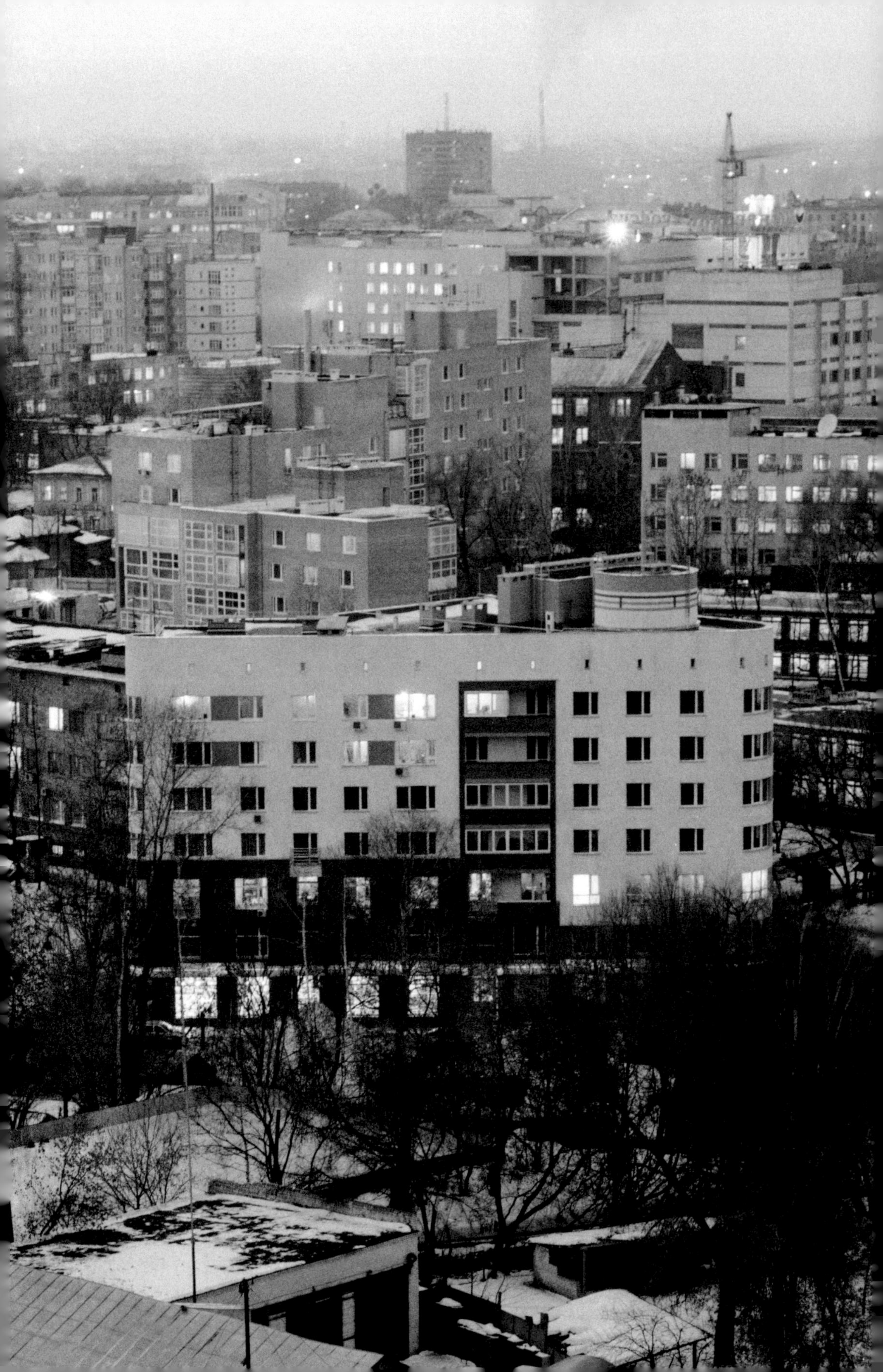

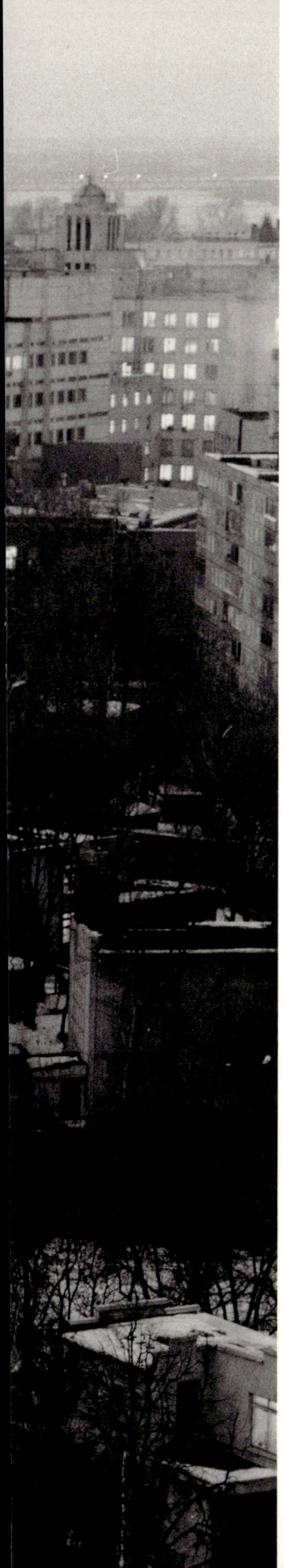

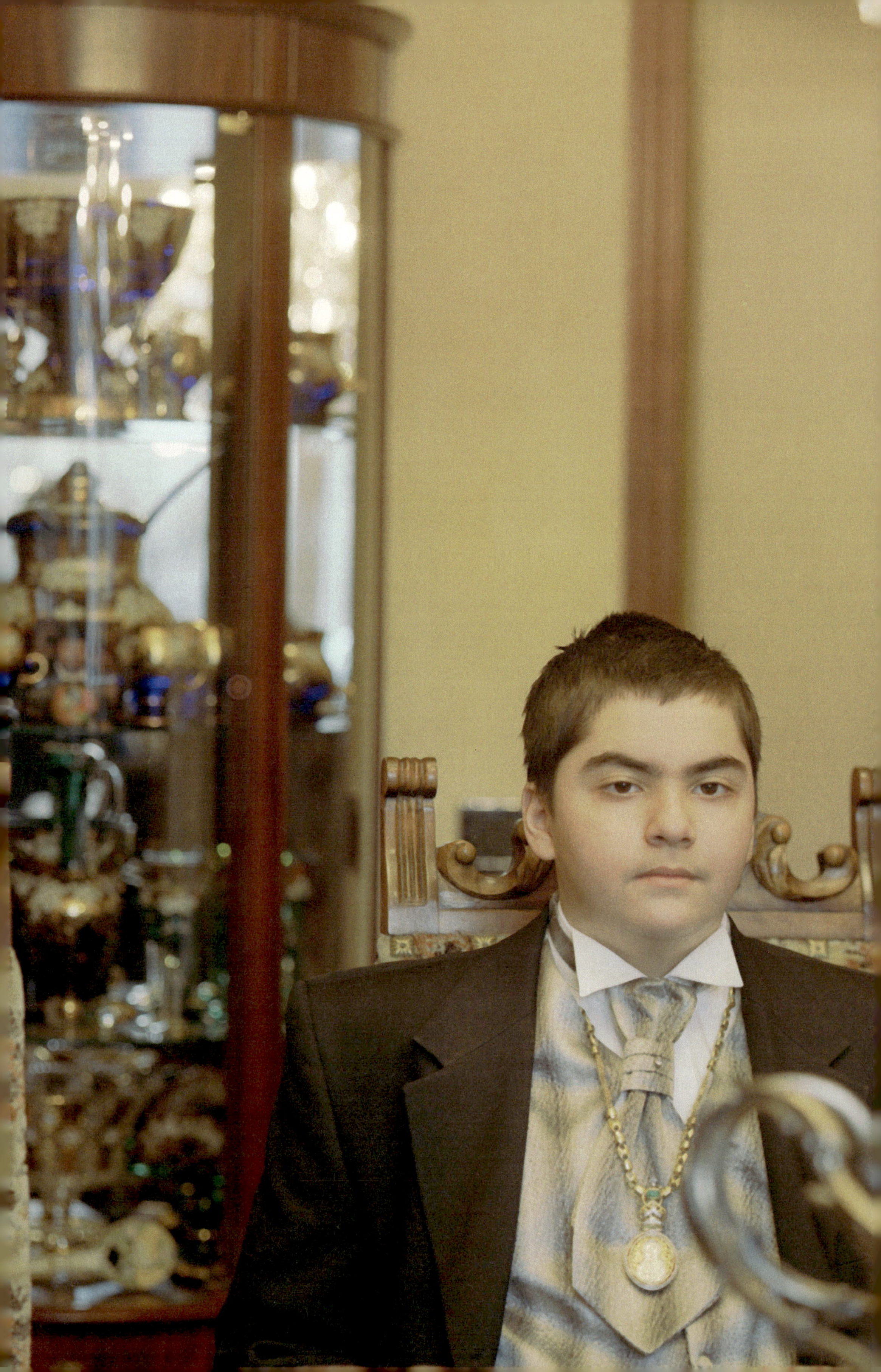

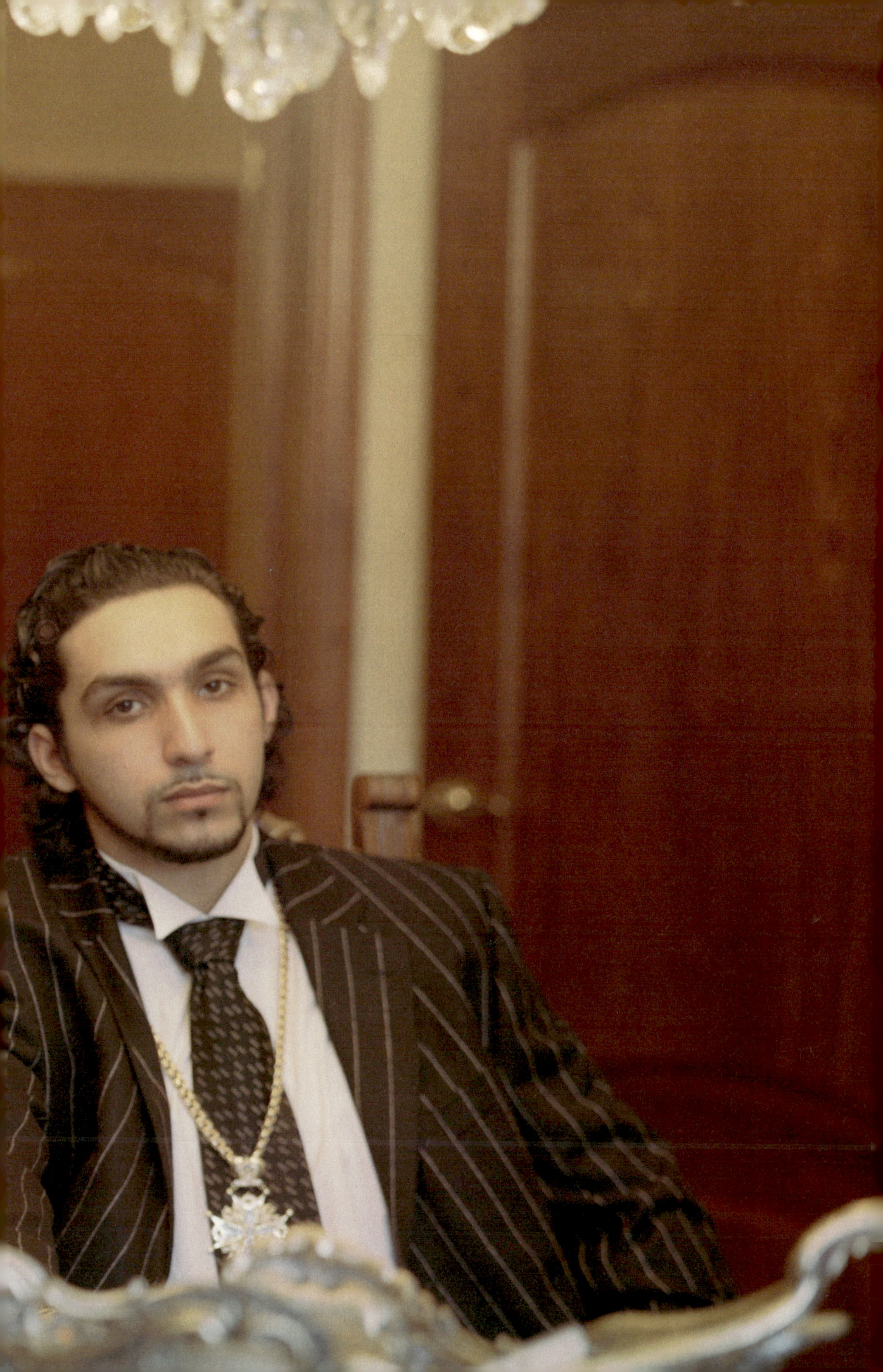

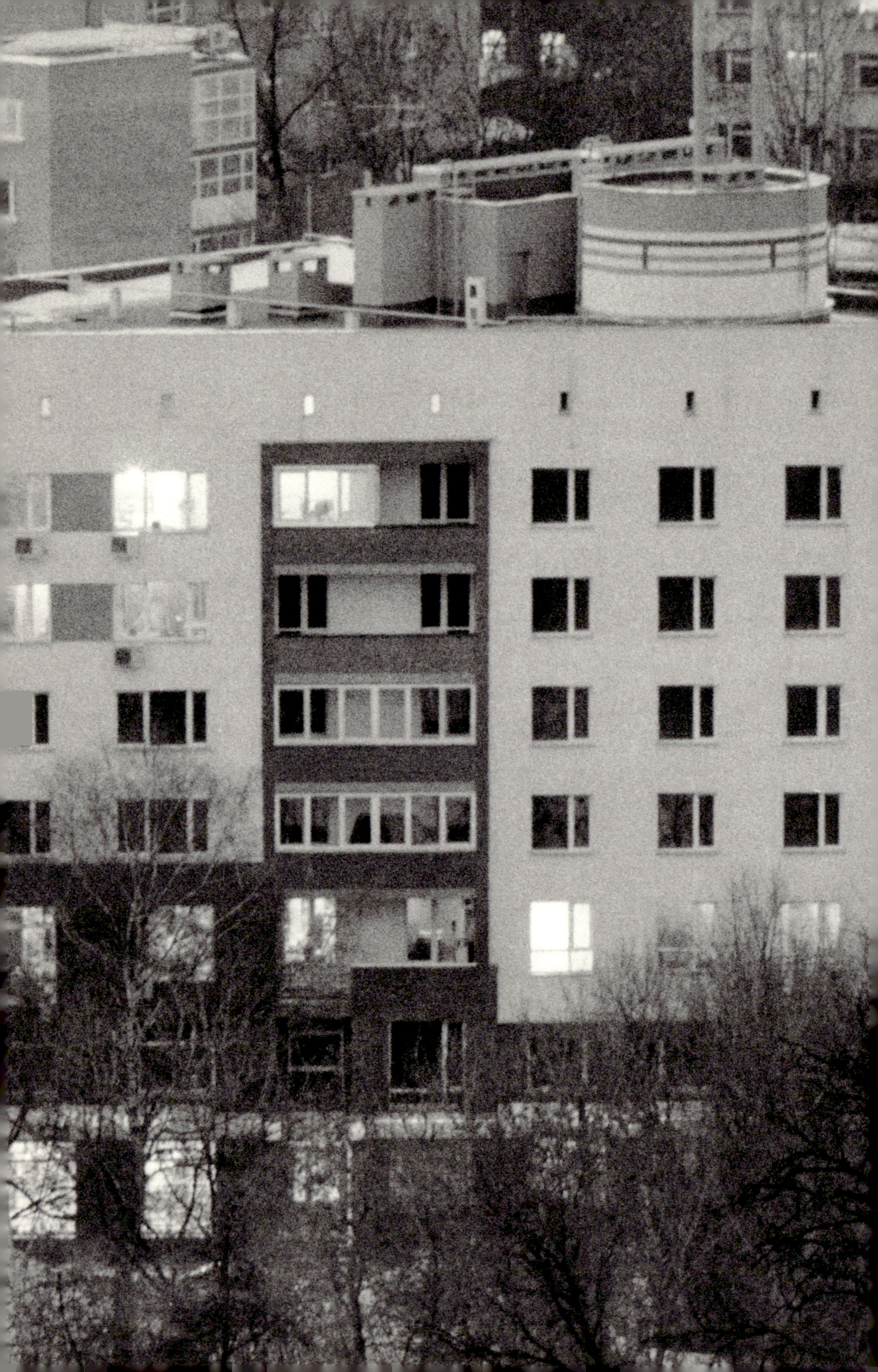

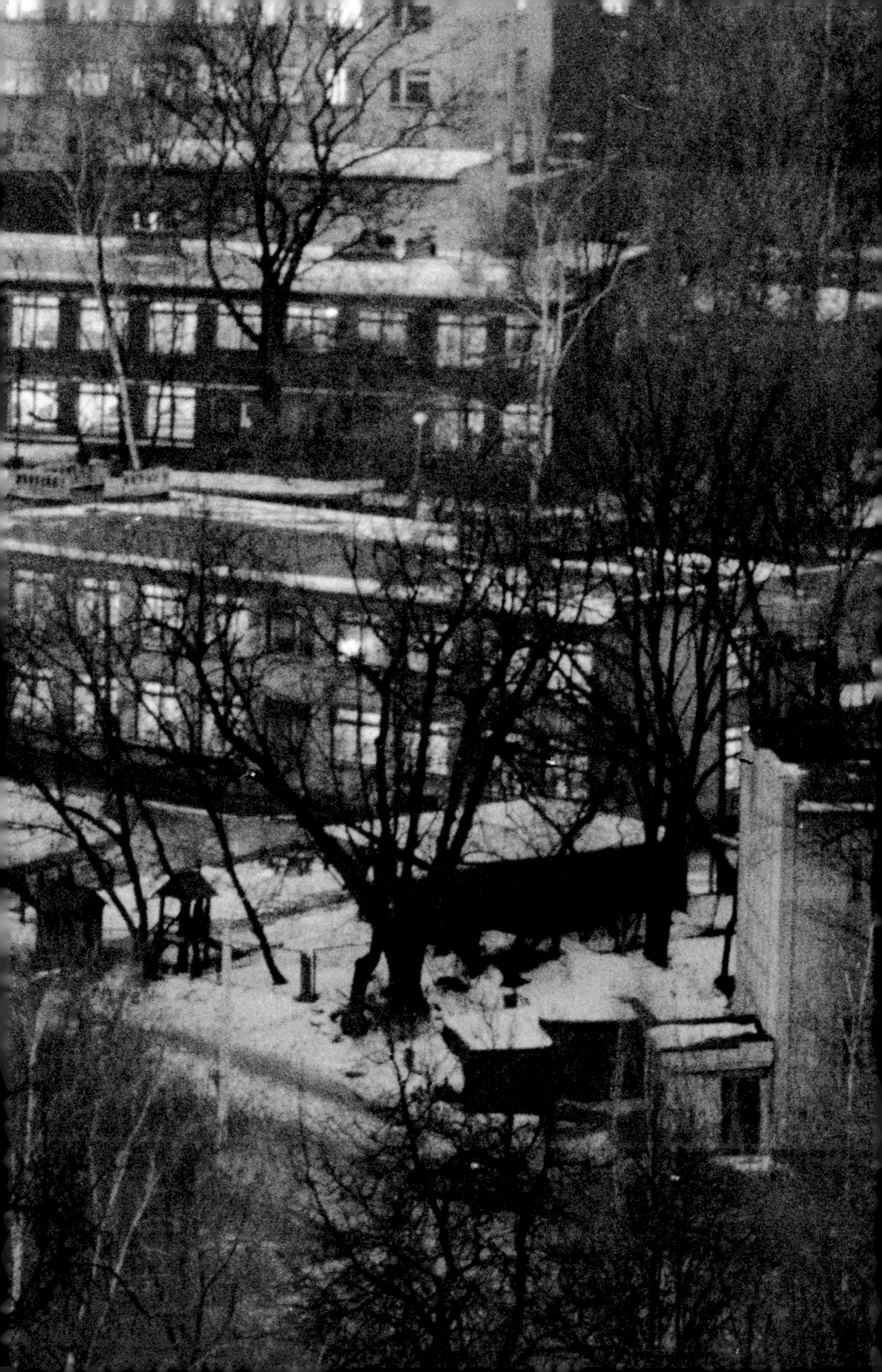

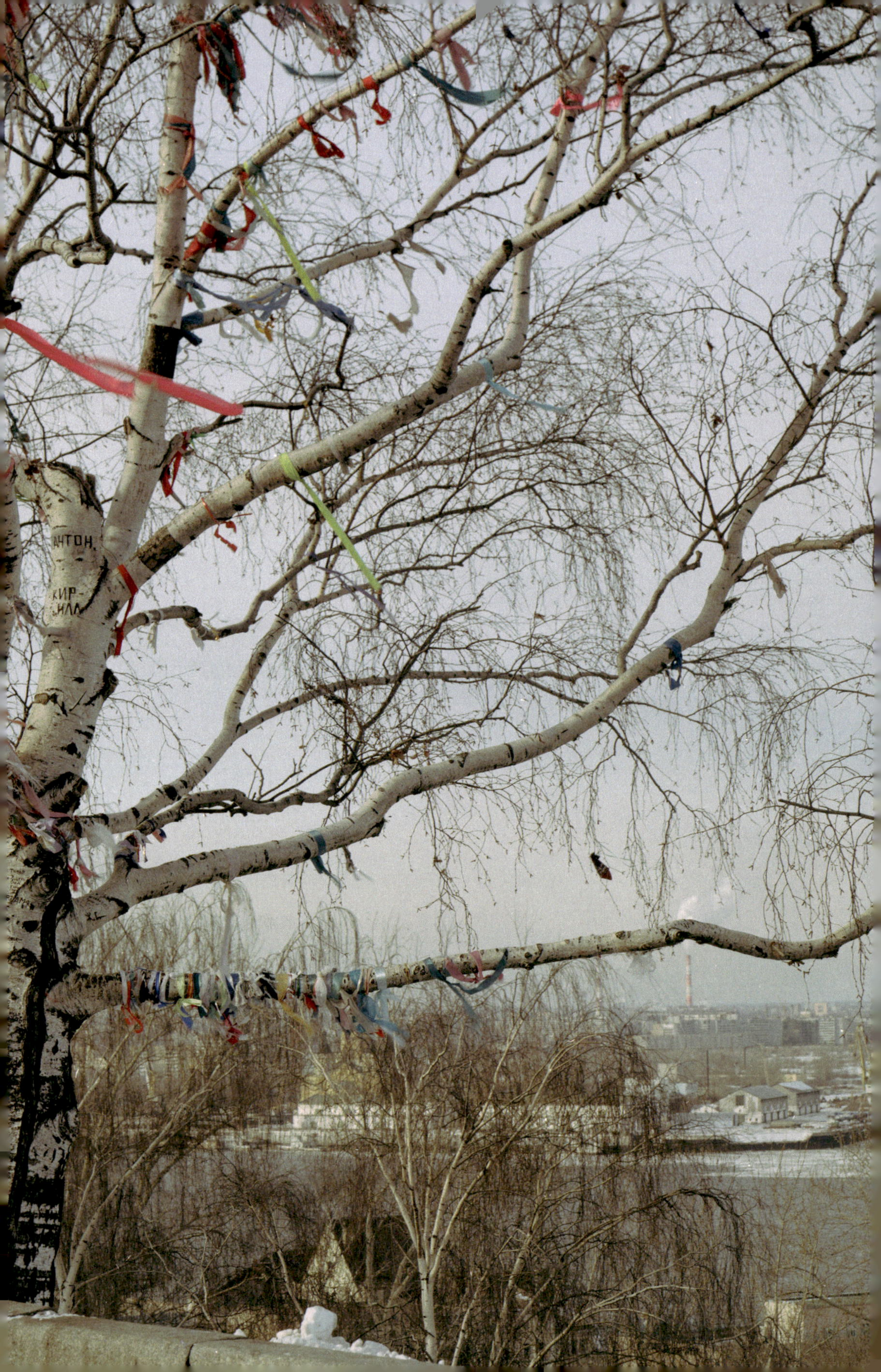

АНТОН
КИР-
ИЛЛ

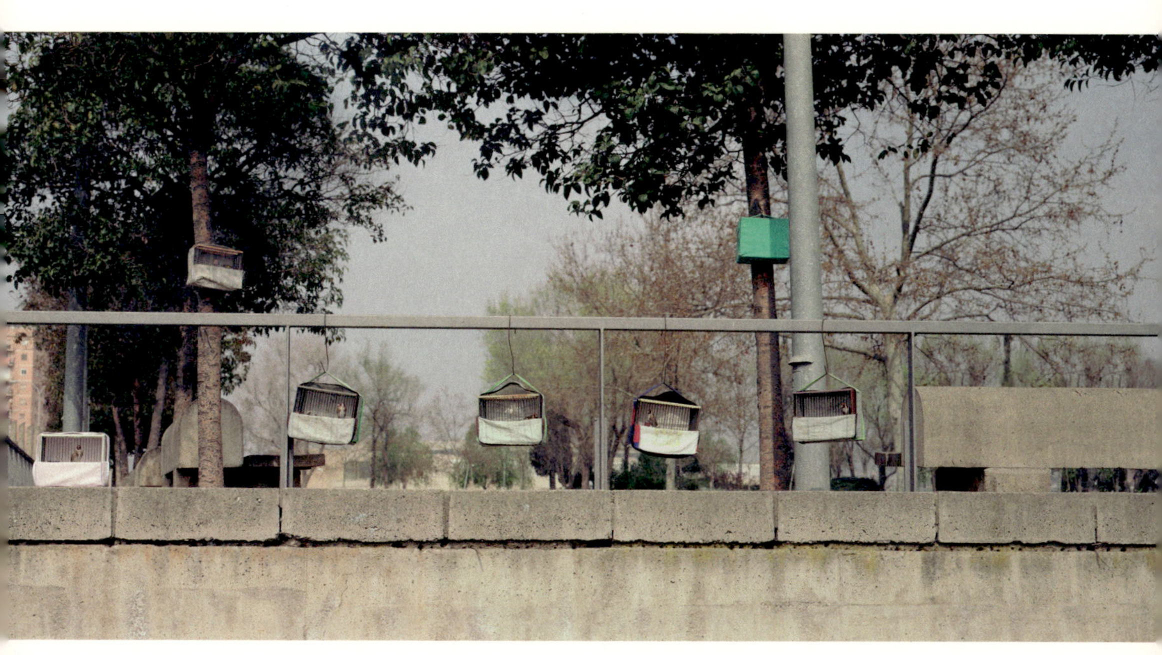

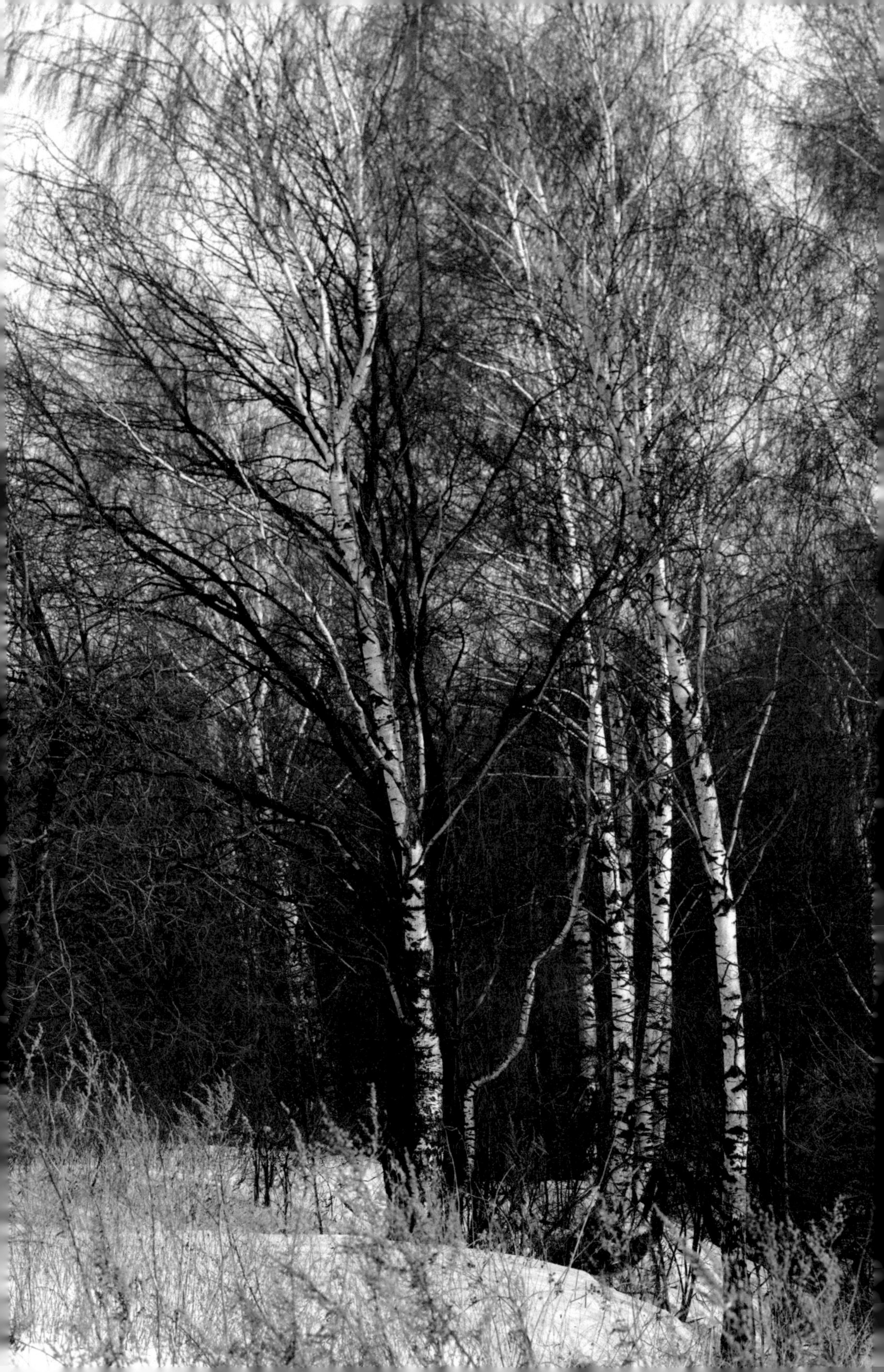

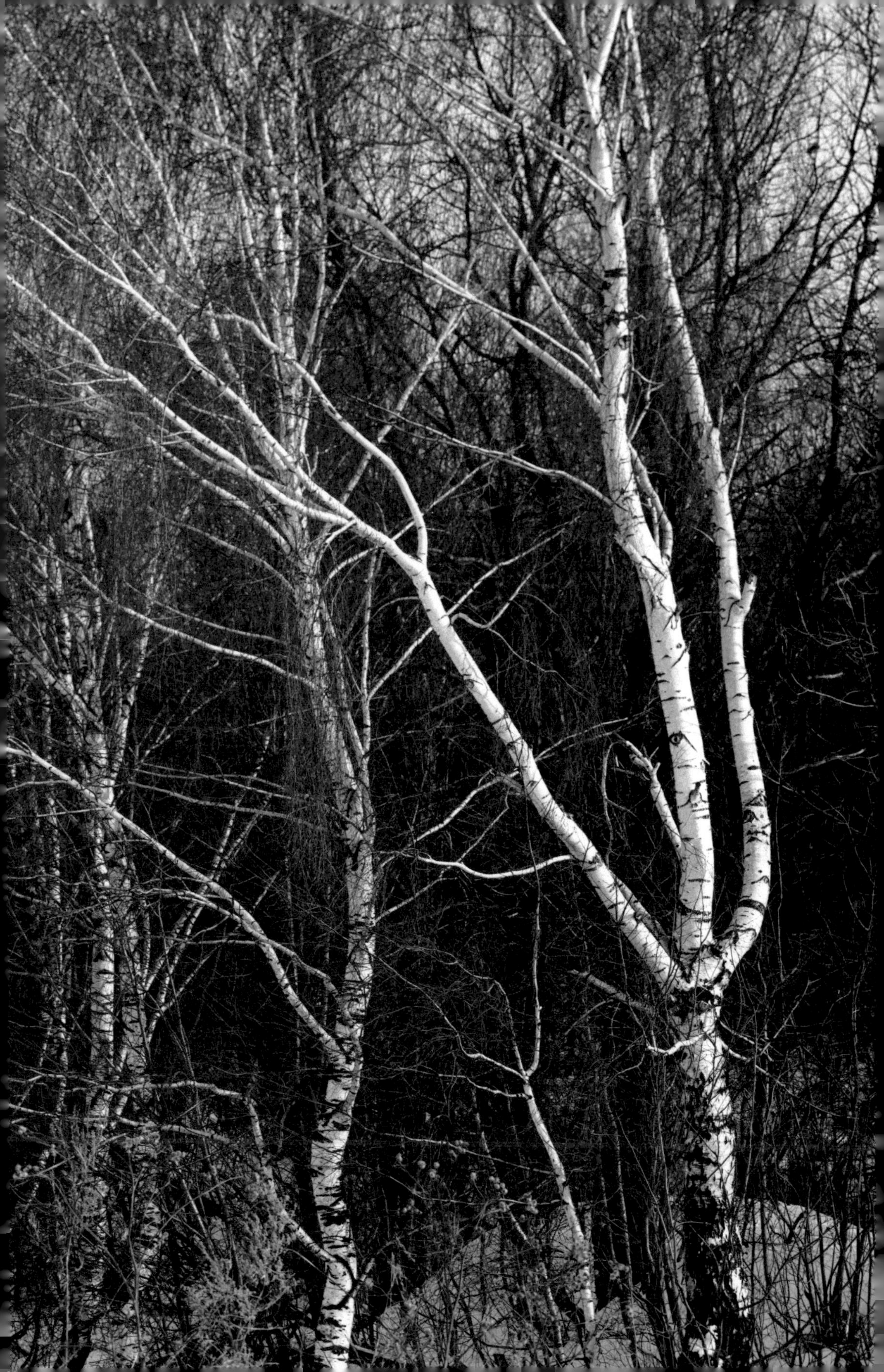

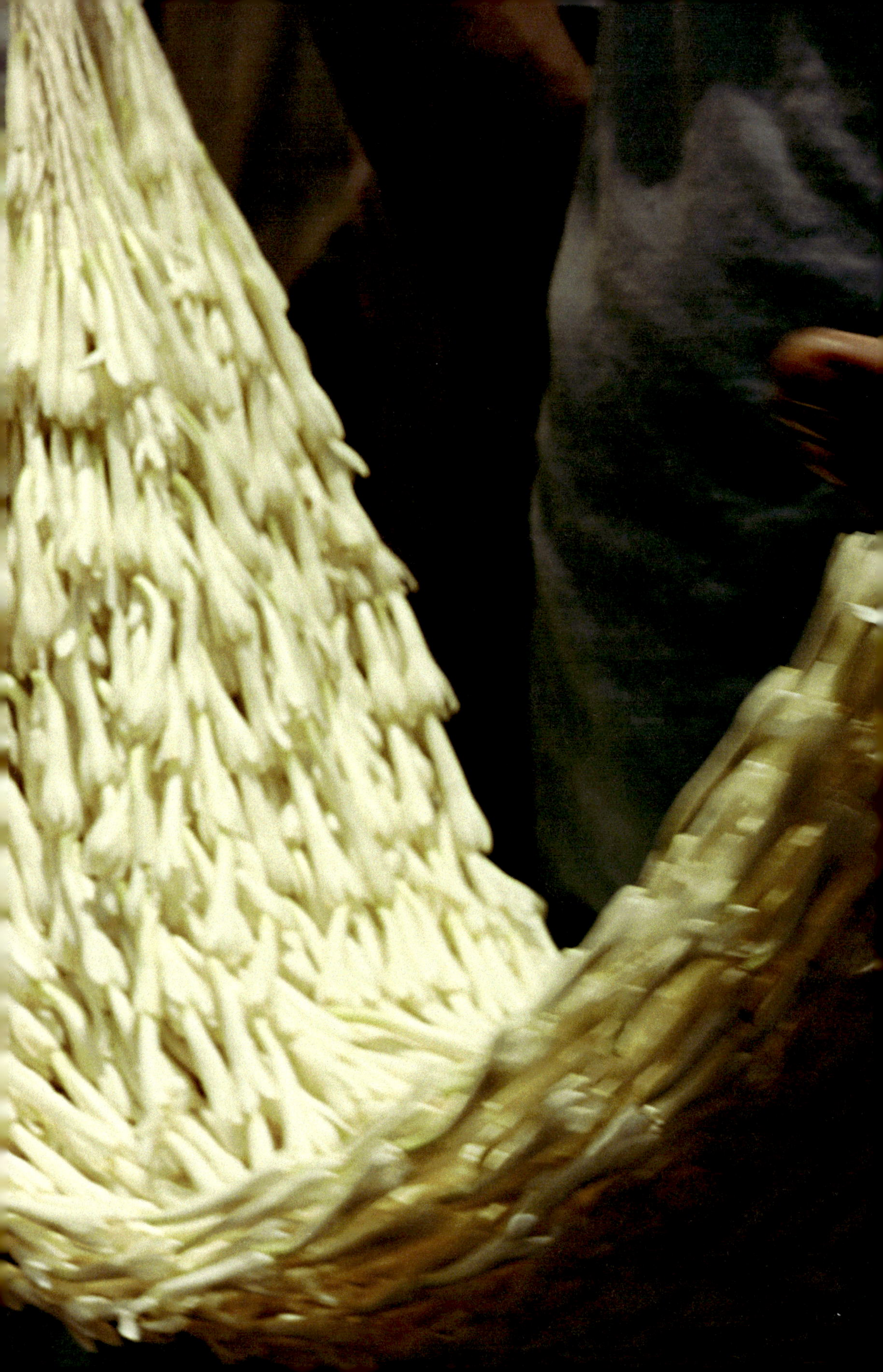

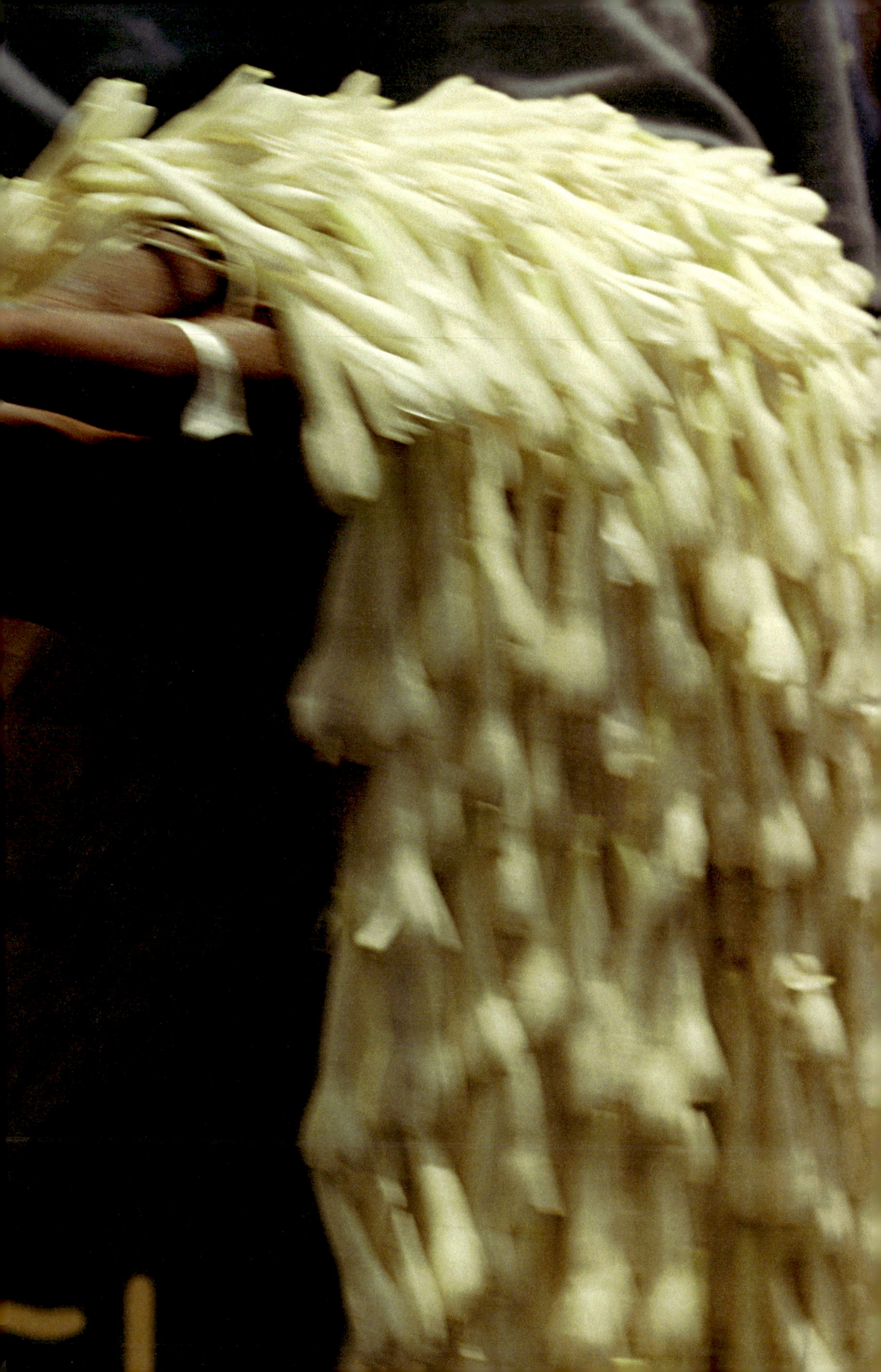

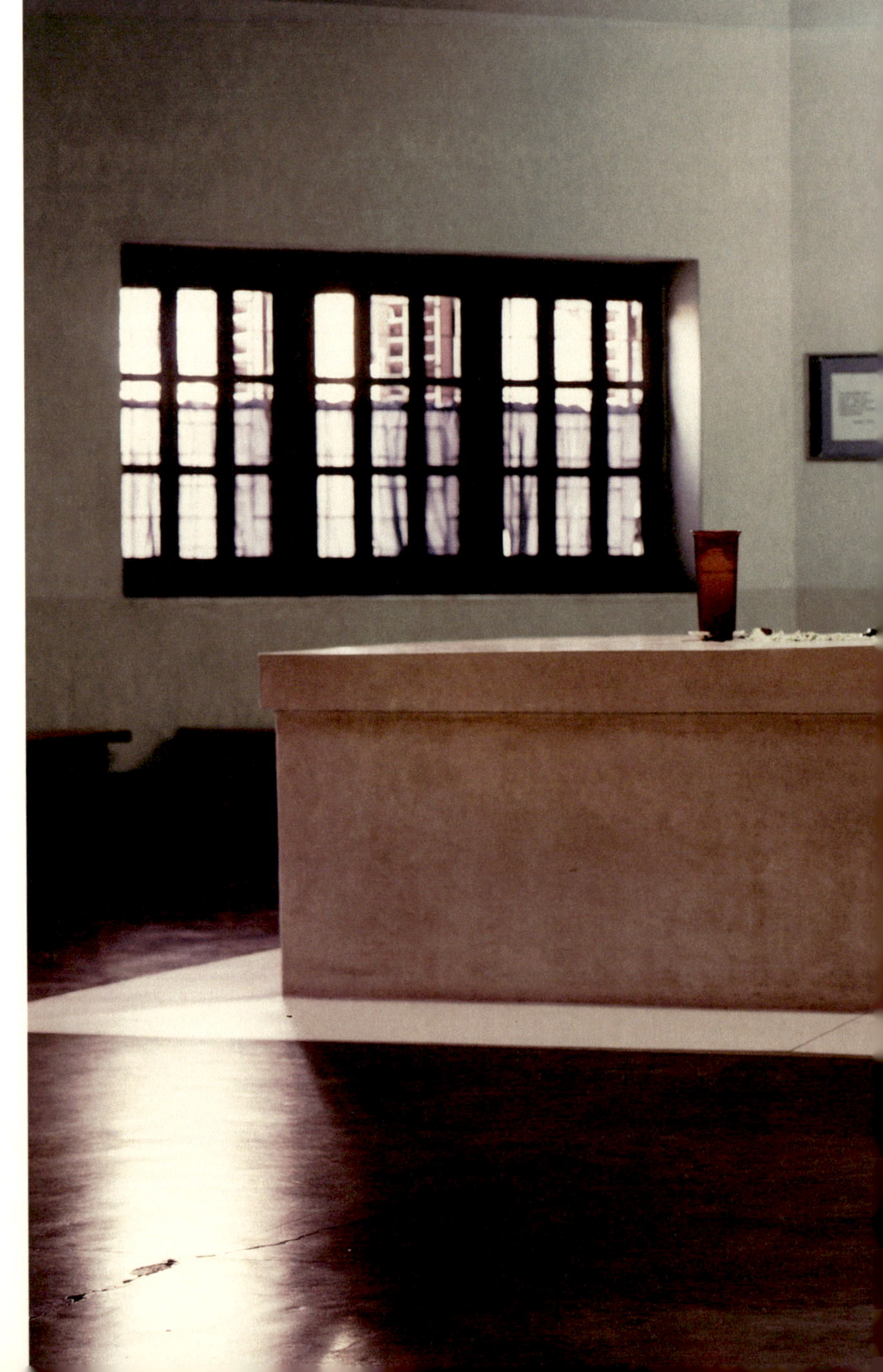

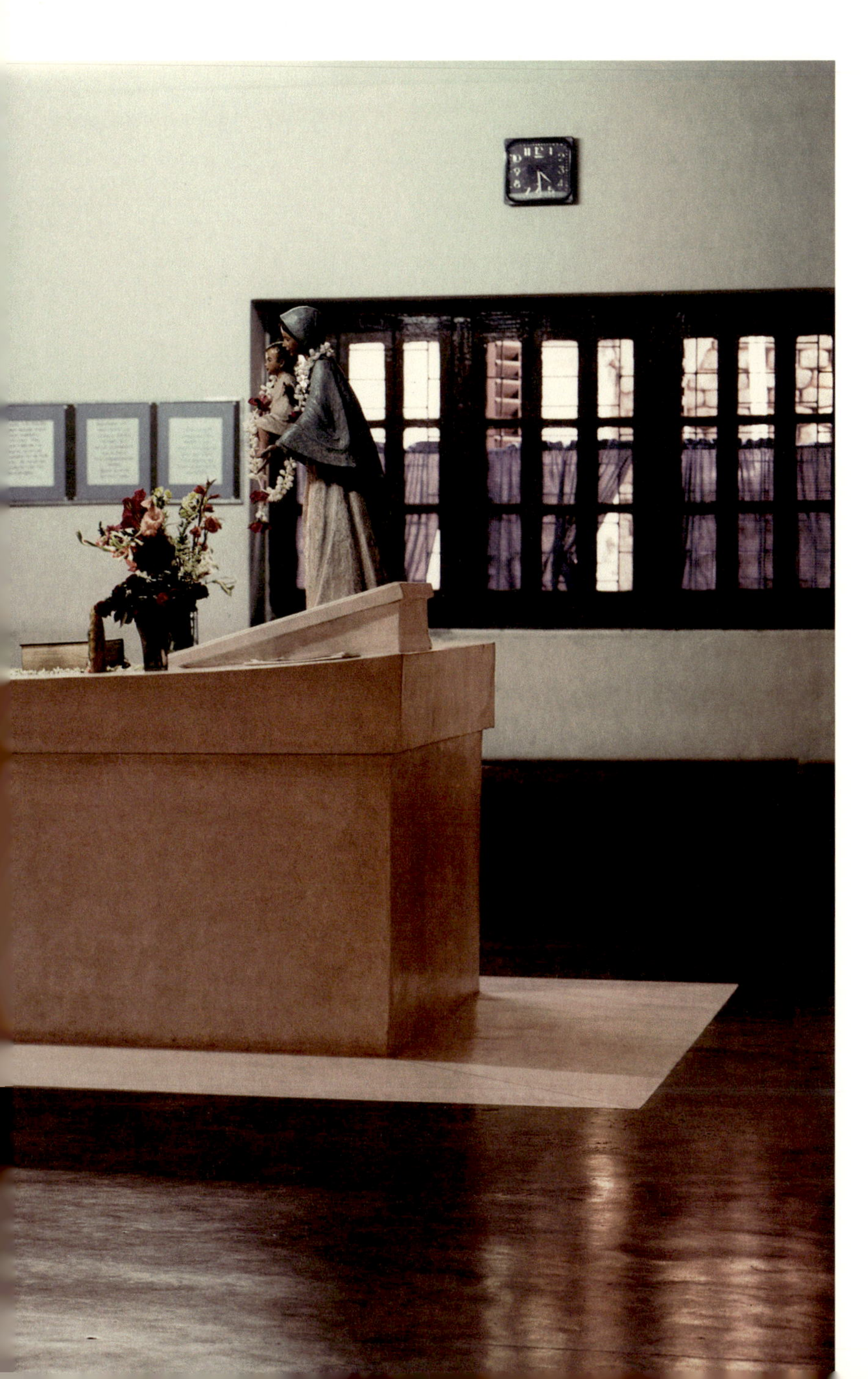

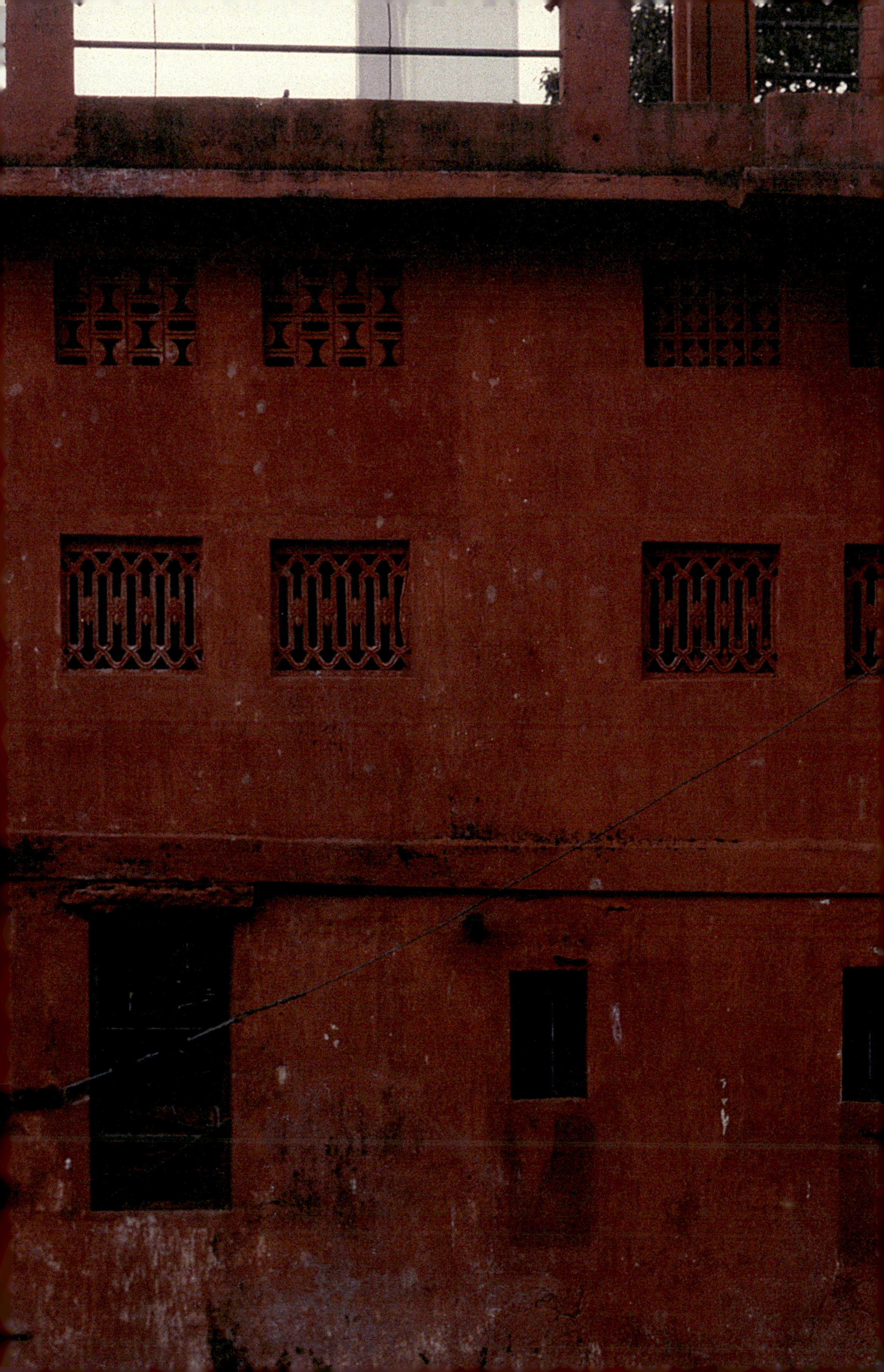

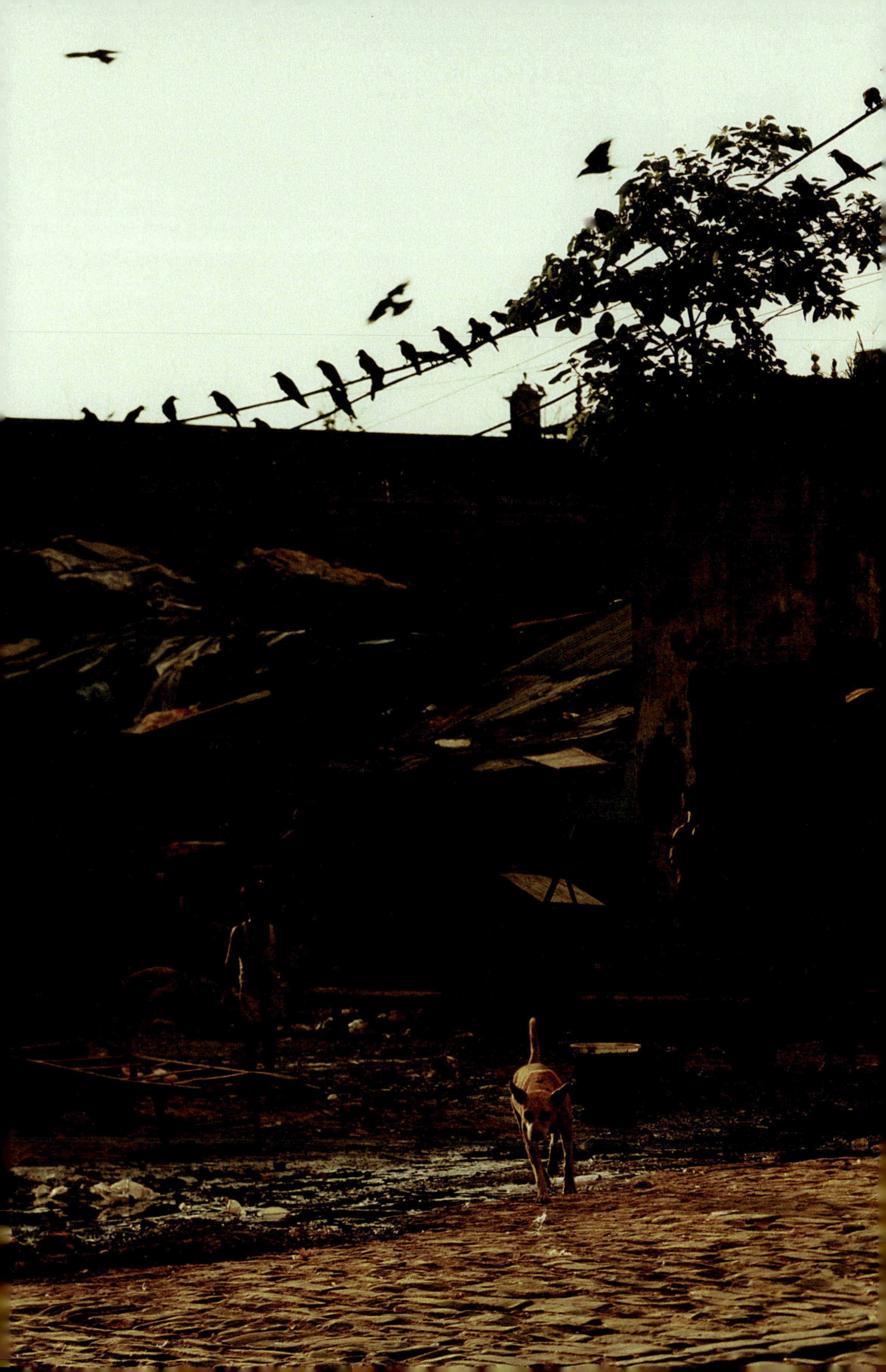

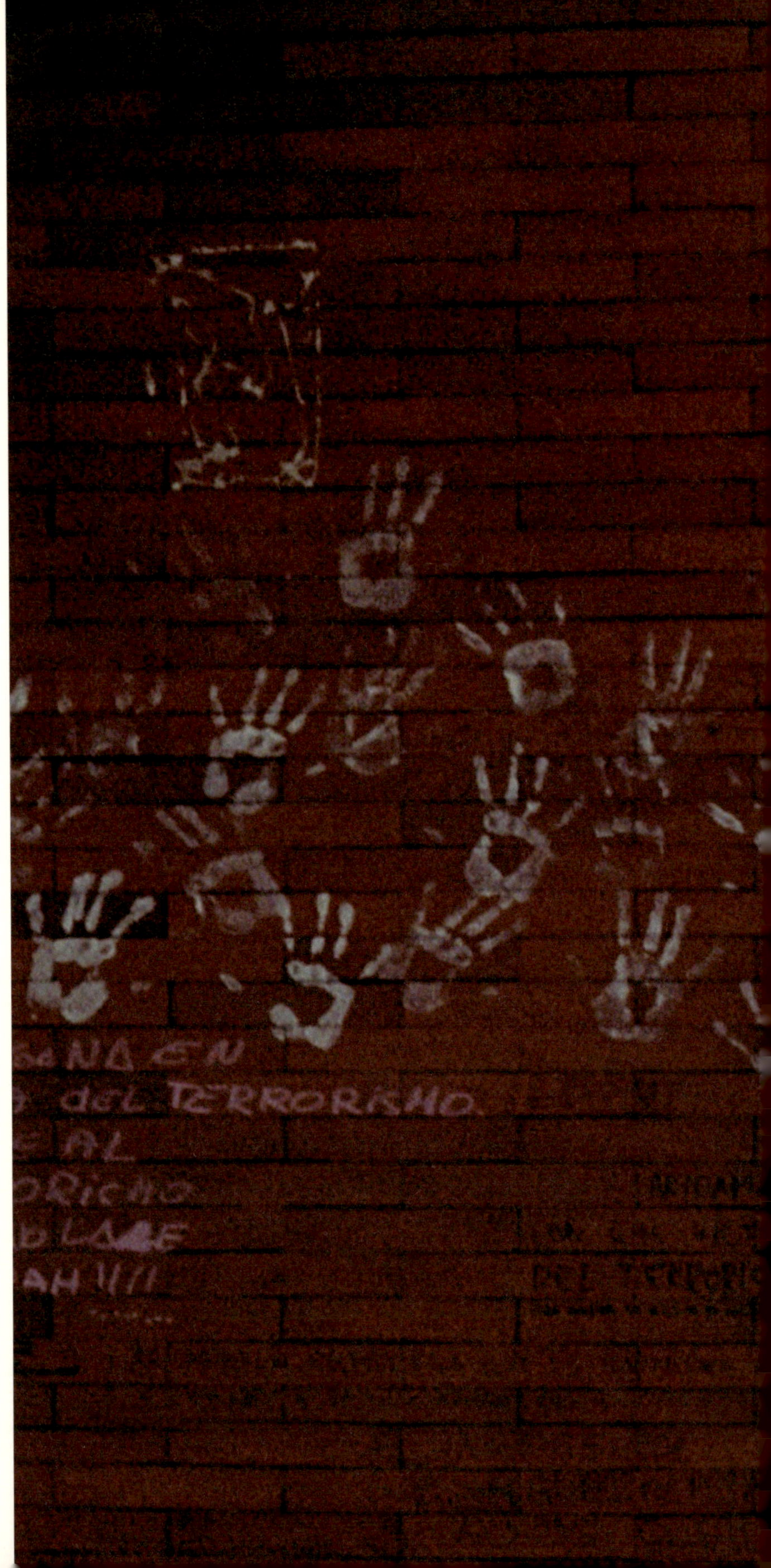

5.48

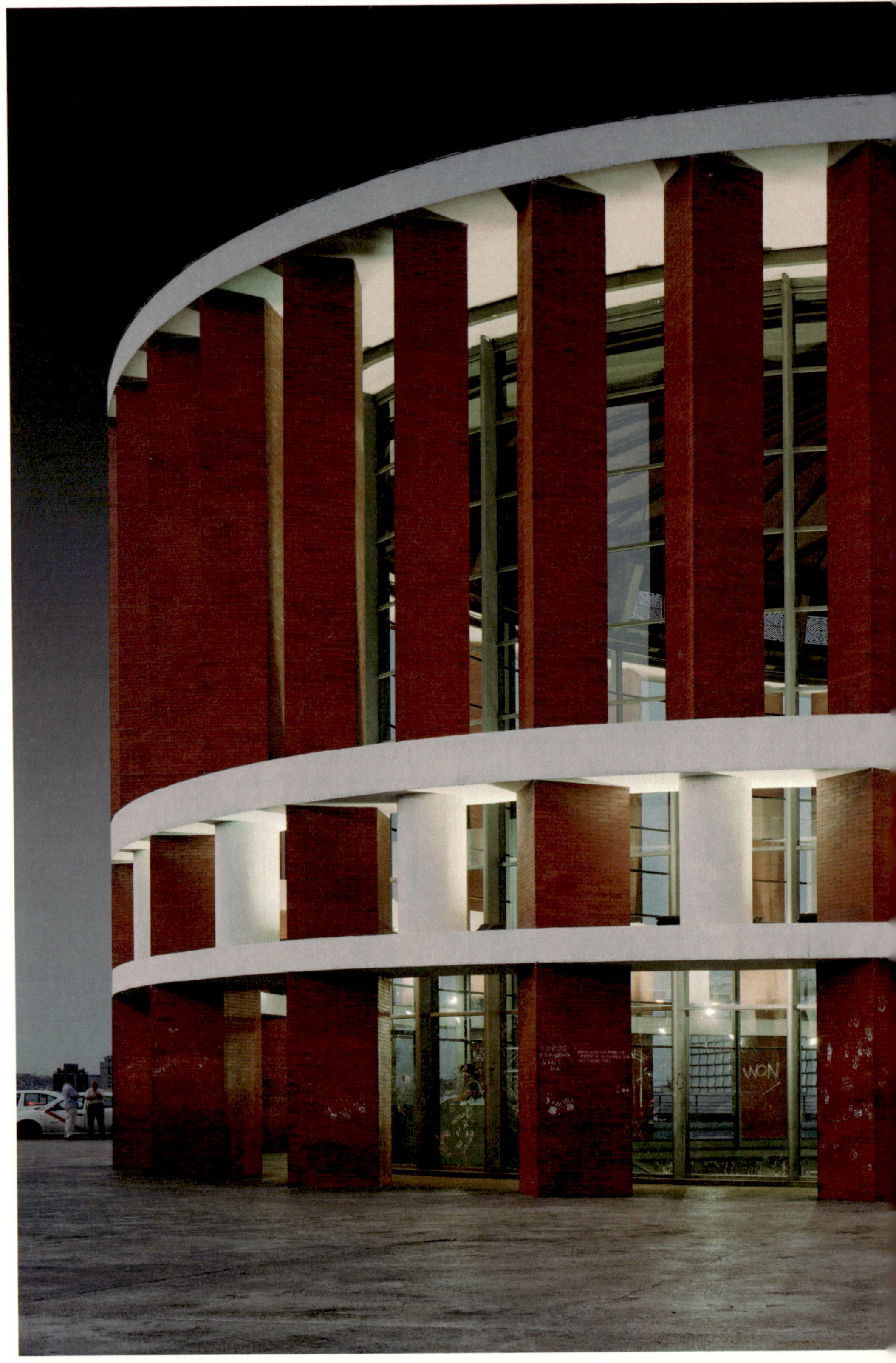

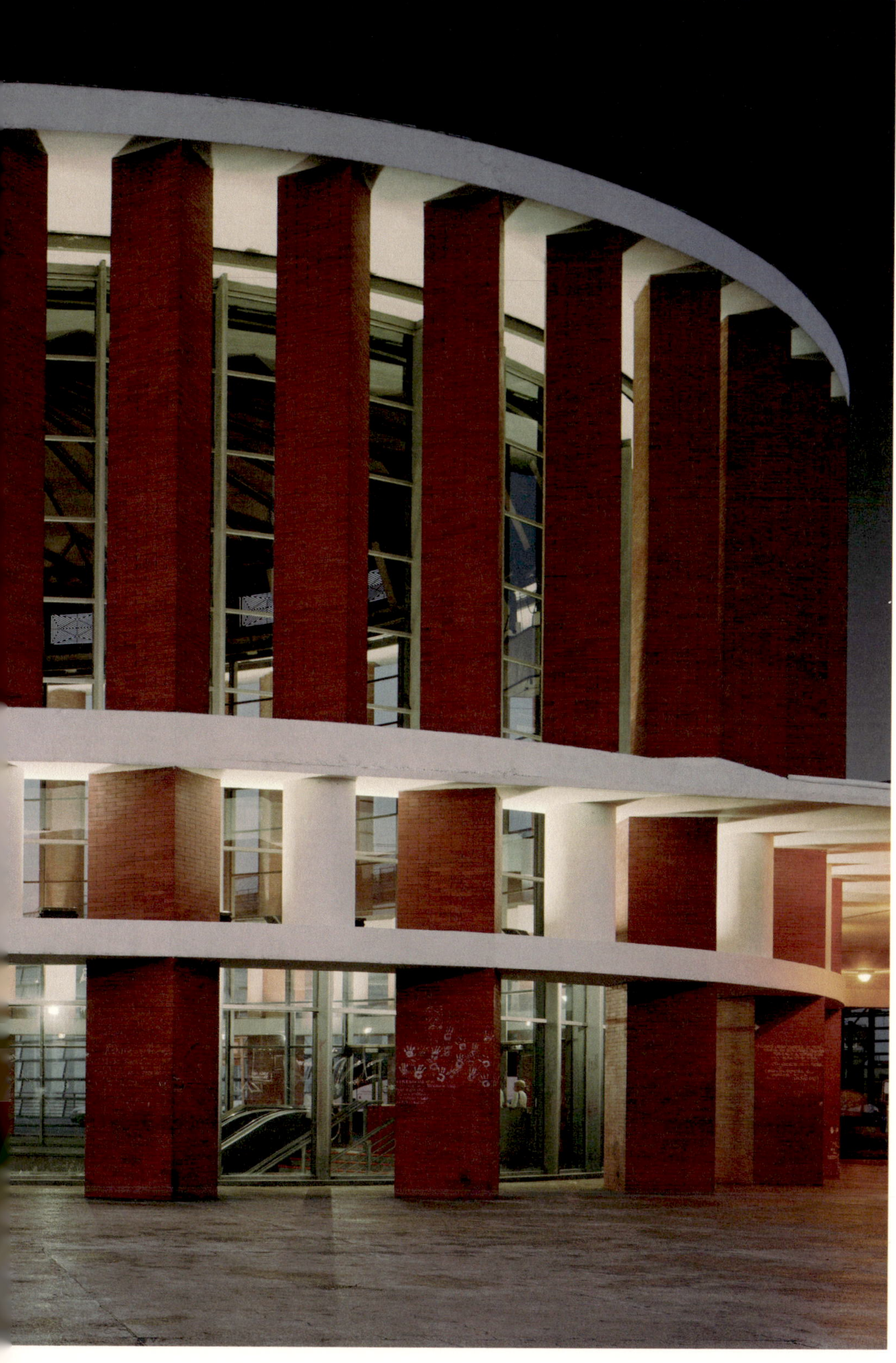

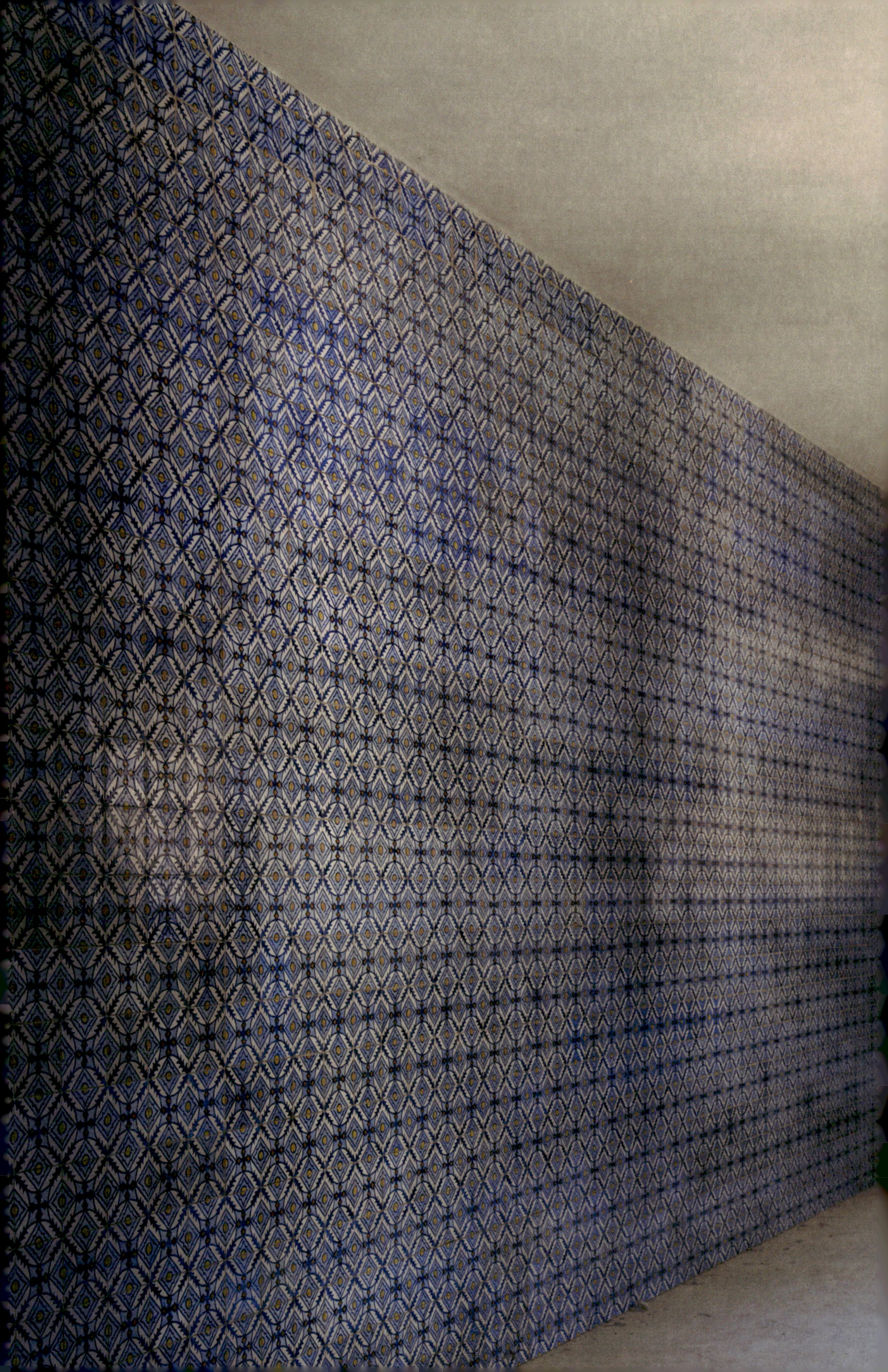

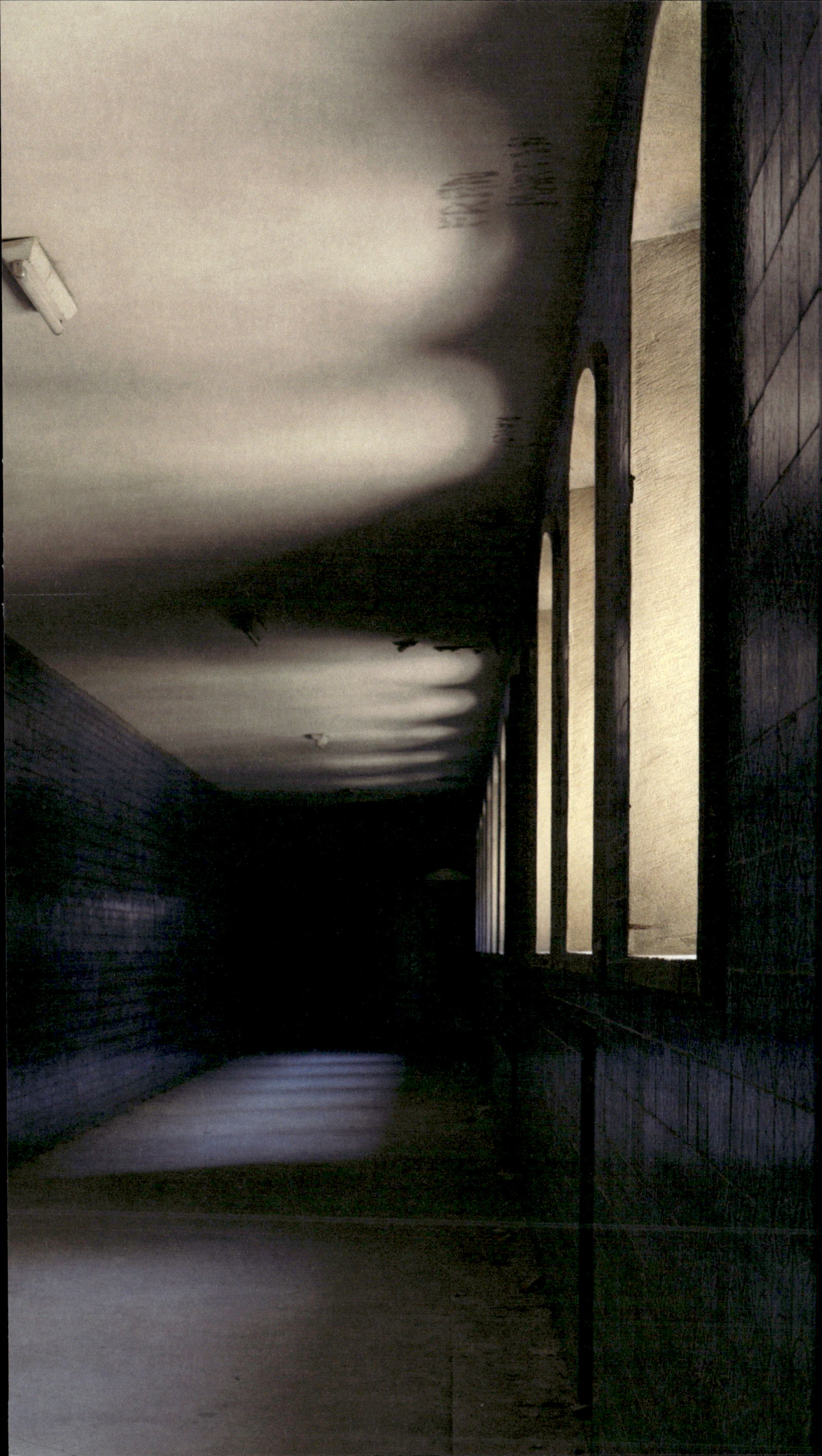

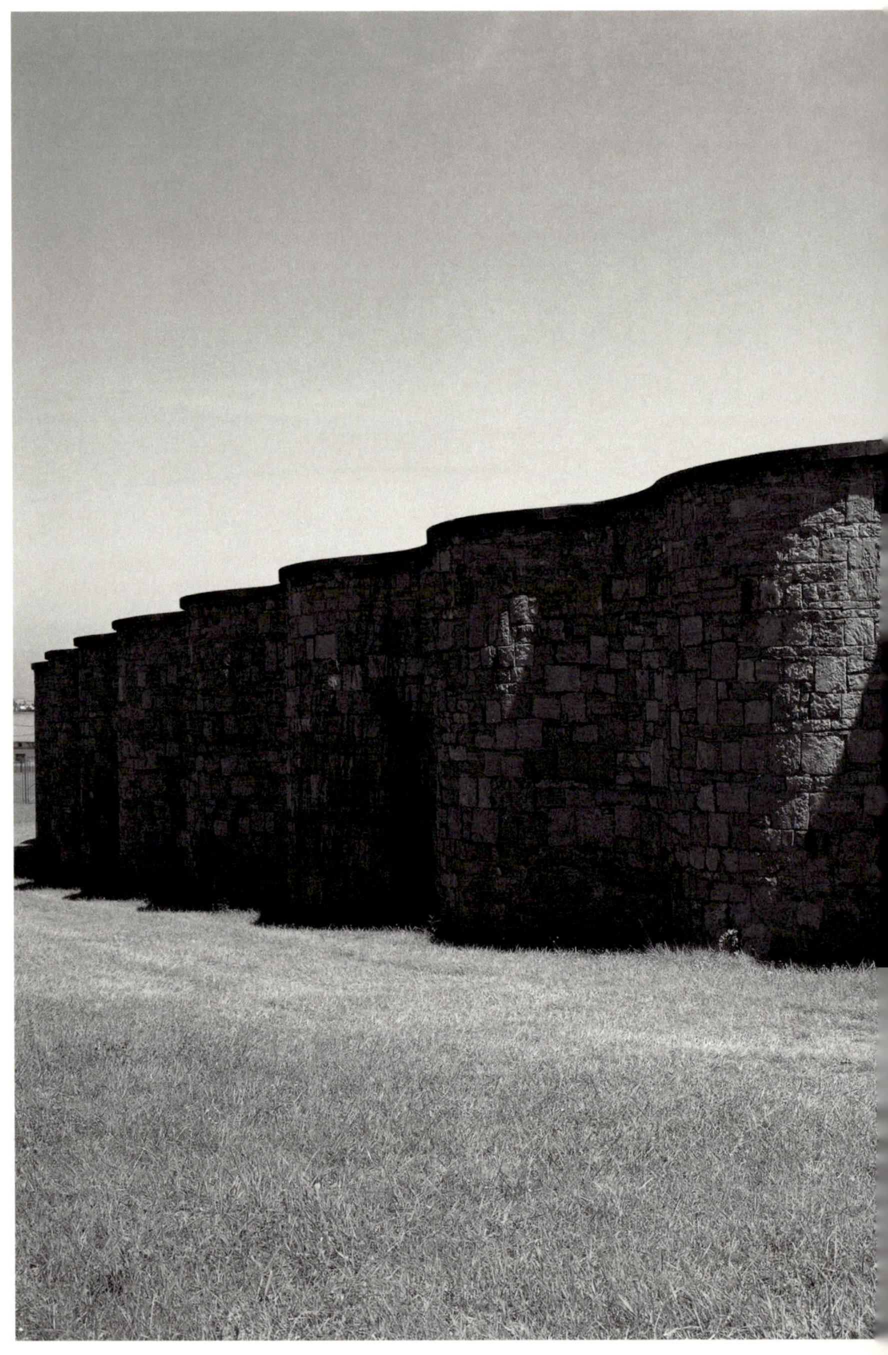

5.54

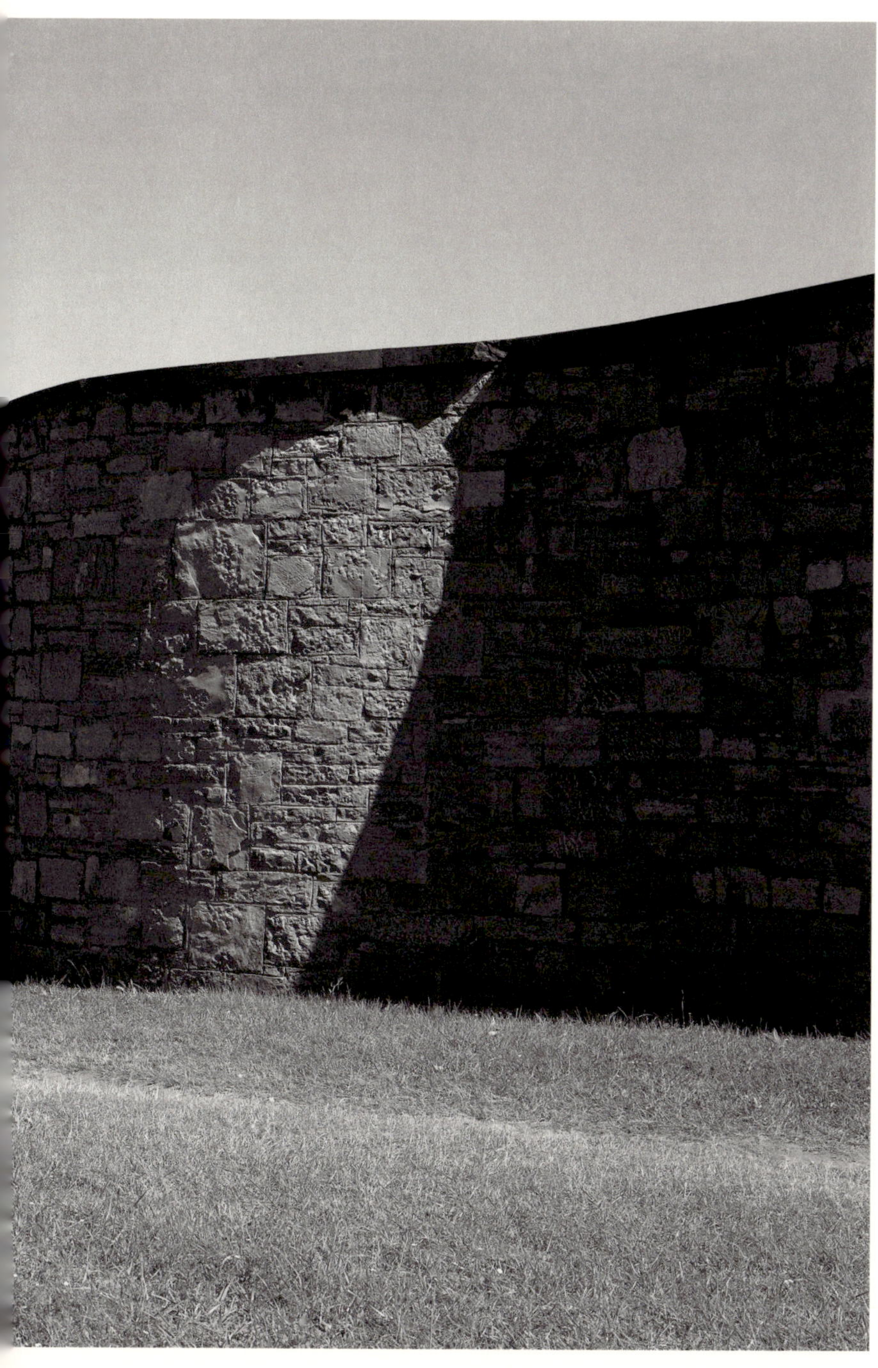

5.55

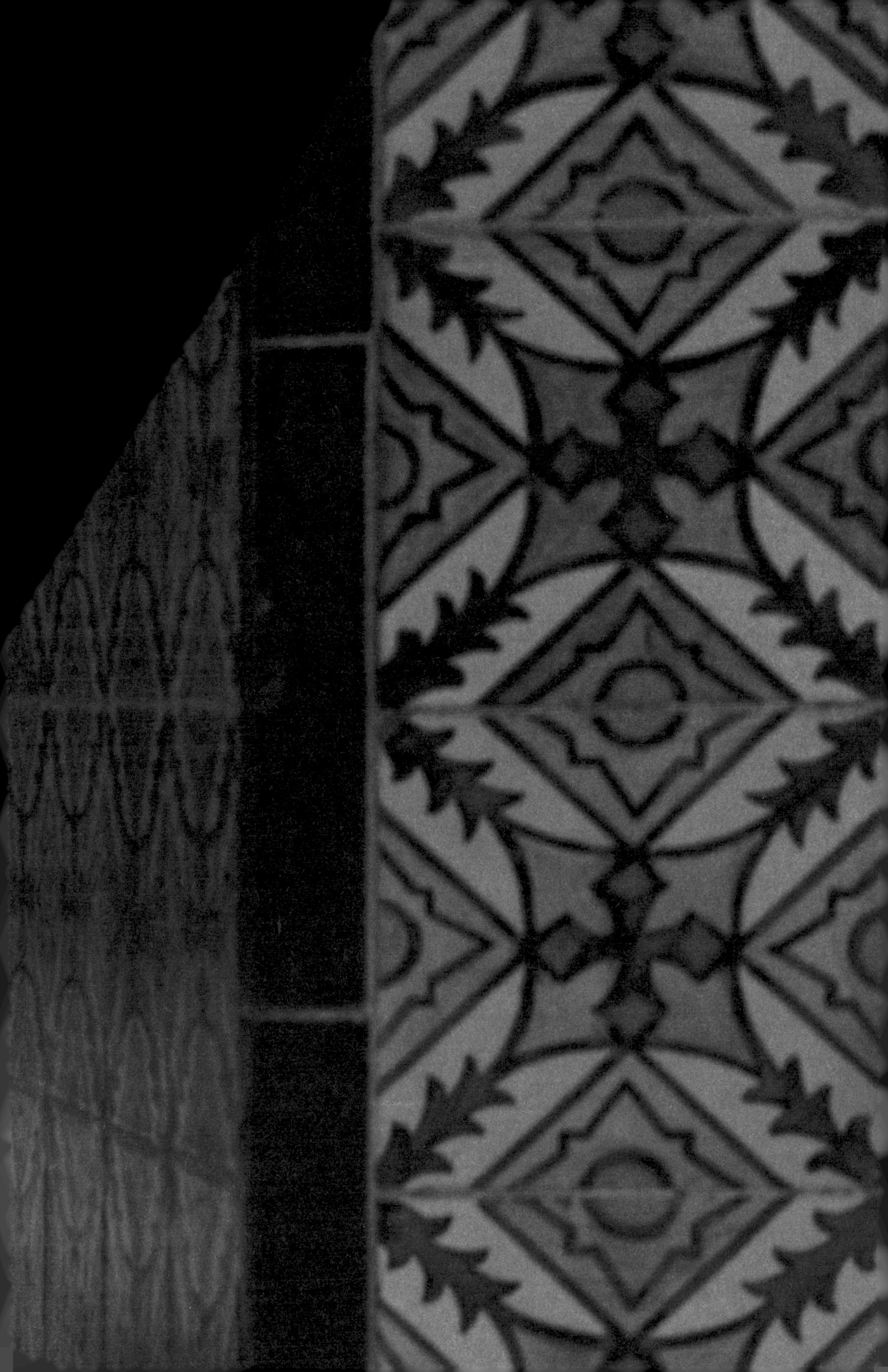

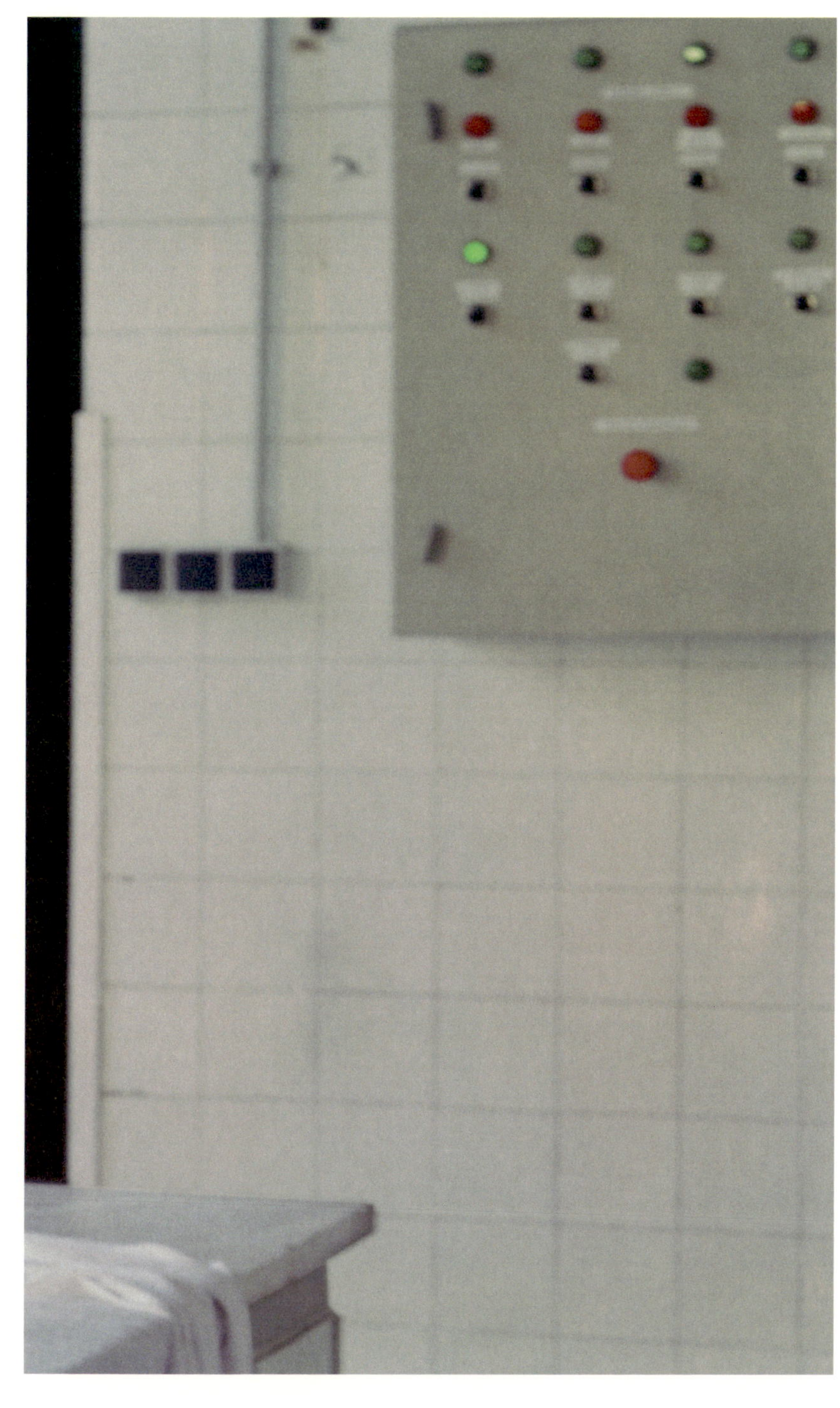

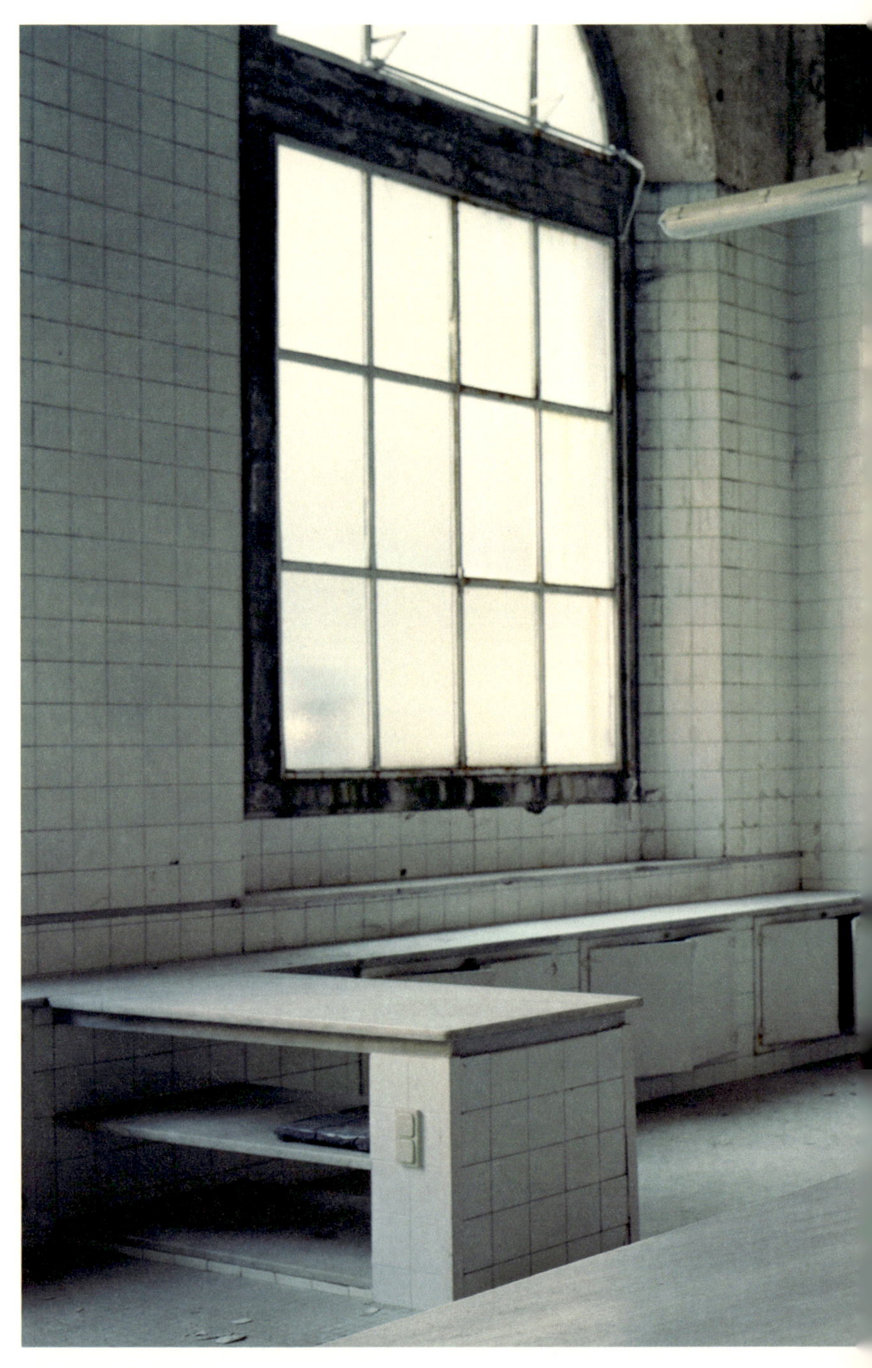

5.60

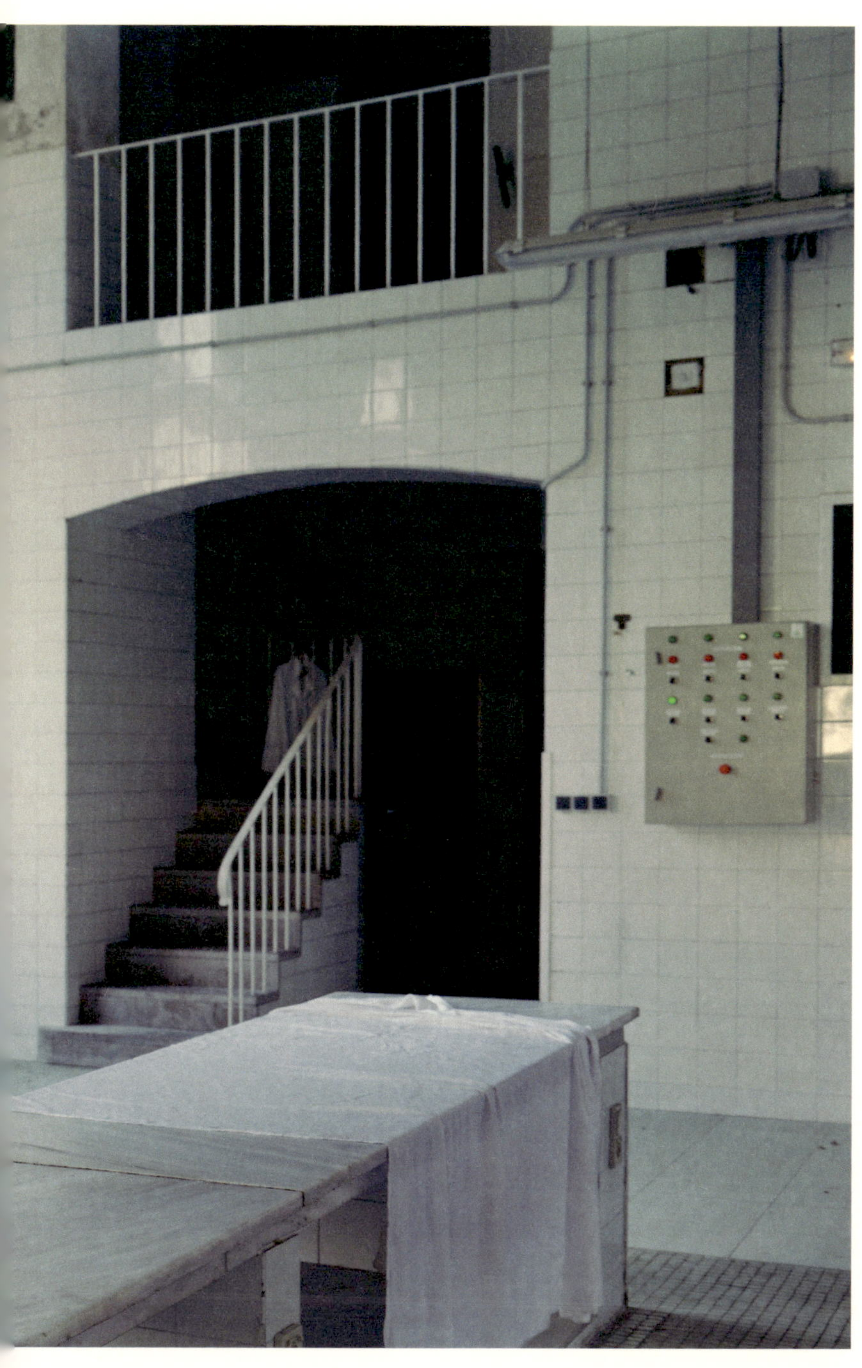

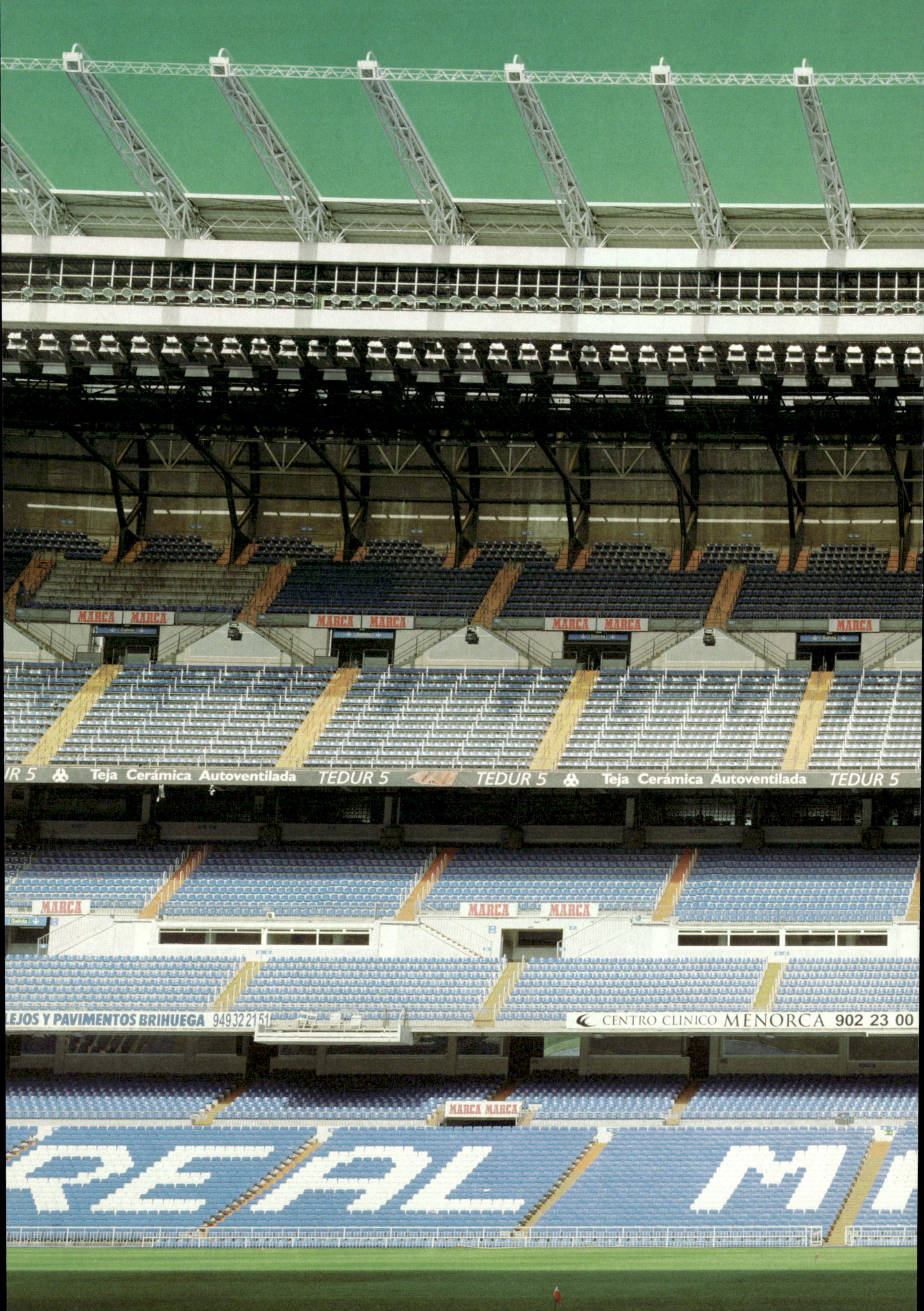

MARCA
Teja Cerámica Autoventilada   TEDUR 5
EJOS Y PAVIMENTOS BRIHUEGA   949 32 21 51
CENTRO CLINICO MENORCA   902 23 00
REAL M

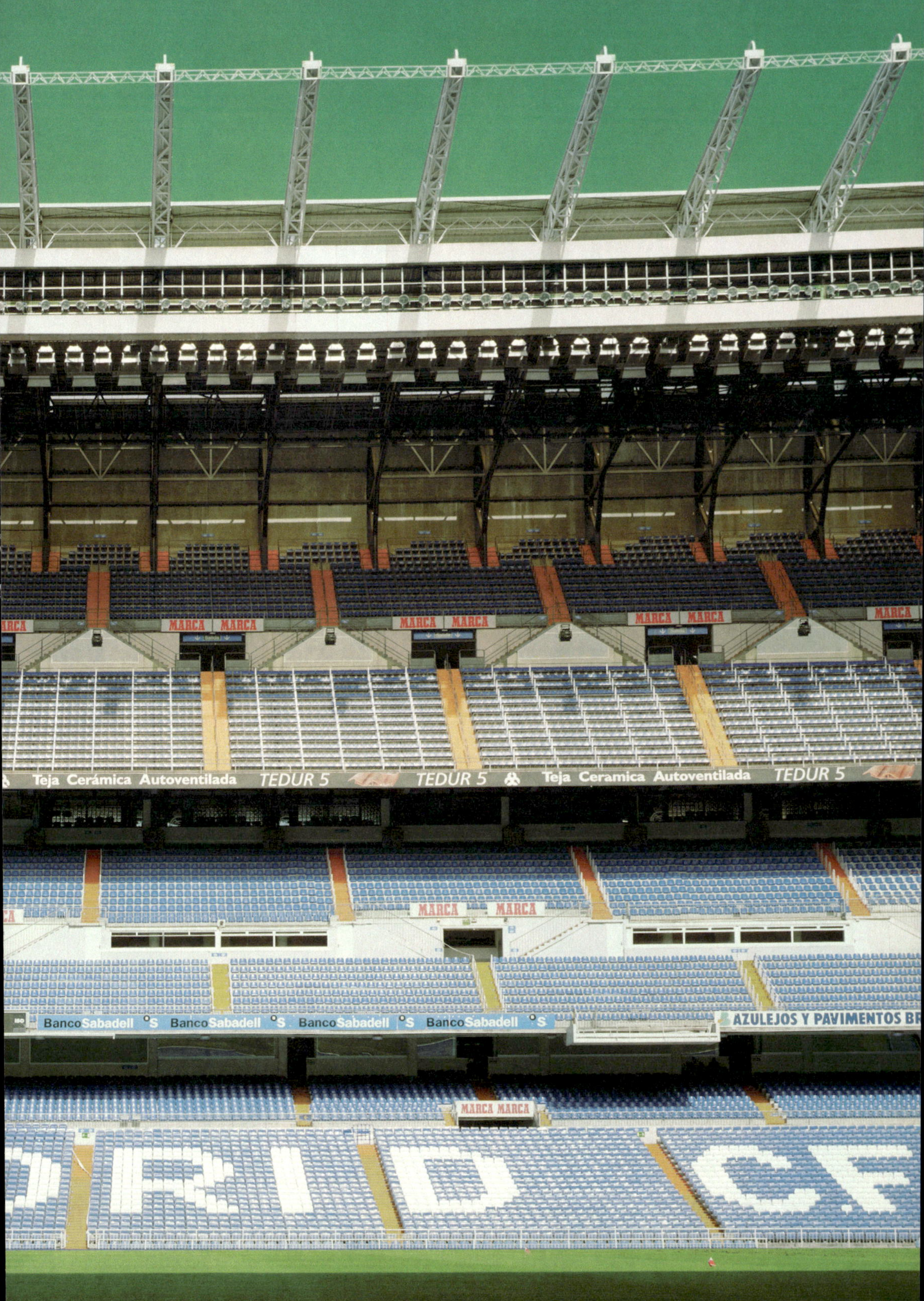
MARCA
MARCA MARCA
MARCA MARCA
MARCA
Teja Cerámica Autoventilada   TEDUR 5   TEDUR 5   Teja Cerámica Autoventilada   TEDUR 5
MARCA   MARCA
Banco Sabadell   S   Banco Sabadell   S   Banco Sabadell   S   Banco Sabadell   S   AZULEJOS Y PAVIMENTOS BR
MARCA MARCA
RID   CF

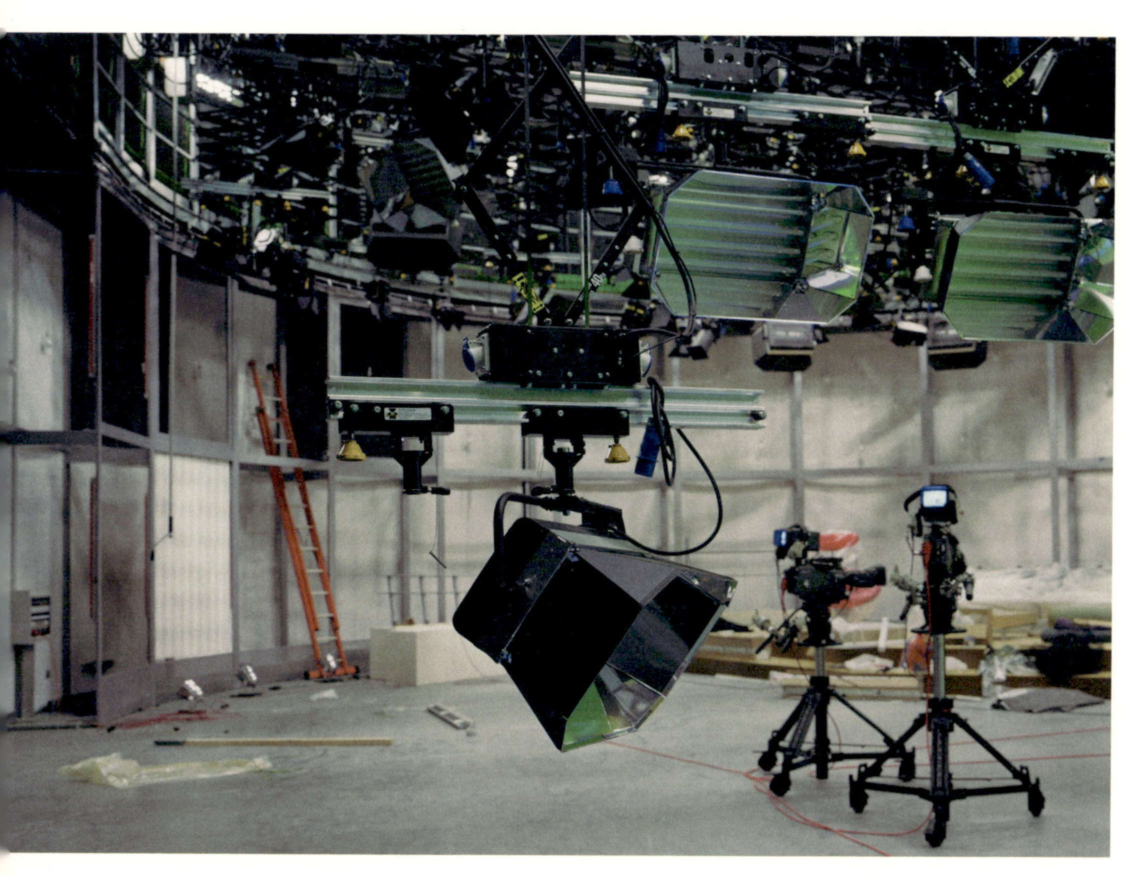

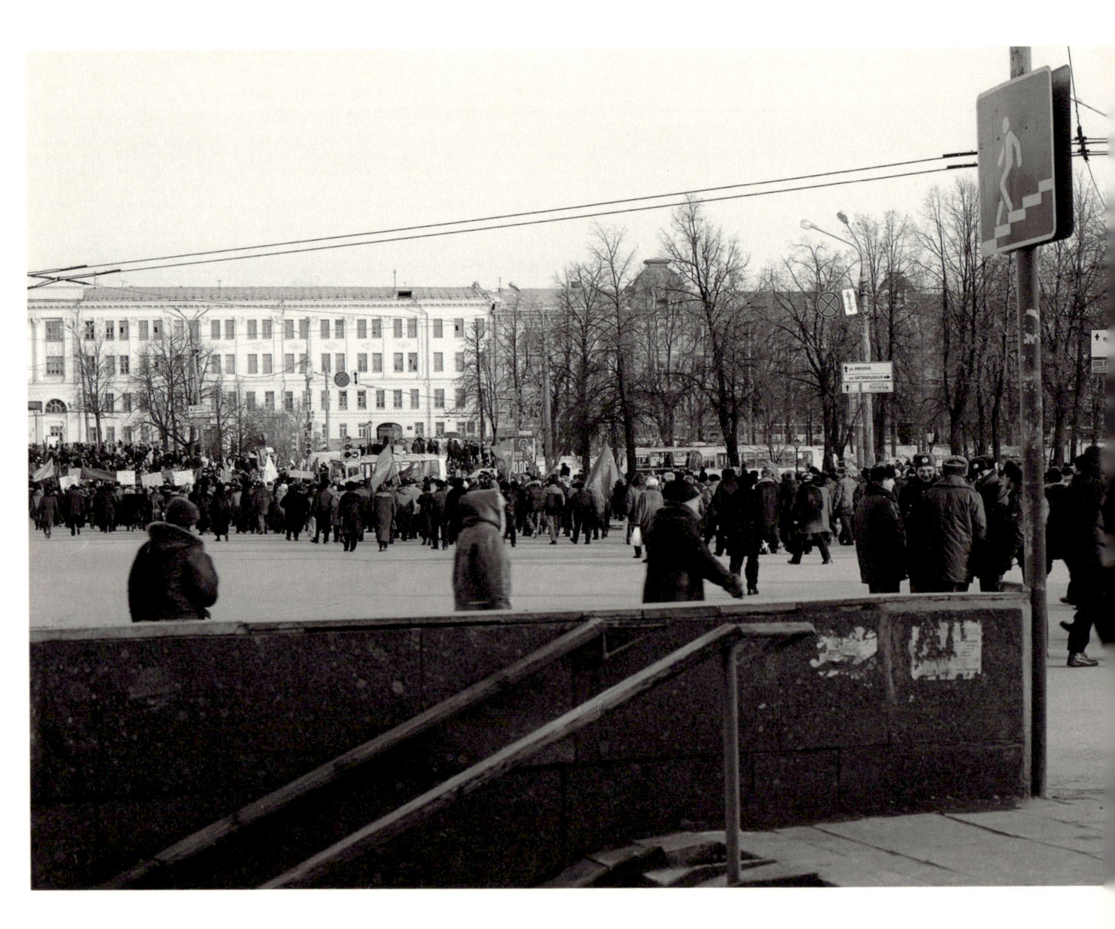

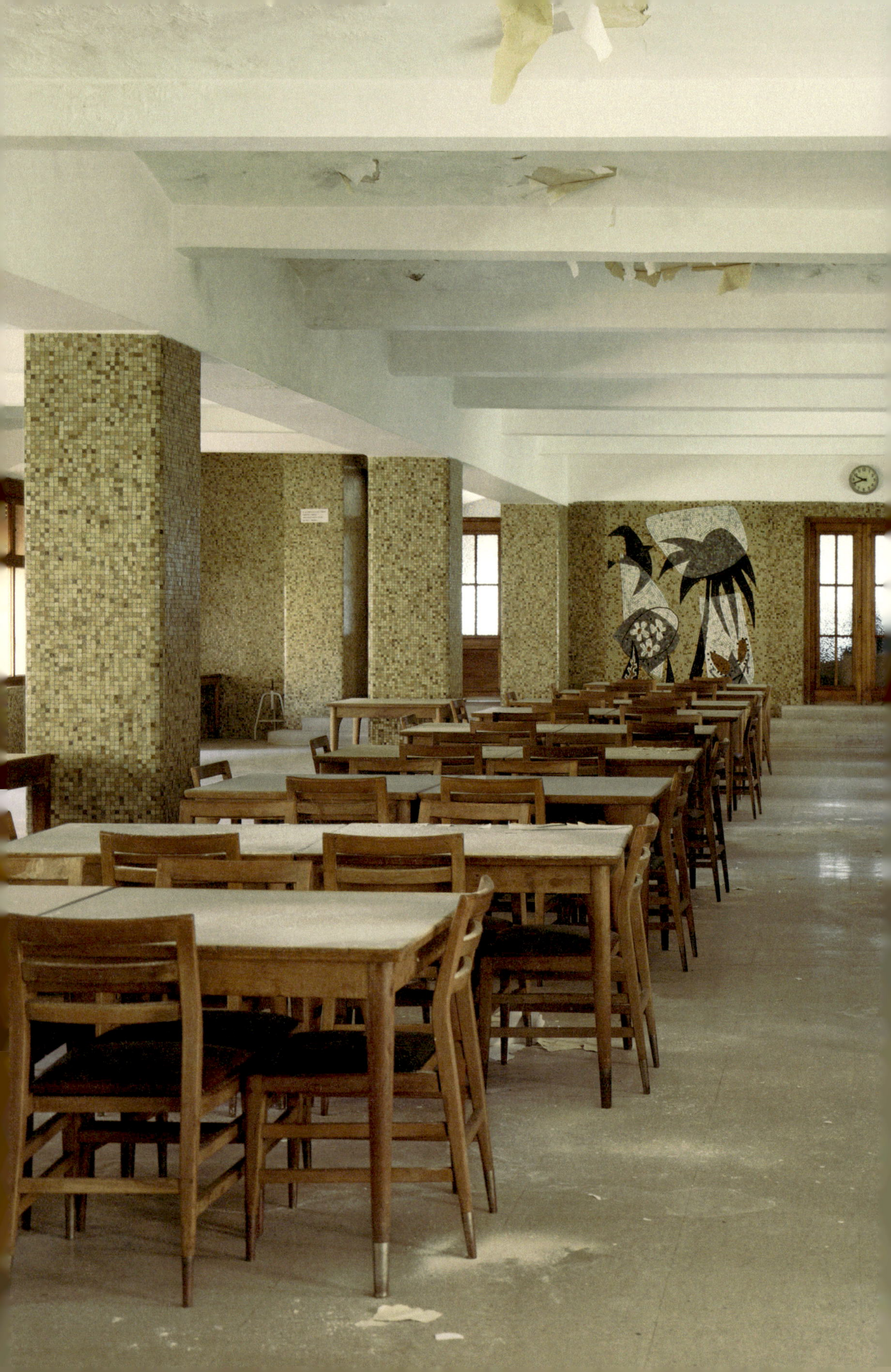

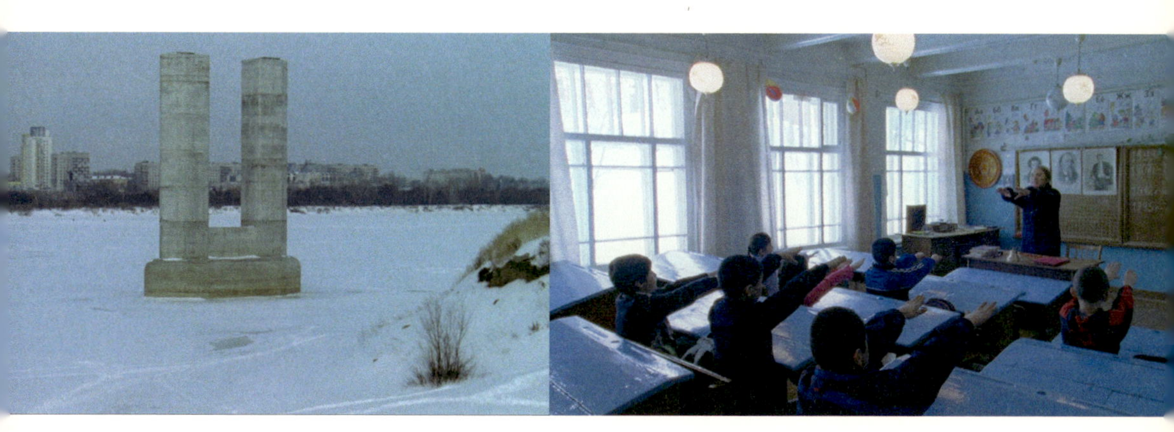

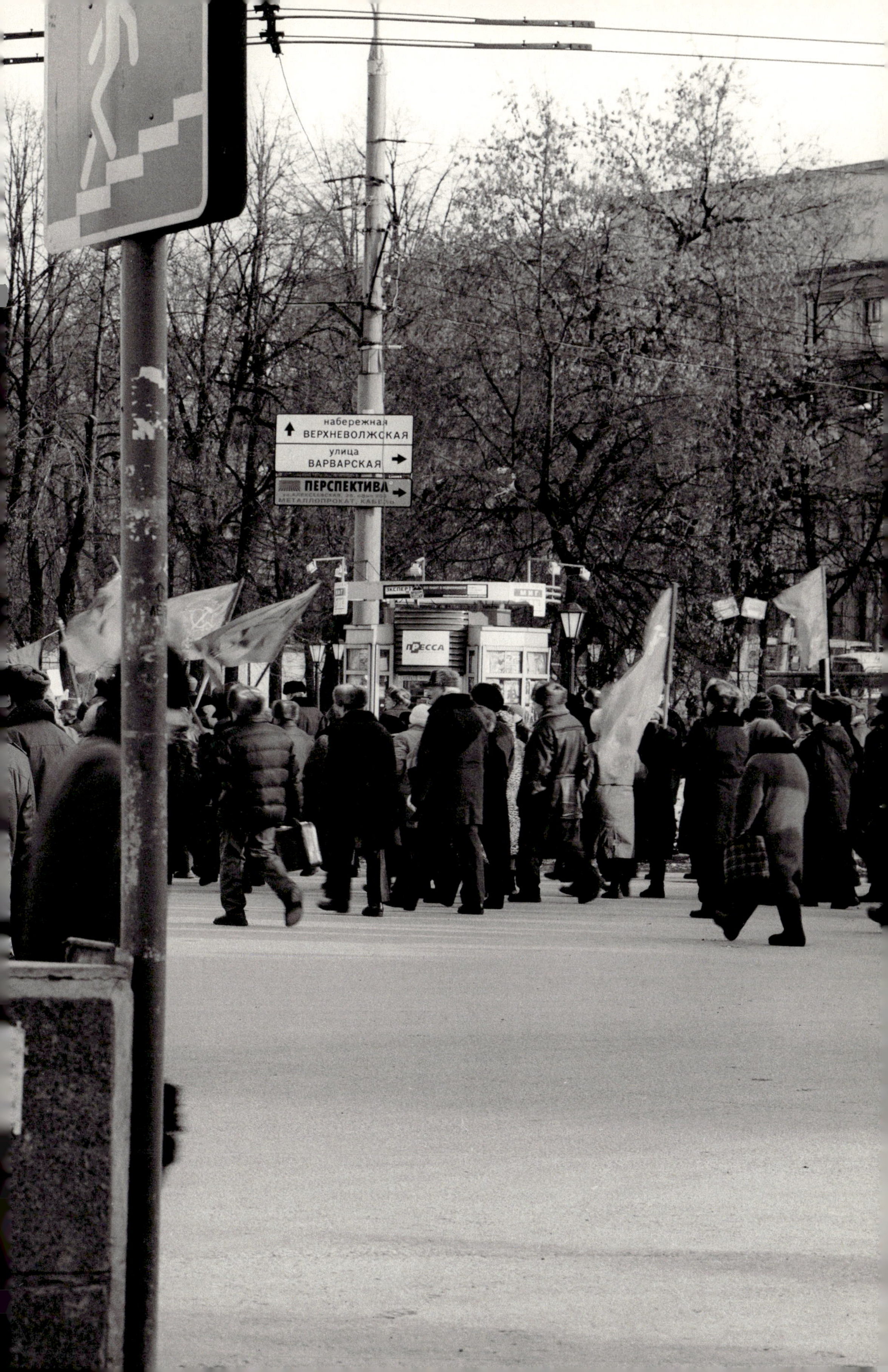

набережная
ВЕРХНЕВОЛЖСКАЯ
улица
ВАРВАРСКАЯ
ПЕРСПЕКТИВА
МЕТАЛЛОПРОКАТ. КАБЕЛЬ
пРЕССА

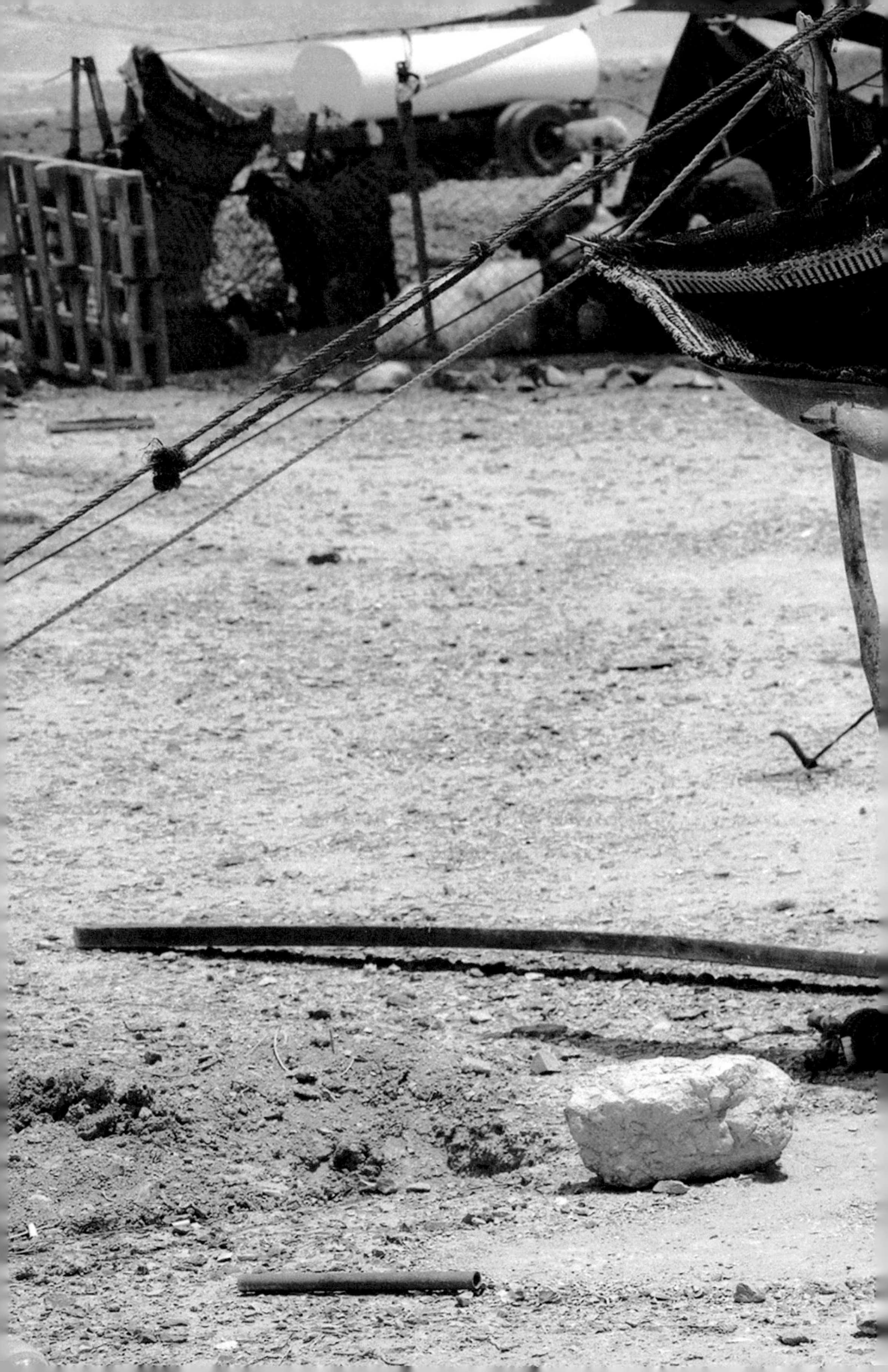

1 Events and Conditions

Unaware of immediate forces around me, it takes an event for sensations to be
triggered and circumstances brought into sharp relief. Events and conditions collide
— on a particularly cold night when I used to sleep in my studio, a line of fire-
coloured posters outside the Indian cinema in Calcutta. On a journey I remember
seeing a man walking on a freezing day beside a tiny Lada car, a vast polluting
Soviet factory and a deformed outsized tree beside him. The moment can be
a very intense thing and very complete way of looking at the past and projecting
into the future.

2 Finding, Transmitting, Receiving

The gypsy musicians playing on the beach have accepted their surroundings,
they only try to change things by music, they feel nature and have chosen to be
beside the sea. The musicians remain oblivious to the foul factory, locally known
as Chernobyl, which funnels its waste into the water through the long pipeline
in the background. Here I am, I brought them here to play and I am transmitting
that, just as I enjoy and am carried along by the music, their inner world lies
seamlessly in my outer one.

3 Ghosts

I found a collection of old photographic cards in a shop in Nizhny Novogorod
in Central Russia. This event coincided with the clearing of my mother's house
after she died in 2004 and with the finding of my childhood drawings made 45 years
ago. I had drawn a ghost standing next to me — an infinite future in which I might
later be a ghost, or a fragile friend to keep me company in the future or the past.
In the old studio photographs, the relationships at a particular point in time
are frozen. These people project their own desire to be remembered, to have
a permanent presence. I simply have no memory of the drawing I had made
of the ghost — though it is as absolutely real to me now as it was then — a jump,
into the past like a bridge in time.

4 Scripts

Before filming there is the script, like a net for catching something. The script
sets the scene for a particular set of circumstances. Each film project has happened
as a mixture of chance and intention, the time and the place have to be right.

5 Pavilions

Nature producing the materials for our environment gets its chance to illuminate
our path in architecture temporary and permanent. Mies van der Rohe used
diverse marbles for his Barcelona Pavilion, these are repeated and mirrored in the
creation of structures. The marble is transformed as part of his visionary modernity.
The tents of the Bedouin in the desert are immense and repetitious works anchored
to the ground using surrounding rocks. Whilst water in the courtyard of the Mies
Pavilion lies still, abstracted and removed from nature, Indians on a night pilgrimage
gather on a bridge over the Ganges, the powerful flow of the river becoming a part
of their ritual cleansing. The task of securing our futures, putting belief on display,
still returns to nature.

Selected Bibliography

WRITINGS BY THE ARTIST

"Filming in Russia. By Hannah Collins", *Vertigo*, Vol 3, No 3 (Autumn), 2006, pp. 42–44.

For the *Giorgio Morandi Catalogue*, Tate Modern, 2001, pp 34–35.

"La Vida en Pelicula — Life on Film", Galeria Joan Prats, September 1999.

Filming Things, Centre nationale de la photographie, Echo Books, 1997, pp. 19, 29, 47, 59, 69, 77, 87–91.

"Signs of Life. Diary Notes by Hannah Collins", 3rd Istanbul Biennial Catalogue, London: British Council, 1992. Reprinted in *In the Course of Time*, San Sebastian: Koldo Mitxelena, 1996.

A Worldwide Case of Homesickness, Dublin: Irish Museum of Modern Art, October 1996. Reprinted as *Filming Things*, 1997.

Desvan, Barcelona: Gallery Joan Prats, 1995.

INTERVIEWS

Gili, Marta, "Gestes", Toulouse: Printemps de septembre, Rendez-vous des images contemporaines, 2003.

"How to Stay Hungry, An Interview with Hannah Collins by Becky Beasley", London: Grey Area Books, March 2003.

Talking Photography, An interview with Shirley Read, Oral History, British Library National Sound Archive, 2003.

Without Walls, The Turner Prize, produced by John Wyver, Illuminations, 1993.

A Conversation with Hannah Collins, " Signs of Life", Michael Corris, 3rd Istanbul Biennal Catalogue, London: British Council, 1992.

Books and Catalogues by the Artist

Shopping, Barcelona: Echo Books, 1996.

A Worldwide Case of Homesickness, Dublin: Irish Museum of Modern Art, 1996.

The Hunter's Space, London: Chisenhale Gallery and Manchester: Cornerhouse
Gallery, 1995.

Legends, London: Matt's Gallery and Institute of Contemporary Arts and
Derry: Orchard Gallery, 1988.

Monographs and Exhibition Catalogues

Blazwick, Iwona, *Excessive Visions*, Barcelona: Centre d'Art Santa Monica,
Departament de Cultura, 1993.

Brea, Jose Luis, *The Land of the Last Men (stories)*, Barcelona: Centre d'Art Santa
Monica, Departament de Cultura, 1993.

Condo, George, *Hannah Collins*, Barcelona: Galeria Joan Prats, 1992.

Cork, Richard, *Secular Shrines, Colindale Hospital Project*, London: Public Art
Development Trust, 1993.

Durand, Regis, *The World of Hannah Collins/Le Monde de Hannah Collins,
Filming Things*, Paris: Centre nationale de la photographie, 1997.

LaVoie, Vicent, *La Mina*, Montreal: VOX, Centre de l'image contemporaine, 2004.

Legallais, Catherine, *A Worldwide Homesickness, In the Course of Time*,
San Sebastian: Koldo Mitxelena Kulturunea, 1996.

Legallais, Catherine, *Le faste étrange des perles et des coraux, Profil d'une collection*,
FRAC Basse-Normandie, 1995.

Noble, Richard, *Bird Land, The Street*, Malaga: CAC Malaga, 2002.

Peran, Marti, *Transitional Spaces, Hotel of Being*, Barcelona: Galeria Joan Prats, 2002.

Renton, Andrew, *An Image taken (away) and a site wherein it may be recalled,
The Hunter's Space*, London: Chisenhale Gallery, 1995.

Stimson, Blake, *Bonjour Madamoiselle Collins, The Street*, Malaga: CAC Malaga, 2002.

Tarantino, Michael, *The Façade of the Objective/La Façade de L'Objective,
Filming Things*, Paris: Centre nationale de la photographie, 1997.

Texts, Articles, Essays

Aliaga, Juan Vicente, "MALAISE", Gallery La Maquina Espanola, Catalogue, 1989.

Allington, Edward, "Hannah Collins", *SLADE*, Issue 3, 2002.

Altaio, Vincenç, "Stonefree", *Tinglado 2*, 1992.

Baqué, Dominique, *En Guise d'épilogue: Admirations, Photographie Plasticienne, L'Extréme Contemporaine*, Paris: Editions du Regard, 2004.

Blazwick Iwona, "The Hunter's Space", *Portfolio*, No 21, 1995.

Blazwick, Iwona and Simon Wilson, *Tate Modern, The Handbook*, London: Tate Publishing, 2001, reprinted 2002, pp. 137.

Bonet, Juan Manuel, *Citadanos*, Arte y Naturaleza, Madrid, 2004.

Brea, José Luis, "Los Ultimos Días", Pabellón de España, Expo Seville, 1992.

Button, Virginia, *A History of the Turner Prize*, London: Tate Publishing, 1997. pp. 98–100.

Cameron, Dan, *To be Or Not To Be*, Barcelona: Centre d'Art Santa Monica, 1991.

Cameron, Dan, "Hannah Collins", *Artforum*, October, 1994.

Campany, David, *Art and Photography*, London: Phaidon, 2003.

Chevrier, Jean-Francois and James Lingwood, *Une Autre Objectivite*, Paris: CNAP, 1989.

Collins, Hannah, *Today, tomorrow and the next day*, Dublin: Irish Museum of Modern Art, 1996.

Corris, Michael, "The Vulnerable Image", *Lapiz*, No 89, 1993.

Combalia, Victória, "Hannah Collins", *El Pais*, 1993.

Durand, Regis, "Le Monde après la photographie", Lille: Musee d'Art Moderne, 1995.

Enwezor, Okwui, "The Unhomely, Phantom Scenes in Global Society", BIACS2, 2nd Seville Biennial, 2006.

Farr, Ian, *Art and Photography*, London: Phaidon, 2003.

Fernandez Cortez, Manuel, "Intierview", *Scope Magazine*, Autumn 2002.

Foster, Alicia, *Tate Women Artists*, London: Tate Publishing, 2004, pp. 188–189.

Frisinghelli, Christine and Manfred Willman, "Revenge of Recollection", *Camera Austria*, 1990.

Grandes, Teresa, "Hannah Collins: el transcurso del tiempo", *Arte y Parte*, Summer, 1996.

Guerra, Carles, "Mesurar La Veritat II de Hannah Collins", *La Vanguardia*,
September 2002.

Guerra, Carlos, *Despues de la Noticia*, Barcelona: Publicaciones CCCB, 2003.

Haworth-Booth, Mark, *European Photography Prize*, Berlin, 1991.

Haworth-Booth, Mark, *Things, A spectrum of Photography 1850–2001*,
London: Victoria and Albert Museum, 2004, pp. 125–126.

Hoet, Jan, *Image 7 Image*, Ghent, 1994.

Horne, Kathryn, "In with the outcasts", *The Times*, 30 September, 2003.

Lavoie, Vincent, *"Histoire Tiede"*, *Parachute*, February 1998.

Legallais, Catherine, "Le Nomadisme Hybride d'Hannah Collins", *Art Press*,
No 165, 1992.

Lingwood, James, *Hannah Collins*, London: Institute of Contemporary Arts, 1988.

Matos, Dennys, "What is the City? Citadanos", *Arte y Naturaleza*, 2004.

Ramirez, Juan Antonio, *Los Géneros de la Pintura*, Madrid: Museo Español de Arte
Moderno, 1994.

Renton, Andrew, *The Street/A Home in Three Places (Somewhere on the Road Between
Jerusalem to Tel Aviv), La Calle/The Street*, Malaga: CAC Malaga, 2003–2004, p. 42.

Riley, Robert R, "La Mina", *Forum*, 2004.

The Photo Book, London: Phaidon, 2001.

Thompson, Jon, *The Sublime Moment: The Rise of the Critical Watchman,
'Sublime: The Darkness and the Light'*, London: Arts Council England, 1999.

Wilson, Simon, *The Turner Prize*, London: Tate Publishing, 1993.

Acknowledgements

The artist would like to thank the following people:

Axel Antas, Rebecca Beasley, Iwona Blazwick,
Francesca Castano, Edouard Chiline, the Chiline family,
Echo Collins, Manuel Fernandez Cortez and the gypsy
community of La Mina, Javier Lopez Gallery,
James Mackay, Avni Patel, Andrew Saint Clair,
Gregory Rukavina.

This book was produced in collaboration Gering & López Gallery, New York.

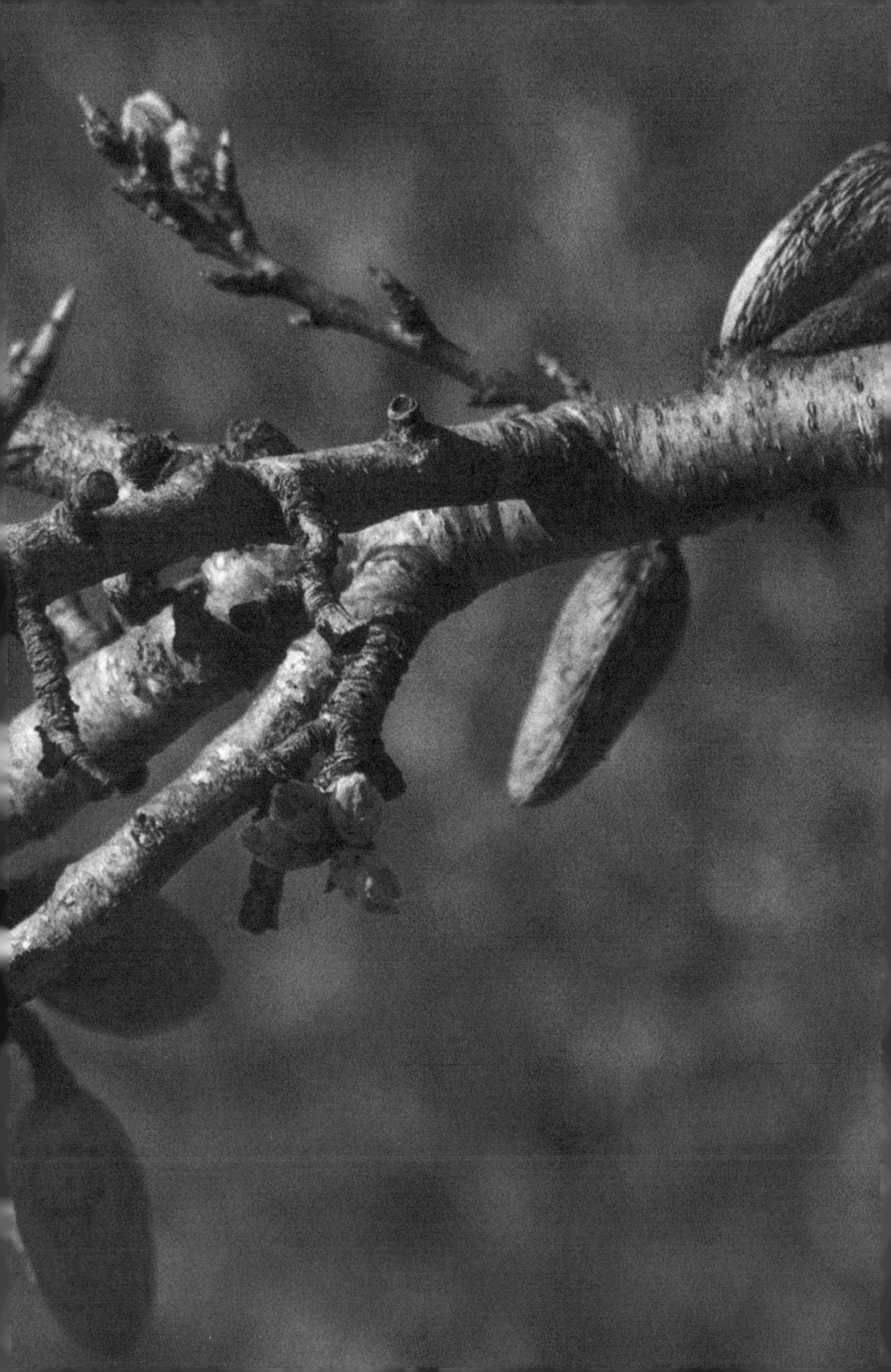

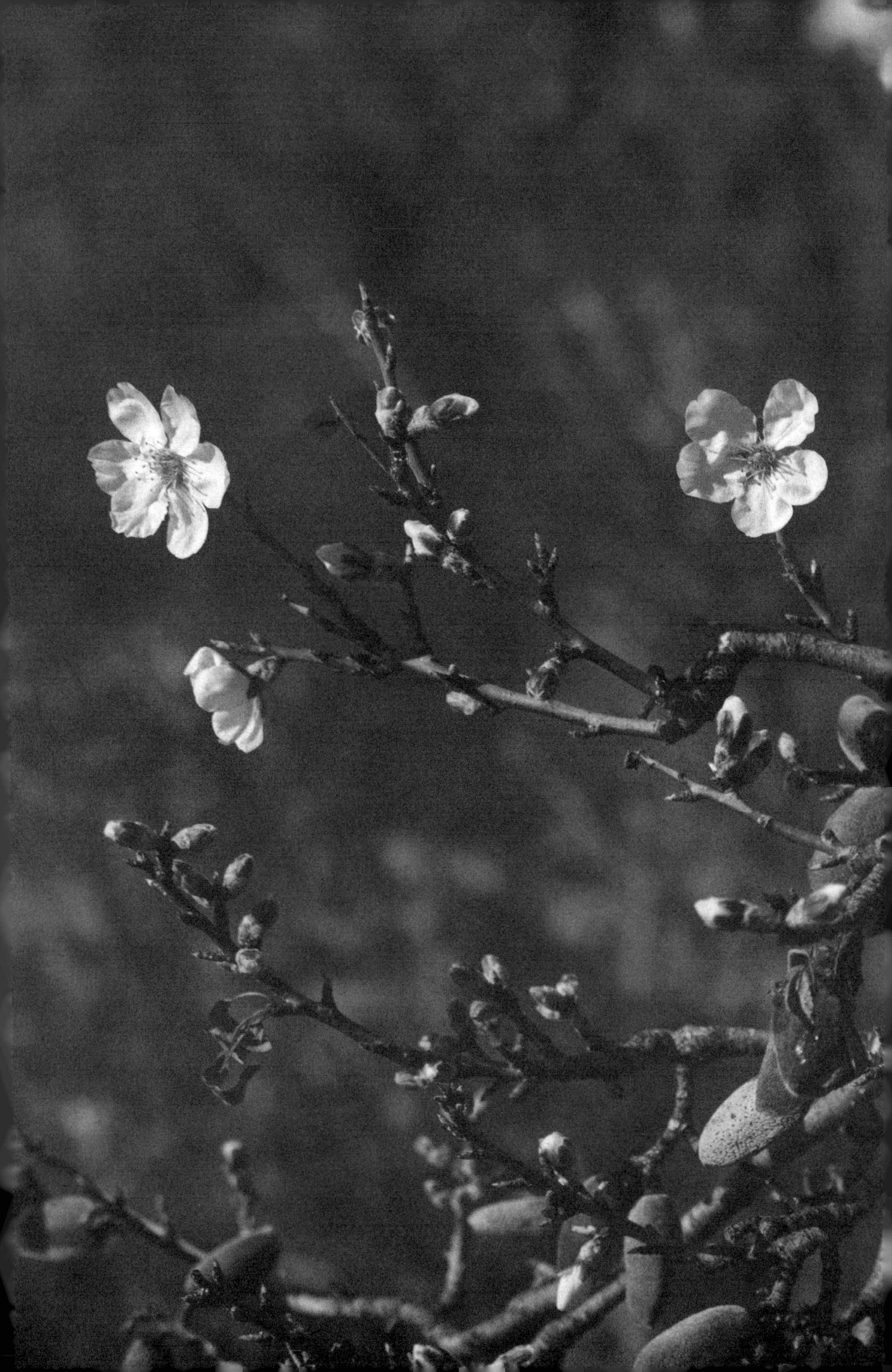